Y0-BVO-431

INTERNATIONAL LAW FOR BUSINESS

INTERNATIONAL LAW FOR BUSINESS

CAROLYN HOTCHKISS

K
1005.4
.H68
1994
West

McGraw-Hill, Inc.
New York · St. Louis · San Francisco · Auckland · Bogotá · Caracas · Lisbon · London · Madrid
Mexico City · Milan · Montreal · New Delhi · San Juan · Singapore · Sydney · Tokyo · Toronto

INTERNATIONAL LAW FOR BUSINESS

Copyright © 1994 by McGraw-Hill, Inc. All rights reserved.
Printed in the United States of America. Except as permitted under the
United States Copyright Act of 1976, no part of this publication may be
reproduced or distributed in any form or by any means, or stored in a data
base or retrieval system, without the prior written permission of the
publisher.

This book is printed on acid-free paper.

1 2 3 4 5 6 7 8 9 0   DOH   DOH   9 0 9 8 7 6 5 4 3

ISBN 0-07-030495-5

This book was set in New Aster by The Clarinda Company.
The editors were Kenneth A. MacLeod, Peitr Bohen, and Bernadette Boylan;
the production supervisor was Friederich W. Schulte.
The cover was designed by Wanda Lubelska.
R. R. Donnelley & Sons Company was printer and binder.

Library of Congress Cataloging-in-Publication Data

Hotchkiss, Carolyn.
    International law for business / Carolyn Hotchkiss.
        p.   cm.
    Includes bibliographical references and index.
    ISBN 0-07-030495-5 (alk. paper)
    1. Commercial law.   2. International business enterprises—Law and
legislation.   3. Trade regulation.   I. Title.
K1005.4.H68   1994
341.7'53—dc20   93-4372

ABOUT THE AUTHOR

Carolyn Hotchkiss has taught at Babson College since 1986 and is currently the Wilson Payne Term Chair and an associate professor of law. She was one of the founding members of the International Law Section of the Academy of Legal Studies in Business and has served as the section president. She has also been the president of the North Atlantic Regional Business Law Association. A graduate of Mount Holyoke College and Columbia Law School, she has practiced law with a large law firm and as an in-house counsel. She is a member of the Bar in New York and Massachusetts. As much as she enjoys writing books, she also enjoys sailing, canoeing, and fly fishing.

To my grandmother, Jeanette Kennan Hotchkiss,
who inspired my lifelong love of books.

CONTENTS IN BRIEF

CONTENTS

xi

PREFACE

At the end of the twentieth century, the marketplace for goods, services, and technology has become global. Even the most traditional local businesses import goods from other countries and use the products of global corporations to enhance their ability to serve their local customers. Business markets are in a time of unprecedented change.

In colleges and universities around the world, students are finding that they must study international business in order to prepare for careers in industries ranging from banking to consumer products. New classes in international marketing, finance, economics, and other subjects have become part of the standard course of study for business students at both undergraduate and graduate levels.

The study of the international legal environment of business is an integral part of the study of global markets. Law provides the ground rules for international trade and investment in goods, services, and technology. An understanding of the ground rules for that trade and investment allows managers to compete successfully in the most competitive global markets. A working understanding of the international legal environment allows managers to make judgments about the political and business risk of doing business in countries around the world. It also serves to help managers to clarify their ethical values in a world of multiple ethical and legal paradigms.

This book is designed to provide a survey of the most significant areas of the international legal environment of business, for students studying business at both graduate and undergraduate levels. It should be useful to students planning careers in many different areas including finance, banking, marketing, entrepreneurship, sales, and operations. The book examines problems in each one of these areas. Although the focus is primarily one of a U.S. businessperson, the book uses cases, examples, and problems relating to a variety of important trading countries.

As you read this book, you will notice that it emphasizes the principles and underlying assumptions of international business and the law. In the current atmosphere of unprecedented change in global business, the principles of the law are the most important factors for students to learn. By the time you use these principles in your careers, the applications are likely to be very different than what we now know. However, the underlying principles will remain useful and relevant, even as new applications develop.

No one person can write a text without the help of many others. Many people have contributed ideas, read drafts, helped me articulate concepts, and otherwise assisted in the writing of this book. Their contributions have immensely enriched the final product.

At Babson, the Board of Research granted me release time to work on preparing the manuscript. Gordon Prichett and Allen Cohen were supportive of my work during their terms as vice president for academic affairs. Mike Fetters, my department chair, was very helpful in the completion of this work. His encouragement, reminders, course releases, and protection were all crucial to the creation of the text. Les Livingstone, when he was department chair, encouraged me to begin this daunting task. I owe a great debt to my colleagues Richard Mandel, Ross Petty, and Toni Lester, who encouraged my writing and my teaching in this area. Toni was the first person other than me to teach from the entire manuscript. I am indebted also to the department secretaries, Sandy Teixiera and Elly Gross, for their help in the production of the book, and to the word processing department for its good humor and efficient service in the face of many rush requests for copies.

I have also profited from academic and professional colleagues. The Boston-based group International Business Advisors and the International Law Committee of the Massachusetts Bar Association have been very helpful in my education on a variety of topics that ended up in the text. Virginia Reiberg spent much time with me on the documentation of commercial transactions. My colleagues in the Academy of Legal Studies in Business have given me much encouragement, and their research across all the areas of international law has been quite helpful. I would particularly like to thank Michael Jones of the University of Massachusetts at Lowell, Carter Manny of the University of Southern Maine, Jere Morehead of the University of Georgia, and Mark Baker of the University of Texas for their early support. Susan Grady, of the University of Massachusetts at Amherst, also deserves special thanks for her reminders to write for my student audience. I would also like to thank my friends, especially Kathy Cole, for putting up with a lot of antisocial behavior on my part while this book was in progress, and my cats Bopper and Whizzer for sitting on the manuscript at crucial points.

I have benefited greatly from the reviews of the manuscript from Mark B. Baker, University of Texas at Austin; Georgia L. Holmes, Mankato State University; Carter Manny, University of Southern Maine; Jere W. Morehead, University of Georgia; Gregory Naples, Marquette University; Richard E. Olson, Washburn University; Dinah Payne, University of New Orleans; Patricia B. Rogers, San Francisco State University; Peter C. Ward, Millsaps College; and Russell L. Welch, University of North Texas. Their constructive comments really helped to make this a better book.

The people at McGraw-Hill were all supportive and helpful in getting this book out. Bernadette Boylan and Ken MacLeod saw it through the production process, but other past and present McGraw-Hill people, including Peitr Bohen, Johanna Schmidt, Michael Ascher, Frank Burrows, and Mary Eshelman provided encouragement along the way.

I wish to express my thanks to the following publishers, who have granted permission for the reproduction of work in this text.

The American Business Law Journal, for F. Cross and B. Winslett, "Export Death: Ethical Issues and the International Trade in Hazardous Products."

The American Journal of Comparative Law, for F. Vergne, "The 'Battle of the Forms' under the 1980 United Nations Convention for the International Sale of Goods."

The Boston College International and Comparative Law Review, for J. Brand, "Aspects of Saudi Arabian Law and Practice."

The California Western International Law Review, for C. Hauscha, "Central Issues of Business Litigation in West German Civil Courts."

The Harvard University Press, for F. Upham, *Law and Social Change in Postwar Japan*.

The Houston Journal of International Law, for J. Schmidt, "Preliminary Agreements in International Contract Negotiation."

The International Lawyer, for P. Lansing and M. Wechselblatt, "Doing Business in Japan: The Importance of the Unwritten Law."

The Northwestern Journal of International Law and Business, for Z. Yuqing and J. McLean, "China's Foreign Economic Contract Law: Its Significance and Analysis."

Finally, this book would not have been possible without the help over the years of my students. Nancy Matthews, Captain Peggy Carson of the U.S. Army, and Sandra King provided research help that ultimately made its way into the text. The graduate students in the International Legal Environment classes and the undergraduate students in the International Law for Business classes were my best critics. They were the first to try out each chapter of the book as it came off my word processor. Their honest opinions of the clarity and flow of the material improved the text immensely.

Carolyn Hotchkiss

INTERNATIONAL LAW FOR BUSINESS

PART ONE

THE INTERNATIONAL LEGAL ENVIRONMENT

GOING GLOBAL

INTERNATIONAL LAW FOR BUSINESS

MAJOR WESTERN LEGAL TRADITIONS

NON-WESTERN LEGAL TRADITIONS

SUPRANATIONAL: THE EUROPEAN COMMUNITY

CHAPTER **1**

GOING GLOBAL

1.1 INTRODUCTION

Jeff Washington had made up his mind. He was going to buy an "American" car. He called his friend Anita Cruz, who had offered to help him choose a car. Together they went to local car dealerships, looking for an all-American car. At the Pontiac dealer, Jeff liked the LeMans model, until Anita pointed out that the LeMans was made in South Korea. They went on to a local Chevrolet-Geo dealership, where Jeff kicked the tires on a GeoPrizm. The dealer called the Prizm a domestic car, but Anita pointed out that it was made in the same plant in California that produces Toyota Corollas, under a joint venture between Toyota and GM. At the Ford dealership, Jeff test drove a Ford Probe. The dealer proudly proclaimed that the car was engineered by Mazda. Finally, Jeff asked Anita about her Eagle Talon, a Chrysler car. Anita explained that it couldn't qualify as a purely American car either, since it was built by a Chrysler–Mitsubishi joint venture.

Jeff didn't know quite what to do. At lunch, Anita said, "You know, Jeff, it's getting really hard to call any product strictly American. With revolutions in communications and transportation, it's easier than ever for every company to look for the best, most cost-effective sources of materials and labor. Political boundaries don't define market boundaries anymore. Businesses are trading and making investments wherever they think they can get a competitive advantage. As consumers, we see the effect of the global market every time we enter a store for basic items like food, clothing, and personal necessities. We also see it every time we look for larger items like cars and appliances, as we found out this morning."

At this point, Jeff interrupted, saying, "But isn't all of this bad for American jobs and American industries?"

Anita replied, "Not necessarily, Jeff. Increased world trade increases competition, which should lead to better products. Keep in mind that the United States is only one country. It's not even the only country in North America, as people from Canada and Mexico will be quick to point out. With increased world trade, U.S. businesses also get the chance to compete in other countries. Many U.S. businesses now realize large percentages of their profits from international operations, and some see their best growth prospects in foreign markets. There will definitely be short-term problems as industries restructure to compete globally, but in the long term U.S. companies will be much better competitors, producing better-quality products at lower prices."

Jeff said, "But wait a minute, Anita. This global market stuff only works if other markets let in U.S. traders and investors on the same terms as we do. A lot of politicians I hear say that doesn't happen."

Anita responded, "Well, in some countries it doesn't. Some countries still have laws, regulations, and commercial practices that restrict trade and investment. There is an extensive legal environment for international trade and investment. The law can be an instrument for unfair restrictions, or it can be a means to facilitate increased trade and increased competition."

Jeff and Anita paid for lunch and left the restaurant. As they got into Anita's Talon, Jeff said, "So what you're telling me is that I have to buy a foreign car?"

Anita said, "Not really. I suggest that you look for the best-quality car you can find. I also think that before you either start your own business or manage someone else's business, you should learn about the legal environment of international business activity. You'll find that knowledge quite useful in the future."

As a reader of this story, no doubt you weren't surprised by the ending, since this is a law text. However, the points of the story are quite serious. The global marketplace is already here. That global marketplace affects many items we purchase every day. In our working lives, the global marketplace may mean new opportunities for personal and career growth, or it may mean layoffs. The global marketplace is a political issue affecting national political debates all over the world. It has even had a profound effect in redrawing the map of the world and creating a new world political order.

To a large extent, law provides the rules of the game for the global marketplace. Countries regulate the way goods, technology, services, money, and people can cross their borders. They enter into treaties and agreements with other countries, simplifying international trade and investment. If a country wants its international trade to grow, it will create a legal environment that makes its people, products, and services more competitive with those of other countries. If it feels the need to protect local jobs, industries, or products, or finds too much money leaving the country, it will create a more restrictive legal environment.

For the business exploring the global marketplace, knowledge of how the international legal system works is crucial. It will enable a manager to anticipate problem areas, analyze developing business situations, and make the decisions that will let a business prosper into the future. The function of this book is to explore the legal environment of international business, focusing on the most significant areas that a manager is likely to encounter in a wide variety of business situations. For the purpose of this text, the most important question is always, "How does the law affect my business plans?" The emphasis is on strategic planning, keeping a business from getting into legal trouble, and learning how to ask the right questions worldwide to get the best information for making management decisions.

1.2 THE GROWTH OF INTERNATIONAL BUSINESS

According to some popular politicians, the global marketplace is a brand new phenomenon, never before experienced by humankind. Of course, that idea is nonsense. Although the extent of the integration of the world economy may be new, international trade and investment have both existed well back into world history. It is well beyond the scope of this book to provide a history of international business, but a few of the more significant chapters are worth mentioning. They provide a useful background for explaining some of the ways the current trading and legal environment has grown into its present form.

ANCIENT TRADING SYSTEMS

Anthropologists will say that almost as soon as people gathered into groups, they began to trade. Originally, marketplaces probably developed on the boundaries between territories, with the group leaders agreeing to give some protection to traders at those market points. Often, the point of trading occurred at a change in climate or geography, where the two groups could grow or produce certain products that would be desirable to others. So, for example, in early Africa, trading sites would be found at the point where deserts turned to savannah, because groups of people in one ecosystem could not survive in the other. Dates, which grew in abundance in desert oases, could be traded for grains or for fish, which would not be found in desert societies. The desert-based traders could not survive the increased humidity and the diseases of the savannah, whereas the grassland traders found the desert environment uninhabitable.

Today, we have only tantalizing glimpses of ancient trading systems, discovered by archaeologists excavating sites around the world. Patterns of widespread trading tend to emerge with increased levels of urbanization. The first extensive trade network of which archaeologists are aware appeared about 3500 BC, in ancient Mesopotamia. Over the next several hundred years, trade routes expanded from what is present-day Iraq and Iran westward into the civilizations of Egypt, then eastward into what is now Pakistan and northward into what is now Uzbekistan. Archaeologists tend to think that societies using widespread trade routes appeared in China between 1500 and 2000 BC, and in several different parts of the Americas between 1000 and 2000 BC.

Even before the advent of the era of Greek civilization, the Mediterranean region was the site of a well organized system of international trade. The Phoenicians were the master traders of the region from roughly 1500 to 400 BC. From their trading centers first on what is now the coast of Lebanon, then later along the shore of the Mediterranean westward as far as present-day Spain, the Phoenicians traded olive oil, wine, pottery, slaves, timber, textiles, and metals. One description of the extent of trade in the Mediterranean comes from the Prophet Ezekiel, in the Old Testament book bearing his name. Before predicting the doom of the city of Tyre, he described its international trade. In part, the description reads:

> The Rhodians traded with you; many coastlands were your own special markets; they brought you in payment ivory tusks and ebony. Edom did business with you because of your abundant goods; they exchanged for your wares turquoise,

purple, embroidered work, fine linen, coral, and rubies. Judah and the land of Israel traded with you; they exchanged for your merchandise wheat from Minneth, millet, honey, oil, and balm. Damascus traded with you for your abundant goods. . . . Arabia and all the princes of Kedar were your favored dealers in lambs, rams, and goats; in these they did business with you. The merchants of Sheba and Raamah traded with you; they exchanged for your wares the best of all kinds of spices, and all precious stones, and gold [Ezek. 27: 15–18, 21–22 (New Revised Standard Version)].

The Greek city-states began competing with the Phoenicians as early as 800 BC, developing extensive trading routes as their civilization grew. The conquests of Alexander the Great created trading routes extending far to the east as well as around the Mediterranean Sea. The Romans built an even more powerful trading empire to the west and north, extending at its peak to Northern Europe and England. This era also saw the opening of overland trade routes between the Mediterranean and China.

Although international business never disappeared in the Dark Ages, it went through a period of some decline when Europe and the Mediterranean became more rural and less politically stable after the fall of the Roman Empire. During the Dark Ages, Arab merchants carried on the traditions of international trade, building extensive trade networks around the Persian Gulf, into Africa, and as far east as India. China during this period was open to foreign trade and foreign traders, doing substantial business with India, on the Malay peninsula, and in Southeast Asia.

MEDIEVAL TRADE

Modern trade and investment practices are found partly in the ancient era, but are mostly rooted in the flourishing world-trading environment of the Middle Ages. The large number of new urban centers across Europe, Africa, and Asia and rapid advances in technology and knowledge allowed international trade to grow around the Mediterranean area, over the Silk Road to China, around the Persian Gulf and to India, and into Southeast Asia. Cities established seasonal and permanent markets, to which merchants from many countries would bring their wares. Of course, political leaders would try to tax the sales at the markets and tax the goods as they passed along roads or rivers on their way to market. One early example of such practices comes from early 11th century Lombardy, in Italy.

Regulations of the Royal Court at Pavia
From the Vulgar Latin
[Pavia, c. 1010–1020]
   2. . . . Merchants entering the kingdom [of Italy] were wont to pay the decima [a 10% tax] on all merchandise at the customs houses. . . . All persons coming from beyond the mountains into Lombardy are obligated to pay the decima on horses, male and female slaves, woolen, linen and hemp cloth, tin and swords. . . .

3. As for the nation of the Angles and Saxons, they have come and were wont to come with their merchandise and wares. And [formerly], when they saw their trunks and sacks being emptied at the gates, they grew angry and started rows with the employees of the treasury. The [parties] are wont to hurl abusive words and in addition very often inflicted wounds upon one another. But in order to cut short such great evils and to remove danger [of conflicts], the king of the Angles and Saxons and the king of the Lombards agreed together as follows: The nation of the Angles and Saxons is no longer subject to the decima. And in return for this the king of the Angles and Saxons and their nation are bound and are obligated to send to the [king's] palace in Pavia and to the king's treasury, every third year, fifty pounds of refined silver, two large, handsome greyhounds, hairy or furred, in chains, with collars covered with gilded plates sealed or enameled with the arms of the king, two excellent embossed shields, two excellent lances, and two excellent swords, wrought and tested.[1]

By the end of the Middle Ages, Europe enjoyed extensive sophisticated trading networks. Along the Mediterranean coast, Venice, Florence, and Genoa prospered by trading regionally and with Africa and Asia. In Northern Europe, by the mid-1300s, eighty cities had gathered into a loose political confederation, known as the Hanseatic League, with common commercial laws and practices, and with enough political and military power to fend off outside princes and pirates. Treaties between political rulers provided protection for trading interests and favorable tax treatment for traders.

TRADE AND COLONIAL POWER

As most students know, when Columbus left on his voyage west from Spain, he intended to discover a new, faster route to Asia, to bring back spices and other commercial cargo for the Spanish kingdom. The technological changes in sailing that made his long-distance voyage possible opened an era of Western domination of world trade. That era, starting more than 500 years ago, is only now perhaps reaching its end.

Spain, Portugal, France, the Netherlands, and England all used naval power to create political and mercantile empires around the world. In the classic mercantile system of this time, the function of distant colonies was to provide raw materials, which would then be finished at home. The distant colonies could then import the finished goods from the mother country. The monarchs of the colonial powers used the promise of becoming great trading companies to encourage merchants to take the risks of exploration and discovery. England in particular granted merchants exclusive rights to exploit geographic areas of interest to the crown. Thus the East India Company or the Hudson's Bay Company would get monopoly rights

---

[1]Robert Lopez and Irving Raymond, eds., *Medieval Trade in the Mediterranean World*, (Norton, 1950) pp. 56–57.

and monopoly profits in return for colonizing and investing and trading in their particular areas. It would be fair to say that the great trading companies of this era were truly the first multinational enterprises.

THE ERA OF MULTINATIONAL ENTERPRISES

The great trading companies were the first business enterprises to make large-scale investments in foreign countries. The combination of investment and trade begun by those companies is now the hallmark of modern international business. During the 19th century, as the industrial revolution produced large accumulations of capital, money became available for investments by private individuals and corporations. The investments often involved transportation or mining interests. For example, the Panama Railroad Company was begun in 1849 with $5 million in U.S. investment. Canal companies, such as those building the Suez and Panama canals, were popular 19th-century foreign investment vehicles. By the end of the century, corporations like General Electric and Standard Oil already had significant overseas operations.

International business in the 20th century, particularly since the end of World War II, has been dominated by businesses engaging in large-scale trade and investment in many countries. Some names, like Royal Dutch Shell, Unilever, Proctor & Gamble, IBM, and Nestlé, are familiar to consumers and merchants. But they represent only a few of the major multinational enterprises. These companies sometimes have annual sales that are larger than the gross national product of countries in which they do business. As you might expect, the size and influence of multinational enterprises create the possibility of political conflict. Throughout this book we will explore the ways in which multinational enterprises structure their businesses and the response of developing countries to the influence of multinational enterprises on their economic, political, and social development.

1.3 THE GROWTH OF INTERNATIONAL COMMERCIAL LAW

International trade could not have grown without the recognition of both merchants' rights and commercial practices by political rulers. In many ways, it is accurate to say that commercial law was the first form of international law. Chapter 2 discusses the ways in which international law affects business today. In the meantime, it is worthwhile to explore the origins of some of the basic principles of commercial law that international businesspeople currently take for granted.

The oldest commercial laws were made to protect foreign merchants and to regulate the transportation of goods. Most of the ancient trading societies we discussed earlier had commercial laws. For example, the first written commercial laws came from the Code of Hammurabi, about 2500 BC. The Code governed all kinds of criminal and civil activities, but it also provided specifically for the safety of foreign merchants and gave them breach-of-contract remedies. For example, one section of the Code stated:

> If any one on a journey intrust silver, gold, precious stone or any treasure of his hand, to a man for transportation, if this man do not bring all that was to be transported to the appointed place, but appropriates them, then this man who did not deliver the goods intrusted to him shall be called to account, and he shall pay the owner of the goods to be transported, fivefold, for all that intrusted to him.[2]

THE LAW MERCHANT

The real growth of commercial law came in the Middle Ages. As the trading fairs evolved in the late 7th century, they developed sets of commercial customs. The merchants traveled to other cities, and many of the customs traveled with them. Over time, those customs gained the force of law, as political leaders recognized that merchants should be allowed to resolve their disputes by their own rules. From the beginning, this "law merchant" had an international flavor, because it existed independently of kings and princes.

By the height of the Middle Ages, the law merchant was a sophisticated and powerful body of rights and customs. An example of the power of merchants may be found in the Magna Carta of 1215, the fundamental document of rights in England. That document provides that:

> All merchants shall have safe conduct to go and come out of and into England, and to stay in and travel through England by land and water for the purposes of buying and selling, free of legal tolls, in accordance with ancient and just customs.[3]

The areas of law covered by the law merchant were extensive. The validity and enforcement of contracts, as well as remedies for breach of contract; practices regarding credit and commercial documents, such as checks, promissory notes, and bills of lading; agency and fiduciary relationships; bankruptcy; partnerships and joint ventures; and even trademarks and patents were all areas of commercial practice covered by the law merchant. Many of the legal doctrines of modern commercial law got

---

[2]Albert Kocourek and John Wigmore, eds., *Primitive and Ancient Legal Systems*, vol. 2. Little Brown, Boston, 1977 (reprint of 1915 original), p. 112.
[3]Quoted from Berman, *Law and Revolution*, 1983, p. 343.

their start and became relatively fully developed during the 12th and 13th centuries, when the law merchant reigned throughout Europe. A lot of the concepts discussed throughout the remainder of this book have their origin in the body of commercial practice known as the law merchant, and are traceable directly to medieval Europe.

One of the purposes of the law merchant was to allow traders to resolve their business disputes outside the regular court systems of the cities and countries in which they traded. At the time, if courts were available to merchants, their quality varied widely, with no guarantee that litigation would be resolved with what we now consider fairness or justice. And, of course, by the time a case could be heard, the aggrieved merchant would probably have moved on to a new trading fair in a new city. So one of the early features of the law merchant was alternative dispute resolution, usually taking the form of merchant courts in the trading fair cities, with merchants acting as judges.

The second hallmark of these merchant courts was speed. If two merchants had a dispute, the case would often be heard the same day the dispute was brought. Courts were said to meet "from day to day," or, in the case of disputes involving sea transport, "from tide to tide." Thus, if a ship arrived carrying damaged cargo, the recipient would have to bring his suit quickly, and the dispute would be resolved before the ship was ready to sail again.

The third hallmark of the merchant courts was informality. Cases were decided on the basis of consensuality and good faith. Parties were held to their promises, unless those promises worked some fundamental unfairness or surprise. Merchants were expected to know what the customs and practices were in their particular trade. Today, we find reflections of those concepts in the commercial law of almost all major international trading nations.

THE NEW LAW MERCHANT

As kings and princes grew more powerful and as nations formed at the end of the Middle Ages, the law merchant tended to be pulled back into national legal systems. In England, for example, many of the concepts of the law merchant remained part of legal practice, enforced through the Equity courts. Throughout Europe, as countries codified their laws, the customs of the international commercial community found their way into local and national laws. Over time, distinctive local practices worked their way into commercial laws, diluting the uniformity of the law from country to country.

During the late 19th century, international lawyers began to attempt to recreate a relatively uniform law for international commercial matters, using treaties among nations. The first successful treaties were in the field of ocean transport, providing relatively uniform rules for carrying goods from country to country. When air transport became widely available in the mid-20th century, the ocean transport concepts were readily adaptable. The air and sea transport treaties are still important factors in current practice, as you will see in Chapter 9.

Today, business leaders and lawyers recognize that the legal environment of both trade and regulation must reflect the increasing internationalization of business. Renewed efforts to create uniform laws governing international transactions have already had some success in the field of sales of goods, and are under way in several other areas, including patents, copyrights, and trademarks. There are even attempts to regulate the investment and business practices of multinational enterprises on an international basis. Much of this book will discuss those efforts, because they are laying the foundation for the new law merchant—in this case, a wide-ranging system of law and regulation governing many different kinds of business activity.

1.4 THE STRUCTURE OF INTERNATIONAL BUSINESS ACTIVITY

Just as the law provides a framework for international business activity, the realities of the marketplace lead businesses to organize their activities in ways that maximize their competitive advantages. Several methods of organizing business activity are common in international business. We will explore three major ways of doing business internationally, looking at the legal parameters for each kind of activity. Although the categories don't always break neatly, most international business activity takes the form of sales relationships, licensing relationships, or investment relationships.

SALES RELATIONSHIPS

The simplest way for a business to "go international" is for it to find customers in other countries and sell directly to them. Direct-selling relationships are popular in both goods- and service-oriented industries. Often, a potential foreign buyer will become acquainted with a product or a service while on a trip overseas, and inquire about contracting for sales. In some cases, a business may display a product at a fair or trade show, either in the home country or abroad, and customers will inquire about purchase. For example, the Nuremberg Toy Fair is a large international trade show that leads buyers and sellers to the same marketplace, resulting in many international sales.

For some businesses, the process of finding customers and learning new markets may be difficult. They may decide to use intermediaries to help them sell their products or services. Two kinds of intermediaries that are frequently part of the structure of international business activity are agents and distributors. Agents act to find buyers for a seller. Generally, they reside in the market the seller wants to reach, and know the market and potential buyers in that market. In some cases, the agent may take orders for the seller; in others, the agent merely helps the buyer and seller to come to terms on the purchase of a product or service. The legal relationship between the seller of goods or services and the agent can be fairly complex.

The second kind of intermediary, the distributor, functions quite differently. A distributor is an independent company that buys the products from the seller, then resells them in the foreign market. The distributor takes the risk that the products won't sell in the foreign market and most likely bears the responsibility for service and warranty problems. The automobile industry, for example, often uses distributors to sell products in overseas markets.

LICENSING RELATIONSHIPS

A business may decide that it is more efficient to have a product manufactured in the foreign country, rather than making the product at home and shipping it abroad. That is one circumstance under which it might decide to license the rights to make and sell its products to another company. Licensing is a particularly effective way for a company to make worldwide use of technology and of intellectual property rights.

A license may take several forms, although it is always a contract allowing another company to make, sell, or use a name or product. A German pharmaceutical company, for example, may license the patent rights it has in a particular drug to a Canadian manufacturer. That would give the Canadian company the right to make the drug. In all likelihood, the German business would also license its trademark rights in the name of the product to the same Canadian company, so that the Canadian company could manufacture and sell the drug in the Canadian, or perhaps the entire North American, market. Similarly, a U.S. film studio might license the copyright rights it holds in a film to a French business, giving that business the right to reproduce and market the film in the European Community countries.

One particularly effective form of licensing in international business is franchising. Both services and goods are the subject of international franchising. Franchising is sometimes a very cost-effective method of expanding to new markets. It involves licensing trademarks for product and business names, and in some cases licensing "know-how" or patents as well. Ready examples of successful international franchisers include McDonalds, KFC, Servicemaster, and Pizza Hut.

INVESTMENT RELATIONSHIPS

When a business looks toward a long-term presence in a market, it may decide to make a direct investment in that market. That investment is likely to take the form of a branch, a subsidiary, or a joint venture. A branch is the simplest form of direct investment. It involves opening an office, a factory, a warehouse, or some other business operation. The branch has no separate legal identity from the rest of the business.

For a variety of reasons, including limiting legal liability, a business may create a separate legal entity, known as a subsidiary. The business, known as the parent corporation, incorporates a separate corporation, known as the subsidiary, in the foreign market. It may own all the stock in the subsidiary, in which case it is known as a wholly owned subsidiary, or the parent may allow other people or businesses, usually in the foreign market, to hold partial ownership of the subsidiary. Many nations regulate foreign ownership of businesses. In some cases they require local ownership, or even local controlling ownership.

International businesses may decide that the best way to enter a new market is with other businesses in a joint venture. For example, General Electric entered the Eastern European marketplace for light bulbs by buying a stake in Tungsram, a Hungarian producer that held a significant share of the market for light bulbs in both Eastern and Western Europe. General Electric got the benefits of established market share, while Tungsram got the benefits of GE's capital and technical strengths. In other joint ventures, two or more businesses may cooperate to create a new legal entity in a market. Many countries around the world require foreign investment to take the form of joint ventures with local investors, rather than branches or wholly owned subsidiaries.

1.5 MULTINATIONAL ENTERPRISES

One form of international business that has played a very large role in creating a truly global marketplace is the multinational enterprise. The term multinational enterprise (MNE) has only come into the business vocabulary in recent decades, to refer to the large businesses that since World War II have dominated international business. The MNE commonly uses more than one kind of organization to compete internationally. In some countries, the MNE may have subsidiaries, branches, or joint ventures, while in other countries it may license others to produce its products or use its name. In still other markets, the MNE may simply sell products from its home base, or have agents or distributors. Forms of doing business are quite flexible, changing over time to reflect the strategy of the business, the competitive environment, and the legal and political environments of various markets. The case below shows one way that a multinational enterprise might structure its activity, and how that structure will have certain legal consequences. As you read the case, try to create a diagram of the organization of this MNE.

BULOVA WATCH CO., INC., v. K. HATTORI & CO., LTD.

508 F. Supp. 1322 (E.D.N.Y. 1981)

FACTS:

Bulova, a New York corporation, sued Hattori, a Japanese corporation, and several of its employees in federal district court, alleging that Hattori engaged in unfair competition, product disparagement, and a conspiracy to raid Bulova's marketing staff in order to gain improper access to Bulova's trade secrets. Hattori moved to dismiss the suit, claiming that since it had separately incorporated a subsidiary in the US, only that subsidiary, not the Japanese parent corporation, could be liable for any wrongful acts.

ISSUE:

Is the Japanese corporation "doing business" in New York and should it therefore be subject to the action of federal courts there?

RESULT:

Yes. Hattori's motion to dismiss the case was denied (although the court dismissed the case against Hattori's employees).

REASONS:

Hattori is a company incorporated under the laws of Japan with its principal offices in Tokyo. It owns all the stock of Seiko Corporation of America (SCA), a New York corporation. SCA owns all the stock of Seiko Time Corp., Pulsar Time, Inc. and SPD Precision, Inc., all New York corporations. Hattori contracts in Japan for the manufacture of its watches and sells them under the Seiko, Pulsar and other brand names to its three American sub-subsidiaries. . . . A very substantial amount of its total revenue is derived from exports of watches and timepieces, the United States being its largest foreign market. In 1980 over four million Hattori timepieces were sold in this country at prices to the consumer of one hundred twenty-five dollars and higher—far more than half a billion dollars at retail. . . .

Hattori sells products to distributors in over one hundred countries around the world. Wholly-owned subsidiaries of Hattori handle distribution of Hattori's products in about ten of those countries, including the United States. In the rest, or the great majority of the countries in which Hattori's products are sold, sales are made by Hattori or its subsidiaries to independent distributors who conduct their own advertising and other marketing activities and maintain their own repair centers pursuant to agreement or arrangements with Hattori. . . .

Hattori's United States subsidiaries sold Seiko-branded products totalling over $50,000,000 in wholesale dollars in 1979 to retail customers and wholesale distributors in the Caribbean, South America and Europe. SCA has also made substantial investments in third countries to assist Hattori in selling its Japanese manufactured timepieces. It owns one hundred percent of the capital stock of Pulsar subsidiaries which it has established in Canada and Europe during the past two years. . . . In 1980, SCA also acquired one hundred percent of the stock of a Brazilian corporation, Seiko Time, Ltd., which in turn acquired all of the stock of Hasc, S.A., a company which sells Hattori's Seiko-branded products in Brazil. . . .

It is no longer a matter of doubt that a foreign corporation can do business in New York through its employees, ... Equally settled is the concept that a corporation may be amenable to New York personal jurisdiction when the systematic activities of a subsidiary in this state may fairly be attributed to the parent. . . .

The parent-subsidiary relationship has not in itself been treated as sufficient to establish personal jurisdiction over the foreign parent. . . . Some additional factor has been needed. . . . Such circumstances include direct and indirect control of the local distributor, . . . treating the subsidiary as an "incorporated division," . . . as an agent, or as both.

. . . [Hattori places] great stock in the formal separation of Hattori from its 100% directly-owned subsidiary and its 100% indirectly-owned subsidiaries. They state that the subsidiaries do not receive loans from the parent, that they generally buy from the parent by letter of credit posted with a Japanese bank abroad, that they do their own advertising (although at times they participate in promotions organized by Hattori), and that the parent has no bank account, office or phone listing in New York, is not licensed to do business here, does not assign its "salaried employees" to New York, and is not involved in the personnel policies or the hiring of personnel by its New York office.

Plaintiff, on the other hand, points to the complete stock ownership by the parent and additionally draws our attention to the interchange and overlap of directors and officers between parent and subsidiaries, to the fact that intercompany loans are made to other Hattori subsidiaries and are assertedly available, if needed, to the New York subsidiaries, that the financial statements of the New York subsidiaries are consolidated in Hattori's reports filed under the securities and exchange law of Japan, and that unrealized profits and losses arising from sales among the consolidated companies are eliminated in the financial statements. It also relies on certain advertising materials produced by Hattori and distributed by the public relations firm of the New York subsidiaries that refer to Hattori's "marketing offices in . . . New York" and an "international network of designated distributors . . . supervised by the Tokyo headquarters."

. . . What is involved here is a series of relatively young sales and marketing subsidiaries abroad, whose purpose is to market a single product—timepieces. There is no manufacturing or product research done by any of these subsidiaries. They do not seem to have developed third country trade except for the purpose of selling Hattori's Japanese manufactured goods. Only very recently have they begun to make some investments in third countries, again to produce further outlets for Hattori's factories in Japan. The use of the wholly-owned subsidiary form here reflects the desire for "unambiguous control" over sales and marketing subsidiaries to insure uniform quality and promotion of the product sold.

Hattori and its American subsidiaries do maintain some independence—about as much as the egg and vegetables in a western omelette. Just as, from a culinary point of view, we focus on the ultimate omelette and not its ingredients, so, too, from a jurisdictional standpoint, it is the integrated international operations of Hattori affecting activities in New York that is the primary focus of our concern.

Although with time the Hattori subsidiaries might well evolve, along with their parent, into the later stages of multinational development, today Hattori is a highly effective export manufacturer and not a fully developed multinational. . . . Large and sophisticated as it may be, it is very much the hub of a wheel with many spokes. It is appropriate, therefore, to look to the center of the wheel in Japan when the spokes violate substantive rights in other countries.

1.6 LAW, BUSINESS, AND ECONOMIC DEVELOPMENT

One of the themes of this book that may already be apparent from this chapter is that the commercial law of the trading nations of the world is moving toward a more compatible status. A contradictory theme that this book will explore throughout its chapters, however, is that the interests of different nations are not always the same, and sometimes may be very different. These national differences are particularly strong in the areas of law relating to economic development.

Since the end of World War II, the world has undergone many political and economic changes. Certainly one of the most significant was the era of decolonialization that took place from the 1950s through the 1970s. Many former colonial powers, such as the United Kingdom and France, granted independence to their former colonies. In countries like Vietnam and Algeria, people fought for independence from their former colonial governments. The new nations of the world found a political voice at the United Nations, where they became the majority of voting members. In the early 1990s, the U.N. underwent another significant expansion as the newly independent nations that once were republics of the Soviet Union became members.

The political voice of the newly independent nations did not translate into economic power. The Chinese referred to the division of power in the world in terms of three worlds. The First World contained the political superpowers, the United States and the U.S.S.R. The Second World was made up of the other relatively developed nations of Western Europe and the economically developed countries of the Pacific Rim. The Third World was the vast majority of nations that were underdeveloped economically, with lower levels of overall industrialization and large numbers of people living in poverty. Although the categories of the First and Second World are probably no longer accurate, especially after the collapse of the Soviet Union, the term "Third World" is still widely used to describe the community of less-developed countries.

It would be a mistake to look on the less-developed countries (LDCs) as one unified group. The LDCs include relatively large economies, such as Brazil, China, and South Korea, but also really poor countries like Zaire and Uganda. Governments range from totalitarian to democratic. In many ways each country has different concerns. However, the LDCs do share some common concerns and interests.

One common concern among the LDCs is that law, particularly international law, reflects only the interests of the developed nations. Their concern is not limited to law affecting business, but it does have some merit in that area. International commercial law grew out of the Mediterranean trading areas and the medieval European trading fairs. That law merchant is the basis for modern attempts to harmonize commercial law around the world, but it does not take into account the experience and history of traders in Africa and Asia.

This concern about the bias of law toward the Western, developed nations might lead a nation to write into its own laws a provision requiring its substantive law to govern any contract disputes between international traders. The nation might also be reluctant to have international commercial disputes involving its citizens decided by commercial arbitration in another country rather than in its own local courts.

The LDCs also worry that international business, especially the MNEs, distorts local political, legal, and economic structures. Given that an MNE may generate more money than the gross national product of the country in which it is doing business, its concerns are not unfounded. On the one hand, an MNE may be beneficial to the host country, bringing new technology, training highly skilled workers, investing large amounts of capital, and accelerating economic development. On the other hand, an MNE may use its power to obtain a monopoly position and distort prices, corrupt public officials, or remove far more money than it invests, worsening the host country's balance of payments.

Political theorists and economists from LDCs are particularly concerned about the role MNEs play in a country's economic development. Many are convinced that the impact of MNEs is to keep the host country dependent rather than to encourage development. These theorists are known as "dependencia" theorists. The dependencia theorists view MNEs as the agents of domination of local economies, exploitation of natural and human resources, and political imperialism by developed nations. They see MNEs as increasing the gap between rich and poor nations, not closing that gap.

The legal and economic theorists of the Third World are trying to change the global legal environment for business, to recognize the needs and concerns of the LDCs. The most successful attempt to date has been in the United Nations, which in 1974 adopted a resolution supporting the creation of a New International Economic Order. Excerpts from that declaration follow.

DECLARATION ON THE ESTABLISHMENT OF A NEW INTERNATIONAL ECONOMIC ORDER

May 1, 1974 U.N.G.A. Res. 3201 (S-VI), U.N. Doc. A/9559 (1974)

We the Members of the United Nations,

. . . Solemnly proclaim our united determination to work urgently for the establishment of a new international economic order based on equity, sovereign equality, interdependence, common interest and cooperation among all States, irrespective of their economic and social systems, which shall correct inequalities and redress existing injustices, make it possible to eliminate the widening gap between the developed and the developing countries and ensure steadily accelerating economic and social development and peace and justice for present and future generations, and, to that end, declare: . . .

4. The new international economic order should be founded on full respect for the following principles:

(a) Sovereign equality of States, self-determination of all peoples, inadmissibility of the acquisition of territories by force, territorial integrity and non-interference in the internal affairs of other States; . . . .

(d) The right of every country to adopt the economic and social system that it deems the most appropriate for its own development and not to be subjected to discrimination of any kind as a result;

(e) Full permanent sovereignty of every State over its natural resources and all its economic activities. In order to safeguard these resources, each State is entitled to exercise effective control over them and their exploitation with means suitable to its own situation, including the right to nationalization or to transfer ownership to its own nationals, this right being an expression of the full sovereignty of the State. No State may be subjected to economic, political or any other type of coercion to prevent the free and full exercise of this inalienable right. . . .

The governments of the developed countries have largely resisted attempts to make binding the concepts of the New International Economic Order. The Organization for Economic Cooperation and Development (OECD), which consists of government representatives from most of the developed nations, has created nonbinding guidelines for the conduct of MNEs, designed to encourage MNEs to behave in positive ways toward their host countries. Many of the developed nations also have trade programs designed to encourage LDCs to build export trade. However, attempts by the U.N. and others to create treaties that would shift wealth from the developed nations to the LDCs, or would restrict the growth of MNEs are largely stalled in the draft stages.

Throughout this book you will see evidence of the division between the developed nations and the less-developed nations. Just as the growth of the new law merchant is one theme of this text, so the continuing divergence of interests between rich and poor nations is another. Both themes will have a major impact on the development of the international legal environment for business into the 21st century.

1.7 THE GLOBAL MANAGER

In the 1980s, a popular bumper sticker on automobiles exhorted people to "Think Globally, Act Locally." That slogan should be the watchword for the global manager of the next century. The people who will lead business toward a truly globalized market are those who do have a global perspective, but are able to act to meet local conditions. There has been much discussion of what businesses and business schools should do to create managers who can function in a global environment, but to date the results are less than adequate. One of the primary functions of this book is to help you learn to be a global manager.

If we were to try to define what it means to be a global manager, we would first need to look at what we know about the future of business. There is very little anyone can predict with great confidence. What we do know is that the factor that will dominate the development of business is change, and that change will be rapid and unexpected. For example, in 1985, who would have thought that by 1990 the Berlin Wall would be gone, East and West Germany would be reunited, and the nations of Eastern Europe would be open for business with foreign companies? Even more startling was the collapse of the former Soviet Union in 1991. Very few people could have predicted the complete disintegration of one of the two world military and political superpowers.

We also know that technological change will accelerate the internationalization of business activity. As businesses grow across political borders, work will be organized differently. Managers are increasingly likely to receive work assignments abroad, and company divisions, projects, teams, and task forces will be organized more and more along international lines. For example, new products may well be developed by a team of managers from key markets, with research and development specialists from offices worldwide.

If these developments hold true, three principles will characterize the successful global manager. First, the global manager will have to be able to anticipate, lead, and implement change. It is not enough simply to react to changes going on around you. Second, the global manager will have to be ready to function in new and unfamiliar markets. It isn't possible to learn in advance all the languages you might have to know over the course of your career or study in advance all the cultures you might experience. The global manager has to be adaptable, and to learn how to ask the right kinds of questions in new situations. Third, the global manager has to be ready to work with people from many different cultures. Your employees, co-workers, suppliers, and customers will come from many different societies, with different personal, business, and social values. Although each of us is a product of our own culture, to work successfully on a global basis managers will have to understand, accommodate, and even sometimes celebrate the differences among us.

Global managers are products of their personal backgrounds, experiences, education and work history. A family background that involved an exposure to many different cultures can be very helpful in developing a global outlook. Traveling in different cultures or being friends with people from a variety of cultures may also help develop a global outlook. Work assignments in different countries may lead to a broader understanding of cultural similarities and differences. Also, the educational process makes a major contribution to a global outlook. Students should seek an exposure to a variety of cultures in the classroom, and try to study abroad or engage in extracurricular activities that teach new ways of looking at the world and its people.

This book will give you some of the skills you need to be an effective global manager. It is not a comparative law book, although it contains many comparisons of business law. Rather, it will examine the common threads to the global legal framework for business and highlight differences and local conditions. To read this book most effectively, you will need to put aside the common belief that the ways of business and law you know are "normal" and what others do is "abnormal." The different ways people around the world have of doing business are just that: different. In your value system, some may be better and some worse, but as a businessperson, you will need to recognize and use the differences to compete effectively on a global basis. When you can analyze business and law objectively, you will be able to manage the global legal environment for your business and will be well on your way to being a global manager.

1.8 CONCLUSION

Both international business and its legal environment have long and rich histories, extending back toward the dawn of civilization. Those histories provide the context for today's expansion of international trade and investment as well as for current attempts to create an international law for business activity. Although technological change has accelerated the growth of the global marketplace, many dimensions of that marketplace have been in existence for many years.

The purpose of this book is to provide a business-oriented understanding of the operating legal environment of international business. It is divided into four parts, each of which is one dimension of the international legal framework for business. The first part, which includes the next four chapters, examines the kinds of national and international legal structures a manager will encounter when doing business internationally. The second part, which consists of the following four chapters, looks at the international dimensions of contracting. The context for these chapters is direct sales transactions, but much of their message is applicable to all forms of doing business. The third part of this book, encompassing Chapters 10 and 11, looks at global and national regulation of cross-border trade. These chapters are applicable to all forms of doing business. The final part of the book, chapters 12 to 15, looks at the different forms of business organization and the legal issues posed by global competition. There is a particular emphasis on licensing and investment relationships and their special problems.

When you have finished reading this book, you should have a good sense of the ways in which law and regulation interact with business strategies and decisions. This text cannot cover all specific situations that might arise, but it will identify the significant pitfalls businesses might find in the legal environment, and, as important, the basis for competitive opportunities the legal environment sometimes creates. You will know how to anticipate many legal problems before they arise and have a context for making appropriate business decisions. Perhaps most importantly, in a legal and business environment that is undergoing rapid change, you will be familiar with a body of principles that will help you manage, and perhaps even lead, that change.

1.9 QUESTIONS FOR DISCUSSION

1. What were the historic reasons for the growth of cross-border trade? Are those conditions different now? If so, how?

2. In your own country, does the law governing domestic business transactions include the basic ideas of the law merchant? Explain.

3. Review the Bulova Watch case earlier in this chapter. Why do you think Hattori chose to organize its business the way it did? Would it have made sense for Hattori to use licensing agreements with independent foreign businesses in order to make and sell watches? Explain.

4. As a field project, go to three different kinds of stores (for example, a clothing store, a hardware store, and a grocery store). Look at the labels or containers on ten different products to see what country each product comes from. What proportion of the products result from international trade? If you compare your results with those of your classmates, can you draw any conclusions about the globalization of markets?

5. Take a personal inventory of the skills and background you already have that will help you become an effective global manager. Identify three steps you will take in the next year to increase your global capabilities.

1.10 FURTHER READINGS

Harold J. Berman, *Law and Revolution*, Harvard, Cambridge, Mass., 1983.

Philip D. Curtin, *Cross-Cultural Trade in World History*, Cambridge, 1986.

Theodore Levitt, "The Globalization of Markets," *Harvard Business Review*, May–June 1983, pp. 92–103.

Michael Porter, *The Competitive Advantage of Nations*, Free Press, 1990.

N.J.G. Pounds, *An Historical Geography of Europe*, Cambridge, 1990.

INTERNATIONAL LAW FOR BUSINESS

2.1 INTRODUCTION

Chapter 1 introduced the background of international trade and the different forms of business common to the international marketplace. The purpose of this chapter is to provide an introduction to international law for international business. Unfortunately, no one body of rules makes up international law for business. Each one of the methods of doing business consists of a complex web of laws and regulations extending from the home country to international organizations. Even a simple transaction may involve several different kinds of law.

For example, suppose that an American buyer for a clothing store in Virginia goes to Italy and purchases 100 men's suits. He returns to the United States, and the Italian seller ships the suits to Virginia one week later. Even if the transaction works perfectly, both national and international law influence the business deal. When the buyer travels, he will need a passport from the U.S. government and may need a visa from the Italian government. He will have to pass through border checks for compliance with Italian and U.S. customs regulations. The purchase of suits is a contractual obligation, which may be governed by a treaty drafted by the United Nations, called the Convention for the International Sale of Goods. In this instance, both Italy and the United States have ratified the treaty. The shipment of goods must clear customs and is subject to tariffs. Here, the tariff status of the suits is determined by U.S. law, but the U.S. law is structured within the framework of another set of treaties and agreements known as the General Agreement on Tariffs and Trade (GATT).

To take the example one step further, suppose that the clothing store believes the suits to be defective. Where can the parties go to resolve their dispute? Would Italian law, Virginia law, or some other law govern any legal proceedings? These questions would be resolved through the application of private international law, or, as it is sometimes called, conflicts of law principles. If the Italian seller obtains a judgment against the Virginia buyer, is that judgment enforceable in American courts? Each country has its own rules on the enforcement of foreign court judgments.

The role of law in international business gets still more complicated when the setting is not a simple sale of goods but a multimillion-dollar investment, joint venture, or other sophisticated transaction. Yet the same ultimate framework applies to these sophisticated business activities as to the simple transaction, albeit in a more complex form. A business crossing national borders needs to be aware of a legal environment consisting of:

- National laws and regulations, including the law of its own country (domestic law) and that of other countries with which it does business

- Private international law

- Public international law, including treaties and commercial customs

- International organizations, with their laws, regulations, and guidelines.

In managing within the legal environment of international business, the key to success is planning. Anticipating problems before they arise will keep a business from having to answer many of the thornier questions posed in international law, and will make doing business around the world a more pleasant and profitable endeavor. We will now examine the different kinds of law affecting international business, to provide a framework for the specific discussions to follow.

2.2 NATIONAL LAW

As the above example illustrates, any business activity crossing a national border is subject to two sets of law: that of the home country, or domestic law; and that of the foreign or host country. All of the categories of law applying to any domestic business transaction—such as contracts, torts, and antitrust law—will apply to the international transaction.

In addition to the standard areas of law applicable to both domestic and international transactions, all nations have a legal interest in activities crossing their borders. A nation can determine what persons, goods, technology, and money may enter or leave the country, and on what terms. Many countries also regulate the terms of foreign investment in land and in businesses.

Each country has a different internal structure for governing international activities. In the United States, Congress and the President divide between them government powers to regulate business activities across national borders. The Constitution gives Congress the power to establish uniform taxes on imports, known as duties or imposts, to declare war, to "define and punish Piracies and Felonies committed on the high Seas, and Offenses against the Law of Nations," and, perhaps its most important power, "to regulate Commerce with foreign Nations." The President, in addition to being commander-in-chief of the armed forces, also possesses under the Constitution the power "by and with the Advice and Consent of the Senate, to make Treaties, providing two thirds of the Senators present concur." The Constitution further provides that those treaties shall be the supreme law of the land.

The relationship of congressional and presidential powers over international business has been tense since the first years of the Constitution. Recent years have seen court challenges over government actions in Vietnam and Central America, charging presidential action without constitutional authority. The basic reach of federal power, however, was articulated in the older case that follows.

UNITED STATES v. CURTISS-WRIGHT EXPORT CORP.

299 U.S. 304 (1936)
United States Supreme Court

FACTS:

In the 1930s, Bolivia and Paraguay engaged in a border war in a region known as the Chaço. In 1934, Congress passed a Joint Resolution authorizing the President to ban or regulate the sale of arms to either country if he found that such actions would contribute to the end of the conflict. The day Congress passed the joint resolution, President Roosevelt issued a proclamation banning the sale of arms to either country.

Curtiss-Wright was convicted of selling fifteen machine guns to Bolivia in violation of the President's proclamation. It appealed, charging that Congress had improperly delegated its authority to the President.

ISSUE:

Did the President have the authority to ban arms sales to Bolivia?

RESULT:

Yes. Conviction affirmed.

REASONS:

As a result of the separation from Great Britain by the colonies, acting as a unit, the powers of external sovereignty passed from the Crown not to the colonies separately, but to the colonies in their collective and corporate capacity as the United States of America. Even before the Declaration, the colonies were a unit in foreign affairs, acting through a common agency—namely, the Continental Congress. . . . A political society cannot endure without a supreme will somewhere. Sovereignty is never held in suspense. . . .

It results that the investment of the federal government with the powers of external sovereignty did not depend upon the affirmative grants of the Constitution. The powers to declare and wage war, to conclude peace, to make treaties, to maintain diplomatic relation with other sovereignties, if they had never been mentioned in the Constitu-

tion, would have vested in the federal government as necessary concomitants of nationality. . . . The power to acquire territory by discovery and occupation, . . . the power to expel undesirable aliens, . . . the power to make such international agreements as do not constitute treaties in the constitutional sense, . . . none of which is expressly affirmed by the Constitution, nevertheless exist as inherently inseparable from the conception of nationality. . . .

Not only, as we have shown, is the federal power over external affairs in origin and essential character different from that over internal affairs, but participation in the exercise of the power is significantly limited. In this vast external realm, with its important and complicated, delicate and manifold problems, the President alone has the power to speak or listen as a representative of the nation. He *makes* treaties with the advice and consent of the Senate; but he alone negotiates. Into the field of negotiations the Senate cannot intrude; and Congress itself is powerless to invade it. . . .

It is important to bear in mind that we are here dealing not alone with an authority vested in the President by an exertion of legislative power, but with such an authority plus the very delicate, plenary and exclusive power of the President as the sole organ of the federal government in the field of international relations—a power which does not require as a basis for its exercise an act of Congress, but which, of course, like every other governmental power, must be exercised in subordination to the applicable provisions of the Constitution. It is quite apparent that if, in the maintenance of our international relations, embarrassment—perhaps serious embarrassment—is to be avoided and success for our aims achieved, congressional legislation which is to be made effective through negotiation and inquiry within the international field must often accord to the President a degree of discretion and freedom from statutory restriction which would not be admissable were domestic affairs alone involved. Moreover, he, not Congress, has the better opportunity of knowing the conditions which prevail in foreign countries and especially this is true in time of war. He has his confidential sources of information. He has his agents in the form of diplomatic, consular and other officials. Secrecy in respect of information gathered by them may be highly necessary, and the premature disclosure of it productive of harmful results. . . .

Congress and the President have delegated much of their authority over international commercial issues to administrative agencies. The Departments of State, Defense, and Commerce are the primary international regulators, although many other agencies involve themselves in international matters. One of the rationales for the lack of American competitiveness in world markets is the patchwork of government agencies regulating international businesses. This book will be replete with examples of the confusion and delay that can result from the American approach to the regulation of international trade.

Other countries have their own internal frameworks for controlling the flow of goods, services, technology, and money across their borders. The institutions of government and their roles in supervising business will vary according to the legal traditions of each country. Chapters 3 and 4 will introduce some of the major legal traditions and some of the ways those traditions affect the relationship of government and business.

2.3 PUBLIC INTERNATIONAL LAW

When most people think of international law, they think first of what is known as public international law. As the name implies, public international law is the set of rules that governs the relationships among countries, and, increasingly, governs international organizations like the United Nations. Public international law deals primarily with questions of war and peace, human rights, and territorial rights. The response of the United Nations to Iraq's 1991 invasion of Kuwait is one good example of the modern use of international law as a set of principles to guide the actions of individual countries.

Public international law has a long history. The rights of nations have been determined, primarily by means of war and diplomacy, for centuries. During this time, a body of widely recognized legal principles has evolved defining the rights of sovereign nations and the limits on those rights. A systematic examination of the major principles of public international law would fill volumes; we will concentrate on the principles that have direct application to international business.

As one example of the use of public international law in business activity, consider the problem of state succession. Suppose that a French bank has loaned money to the government of the U.S.S.R.: Now that the U.S.S.R. has collapsed, does the new Russian government have to pay the debt? If a U.S. company had a contract to provide electrical equipment to the government of Iran under the shah, does the new Islamic government of Iran succeed to those obligations after its successful revolution against the shah? As a general rule, the answer is yes. On the other hand, there are many examples of countries that have repudiated the debts of former governments. For example, the Soviet government refused to pay bonds incurred under the czar, and only acknowledged those obligations in the late 1980s. After the United States assumed control of Cuba from Spain, it refused to recognize Spanish debts incurred on Cuba's behalf at an earlier time.[1]

As the example above suggests, perhaps the most difficult question of international law pertains to its enforcement. Who decides whether a nation has violated international law? How does a nation enforce the rules of public international law against another nation? There is no wholly satisfactory answer to the question, but alleged violations of international law are often resolved through diplomacy, arbitration, or the United Nations. In particular, the International Court of Justice, the judicial agency of the United Nations, hears claims one nation may have that another has violated international law. It has, however, no enforcement power, and must rely on diplomatic or economic sanctions against violators of international law. In the example of the Soviet debt repudiation, time and financial need are solving the problem. In order to return to the international bond markets, the government of the former Soviet Union found it advantageous to reach agreements with its creditors.

The primary sources of international law are international custom and treaties or other agreements between nations. The body of legal principles developed from these sources both gives rights to and limits the rights of nations.

TREATIES AND INTERNATIONAL AGREEMENTS

Many of the principles of international law derive from treaties or other agreements among nations. Treaties establish international organizations like the United Nations and the European Community; establish trading frameworks like the Canada-United States Free Trade Agreement and the United Nations Convention on the International Sale of Goods; and resolve specific disputes among nations, as in signing the arms-reduction treaties between the former Soviet Union and the United States.

---

[1]Theroux and Peele, "China and Sovereign Immunity: The Huguang Railway Bonds Case," 2 *China Law Reporter* 129, 133–134 (1982–1983).

Treaties are essentially contracts between sovereigns. They may be bilateral—between two nations—or multilateral—among many nations. They may be self-executing, meaning that no internal legislation is needed to bring them into force, or they may need further legislation in each country, for regulations or appropriations.

In the United States, the President has the constitutional power to negotiate treaties, but must submit them to the Senate for its "advice and consent," signified by a two-thirds vote for ratification. A ratified treaty becomes federal law, superseding any contrary state laws and any prior federal legislation. In other countries, treaties may need ratification by national legislatures, or even by national referendum. For example, in 1992, the Danish people narrowly defeated the European Community Treaty on Monetary and Political Union, known as the Maastricht Agreement. An Irish referendum on the same agreement approved the treaty by a wide margin. Chapter 5 will cover these events in more detail.

As a practical matter, the treaty provisions of the U.S. Constitution have produced ongoing tension between Congress and the President. Recall, for example, President Wilson's inability to obtain Senate ratification for the League of Nations at the end of World War I. The process of ratification is also cumbersome; it can take months. The treaty provisions of the Constitution sometimes create frustration for other countries, especially when the President negotiates an agreement that the Senate later rejects or amends to the point of unacceptability.

In part to cope with some of the problems inherent in the treaty process, the President also makes executive agreements with other nations. In some instances, Congress will authorize the President to negotiate agreements, particularly in the area of commerce. In other instances, the President will enter into executive agreements with other nations on the basis of his general constitutional powers as commander-in-chief or to conduct foreign affairs. As a matter of international law, executive agreements and treaties are both considered equally binding obligations of the United States.

The subjects of executive agreements range from the resolution of claims by or against the United States (such as the Algerian agreement ending the embassy hostage crisis in Iran) to the employment of local civilians at military bases overseas (such as the agreement with the Philippines on this subject). In the past few decades, the use of executive agreements has grown exponentially. Whereas the United States may enter into ten to twenty treaties per year, the President will make literally hundreds of executive agreements.

Because each executive agreement represents a national commitment of the United States, Congress has expressed its concern, and sometimes outrage, at presidential use of the agreements to circumvent the checks and balances of the Constitution's treaty powers. Legislation passed in the 1970s requires the President to report all executive agreements to Congress within 60 days of signing.

CUSTOM AND GENERAL PRINCIPLES

The bulk of international law consists not of formal written agreements, but of custom and tradition. It can be difficult to determine what constitutes a custom. Courts often refer to custom in terms of the principles of "civilized nations," by which they probably mean Western, free-market oriented, or developed nations.

Commercial practice is one area in which the laws of various nations do converge. As Chapter 1 discussed, the law merchant is an evolving set of rules of international commerce, developed and practiced by traders since the rise of commerce in the Middle Ages. Today, although the details may vary in different countries, large areas of laws concerning contracts, shipping, and payment are similar regardless of whether the legal system is Western or Eastern, free-market or socialist. Chapters 6 to 9 examine the subjects of the law merchant in detail.

2.4 LIMITS ON NATIONAL POWER

Two of the most important principles concerning the rights of nations to regulate people and businesses are the concepts of nationality and jurisdiction. From these two ideas come the bases for the regulation of multinational business activity, and for the respect that one nation will show for the acts of another.

NATIONALITY

Historically, nationality has been an extremely important concept. A country has a customary right to act to protect the interests of its nationals at home and abroad. Nationality is a somewhat broader concept than citizenship. A person is a national of the country to which she owes allegiance and to which she looks for protection.

People generally acquire nationality at birth, becoming a national of the place of birth or of the same country as one or both parents. A person may change nationality by emigrating to or by becoming a permanent resident of another country. Each country has different standards for determining whether a person is its national and when a person loses status as a national.

A more difficult question is the nationality of corporations, especially multinational businesses. In exercising control over corporate activities, nations do look to several different factors, including the nationality of shareholders, bondholders, officers, directors, and employees; the place of incorporation; the place of the headquarters or center of business activity, or the place of most significant contacts.

With so many possible bases for claiming corporate nationality, more than one government may seek to protect the interests of business nationals against violations of international law. The resolution of just this problem is the subject of the *Barcelona Traction* case that follows.

CASE CONCERNING THE BARCELONA TRACTION, LIGHT AND POWER COMPANY, LIMITED (NEW APPLICATION: 1962) (BELGIUM v. SPAIN)

[1970] I.C.J. Rep. 4
International Court of Justice

FACTS:

Barcelona Traction was incorporated as a holding company in Canada in 1911. It formed several subsidiary corporations under Canadian and Spanish law, and engaged in producing and distributing electric power in Spain. After World War I, most of its stock was controlled by Belgian nationals, largely by one Belgian financial group.

The Spanish Civil War in 1936 caused Barcelona Traction great difficulty in meeting bond payments, and currency problems throughout World War II continued to create problems for the company in meeting its obligations to its bondholders. In 1948, three Spanish bondholders petitioned a Spanish court for a declaration of bankruptcy. The court granted the petition, seized the assets of the company, and appointed Spanish directors and administrators for the subsidiaries involved. In 1949, the Spanish court authorized the sale of new stock for the subsidiaries, which were sold to a Spanish company by auction in 1952.

The Canadian courts refused to recognize the validity of the bankruptcy proceedings in Spain. The Canadian board of directors continued in office until a Canadian court appointed a receiver for the company.

Belgium, Canada, Great Britain, and the United States protested Spain's actions through diplomatic channels, to no avail. Belgium commenced an action against Spain in the International Court of Justice in 1958, alleging that the actions of the Spanish courts violated international law, and

seeking compensation for the Belgian shareholders. The countries discontinued the action in 1961 to make another attempt at settlement, but Belgium refiled the action in 1962 when those attempts failed.

ISSUE:

Does Belgium have the right to protect the interests of Barcelona Traction against violations of international law?

RESULT:

No. Canada is the only government that may negotiate on behalf of the corporation.

REASONS:

42.[2] It is a basic characteristic of the corporate structure that the company alone, through its directors or management acting in its name, can take action in respect of matters that are of a corporate character. The underlying justification for this is that, in seeking to serve its own best interests, the company will serve those of the shareholder too. Ordinarily, no individual shareholder can take legal steps, either in the name of the company or in his own name. If the shareholders disagree with the decisions taken on behalf of the company, they may, in accordance with its articles or the relevant provisions of the law, change

---

[2]Like many courts around the world, the ICJ numbers the paragraphs of its decisions.

them or replace its officers, or take such action as is provided by law. Thus to protect the company against abuse by its management or the majority of its shareholders, several municipal legal systems have vested in shareholders (sometimes a particular number is specified) the right to bring an action for the defence of the company, and conferred upon the minority of shareholders certain rights to guard against decisions affecting the rights of the company vis-a-vis its management or controlling shareholders. Nonetheless the shareholders' rights in relation to the company and its assets remain limited, this being, moreover, a corollary of the limited nature of their liability. . . .

51. On an international plane, the Belgian Government has advanced the proposition that it is inadmissable to deny the shareholders' national State a right of diplomatic protection merely on the ground that another State possesses a corresponding right in respect of the company itself. . . . In fact the Belgian Government has repeatedly stressed that there exists no rule of international law which would deny the national State of the Shareholders the right of diplomatic protection for the purpose of seeking redress pursuant to unlawful acts committed by another State against the company in which they hold shares. This, by emphasizing the absence of any express denial of the right, conversely implies the admission that there is no rule of international law which expressly confers such a right on the shareholders' national State. . . .

70. In allocating corporate entities to States for purposes of diplomatic protection, international law is based, but only to a limited extent, on an analogy with the rules governing the nationality of individuals. The traditional rule attributes the right of diplomatic protection of a corporate entity to the State under the laws of which it is incorporated and in whose territory it has its registered office. These two criteria have been confirmed by long practice and by numerous international instruments. This notwithstanding, further or different links are at times said to be required in order that a right of diplomatic protection should exist. Indeed, it has been the practice of some States to give a company incorporated under their law diplomatic protection solely when it has its seat *(siege social)* or management or centre of control in their territory, or when a majority or a substantial proportion of the shares has been owned by nationals of the State concerned. . . .

71. In the present case, it is not disputed that the company was incorporated in Canada and has its registered office in that country. The incorporation of the company under the law of Canada was an act of free choice. Not only did the founders of the company seek its incorporation under Canadian law but it has remained under that law for a period of over 50 years. It has maintained in Canada its registered office, its accounts and its share registers. Board meetings were held there for many years; it has been listed in the records of the Canadian tax authorities. Thus a close and permanent connection has been established, fortified by the passage of over half a century. This connection is in no way weakened by the fact that the company engaged from the very outset in commercial activities outside Canada, for that was its declared object. Barcelona Traction's links with Canada are manifold. . . .

76. In sum, the record shows that from 1948 onwards the Canadian Government made to the Spanish Government numerous representations which cannot be viewed otherwise than as the exercise of diplomatic protection in respect of the Barcelona Traction company. Therefore this was not a case where diplomatic protection was refused or remained in the sphere of fiction. It is also clear that over the whole period of its diplomatic activity the Canadian Government proceeded in full knowledge of the Belgian attitude and activity.

77. It is true that at a certain point the Canadian Government ceased to act on behalf of Barcelona Traction, for reasons which have not been fully revealed, though a statement made in a letter of 19 July 1955 by the Canadian Secretary of State for External Affairs suggests that it felt the matter should be settled by means of private negotiations. The Canadian Government has nonetheless retained its capacity to exercise diplomatic protection; no legal impediment has prevented it from doing so; no fact has arisen to render this protection impossible. It has discontinued its action of its own free will. . . .

96. The Court considers that the adoption of the theory of diplomatic protection of shareholders as such, by opening the door to competing diplomatic claims, could create an atmosphere of confusion and insecurity in international economic relations. The danger would be all the greater inasmuch as the shares of companies whose activities are international are widely scattered and frequently change hands.

The *Barcelona Traction* case holds some important lessons for investors in multinational enterprises. With the nationality of the corporation determined by the place of incorporation and connection, investors may be forced to resort to the legal processes of that country to protect their interests. They have no remedy in international law.

JURISDICTION

Perhaps the most significant limit in international law on the right of nations to control business activities is the concept of jurisdiction. Jurisdiction takes two forms: power over the subject matter of a dispute and power over the persons involved in the dispute. In the international business context, most disputes center around the issue of personal jurisdiction. A manager might frame the question as: "When might I get dragged into court in a foreign country?"

The traditional bases for the exercise of jurisdiction over a defendant have been consent, appearance, and presence. Consent is relatively straightforward, and is generally a matter of contract between the plaintiff and defendant. Appearance in court to contest a dispute also generally confers jurisdiction over the person, although some nations still recognize limited or conditional appearances, for the sole purpose of contesting the jurisdiction of the court. Presence generally involves the ability to find the defendant within the territory covered by the court. In the case of a business, presence means continuous business activity.

If a defendant is absent from the country of the court, domicile becomes the key legal basis for jurisdiction. Domicile, a concept closely related to that of nationality, is that place of permanent residence to which one intends to return when away. A person may have more than one residence, but only one domicile. Some countries treat a corporation's domicile as its place of incorporation, but the more prevalent practice is to look for the center of its business activities (*siege social* in French, *sitz* in German).

Another basis for jurisdiction over defendants is the presence of property within the territory of the court. In many countries, the presence of property establishes the power of the courts to hear all claims against a defendant, including those not involving the property.

A more controversial basis for jurisdiction, asserted most notably by the French Civil Code, is the nationality of the parties. French courts will hear complaints brought by French nationals against foreign defendants, even if the transaction took place outside of France and the French national does not reside in France. Similarly, a French national, even if nonresident, may be sued in French courts on obligations incurred inside or outside of France. This approach to jurisdiction has not found wide acceptance.

Most countries now have some form of "long-arm jurisdiction," enabling their courts to hear cases arising out of transactions taking place in the country by a defendant outside the country. These long-arm provisions generally allow a court to reach outside national boundaries to find a defendant who contracted within the country or committed a tort within the country. The defendant is not subject to general jurisdiction, but only jurisdiction related to the activity within the country hearing the case. These long-arm statutes raise some questions of the fundamental fairness of proceedings against the defendant, and may open an avenue to attack the enforcement of a foreign judgment.

EXTRATERRITORIAL JURISDICTION

A more difficult question of jurisdiction is that of the power of a nation to regulate activities occurring beyond its borders. Governed by principles of public international law, the question of legislative jurisdiction extends to economic legislation and to criminal law.

A nation, as a function of its sovereign power, has the fundamental right to regulate activities within its territory. A second right under international law is the right to regulate the activities of its nationals and punish violations of law they commit, even if the problem occurs outside the territory. Thus, an American national who commits tax fraud under American law may be indicted, even if the fraud took place abroad.

Beyond these two fundamental bases, the right of a nation to affect conduct beyond its borders is not clear. Some, but not all, governments claim the right to apply their law to conduct abroad that prejudices national security or other public policy interests. Some governments claim the right to act when the victim of a foreign action is its national. Not all nations accept these bases for government action. As Chapter 13 will discuss, they have been particularly problematic in the areas of antitrust law, provoking diplomatic incidents on several occasions.

Finally, in a few instances, any nation that can gain custody of a defendant may try and punish him. This universal jurisdiction is applicable in the case of piracy, slave trading, and crimes against humanity. There is considerable movement to add to the list of universal crimes acts of air piracy, genocide, and severe torture, but at this time such actions are not universally regarded as violations of the law of nations.

2.5 INTERNATIONAL ORGANIZATIONS

The future of international law may lie with international organizations. Whether the problem is the regulation of pollutants, such as chlorofluorocarbons (CFCs) or acid rain; nuclear energy; business exploitation of the sea floor; or the marketing practices of multinational corporations, the legal problems associated with business activities do not fit neatly within national boundaries. In some cases the only solutions to business problems may be regional or global solutions.

Although nations have always entered into alliances and treaties with other nations, the 20th century is the first to see the creation of independent organizations, generally with their own purpose delegated by the member nations, the ability to act relatively independently of the treaty processes of the member nations, and their own internal structure and bureaucracy. The first modern attempt at a true international organization was the League of Nations, which came into existence at the close of the World War I, and was largely unsuccessful at preventing World War II.

At the close of World War II, the victorious nations sought to prevent a repeat of the conditions that led to the worldwide economic depression of the 1930s and the subsequent war. Several international organizations were the product of the collaboration at the end of the war.

THE UNITED NATIONS

At a conference in San Francisco in 1945, the United Nations Charter came into existence. Ratified as a treaty by the United States and other nations, it led to the organization that has expanded to include most of the nations of the world.

The U.N. is the largest international organization in existence, with an executive branch, the Secretariat; a legislative branch, the General Assembly; and a judicial branch, the International Court of Justice. It also has a very large bureaucracy, including agencies working in such areas as public health, economic development, population research, and meteorology.

Although the U.N. is publicly best known for acrimonious political debates and for its dispersement of peacekeeping forces to areas of battle around the world, it has also played a growing role in the development of international business law. In particular, the United Nations Commission on International Trade Law (UNCITRAL) has slowly but successfully brought free-market and Socialist nations together to unify several areas of commercial law. The U.N. Convention on the International Sale of Goods (CISG), which will be discussed in Chapters 6 and 7, is one example of UNCITRAL's successful work. The nations adopting the CISG include not only developed nations like the United States, France, and Italy, but Socialist and developing nations as well, like the People's Republic of China and Argentina.

ECONOMIC ORGANIZATIONS

The Western powers tried to establish an organization to secure world peace, but they also realized that the great economic depression of the 1930s helped lead the world to the point where war became an acceptable course of action. At a conference in Bretton Woods, New Hampshire, these nations created an international economic structure designed to establish a controlled world economic order. The framework of organizations included the International Monetary Fund, the World Bank, and a trade organization that became the General Agreements on Tariffs and Trade (GATT).

The International Monetary Fund (IMF) has as its purpose the stabilization of currency and foreign exchange. It acts in some ways like a worldwide central bank, especially as a lender of last resort to nations having foreign exchange problems.

The IMF has played a large role in the developing world. It often conditions its loans on harsh financial measures in debtor nations, such as wage and price controls and reductions in government spending. IMF restrictions have caused political problems for leaders in such countries as Mexico and Argentina. For example, the imposition of IMF controls caused massive riots and a political crisis in Venezuela in 1989. On a business level, IMF conditions can cause difficulty with loan and payment arrangements on private contracts in developing nations, so IMF involvement is a factor in analyzing potential business markets.

The World Bank, by contrast, has had a somewhat quieter history. It makes loans to developing countries, primarily to fund infrastructure projects. To belong to the World Bank, a nation must also be a member of the IMF, so there has been some interplay between World Bank loans and IMF economic controls.

At the Bretton Woods conference, the participants envisioned the establishment of an international trade organization, designed to prevent the disastrous trade wars that led directly to the worldwide depression of the 1930s. When it became apparent that the U.S. Senate would not ratify the proposed International Trade Organization, the governments created a set of agreements (in the case of the United States, executive agreements, not ratified by the Senate) establishing a framework for the reduction of tariffs and trade barriers. The General Agreements on Tariffs and Trade (GATT) have proved to be an extremely useful vehicle for preventing tariff and trade wars, although its continued usefulness is currently at risk. Chapters 10 and 11 will discuss the GATT and its principles in detail.

REGIONAL ORGANIZATIONS

The decades since World War II have seen the rise and sometimes fall of a variety of regional political and economic organizations. For some organizations, like the European Community, the original purpose was to increase trade among members. For others like the Organization of American States (OAS) or the Association of South East Asian Nations (ASEAN), the original purpose of the regional organization was to enhance collective security. Over time, the trade-based regional organizations have tended to develop political objectives, while the security-based organizations have started to discuss trade issues.

The most important regional organization (which is the subject of Chapter 5) is the European Community. It is beginning to be widely emulated in other parts of the world. Both Central and South American nations have formed similar organizations, without the same degree of success, and there is now an organization of African countries whose objective is to create an African community. If the movement toward a single European market is successful, businesses should expect to see the revival and growth of similar economic organizations in other parts of the world.

2.6 PRIVATE INTERNATIONAL LAW

In discussing the role of international law in business, courts consider two different kinds of international law. As the text discusses above, public international law regulates the way that nations treat each other and each other's nationals. The second kind, of more immediate importance to specific business transactions, is private international law. Private international law is really another form of national law, this time dealing not with movement across borders, but with the effect of another nation's laws in its own courts.

In a contract dispute between an American seller and a Japanese buyer, whose law governs the transaction? Will a Swedish court enforce a judgment against a Swedish company obtained in an American court? Although the laws of the nation in which a court is resolving the problem may govern the result, the general principles of comity and reciprocity will influence the outcome of the case. The following case is the classic explanation of the concept of comity. Note carefully how it differs from the concept of reciprocity.

HILTON v. GUYOT

159 U.S. 113 (1895)
Supreme Court of the United States

FACTS:
The representatives of a French firm brought an action in a federal district court against two U.S. partners to collect on a judgment obtained in France. Nearly $200,000 of the French judgment remained unpaid. In the federal court, the defendants denied they owed the money, and claimed that the French judgment against them had been

procured by fraud. The plaintiffs prevailed in the lower courts, and the defendants appealed to the Supreme Court.

ISSUE:
Are there any grounds on which the defendants may challenge the French judgment?

RESULT:
Yes. Decision reversed and remanded for a new trial.

REASONS:
International law, in its widest and most comprehensive sense,—including not only questions of right between nations, governed by what has been appropriately called the "law of nations," but also questions arising under what is usually called "private international law," or the "conflicts of laws," and concerning the rights of persons within the territory and dominion of one nation, by reason of acts, private or public, done within the dominions of another nation,—is part of our law, and must be ascertained and administered by the courts of justice as often as such questions are presented in litigation between man and man, duly submitted to their determination. . . .

No law has any effect, of its own force, beyond the limits of the sovereignty from which its authority is derived. The extent to which the law of one nation, as put in force within its territory . . . shall be allowed to operate within the dominion of another nation, depends upon what our greatest jurists have been content to call "the comity of nations." Although the phrase has been often criticised, no satisfactory substitute has been suggested.

"Comity," in the legal sense, is neither a matter of absolute obligation, on the one hand, nor of mere courtesy and good will, upon the other. But it is the recognition which one nation allows within its territory to the legislative, executive, or judicial acts of another nation, having due regard both to international duty and convenience, and to the rights of its own citizens, or of other persons who are under the protection of its laws. . . .

In view of all the authorities upon the subject, and of the trend of judicial opinion in this country and in England . . . , we are satisfied that where there has been an opportunity for a full and fair trial abroad before a court of competent jurisdiction, conducting the trial upon regular proceedings, after due citation or voluntary appearance of the defendant, and under a system of jurisprudence likely to secure an impartial administration of justice between the citizens of its own country and those of other countries, and there is nothing to show either prejudice in the court, or in the system of laws under which it was sitting, or fraud in procuring the judgment, or any other special reason why the comity of the nation should not allow it full effect, the merits of the case should not, in an action brought in this country upon the judgment, be tried afresh, as on a new trial or an appeal, upon the mere assertion of the party that the judgment was erroneous in law or in fact. The defendants, therefore, cannot be permitted, upon that general ground, to contest the validity or the effect of the judgment sued on.

[The court then examined the effect that an American judgment would have in a French court, concluding that a French court would review the merits of a case before giving effect to a judgment rendered in a foreign country.] . . . The reasonable, if not the necessary, conclusion appears to us to be that judgments rendered in France, or in any other foreign country, by the laws of which our own judgments are reviewable upon the merits, are not entitled to full credit and conclusive effect when sued upon in this country, but are prima facie evidence only the justice of the plaintiff's claim.

In holding such a judgment, for want of reciprocity, not to be conclusive evidence of the merits of the claim, we do not proceed upon any theory of retaliation upon one person by reason of injustice done to another, but upon the broad ground that international law is founded upon mutuality and reciprocity, and that by the principles of international law recognized in most civilized nations, and by the comity of our own country, which it is our judicial duty to know and to declare, the judgment is not entitled to be considered conclusive.

CONFLICTS OF LAW

A question that appears whenever a business transaction crosses a territorial border is choice of law. On a basic level, the problem exists from state to state: If a sales representative from Missouri has a car accident in Iowa, which state's law governs a subsequent lawsuit? Should it matter whether the victim sues in Missouri or in Iowa? Choice of law is a more complex issue from one nation to another. If a business in Georgia ships a defective product to England where that product injures a consumer, what law governs any subsequent action? Should it matter whether the lawsuit takes place in Georgia or in England? Should it matter if the accident takes place in Hungary, or Singapore, instead of England? Politics, prejudice, and public policy interests may lead to inconsistent results based on what other nations are involved.

The study of conflicts of law has long been a legal theoretician's delight, and thus a manager's nightmare. There are no universal rules for choosing the appropriate law to govern a dispute; rather, different states and countries employ a variety of techniques. These techniques have changed over time.

Historically, choice of law questions have had a territorial foundation. A dispute over property, for example, was generally governed by the law of the place of the property. A tort suit was generally governed by the law of the place where the tort occurred. A contract suit might have been governed by the law of the place where parties concluded the contract, or by the law of the place of performance.

In the 1960s these territorial rules began to fall apart, replaced by several approaches, such as "most significant contacts," "interest analysis," "the better rule," and "the center of gravity" approach. Some of the reasons for the changes may be illustrated by the following case.

BABCOCK v. JACKSON

12 N.Y.2d 473 (1963)
New York Court of Appeals

FACTS:

Babcock and Jackson were both residents of New York who left Rochester on an automobile excursion to Canada. While in Ontario, Jackson lost control of the car and crashed it into a stone wall, injuring Babcock. Babcock sued in New York, alleging that Jackson was negligent in operating the vehicle. Jackson claimed that Ontario law, as that of the place of the tort, should govern the suit.

Ontario at that time had a "guest statute," providing that "the owner or driver of a motor vehicle . . . is not liable for any loss or damages resulting from bodily injury to, or the death of, any person being carried in . . . the motor vehicle."

The trial court agreed with Jackson and dismissed the suit. The Appellate Division affirmed the dismissal. Babcock appealed to the Court of Appeals, the highest state court in New York.

ISSUE:

Should the court apply Ontario law to the lawsuit in New York?

RESULT:

No. Jackson's motion to dismiss the complaint was denied.

REASONS:

The question presented is simply drawn. Shall the law of the place of the tort *invariably* govern the availability of relief for the tort or shall the applicable choice of law rule also reflect a consideration of other factors which are relevant to the purposes served by the enforcement or denial of the remedy?

The traditional choice of law rule . . . has been that the substantive rights and liabilities arising out of a tortious occurrence are determinable by the law of the place of the tort. . . . It had its conceptual foundation in the vested rights doctrine, namely that a right to recover for a foreign tort owes its creation to the law of the jurisdiction where the injury occurred and depends for its existence and extent solely on such law. . . . [T]he vested rights doctrine has long since been discredited because it fails to take account of underlying policy considerations in evaluating the significance to be ascribed to the circumstance that an act had a foreign situs in determining the rights and liabilities which arise out of that act. . . . More particularly, as applied to torts, the theory ignores the interest which jurisdictions other than that where the tort occurred may have in the resolution of particular issues. It is for this very reason that, despite the advantages of certainty, ease of application and predictability which it affords . . . there has in recent years been increasing criticism of the traditional rule by commentators and a judicial trend toward its abandonment or modification.

Significantly, it was dissatisfaction with "the mechanical formulae of conflicts of law" . . . which led to judicial departure from similarly inflexible choice of law rules in the field of contracts, grounded, like the torts rule, on the vested rights doctrine. According to those traditional rules, matters bearing upon the execution, interpretation, and validity of a contract were determinable by the internal law of the place where the contract was made, while matters connected with their performance were regulated by the internal law of the place where the contract was to be performed. . . .

. . . The "center of gravity" or "grouping of contacts" doctrine adopted by this court in conflicts cases involving contracts impresses us as likewise affording the appropriate approach for accommodating the competing interests in tort cases with multi-State contacts. Justice, fairness and "the best practical result" . . . may best be achieved by giving controlling effect to the law of the jurisdiction which, because of its relationship or contact with the occurrence or the parties, has the greatest concern with the specific issue raised in the litigation. The merit of such a rule is that "it gives to the place 'having the most interest in the problem' paramount control over the legal issues arising out of a particular factual context" and thereby allows the forum to apply "the policy of the jurisdiction 'most intimately concerned with the outcome of [the] particular litigation.'". . .

Comparison of the relative "contacts" and "interests" of New York and Ontario in this litigation, vis-a-vis the issue here presented, makes it clear that the concern of New York is unquestionably the greater and more direct and that the interest of Ontario is at best minimal. The present action involves injuries sustained by a New York guest as the result of the negligence of a New York host in the operation of an automobile, garaged, licensed and undoubtedly insured in New York, in the course of a weekend journey which began and was to end there. In sharp contrast, Ontario's sole relationship with the occurrence is the purely adventitious circumstance that the accident occurred there.

New York's policy of requiring a tort-feasor to compensate his guest for injuries caused by his negligence cannot be doubted—as attested by the fact that the Legislature of this State has repeatedly refused to enact a statute denying or limiting recovery in such cases. . . . Per contra, Ontario has no conceivable interest in denying a remedy to a New York guest against his New York host. . . . The object of Ontario's guest statute, it has been said, is "to prevent the fraudulent assertion of claims by passengers, in collusion with the drivers, against insurance companies". . . .

Although this case may have had a clear "center of gravity," other cases may not be so clear. Often times, the choice of law becomes a matter of litigation, with an outcome depending on the result desired by the forum state. Some countries allow the victim in a tort case to choose the applicable law; courts in other countries will almost always choose to apply their own law.

Managers have some techniques available to help plan for choice of law problems. In the contract area, courts will often recognize and respect choices the parties make in their contract. Thus, a manager's best weapon against the uncertainty of conflicts doctrine is simply to specify what law will govern the transaction. Chapter 7 will examine this problem and solution in more detail.

In tort problems, the best preventive measure is to consider the tort law in a potential market as one factor in the decision to do business. If the substantive law of that market seems too onerous, the business should consider whether or not it really wants to enter that market or whether some devices might be available to insulate the foreign company from liability.

ENFORCEMENT OF FOREIGN JUDGMENTS

The second branch of private international law deals with the recognition that the courts of one country will give to the judgments of the courts of another country. In the event of a dispute over an international transaction, the winner will sometimes need to go to another country to find the loser's assets. The winner would prefer not to have to relitigate the merits of the dispute, but to have the original judgment recognized and enforced.

Hilton v. Guyot, earlier in this chapter, sets out the general principles that American courts will use in examining the judgments of courts in other countries. Comity and reciprocity are the watchwords for courts looking at foreign judgments. Of the two concepts, reciprocity is the one observed most frequently around the world. The issue of reciprocity may be handled by treaty. For example, the nations of the European Economic Community have agreed to recognize each other's judgments. If no treaty controls, a court in one country will look at the approach of the other country toward the first country's nationals.

In the United States, the problem of enforcement of foreign judgments is complicated by the limits on the kinds of cases federal courts may hear and on the application of federal law. In many commercial matters, a federal court will apply state law, including the law of recognition of judgments. State courts have formulated their own approaches to the *Hilton* analysis. Some have, at various times, been reluctant to enforce judgments rendered in courts in socialist countries, while others have been more willing than the Supreme Court to give binding effect to foreign judgments.

In order to encourage some uniformity in the state law enforcement of foreign judgments, the National Conference of Commissioners on Uniform

State Laws drafted a Uniform Foreign Money-Judgments Recognition Act. As of the writing of this book, seventeen states have adopted the Uniform Act. The act rejects the requirement of reciprocity in favor of an approach based on a presumption of the validity of the foreign judgment.

Uniform Foreign Money-Judgments Recognition Act (1962)

Sec. 3. [Recognition and Enforcement].—Except as provided in section 4, a foreign judgment meeting the requirements of section 2 is conclusive between the parties to the extent that it grants or denies recovery of a sum of money. The foreign judgment is enforceable in the same manner as the judgment of a sister state which is entitled to full faith and credit.

Sec. 4. [Grounds for Non-recognition].

(a) A foreign judgment is not conclusive if

(1) the judgment was rendered under a system which does not provide impartial tribunals or procedures compatible with due process of law;

(2) the foreign court did not have personal jurisdiction over the defendant; or

(3) the foreign court did not have jurisdiction over the subject matter.

(b) A foreign judgment need not be recognized if

(1) the defendant in the proceedings in the foreign country did not receive notice in sufficient time to enable him to defend;

(2) the judgment was obtained by fraud;

(3) the [cause of action] [claim for relief] on which the judgment is based is repugnant to the public policy of this state;

(4) the judgment conflicts with another final and conclusive judgment;

(5) the proceeding in the foreign court was contrary to an agreement between the parties under which the dispute in question was to be settled otherwise than by proceedings in that court; or

(6) in the case of jurisdiction based only on personal service, the foreign court was a seriously inconvenient forum for the trial of the action.

The effect of the Uniform Act is to have courts begin a case with a presumption in favor of the foreign money judgment. It will be difficult for the defendant in an enforcement action to overcome the presumption of the judgment's validity. Businesspeople will have limited reasons for attacking the judgment. The following case illustrates the perils a manager faces by choosing to ignore court proceedings in other countries.

BANK OF MONTREAL v. KOUGH

612 F.2d 467 (9th Cir. 1980)

FACTS:

Kough, a California resident, was a shareholder, officer, and director of Arvee Cedar Mills, Ltd., a corporation organized and located in British Co-lumbia. Kough personally guaranteed loans made by the Bank of Montreal to Arvee. When Arvee defaulted on the loans, the bank sued Kough on his guarantee in British Columbia. Kough was personally served with notice of the suit at his home in California, but did not appear to contest the Canadian court action against him. The Court entered a default judgment of $842,278.75 against Kough.

The bank sued in the federal district court in California to enforce the Canadian money judgment. Kough claimed that the court should not enforce the judgment first, because he received notice of the suit in California, not British Columbia; and second, because a California judgment would not have conclusive effect in British Columbia. He also added several counterclaims against the bank.

The district court ruled in favor of the bank, based on the Uniform Foreign Money Judgments Recognition Act (UFMJRA), and Kough appealed.

ISSUE:
Should the court enforce the British Columbia judgment against Kough? May he assert his counterclaims against the bank in California?

RESULT:
Yes. The judgment did not violate concepts of due process, nor is reciprocity required. No. Kough had his opportunity to make counterclaims in the British Columbia lawsuit. Judgment against Kough affirmed.

REASONS:
The Supreme Court has repeatedly recognized that a constitutionally valid judgment which is entitled to full faith and credit in sister states may be entered by a state court as long as there is "a sufficient connection between the defendant and the forum state as to make it fair to require defense of the action in the forum," and provided that the defendant has received "reasonable notice" of the proceedings against him. . . .

This appeal involves the recognition by California of the judgment of a Canadian province, not a sister state, but the language of [the UFMJRA] . . . seems to us to leave the door open for the recognition by California courts of foreign judgments rendered in accordance with American principles of jurisdictional due process.

With respect to both minimum contacts with the forum state and adequate notice, those principles were satisfied in this case. Kough did have substantial contacts with British Columbia not only by means of the execution and breach of the guarantee there, but also by prior negotiations there involving the guarantee and by other promissory notes to the Bank previously executed. Since Kough was served at his California residence, no question can be seriously raised as to the adequacy of the personal service. . . .

Kough also invokes the doctrine of reciprocity to defeat the recognition of the Canadian judgment. He predicates this argument upon his contention that British Columbia would refuse to recognize a default judgment rendered against one of its citizens in the United States under similar circumstances. . . .

The difficulty with appellant's argument is that the section of the Uniform Act specifically dealing with the circumstances where recognition should or may be denied . . . makes no mention of reciprocity, and we find nothing in the Act which authorizes us to read such a prerequisite into the statutory scheme by implication.

[The court then discussed Kough's counterclaims, holding that they "were so intimately intertwined" with the bank's claims against Kough that the Canadian court decision should be conclusive on the counterclaims as well as the main claims.]

The *Kough* case holds two important lessons for managers. The first is that since the recognition of foreign judgments is a state law, not federal law matter, court decisions may vary from state to state. Some states will follow the *Hilton* criteria, some are bound to follow the Uniform Act, and some will follow the ideas in the Uniform Act, even where the state has not adopted the Act. If there is a trend, it is toward more frequent enforcement of foreign judgments.

The second lesson of *Kough* is that a business ignores a foreign action at its peril. A decision to default abroad is a calculated risk, and probably not a good risk. That decision may lead both to an enforceable judgment against the business and to the loss of the opportunity to assert claims against the other party.

The problems of enforcing foreign judgments increase when the judgment involves some remedy other than money. Generally, courts are extremely reluctant to enforce injunctions, specific performance, or other equitable remedies. Courts are also reluctant to enforce either tax or criminal law judgments from other countries. However, if a country has a treaty calling for reciprocal tax collections or for extradition for criminal acts, the courts will follow the terms of the treaty. Thus, there is a wide network of tax treaties and extradition treaties allowing for the collection of revenues and the return of criminals to the judgment country. Some of these treaties will be discussed later in this book.

2.7 CONCLUSION

This chapter has introduced the different kinds of law that affect international business. Obviously, the laws of each nation touched by an international transaction will apply. Each nation will also have its own rules for resolving the problems caused by acts taking place outside its borders but affecting its interests. The rules of private international law will influence business transactions. Finally, the rules of public international law have a direct effect on business, either through treaties or through the law merchant.

You should leave this chapter with two main lessons. First, international law has a heavy component of politics. What seems to be a simple legal issue may turn into a diplomatic dilemma requiring lengthy negotiation. The interest of the business may be subordinate to the interest of the nation. As in *Barcelona Traction*, when the politicians lose interest, investors and traders may lose money.

Second, a business needs to anticipate problems and plan for them. Choice of law, choice of forum, jurisdiction, and remedies are all manageable problems, if you think about them in advance. Much of the rest of this book will be devoted to preventive law—the successful ways to avoid expensive and uncertain litigation in unfamiliar legal systems.

2.8 QUESTIONS FOR DISCUSSION

1. After a cloud of toxic gas escaped a chemical plant in India, many of the victims filed suit against Union Carbide Corporation in the United States and in India. The government of India then brought suit in the

United States against Union Carbide. It sued in parens patriae, that is, on behalf of all Indian nationals. Its suit replaced all individual suits in any court by an Indian national. By depriving Indian nationals of their individual days in court, does the government's action violate international law?

2. Does the logic of the Barcelona Traction case make sense when applied to large multinational enterprises? Are there better solutions? Explain.

3. Manitoba Outfitters is a Canadian business with a successful product line of winter outdoor clothing and equipment for winter recreation. The company is considering starting a mail order operation to sell its clothing and equipment to Canadian and U.S. customers. Customers would place orders by calling or writing the Manitoba headquarters, and orders would be shipped postage paid to the customers. Prepare a brief memo to the president of the company explaining what law might apply to a dispute (a) with a customer over defective merchandise, or (b) with a U.S. person who has been injured by defective merchandise. Would the company have to be ready to defend itself in all U.S. states and Canadian provinces? Explain.

4. As a class project, take a survey of your class, asking each person for his or her nationality and domicile. Are there people for whom the two are different? Are there people with more than one nationality? What consequences does dual nationality have?

2.9 FURTHER READINGS

For a good discussion of international law in a business-oriented context, see Henry J. Steiner and Detlev Vagts: *Transnational Legal Problems,* 3d ed. Foundation Press, Mineola, N.Y., 1986.

Each of the international organizations mentioned in this chapter has numerous publications available to the public through its public affairs office. The U.N. office in New York and the EC office in Washington, D.C., have many useful publications for students interested in the history, structure, and activities of these organizations.

MAJOR WESTERN LEGAL TRADITIONS

3.1 INTRODUCTION

Managers doing business in the global marketplace need to be aware that American attitudes toward law and toward lawyers in business are probably not shared by managers in other countries. Differences range from matters of style to those of the fundamental substance of the law. For example, lawyers in the United States often sit at the negotiating table with executives during contract negotiations. By contrast, in Japan, the presence of lawyers may be seen as a sign of the negotiating manager's lack of authority to conclude the deal. On a more substantive level, a typical American assumption that loans should be repaid with interest violates a fundamental tenet of Islamic law, where a contract calling for interest payments may be void.

An American trader carrying American assumptions about law into business transactions in foreign countries may find numerous pitfalls and surprises, and may even jeopardize business relationships. Although it is not possible to know the law of every country, you can be aware of possible differences in attitudes toward law and lawyers. You could also know how to ask the kinds of questions that will reveal those differences before you deal with executives in other countries.

The purpose of Chapters 3 and 4 is to introduce you to several different ways of thinking about law and its role in business. These different ways of thinking about law can be grouped into legal traditions. In some instances, many different countries derive their legal systems from one legal tradition. For example, the civil law tradition is the source for the legal systems of most of Europe and Latin America. Although specific laws and legal structures will vary among countries, the underlying attitudes and principles have the same historical source.

In order to give you an understanding of the practical application of major legal traditions, Chapters 3 and 4 will present examples from five different countries, all major current and future trading partners of the United States. They are also good examples of how a country will use a legal tradition as a basis for its legal system, and how different legal traditions can combine in a country, due to wars, colonialism, or ethnic interests.

WESTERN LEGAL TRADITIONS

Most of Europe and the Western Hemisphere share a common set of legal ancestors, dating back to ancient Greece and to the Roman empire. From these common roots grew three legal traditions: the common law, the civil law, and Socialist law. In the late 1980s, the Socialist legal tradition in force across Central and Eastern Europe collapsed, leaving legal uncertainty in its wake. It appears now that many of the former Socialist law countries will look to the civil law tradition as they develop new, free market–based legal systems.

3.2 THE COMMON LAW TRADITION: CANADA

THE COMMON LAW

American students are already familiar with the common law. It is the framework for the law we know from television, movies, and books, as well as from our own experience. The United States shares the fundamental principles of its law and legal system with Canada, Australia, New Zealand, Great Britain (except Scotland), and other areas once colonized by the English.

As a legal system, the common law dates back to the Norman conquest of England in 1066. At that time, disputes were resolved locally, and local custom determined legal rights. With the unification of England came attempts to make legal rights and duties uniform throughout the kingdom. The king's judges, traveling from town to town, began to apply the same reasoning to similar cases, and from those cases develop law common to the kingdom.

SOURCES OF LAW

Although each common law country recognizes legislation as a major source of law, the primary focus of the common law is the case. In common law countries, vast areas of law, such as contracts, torts, and agency, are controlled by collections of principles deduced from specific disputes resolved in an adversary process. The law in these areas evolves over time as judges apply the reasoning of prior cases to new facts.

A key concept in the common law is that similar disputes should achieve similar legal results. Thus, parties to a dispute will search for earlier, similar cases with favorable outcomes. Those earlier cases have precedential value to a current dispute. If an earlier case is from a higher court in the same jurisdiction, a subsequent judge generally must follow the earlier decision.

Precedents in common law countries provide the stability needed for people and businesses to plan future actions. Courts in common law countries follow the ancient legal maxim, *stare decisis et non quieta movere* (adhere to precedents and do not unsettle established things), which is known as the principle of *stare decisis*. As a result, once a court decides a case, later courts will rarely declare it wrong and change the rule. For example, the United States Supreme Court decided in the 1896 case of *Plessy v. Ferguson*[1] that segregated accommodations for blacks did not offend the Constitution if those accommodations were separate but equal. For the next 58 years, victims of discrimination sought to distinguish the facts of their

---

[1]163 U.S. 537 (1896)

cases from those of *Plessy*. Only in 1954, in the case of *Brown v. Board of Education*,[2] did the court conclude that its earlier decision was wrong and overrule it.

The value of precedent is obviously much stronger in countries with only one court system than in countries having parallel state and federal systems. The United States, for example, has state courts with defined areas of competence and federal courts with defined areas of competence. A decision from the Supreme Court of Ohio will not bind the Supreme Court of Indiana, hearing a case with similar facts. By contrast, a decision of the Court of Appeal in England will control lower court decisions nationwide.

Legislation and its accompanying regulations are another major source of law in common law countries. Cases provide rules for individual, specific circumstances, whereas legislation and regulation provide blanket rules. Legislation overrides case results, although in some countries, like the United States, the power of legislators to make rules is limited by a constitution.

Finally, tradition is a major source of law in common law countries. The customary practices of an industry or of government institutions influence the way a judge will look at a particular case.

THE CANADIAN LEGAL SYSTEM AND THE COMMON LAW

Canada provides an interesting example of the evolution of a legal system based on the common law tradition. In many ways, its legal system will seem familiar to American students, yet Canada is surprisingly different.

Canada is the second largest country on earth. It is rich in natural resources and has a sophisticated work force and well-developed industrial and agricultural sectors. It is the United States' most important trading partner.

Canada and the United States have many common bonds. They both were once English colonies. Both also have areas once colonized by other powers, especially France (Louisiana and Quebec). Both countries are considered common law countries, although some law in each country follows the civil law tradition inherited from the French.

GOVERNMENT INSTITUTIONS

Canada is a federal system, with a national government and ten provincial governments. It got its own constitution in 1982, by act of the British Parliament. The 1982 constitution for the first time gave Canada the right to

---

[2] 347 U.S. 483 (1954).

structure its own government, and for the first time granted to Canadians a set of fundamental personal rights, the Canadian Charter of Rights and Freedoms. The 1982 constitution also preserves the rights of the province of Quebec to its culture, language, and governing institutions.

Throughout the 1980s, Canada governed itself under a threat by the province of Quebec to secede from the rest of the country. In response to pressures from Quebec and from other provinces, there were several attempts to change the constitution both to preserve the special status of Quebec and to preserve a viable federal system of government. In October 1992, the people of Canada voted down amendments to the Canadian constitution. As this book went to press, the government of the province of Quebec was expected to schedule a referendum on secession.

The main legislative body is a bicameral parliament, with a popularly elected House of Commons and a Senate whose members are appointed until age 75. As a parliamentary system, the House of Commons elects a prime minister and cabinet, who form the executive branch of the government. As a functional matter, the minister of justice selects judges for most of the federal and provincial courts, although technically the appointments of judges and senators come from the queen of England, acting through her appointed Governor-General of Canada.

Canada follows the principle of legislative supremacy, which means that a law within the area of competence of parliament or a provincial legislature will override any previous case law and will control subsequent cases. Unlike the limitations imposed on Congress by the United States' Constitution, the Canadian parliament can choose to override the Charter of Rights and Freedoms.

In addition to cases and statutes, Canada recognizes two other sources of law. The most important additional source of law is custom and convention. Consistent practice, whether in a particular industry or by the government, may provide a basis for resolving disputes. Custom is especially important in Canadian constitutional law.

The second additional source of law is the royal prerogative. Over time, the Crown has given away many of its powers, yet it still maintains the authority to govern through the governor-general on the federal level and the lieutenant governor in each province. By custom, the Crown exercises its power in consultation with the elected Ministers.

COURTS AND LAWYERS

Canadian courts resolve disputes in ways that are quite familiar to American students. The case that follows illustrates how the Canadian Supreme Court views its role in developing law, and is an excellent example of the sources common law judges use in resolving disputes. Note that the court's decision uses a more conversational style than a U.S. decision would use. The personalized reasoning is more typical of British courts.

HARRISON v. CARSWELL[3]

62 D.L.R. (3d) 68, 81–83 [1975]
Supreme Court of Canada, 1975

FACTS:

Mrs. Carswell was picketing her employer, Dominion stores, at a privately owned shopping center in Winnipeg. When Harrison, the mall manager, asked her to leave, she refused. She was
convicted of four counts of trespass under the
Manitoba Petty Trespasses Act, and fined $10 for
each violation. The Manitoba Court of Appeal set
aside the conviction and the prosecutor appealed
the case to the Supreme Court.

ISSUE:

Does the right to picket in support of a lawful
strike extend to picketing on privately owned
property open to the public?

RESULT:

No. Conviction reinstated.

REASONS:

It is urged on behalf of Mrs. Carswell that the
right of a person to picket peacefully in support of
a lawful strike is of greater social significance
than the proprietary rights of the owner of a shopping centre, and that the rights of an owner must
yield to those of the picketer. The American example has been cited, but I cannot say that I find the
American cases to which we have been referred of
great help. . . .

The submission that this Court should weigh
and determine the respective values to society of
the right to property and the right to picket raises
important and difficult political and socio-eco-
nomic issues, the resolution of which must, by
their very nature, be arbitrary and embody personal economic and social beliefs. It raises also
fundamental questions as to the role of this Court

under the Canadian Constitution. The duty of the
Court, as I envisage it, is to proceed in the discharge of its adjudicative function in a reasoned
way from principled decision and established concepts. I do not for a moment doubt the power of
the Court to act creatively—it has done so on
countless occasions; but manifestly one must
ask—what are the limits of the judicial function?
There are many and varied answers to this question. Holmes, J., said in *Southern Pacific Co. v.
Jenson* (1917), 244 U.S. 205 at p. 221: "I recognize
without hesitation that judges do and must legislate, but they can do it only interstitially; they are
confined from molar to molecular actions." Car-
dozo, *The Nature of the Judicial Process* (1921), p.
141, recognized that the freedom of the Judge is
not absolute in this expression of his view:

> This judge, even when he is free, is still not wholly
> free. He is not to innovate at pleasure. He is not a
> knight-errant, roaming at will in pursuit of his own
> ideal of beauty or of goodness. He is to draw his in-
> spiration from consecrated principles.

The former Chief Justice of the Australian
High Court, Sir Owen Dixon, in an address delivered at Yale University in September, 1955, "Concerning Judicial Method," had this to say:

> But in our Australian High Court we have had as yet
> no deliberate innovators bent on express change of
> acknowledged doctrine. It is one thing for a court to
> seek to extend the application of accepted principles
> to new cases or to reason from the more fundamen-
> tal of settled legal principles to new conclusions or to
> decide that a category is not closed against unfore-
> seen instances which in reason might be subsumed
> thereunder. It is an entirely different thing for a
> judge, who is discontented with a result held to flow
> from a long accepted legal principle, deliberately to
> abandon the principle in the name of justice or of so-
> cial necessity or of social convenience. The former
> accords with the technique of the common law and
> amounts to no more than an enlightened application

---

[3]Students of U.S. law may know that the question of
picketing and leafleting in shopping malls has been particularly vexing for the U.S. Supreme Court. See, e.g.,
Prune Yard Shopping Center v. Robins, 447 U.S. 74
(1980).

of modes of reasoning traditionally respected in the courts. It is a process by the repeated use of which the law is developed, is adapted to new conditions, and is improved in content. The latter means an abrupt and almost arbitrary change.

. . . Society has long since acknowledged that a public interest is served by permitting union members to bring economic pressure to bear upon their respective employers through peaceful picketing, but the right has been exercisable in some locations and not in others and to the extent that picketing has been permitted on private property the right hitherto has been accorded by statute. For example, s. 87 [since rep. & sub. 1975, c. 33, s. 21] of the *Labour Code of British Columbia Act, 1973* (B.C.) (2nd Sess.), c. 122, provides that no action lies in respect of picketing permitted under the Act for trespass to real property to which a member of the public ordinarily has access.

Anglo-Canadian jurisprudence has transitionally (sic) recognized, as a fundamental freedom, the right of the individual to the enjoyment of property and the right not to be deprived thereof, or any interest therein, save by due process of law. The Legislature of Manitoba has declared in the *Petty Trespasses Act* that any person who trespasses upon land, the property of another, upon or through which he has been requested by the owner not to enter, is guilty of an offence. If there is to be any change in this statute law, if A is to be given the right to enter and remain on the land of B against the will of B, it would seem to me that such a change must be made by the enacting institution, the Legislature, which is representative of the people and designed to manifest the political will, and not by this Court.

The Canadian lawyer functions in ways quite familiar to American managers. Many advise on the legal aspects of business choices and draft contracts. Others appear in court or advocate clients' positions with regulatory agencies.

A prospective lawyer attends law school for three years after first completing an undergraduate program. After finishing law school, the future lawyer spends one year serving "articles of clerkship," working for a practicing lawyer, before becoming eligible for admission to the bar. All Canadian lawyers are allowed to practice as barristers (litigators) and solicitors (counselors), and must belong to the Law Society of their province. An experienced lawyer who has practiced with distinction may be granted the status of Queen's Counsel, which allows the lawyer to add the letters "Q.C." after his or her name. Canadian law firms work primarily in each province, although the past few years have seen the first attempts at forming nationwide law practices.

THE REGULATORY ENVIRONMENT

Canada has experienced much of the same growth in business regulation as the United States. Ministries, councils, and both ad hoc and permanent boards and commissions may all regulate business activities. These administrative agencies exist on both the national and provincial levels. Agencies may have rule-making functions, administrative functions, or adjudicative functions.

One feature of the regulatory environment is some uncertainty about the possibility of judicial review of erroneous administrative acts. Parliament and provincial legislatures have explicitly attempted to strip courts of jurisdiction to review agency actions in several areas, while the courts have attempted to expand their ability to review actions.

FOCUS ON CONTRACTS

Canadian contract law has many of the same roots as contract law in the United States. English courts developed many of the major principles of law, such as offer, acceptance, and consideration, as well as the basic ways Canadians and Americans think about the role of contracts in business transactions. On the whole, the terminology and concepts of Canadian contract law will be quite familiar to Americans.

However, an executive doing business in Canada should not assume that the rules are all those of the United States. The largest exception is the province of Quebec, which uses an entirely different framework to discuss contractual obligations. Specific contract rules may vary among provinces. For example, some provinces have abolished much of the Statute of Frauds.[4] The case that follows illustrates a familiar rule of contract law, with perhaps a different application than an American business might expect to see.

PETROGAS PROCESSING LTD. v. WESTCOAST TRANSMISSION COMPANY, LIMITED

[1988] 4 W.W.R. 699
Alberta Queen's Bench, 1988

FACTS:
Petrogas agreed to sell natural gas to Westcoast, which would in turn sell the gas to Northwest Pipeline Corp., a U.S. distributor, for ultimate resale in the Pacific Northwest region of the United States. The contract contained a price schedule for the gas, as well as a "take or pay" provision requiring Westcoast to pay for a certain minimum amount whether or not it actually purchased that amount.

In 1975, the Canadian National Energy Board (NEB) imposed price controls on natural gas for the export market. The price set for natural gas was so high that demand for Canadian gas fell in the United States. From 1978 through 1985, Westcoast did not purchase the minimum amounts it was obliged to purchase under the contract.

Petrogas sued to enforce the take or pay provision, asking the court for $172,925,479 plus interest. Westcoast claimed that it should be excused

---

[4] The doctrine that requires that some contracts be written in order to be enforceable.

from payment based upon the subsequent illegality of the pricing portion of the contract, and based upon frustration of the contract.

ISSUES:

Did performance of the contract terms become illegal? Was the contract frustrated by the price controls on natural gas?

RESULT:

Yes. Yes. Action against Westcoast dismissed.

REASONS:

Supervening illegality occurs when, after the making of a contract, a change in the law renders it illegal to perform the contract in accordance with its terms. The change in the law, to qualify as a frustrating event, must be one which was not foreseen by the parties and for which no express or implied provision is made in the contract. In addition, the illegality must not be temporary or trifling in nature when viewed in the context of the contract as a whole. If these conditions are met, the contract is automatically discharged by frustration the moment performance in accordance with its terms becomes illegal.

From 1st November 1975 onward the parties were compelled to abide by the prices imposed from time to time under the Natural Gas Pricing Agreement Act in respect of all gas sold by Petrogas and purchased by Westcoast. To that extent, the terms of the contract were inoperative. It was thereafter illegal for the parties to comply with the provisions of the contract in respect of the price of gas sold and received. . . .

It need hardly be said that the provisions of the contract relating to price were material. The two most important areas of the contract concerned volumes and prices. The imposition of a regulated price nullified the terms of the contract with respect to the price of gas sold and purchases by the parties. . . . Price regulation made performance of a fundamental term of the contract illegal. That illegality was continuous and permanent; it was neither trifling nor temporary. . . .

I have concluded that the contract was discharged by supervening illegality on 1st November 1975. On that date it became legally impossible for the parties to perform a significant part of the contract. The imposition of regulated field prices was an unforeseen event for which the contract made no provision.

In addition to the narrow ground of supervening illegality, Westcoast relies upon the broader submission that the comprehensive scheme of price regulation imposed by the federal and Alberta governments so significantly altered the nature of the then outstanding contractual rights and obligations as to make continued performance a thing radically different from what was originally undertaken, with the result that it would be unjust to hold Westcoast to its contractual obligations in the changed circumstances. Consideration of this argument must begin with an examination of the commercial setting in which the contractual obligations were assumed and a review of the relevant terms of the contract.

Petrogas undertook to sell and Westcoast agreed to buy a large quantity of natural gas over a lengthy period of time. Petrogas intended to construct a plant to process the gas to be sold under the contract and required a minimum assured revenue flow in order to justify the large capital investment. Petrogas knew that Westcoast intended to resell virtually all of the gas taken under the contract to a single purchaser at the international border for ultimate sale to consumers in the Pacific North West region of the United States.

The contract was made in an economic climate which was substantially free from government regulation. There were no statutory or other restraints on the negotiation of price. The export price which Westcoast proposed to charge its customer was subject only to regulatory review by the N.E.B. to ensure that it was "just and reasonable in relation to the public interest." I believe it is fair to assume that the terms of the contract relating to volumes and prices reflected the views held by the parties in 1959 of the actual and foreseeable economics of the natural gas market. . . .

The evidence shows that the market for natural gas in the Pacific North West region of the United States was particularly sensitive to price. Other energy sources, such as fuel oil and electricity, were readily available. A large proportion of the market was comprised of industrial users with the capacity to convert to alternate energy sources in response to unrealistically high gas prices.

The export price set by the N.E.B. from 1st January 1975 onward was insensitive to the market. It was based on the equivalent energy value of crude oil imported into eastern Canada, the cost of which escalated dramatically between 1973 and 1984. In addition, the N.E.B. set a uniform export price for all gas exported to the United States regardless of ultimate market conditions. The N.E.B. refused to alter its policy despite knowledge that the export price was having a particularly adverse effect on the market for Canadian gas in the Pacific North West. . . .

In my opinion the imposition of price regulation made performance of the contract a thing radically different than what was originally undertaken by the parties. The pervasive and overwhelming effect of regulation was not something which the parties did or could have foreseen when the contract was made. It was not expressly or impliedly covered by the contract. Price regulation did not, in my view, merely render performance by Westcoast more expensive or more onerous. It effected a fundamental change in the nature of the contract. The commercial basis of the contract was destroyed by government intervention and it would be unjust to hold Westcoast to its take or pay obligations in circumstances where the complementary provisions of the contract relating to price have been rendered inoperative.

In the result, I find that the contract was discharged by frustration on both the narrow ground of supervening illegality and the broad ground that price regulation made performance of the contract a fundamentally different thing than what the parties originally agreed upon.

Much of the area of contract law that is covered in the United States by the Uniform Commercial Code is covered in Canada by case law. Canadian law concerning the sale of goods is based on the British Sale of Goods Act of 1893. In order to bring sales law along with the needs of modern commerce, Canadian courts have developed new doctrines of law, such as unconscionability, and modernized other areas of law covered by the act, such as warranties.

CONCLUSION

Canada shares its approach to law and its outlook on the role of law in business with the other common law countries. An American trader doing business in Canada will be on familiar ground in all the provinces except Quebec. However, Canada has a very different political history than the United States, and has many substantive rules of law that differ in some fashion from the rules of law in the United States. Later chapters in this book will discuss some areas of Canadian law and practice that may pose hazards for foreign businesses.

3.3 THE CIVIL LAW TRADITION: WEST GERMANY

The common law may provide a familiar way of thinking about law for U.S. students and business executives but the civil law tradition is far more prevalent around the world. The civil law tradition extends across Europe,

Central and South America, parts of Asia, the Middle East and Africa, and, in North America, Mexico, Louisiana, Puerto Rico, and Quebec. As you might expect from the diversity of countries having a civil law legal tradition, there is wide variety in the way different countries have developed the tradition. As you might also expect, there are historical linkages between the legal systems of many countries and those of the former major colonial powers.

When lawyers think of civil law countries, they tend to think of civil codes. The codes are large, comprehensive statutes. In some countries, they may try to cover every aspect of the legal system; in others, they cover more limited aspects, such as the obligations that individuals owe each other in tort and contract. In these countries, the codes will be supplemented by a substantial body of other statutory law. What ties the civil law countries together is that codes have a profound influence on the way law is shaped and on the way new law is made.

The civil law tradition has a long history, extending back to the Roman Empire. The Romans had statutes, lawyers, and commentators on the law, and took their laws with them when they conquered other lands. By the sixth century, the focus of the empire had shifted to Constantinople (Byzantium), where one of the last emperors, Justinian, compiled the document that became the foundation document of the civil law tradition.

Justinian's Code, correctly known as the *Corpus Juris Civilus*, was a restatement of what Justinian and his scholars believed to be the best of Roman law. The Code was a comprehensive document, supposedly covering all necessary areas of the law. Enough of the Justinian Code survived the upheavals of the Middle Ages so that when the universities began to revive higher learning at the end of the 11th century, the lectures on the Code at the University of Bologna attracted scholars from all over Europe. These scholars took the ideas of the Code home, where they became incorporated into local legal systems.

The modern civil law tradition grew from an age of nationalism, influenced by the politics of the Enlightenment and the spirit of scientific inquiry. National leaders found that one way to unify a nation was to develop a comprehensive codification of the law, based on national conditions and national needs. The earliest codes were enacted in Scandinavia, in the 17th and 18th centuries. The most influential national codes, however, were put in place in the 19th century.

The French Civil Code of 1804, which is also known as the Napoleonic Code, has had the widest influence of any of the civil codes. Napoleon considered the Code to be one of his greatest achievements, and, as the contemporary advertisement would say, when he expanded the French empire militarily, "he wouldn't leave home without it." Thus, wherever Napoleon went, his officials put into place the Napoleonic Code. Also, in the 19th century France was a major colonial power, with colonies in Asia and Africa. The French government installed the Napoleonic Code in the colonies. Between conquest and colonization, much of the world was exposed to the ideas and the structure of the Code.

Napoleon's Code was revolutionary in two major ways. First, it reflected the political ideas of the Enlightenment. Its three major emphases were the security of private property, the freedom to contract, and the value of the traditional family. In particular, the Code altered the values of traditionally feudal societies, by placing into the area of private law matters of property, contract, and family. Second, the Code was meant to be read and understood by common people. In response to the ideas of the Enlightenment, the average citizen was to be able to determine what the principles of law were, and how he should act in accordance with the law.

In contrast to the French, the Germans adopted their comprehensive Civil Code in 1896, as an attempt to bring scientific reasoning to the law. The German Code is much more detailed than the French Code, and is more technically oriented. Where the French Code is in many areas an exposition of broad principles, the German Code is much more specific. The German Civil Code has not had the widespread influence of the French, but was important in the development of law in China, Japan, and many countries of Eastern and Central Europe.

With the end of the Cold War and the rise of a strong European Community, Germany has once again become a key world power. It is playing a leading role in developing a unified European political system. It is heavily involved with the reconstruction of Eastern Europe and the former Soviet Union. It is a financial and technological leader among the developed nations. Germany's influence on the shape of global business is already substantial and will probably increase in the future. Thus, it is important for managers to have some sense of the way Germans look at law, and how businesses interact with the German legal system. The features of that system will be unusual for managers used to common law traditions, but will share some basic similarities with the legal traditions of other civil law countries.

GERMAN GOVERNMENT

Germany, with approximately 78 million people, is located in the heart of Europe. From 1945 to 1990, it was two countries: East Germany, a hard-line Communist power, and West Germany, a democratic republic. The two countries resulted from the division of German territory by Allied occupying armies after World War II. The reunification of the two countries, symbolized best by the dramatic fall of the Berlin Wall, resulted in a treaty between the two countries, where the former East German territories agreed to become part of the existing West German legal system.

The German constitution *(Grundgesetz)* establishes a federal structure of government. Political authority is divided between the sixteen German states *(Länder)* and the federal government. The federal government has the exclusive authority to make laws in the areas of defense, foreign affairs, currency, nationality, and intellectual property. It has concurrent authority with the states in the areas of criminal law, labor law, social security, the economy, and agriculture. The states may only legislate if the federal government has not done so. The states have exclusive authority over education, culture, and local administration.

The legislative authority of the federal government rests in the two houses of the legislature, the *Bundestag* and the *Bundesrat*. The *Bundestag* functions as a parliament, with its members directly elected by the people, for four-year terms. No political party may get seats in the *Bundestag* unless it receives 5 percent of the popular vote. By contrast, the *Bundesrat* is composed of representatives sent by the governments of the states, who vote as their state government instructs them. The *Bundesrat* has the power to object to some legislation, and to veto legislation that significantly affects the interests of the states.

The most powerful politician in Germany is the chancellor, who makes public policy and appoints the heads of government agencies to carry out the law. The chancellor is chosen by vote of the *Bundestag*. He functions in much the same way as an American president.

Germany also has a federal president. The president functions as the ceremonial head of state and validates the laws passed by the legislature and the selection of the chancellor and of the ministers. The president does not have a significant influence on law or public policy.

SOURCES OF LAW

Like most countries coming from the civil law tradition, Germany has legislation as its dominant source of law. In the civil law, legislation may be divided into two categories. The first is public law, which regulates the relationship between individuals and the government. Criminal codes, administrative law, and tax law would be examples of public law in a civil law system. Private law is the law that governs the relationships among persons.

The German Civil Code *(Bürgerliches Gesetzbuch)* is the centerpiece of German private law, with more than 2300 sections covering the relationships between individuals. The Code is divided into an introduction and five books. The first book is general, with rules that will apply throughout the Code, such as the basic principles of agency relationships, legal capacity, and some contract rules. The second book covers legal obligations, which includes much of what common law systems would call torts and much of contract law. The third book covers property, the fourth family law, and the fifth the law of inheritance and succession.

Germany has extensive legislation in three other areas of private law that affect business activity. The first is corporate formation. In many common law countries, the legal duties of managers and directors are developed through case law, but in Germany, as in many civil law countries, those duties are specified by statute.

Germany also has extensive statutory regulation of labor law. The German workplace is characterized by a protective environment for workers, with extensive social insurance programs, protection against unjust dismissal, and strong union protection. Executives from other countries, particularly the United States, are often surprised that German law mandates worker participation on the boards of directors of some corporations. This practice, known as co-determination, has been in place for many years in Germany, and may soon extend throughout Europe.

Of great significance for businesses is the German Commercial Code *(Handelsgesetzbuch)*. The Commercial Code supplements the Civil Code by providing specialized sets of rules for merchants doing business in Germany. In some ways it is not dissimilar to the Uniform Commercial Code of the United States. It provides rules for a wide variety of commercial settings, including negotiable instruments, warehousemen, banking, common carriers, and sales of goods. It also regulates business names, the duty to keep accounts, and several forms of commercial agency.

Just from this brief description of German codes it is easy to see that legislation is the primary source of law in Germany. When a German lawyer or manager looks to resolve a legal problem, the first source of law will be the relevant code or statute. Courts have a less important role to play, although their decisions have increased in number and importance in recent years.

The first function of courts in a civil law country is to interpret the relevant code or statute. If there is no statutory provision that covers the situation before the court, its function is to determine whether there is a custom that is common in the situation. Looking for customary practice can be very helpful, as there is often a widely accepted business practice dealing with the disputed situation. If there is no custom, then the judges must create law. In the German system, judges look to maintain consistency with existing law, and rely heavily on the writings of scholars in looking at such situations.

Technically, a court ruling is binding only on the parties before the court and does not have the power of precedent as in common law countries. As a practical matter, earlier court decisions covering the same or similar subjects can be very persuasive to later judges. Some judges are highly esteemed by other judges, and their opinions carry great weight. Thus, German lawyers looking for the answers to legal questions will often seek out earlier cases before the courts, and managers who want to avoid legal problems will give some consideration to earlier, similar decisions. There are also some provisions of the German Civil Code that are quite general, as a matter of principle, and not at all specific. In these areas, court decisions have been the main way the law has developed and lawyers and managers have had to rely on judge-made law in resolving legal problems.

COURTS AND LAWYERS

To someone accustomed to common law courts, the German court system will look complex and unusual. Courts exist at both federal and state levels, and their power to hear cases is carefully prescribed. The federal level has six courts. Five are divided by subject matter into courts for tax, social matters, labor, administrative law, and general law. The sixth is a federal constitutional court, which is restricted to deciding matters affecting the constitution, such as disputes between the states and the federal government.

The five regular federal courts are appeals courts, hearing cases brought from courts based in the states. Each state maintains a court system with five court divisions, containing trial courts and a first-level court of appeals.

In a business dispute, the parties are likely to appear before the district court *(Landgericht)* in their state. The district court is divided into three divisions: civil, criminal, and commercial. The case will go to the commercial division, where it will be tried before three judges, two of whom are businesspeople, not law-trained judges. These judges take an active role in the trial. Rather than having the lawyers examine and cross-examine witnesses, as is usual in common law countries, Germany follows the civil law tradition of an inquisitorial trial. The judges ask the witnesses questions, help the parties frame the issues, and resolve both factual and legal issues. There is no jury. Appeals stay at the state level, going to a state court of appeal *(Oberlandesgericht)*. Only when the state appeals are exhausted can the losing party appeal to the federal court having general jurisdiction *(Bundesgerichtshof)*.

CHRISTOPH HAUSCHA, "CENTRAL ISSUES OF BUSINESS LITIGATION IN WEST GERMAN CIVIL COURTS,"

19 Cal. Western Int'l L. Rev. 47, 53–55 (1988).

Foreign attorneys are not the only ones who are frequently disappointed after attending an oral hearing in a German civil court. Procedurally, the only important thing to happen in court is that the attorneys read their formal proposals, which consist of the suggested operative part of the judgment. Although nothing else is required, usually the court will discuss the case informally with both sides at the hearing. This is a habit that has developed in daily practice without being described anywhere in the ZPO [Code of Civil Procedure]. Apart from the above, there is no formal pleading, no jury, and clients frequently do not attend the hearing in person.

The ZPO, however, clearly states that parties will plead in court, and written proceedings will only be the exception. But in practice most cases have already been decided when attorneys appear for the oral hearing. Civil litigation in German court practice essentially takes place in writing. Therefore, parties have to think about their tactics and arguments when preparing their written briefs. They should not leave arguments for the oral hearing that are complicated, hard to explain, or based on a legal theory that the judges might not immediately understand. A judge's legal education trains him to compare the arguments in the written briefs to determine the few crucial points that need evidence or proof. The result of this highly developed and sophisticated way of analyzing written briefs is that frequently the case is over before the oral hearing has even started.

It is essential to bear this in mind when preparing written briefs. The court's opinion will often be close to final by the time of the oral hearing, and the attorney will have a difficult time try-ing to change the judge's mind. Judges may not like to reveal that they have changed their opinion on the law at such an advanced stage of the proceeding merely because of a lawyer's oral argument. . . .

In most cases the court only holds one hearing, which often lasts less than 1 hour and rarely more than half a day. Therefore, whatever can be said in writing should be said in writing and should be submitted to the court well in advance of the hearing.

German lawyers go through a rigorous education process consisting of a theoretical study for a minimum of $3^1/_2$ years, followed by a state examination and a 30 month period of practical training, followed by a second state examination. Fees for legal work are specified by statute, although the lawyer and client may agree in writing to a higher fee. To charge a lower fee than the statute sets is unethical, as is the U.S. practice of contingent fees. Under the German system, the losing party to a litigation pays the attorney's fees of the winner. Since the statutory fees are based on the amount of the lawsuit, in a large lawsuit the payment of the victor's fees can be a substantial obligation.

An important group of legal professionals in civil law countries are notaries. Notaries in Germany are lawyers who have gone through all the training and examinations of the legal profession. By law, notaries have the exclusive right to perform certain functions, such as attesting to signatures, and to certain kinds of agreements. Some contracts, such as those for the sale of real estate, must be drafted and certified by a notary. The notary's function is to advise the parties of the consequences of their acts, to be sure that no party is disadvantaged because of inexperience, and to be sure that agreements are clearly and unambiguously written.

THE REGULATORY ENVIRONMENT

As one might expect in a country in which legislation is the primary source of law and courts play a secondary role, Germany has a large corps of civil servants dedicated to carrying out the law. Government employees include railway and postal workers, educators, public utilities workers, and police, as well as employees of government ministries in both the state and federal governments. The roster of state workers has temporarily been expanded by the reunification with East Germany, which included the assumption of ownership of the state-owned enterprises of East Germany.

As of 1993, the most interesting of the German government agencies may well be the Trust Agency *(Treuhandanstalt),* which is the largest holding company in the world. It was created by the 1990 Unification Treaty between East and West Germany and by the Trusteeship Act, and was charged with privatizing East German businesses. Its task is to run the businesses until they can be privatized, set the terms under which the businesses will be sold, and distribute the profits to the federal government and the appropriate state. The agency has enormous power within the former East German states, setting employment policies and wages. It is looking all over the world for investors for the state-owned enterprises of the East German states.

FOCUS ON CONTRACTS

In many ways, German contract law handles contract situations in ways that are quite comfortable for common law lawyers. However, the conceptual framework of the law is different in civil law than in common law systems, and the actual rules in some areas are different from those in common law systems.

Contract Formation

The starting point for German contract law is the Civil Code. Unlike common law systems, where most of the rules of contract behavior have developed through litigation, in civil law countries they tend to lay down the basic principles of contract obligations in their civil code. Those codes have also reached some different conclusions about the basic formation of contracts from the common law decisions.

German contracts are formed by an offer and an acceptance, which must correspond to each other. Conceptually, German law talks of these actions as "expressions of will" by the parties (BGB Sec. 133). Thus, as in common law countries, mere advertisements, price inquiries, circulars, or catalogs are not legally binding contract offers, but are invitations to others to make offers.

There are three areas of contract formation that might surprise managers from common law countries. First, unless an offer specifies otherwise, it must be held open for a reasonable time (BGB Sec. 145). Second, the mailbox rule, familiar to common law lawyers and managers, does not apply. An acceptance is effective when it is received by the offeror, not when it is sent to the offeror (BGB Sec. 130).

Finally, German law does not contain the concept of consideration. In the common law, most contracts require a bargained-for exchange in order to be binding. In Germany, as in most civil law countries, agreements to make gifts and agreements to hold offers open are examples of legally enforceable expressions of will. The absence of consideration as a legal requirement can have a large impact on the process of negotiating complex commercial agreements. Chapter 6 will discuss further the problems posed by letters of intent and preliminary agreements.

German law, like U.S. law, imposes some special obligations on merchants engaged in contractual transactions. For example, where the usual rule in both civil and common law systems is that silence does not constitute an acceptance, a merchant must make clear that he will not fill an order: If he remains silent, he has undertaken the obligation to send goods (HGB Sec. 362). Also like U.S. law, a merchant may use letters of confirmation as evidence of a contract. If the merchant recipient of such a letter fails to object, she will be deemed to have accepted the contract terms contained in the letter of confirmation.

German law also includes a statute regulating the terms of standard form contracts, such as those a consumer might have to sign when purchasing furniture or opening a bank account. Historically, such contracts between merchants and consumers have been one-sided, with the more sophisticated merchants using the contract form to disclaim responsibilities and liability. The General Conditions of Business Act (*Gesetz zur Regelung des Rechts der Allgemeinen Geschaftsbedingungen*) prevents merchants from disclaiming all liability for defective goods and protects consumers in situations in which historically they have not had real bargaining power.

Performance and Breach

As a practical matter, the law of performance and breach is not substantially different in common law and civil law systems. However, the way the two legal traditions articulate the legal concepts is different, and there are a few areas of divergent law. As one might expect, civil law systems use the civil code to define contract performance and breach. The German Civil Code has a complex set of provisions detailing the rights and duties of contracting parties under a variety of circumstances. Some legal scholars group the detailed provisions into three categories describing breach of contract: impossibility, delay, and a positive breach, such as shipping defective goods.[5] Within each category the parties to a contract have different rights in different situations.

Throughout German contract law runs a very strong principle of good faith in contractual dealings. Section 242 of the Civil Code, titled *Treu unde Glauben*, states a broad principle of good faith and fair dealing in contractual relationships. German courts have used this section extensively to deal with sharp business practices, and what would, in the United

---

[5]*See* N. Horn, H. Kotz, and H. Leser, *German Private and Commercial Law*, Oxford 1982, pp. 90–108.

States, be called unconscionable contracts. It has also served as a philosophical underpinning for moves to expand the concept of impossibility from the traditional civil law definition of actual or legal impossibility to a concept that is much closer to commercial impracticability. In this usage, Germany stands in sharp contrast to other civil law countries, like France, where impossibility is a very limited excuse for lack of contract performance.

German contract law gives contract parties much more flexible remedies for breach of contract than the traditional common law remedy of damages only. In German law, a buyer of goods has the option of making price adjustments for defective or lower quality goods or of rejecting them. This legal remedy mirrors actual business practice far better than the common law insistance on acceptance or rejection. If a seller ships goods to a buyer and the goods are of a lower quality than called for in the contract, the goods can often still be resold, but at a lower price. German law, like most civil law, allows the buyer to reduce the contract price and take the goods. Ensuing litigation, then, is only over the appropriate amount of the price reduction.

German law also follows widespread civil law tradition in allowing specific performance as a standard contract remedy. Traditionally, in common law systems, specific performance is a remedy only in cases where goods are unique or specially manufactured, or in real estate cases. Throughout German civil law, a party may ask for specific performance even for fungible goods.

CONCLUSION

German law is one of the main strands of the civil law tradition. Its codes, which are its primary source of law, cover many areas of law that have been developed by case law in common law systems. German contract law, although it often yields results that are quite familiar to managers from most Western countries, conceptualizes law and its interaction with business quite differently than the common law would.

Germany, especially as it integrates the former East German states, is becoming an even more influential power in Europe. German businesses are leading the investment charge into Eastern Europe and the former Soviet Union. Germany has a central role in developing the law of the European Community, which is the subject of Chapter 5. It is an economic power of great importance in trade in all parts of the world. Its legal system comes from a historic and widely influential legal tradition that governs more countries than any other legal tradition.

3.4 THE SOCIALIST LEGAL TRADITION

Although legal theoreticians disagree about its conceptual shape, few would disagree that one of the most influential legal traditions of the 20th century was the Socialist legal tradition. It started with the Russian Revolution of 1917 and, at its zenith, provided the conceptual framework for the legal systems of the Soviet Union, China, the nations of Eastern Europe, Cuba, and several countries in Africa and Asia. With the collapse of the Soviet-style governments in Eastern Europe, then the collapse of the Soviet Union, the Socialist legal tradition is largely fading away in Western countries. The tradition still shapes the legal system in China, as Chapter 4 will discuss, and in some other countries, but it is under some political strain. It is likely, however, that even as the Socialist legal institutions are dismantled around the world, some of the ideas of the tradition will remain influential in parts of Eastern Europe, the former Soviet Union, and a few other nations.

SOCIALIST LAW AND CIVIL LAW

On the surface, Socialist legal systems look very much like civil law legal systems. The primary sources of law are the extensive codes, which are structured very much like the civil codes. The legislature is the primary branch of government, and the judiciary is secondary in importance to the legislative power. This structure is not surprising, since the founding fathers of the Socialist legal system were trained as civil law lawyers, and prerevolutionary Russia was essentially a civil law country.

What distinguishes Socialist legal systems from their counterparts is the role of ideology. Unlike a civil law code, which can be used by governments of widely differing political viewpoints, Socialist legal codes are designed to achieve personal and societal transformation. The legal system is not just a set of institutions, but the means to the end of achieving a Communist society, where each gives according to his abilities and takes according to his needs.

The main ideological characteristics built into the Socialist legal tradition are the building blocks of Communist society. The legal system provides for state ownership of the means of production and distribution, including most businesses. It also calls for state ownership of land, and in most cases for collective use of land. Thus, the historically Socialist countries tend toward large industrial complexes rather than small businesses, and collective rather than individual farms. There is at best limited tolerance of private property rights. The Socialist legal tradition is one of strong central government control. The codes support the centralized economic planning characteristic of Socialist states, allowing the central government to set national, uniform standards for business activities.

At the center of the Socialist legal tradition, although not specifically designated as a source of law, is the Communist party. The party is the keeper of the ideology of the state, and through its power to nominate officeholders, staff the bureaucracy, and monitor workplaces, it determines the norms that become law. China is still a good example of the parallel structure of the legal system and the party, as Chapter 4 will discuss.

THE SOCIALIST TRADITION IN A POST-COMMUNIST WORLD

Very few events in recent political history were as dramatic as the disintegration of the Communist empire in the late 1980s and early 1990s. First Poland, then East Germany, Czechoslovakia, Hungary, Romania, Bulgaria, and finally the former Soviet Union cast off the yokes of Communist economic and political systems to seek their own ways to economic and political freedom. Although the circumstances of the revolution were different for each country, each country has set out to radically restructure its legal system.

In most countries the Socialist legal tradition will give way to a civil law system, although several of the Asian republics of the former Soviet Union are more likely to rely on Islamic law. In several countries, most notably Poland, Hungary, and the Czech Republic, the legal restructuring is well under way. Each country is following a different path, but the legal reforms have four common themes.

First, each country is legalizing private property rights. New laws give people the right to own land, individual farms, and businesses. The state-owned businesses are being privatized by selling them off to existing managers, employees, citizens, or foreign investors.

Second, the countries are passing laws reforming their monetary systems. The new laws aim to make currencies convertible on foreign exchange markets, create private banks, and establish money supply and interest regulation.

Third, the former Socialist countries are legislating the protection of domestic and foreign investment. Several countries have started stock exchanges, and 1990 saw four new laws protecting and encouraging foreign investment.

Last, the former Socialist countries are rewriting their commercial law. In some cases, such as in Poland, commercial law for the new market economy comes from the pre-Soviet commercial and civil codes. Several nations are now engaged in drafting new corporation and partnership laws, antitrust laws, and contract laws.

For the next several years, the legal systems of all the former Socialist countries will not provide much certainty or predictability for managers trying to assess the legal environment. Some countries, notably Poland, Hungary, the Czech Republic, and the Baltic countries, will move relatively smoothly toward Swedish-style social democracies, but other countries still face substantial political obstacles. Some countries are still headed by former Communists who still believe in the Communist system, and other countries will encounter ethnic strife and even civil war. Therefore, although the former Soviet bloc provides exciting business opportunities for foreign businesses, it also carries varying degrees of risk, along with uncertainty about what the new legal systems will eventually look like.

3.5 CONCLUSION

The business executive or entrepreneur has certain expectations about the way her home legal system will interact with business. When she goes to court, she knows how judges will act, and how they will see their role in making law. She is familiar with the legislative and regulatory process, and will know how to manage in a familiar legal and regulatory environment. When she starts doing business in other countries, however, all of those expectations are subject to change.

The Western legal traditions share some common characteristics, but they also differ. The civil law tradition is the most widespread and influential, but the common law tradition is also important. Even within a legal tradition, the particulars of the law will change in different countries. A prudent manager will learn about the legal system before entering a new market, and anticipate how that market's legal tradition influences the way government interacts with business.

3.6 QUESTIONS FOR DISCUSSION

1. Doug McKenzie, a Canadian lawyer, is sitting in his office in Vancouver, and Uta Schmidt, a German lawyer, is sitting in her office in Berlin. Each is faced with the difficult legal problem of clients who signed a letter expressing their intent to negotiate a complex contract. Relying on the letter, the clients incurred expenses. When the negotiations fell apart, the clients suffered damage. What methods would each lawyer use to find out whether his or her clients had a legal basis for a lawsuit? Explain.

2. How do the training and functions of judges differ in common law and civil law countries? Which tradition do you think is more sensible? Explain.

3. Suppose you were asked to advise one of the newly democratic countries of Eastern Europe about its new legal system. What tradition would you recommend as a foundation for the system? Explain.

4. Compare the civil law and common law approaches to remedies for breach of contract. Which do you think is more consistent with the traditions of the law merchant? As a businessperson, which approach makes more sense to you? Explain.

3.7 FURTHER READINGS

Burkhard Bastuck, "Unity, Law and Freedom: Legal Aspects of the Process and Results of German Unification," 25 *International Lawyer* 251 (1991).

Francis Gabor, "The Quest for Transformation to a Market Economy: Privatization and Foreign Investment in Hungary," 24 *Vanderbilt Journal of Transnational Law* 269 (1991).

Gerald Gall, *The Canadian Legal System,* Carswell, Toronto, 1983.

M. A. Glendon, M. W. Gordon, and C. Osakwe, *Comparative Legal Traditions,* West, St. Paul, Minn., 1985.

N. Horn, H. Kotz, H. Leser, and T. Weir (trans.), *German Private and Commercial Law: An Introduction,* Clarendon Press, Oxford, 1982.

Ralph Lake, "Letters of Intent: A Comparative Examination under English, French and West German Law," 18 *George Washington Journal of International Law and Economics* 331 (1984).

"Selected Bibliography [on legal change in Eastern Europe]," 58 *Chicago Law Review* 859 (1991).

CHAPTER **4**

NON-WESTERN LEGAL TRADITIONS

4.1 INTRODUCTION

As the Western legal tradition formed nearly 1000 years ago, other legal traditions were already flourishing in such places as India, China, and other parts of Asia and Africa. Today, many parts of the world retain legal systems based partially or wholly on ways of thinking quite different from Judeo-Christian ideas and traditions. Since World War II, countries with non-Western–based legal systems have become increasingly important trading partners for the United States. The nations of the Pacific Rim, the Middle East, and much of Africa view law and its role in business in very different ways than countries in Europe and the Americas.

It is difficult to group the non-Western legal traditions as easily as the two major Western traditions, both of which look to Greece and Rome for their inspiration. There are many different legal traditions across Asia, Africa, and the Middle East. Sources of law range from the Islamic and Hindu religions to the customs of the Tswana tribe in Botswana. Thus, contemporary outlooks on law vary widely from country to country.

Another important factor in the development of non-Western legal traditions is the role of Western colonialism. In many countries of Africa, Asia, and the Middle East, Western powers like France, Germany, Portugal, Spain, and England dominated legal and political systems over time periods ranging from decades to centuries. Western powers left their marks on the legal system and tradition of many countries. Some countries have accommodated a mix of traditional and Western legal outlooks relatively easily. Others, such as Egypt, have had a much more difficult time finding the proper role for each of the influences on its legal system.

We will not survey all non-Western legal systems. Rather, we will introduce other ways of thinking about law, and examine the ways different viewpoints influence business negotiation, decision making, and governance. As examples, we will examine the legal traditions of three of the United States' important present and future trading partners: Saudi Arabia, Japan, and the People's Republic of China.

4.2 SAUDI ARABIA AND ISLAMIC LAW

Islamic law, in terms of its geographic reach and its growth, is the most important non-Western legal tradition in the world today. Islam is one of the world's major religions, and it is growing rapidly in influence. From Indonesia and Malaysia in the Pacific, to Pakistan and the republics of the former Soviet Union across Central Asia, to Egypt and Algeria in North Africa, Islam influences legal and political structures. The resurgence of Islamic fundamentalism in the 1980s has led many nations to reexamine and change laws and legal institutions to follow Islamic religious tenets more closely. Other nations have experienced civil unrest and even civil war in their attempt to find the proper role for Islam in legal and political life.

Saudi Arabia has followed the Islamic legal tradition for its entire national history. It is an important example of the Islamic legal tradition both because it has important trading relationships with many other nations and because its legal tradition has not been subject to the effects of Western colonialism. The kingdom of Saudi Arabia lies between the Red Sea and the Persian Gulf, on the Arabian Peninsula. Since the discovery of oil in the 1930s, Saudi Arabia has grown to be an important trading partner of the United States. It is the largest exporter of oil in the world and has more proven oil reserves than any other country.

In Saudi Arabia, Islam is the law of the land. Unlike many other Islamic countries, Saudi Arabia has not codified or secularized its legal system. It has successfully brought a fundamentalist Islamic legal tradition into a modern, technologically developed state. In order to understand the legal environment of business in Saudi Arabia, you need to understand the nature of Islam and Islamic law.

ISLAMIC LAW

The Islamic religion began early in the 7th century, when the Prophet Muhammad, a trader in the city of Mecca, began preaching his messages from God (Allah). Muhammad and his followers fled Mecca in 622 AD, only to return 8 years later to rule Mecca and found a religious empire. The date of Muhammad's trip from Mecca, called the *hijra,* is the starting date for the Islamic calendar used in much of the Middle East.

While Europe sank into the Dark Ages, Islamic culture thrived. Islamic mathematicians, philosophers, and writers made important contributions to the growth of culture, and Islam spread its influence from the Arabian peninsula into Africa, Asia, and Spain. Today, countries from the Philippines to the former Soviet Union have substantial Islamic populations still following Islamic cultural and legal traditions, and Islamic traditions dominate the legal and social environment of most Arab nations.

The word "Islam" translates into English as "submission" or "surrender." Muslims submit to the will of God, who decrees what is proper and what is improper. God's commandments, as revealed to Muhammad, provide a path, or *shari'a,* for true believers to follow. The *shari'a* is not explicitly a legal matter. It provides ethical and moral precepts as well as the rules of public order.

The idea of law in Islamic societies is quite different from that in most Western cultures. Where most Western nations see law as an expression of the will of the people acting through their legislatures, Islamic law is the product of divine revelation. It cannot be changed, as it is the only path for believers to follow. The immutability of the law requires Islamic nations to look to very different sources of law to resolve disputes and to govern.

J. BRAND, "ASPECTS OF SAUDI ARABIAN LAW AND PRACTICE"

9 Boston College International & Comparative Law Review 1, 2–6 (1986)

I. SOURCES OF LAW

Muslims believe Islam's law is God's law as revealed in the Quran. Thus, the ultimate source of law in Saudi Arabia is the Quran, a holy book of 6,237 verses. Fewer than two hundred, or about three percent, have legal relevance and most of these concern family law and inheritance. Not more than eighty deal with what Westerners would think of as legal issues. Is this not a narrow base on which to build a modern legal system?

The base is far broader. No legal system that has lasted thirteen centuries could derive from only a handful of religious verses. In addition to the Quran, the sources of law are those traditions of the Prophet Muhammad recognized as having legal significance, the consensus of Islamic scholars, and, except in the more conservative Islamic societies and among them especially Saudi Arabia, modern interpretations through the use of analogy.

First, the Quran. It is a holy book that contains God's ordinances as revealed to the Prophet Muhammad during the period 610 A.D. to 622 A.D. It is revered by Muslims as containing the very words of God: "Your companion [Muhammad] errs not, nor is he deceived. Whatever he utters is not of his own whim and fancy. It is naught else but a divine revelation revealed unto him." Few verses indeed deal with legal matters. Most are religious direction which set general goals for Muslim life and prescribe proper conduct for daily activity. This should be no surprise, since Islamic belief does not separate faith from law. In no Islamic society today is this more pronounced and observed than in Saudi Arabia, where the national constitution is the Quran.

Traditions, called the *sunna,* constitute the second source of Islamic law. *Sunna* translated from the Arabic as "habitual practice" or "trodden path" and is defined in a legal context to mean the speech or deeds of the Prophet or those practices he is said to have approved. To draw an analogy to religious sources more familiar to Westerners, the Quran is the Old Testament and the *sunna* the New Testament. As a record of the deeds and acts of human experience, the *sunna* is a source of law not dissimilar in origin to the early sources of the common law; for example, the Law Merchant.

The Quran and the *sunna* were the sources of law and in general constituted the first legal system during the first, short period of Islamic law—that from its beginning until Muhammad's death in 632 A.D. Thereafter, consensus, or *ijam,* evolved as a theological and legal device to fill gaps the Quran and the *sunna* had left in the law. Its evolution is justified on the deduction from Quranic teaching that God would not permit his people universally to be wrong. Thus, consensus is not precedent, which is not a source of law in Islamic jurisprudence, but the universal contemporaneous agreement of Muslim authorities.

In the more liberal Islamic schools of jurisprudence, today's scholars or judges, assuming they were in universal agreement, could reach consensus and thereby create a source of law to deal with newly arising legal issues. This method is not acceptable to the conservative Hanbali school which prevails in Saudi Arabia. The Hanbali school believes that consensus may arise only through the universal agreement of the Prophet's contemporaries and his early followers, not contemporaries alive and agreeing today.

The fourth source of law, analogy or *quiyas,* is also recognized only by the more liberal schools. Here again the justification for applying human reasoning is adduced from the Quran: "Lo! In the creation of the heavens and the earth and [in] the difference of night and day are tokens for men of understanding," meaning that man's rational process may interpret divine authority—the tokens of understanding, analogy to God's works, are given to those who are able to use them.

While all schools accepted the first two sources of the Quran and the *sunna,* disagreements over the remaining two, both of which involve human reasoning, led to the development of four different schools of jurisprudence. Three of these, the Hanafi, Shafi and Maliki, each named for its ancient proponent, are liberal in their acceptance of the sources of law. The Hanbali, however, accepts as sources of law only the Quran, the *sunna*, and the consensus of the Prophet's companions and early followers. Contemporaneous consensus—indeed any consensus achieved after the time of the Prophet—and analogy are not recognized as sources of law by the Hanbalis. This conservative doctrine parched the well from which law was or could be drawn, and the well quite probably would have gone dry had it not been for modern legislation. Arid as this prospect was, it was made even more barren in the ninth century by an agreement of Islamic scholars which determined that the sources of law could not thereafter be interpreted by the process of independent reasoning or *ijtihad*. This agreement is known to Muslims as "closing the gate of *ijtihad*." The gate closed in the ninth century, the sources of law in Saudi Arabia are now regarded as immutable and not subject to *ijtihad* from that time.

The Hanbali school, the official school of Saudi Arabia, is the least widespread of the four schools; elsewhere it is found only in parts of Pakistan, Syria and Iraq. Today the relatively liberal Hanafi school, which was founded in Iraq, prevails in upper Egypt, Lebanon, Turkey and parts of Syria. With followers as well in Sudan, Jordan, India, Libya, Pakistan, Afghanistan and Iraq, the Hanafi is the predominant school in most of the Middle East and accounts for nearly a third of the world's Muslims. The Shafis are found in East Africa and Southeast Asia; the Malikis in Northern and Central Africa. Lines of division are not precise. Malikis, for example, live in Kuwait and Bahrain, and there are adherents of the Shafi school in Egypt, Syria, Lebanon, Jordan, and Iraq.

The small Hanbali school, which developed in the eighth century not long after the split of the Muslim world into *sunni* and *shiite* factions aligned according to their separate choices for the Caliphate, the Prophet's successor, fell into disfavor and was rejuvenated early in the eighteenth century by the Wahhabi movement. The movement's principal, Muhammad Ibn Abdul Wahhab, and the ancestor of Saudi Arabia's founder, Muhammad Ibn Saud, joined forces. Muhammad Ibn Saud became the political head of the Wahhabis and Ibn Abdul Wahhab the religious leader. Ibn Abdul Wahhab's limitation of the accepted sources of law to the Quran, the *sunna*, and that consensus established by the Prophet's companions became a tenet of the movement and of its present-day nation-state, Saudi Arabia.

SAUDI GOVERNMENT

Saudi Arabia has organized its legal system to implement the *shari'a* as law. The government has only two branches: executive and judicial. It has no legislature, as only God can make laws for the conduct of people and society.

The king is the ultimate political authority in Saudi Arabia. He appoints all judges, senior government officials, governors, and military officers above the rank of colonel. He is the court of last resort and has the power to pardon. He enacts or endorses all government regulation.

Although there is no formal document delineating the king's powers, his broad authority is limited by the Quranic injunction to rule in consultation with his people, as well as the need to retain the support of Saudi religious scholars. The king has a consultative council, composed of secular and religious leaders, to advise him, and a council of ministers to formulate and administer government policy.

SAUDI COURTS AND LAWYERS

Saudi Arabia has retained traditional Islamic courts to deal with civil, criminal, and domestic relations disputes. The judges in these *shari'a* courts, known as *qadis*, have religious training as well as legal training. The *qadi* controls court proceedings to a degree unknown in Western legal systems, because the system does not rely on formal written pleadings and procedures. Rules of procedure and substantive rules of proof are provided by the Quran and the traditions of the Prophet. As a result of the religious aspects of the *shari'a* courts, secularly trained lawyers are not an important part of the Saudi Arabian legal system.

The following description of an actual *shari'a* trial from the 1960s gives some indication of culture clash between Western values and an Islamic legal system.

J. BRAND, "ASPECTS OF SAUDI ARABIAN LAW AND PRACTICE"

9 Boston College International & Comparative Law Review 1, 9–10 (1986)

In a hot, crowded courtroom in the Saudi Arabian oil town of Abqaiq, the defendant and the plaintiff stood before the *qadi*—the judge—waiting for the trial to continue. The defendant, an American employee of the Arabian American Oil Company (Aramco), was plainly nervous. He was on trial in a foreign court, whose laws and procedures were a total mystery to him, and he was accused of a serious matter: assaulting and slandering the plaintiff, a Saudi Arab co-worker. He had denied the charge, but if found guilty he might be jailed or he might be deported, thus losing a job he had held for years.

"To prove your claim under our law," the *qadi* was saying to the plaintiff, "you are required to present two witnesses to testify to the truth of your complaint. You have presented one witness. Do you have a second?"

The plaintiff said he did not. "Then you must have one right left to you," the *qadi* said. "You must demand the oath."

"I demand the oath," said the plaintiff.

The defendant turned to the Aramco lawyer representing him and whispered: "What is the oath?"

The lawyer hesitated, wondering if, in just a few seconds, he could adequately explain this ancient, solemn cornerstone of *shari'a* law. "It's like this," he said finally. "To a Muslim, lying under oath is one of the most serious sins that a man can commit. So he is asking you to swear that you are innocent. If you do not take the oath you will immediately be found guilty. But if you do, it must be the truth."

The defendant quickly decided. "I'll take the oath," he said.

A moment later, in English, he repeated after the *qadi* the oath prescribed for Christians:

"I (defendant's name) in the Name of God Who gave Jesus, Son of Mary, the Holy Bible and with His Will made Him cure the sick, the leper, and the deaf, swear that I did not kick (plaintiff's name) in the right leg nor did I call him the son of a bastard."

As soon as he finished the oath the American was adjudged not guilty and released—freed by an unusual aspect of an unusual system of law, the noble *shari'a*, a code of law that has guided Muslim courts for 1,300 years (Reprinted from Baroody, *Shari'ah—the Law of Islam*, Case & Comm., March–April 1967, at 3).

In this brief excerpt from a trial, you can see that two rules of Islamic law determined the outcome of the case. Both the requirement of two witnesses and the defense of the oath stem from the traditions of the Prophet. Note that the possibility of determining the litigation by an oath is not unique to Islamic law, but can be found in some civil law countries.

THE REGULATORY ENVIRONMENT

Even though Saudi Arabia has no legislature and, thus, no legislation, it does extensively regulate business activities. All regulation, however, must be in accordance with the *shari'a,* or the path for believers in Islam.

The primary form of regulation is the administrative decree (*marsum*). Decrees originate in the ministries, then are approved by vote of the council of ministers. If the king approves the proposed regulation, the text is published in the *Official Gazette,* and the regulation goes into effect the next day.

Saudi Arabia also has unpublished regulations, issued as resolutions or circulars by the various ministries. These regulations are issued to interested parties upon request, but are effective without any official publication. If a decree conflicts with an unpublished regulation, the decree prevails. These unpublished regulations often create problems for unwary foreign businesses.

The king has established several agencies to resolve disputes arising from administrative regulations. The three most important, for business purposes, are the Supreme Commission on Labor Disputes, the Commission for the Settlement of Commercial Disputes, and the Board of Grievances. The Supreme Commission on Labor Disputes has exclusive authority over all disputes relating to labor contracts. The Commission for the Settlement of Commercial Disputes resolves disputes between private parties concerning commercial regulations. Finally, the Board of Grievances hears disputes involving government actions or inactions, including decisions to withhold operating licenses, the taking of bribes by government officials, and attempts to enforce judgments obtained abroad.

Government regulation covers many areas of business activity in Saudi Arabia. The government has attempted to accomplish substantial economic development, yet maintain traditional Islamic values. Administrative decrees in the form of 5-year plans establish priorities for economic development and establish a central bank (the Saudi Arabia Monetary Agency) with powers to regulate currency and banking. Administrative decrees regulate foreign investment, government procurement, the conduct of Saudi agents for foreign companies, and the employment of foreign workers.

The law outlined in this section represents only a few of the areas of regulation that may apply to foreign businesses wishing to operate in the kingdom of Saudi Arabia. One theme that runs throughout the legal environment of Saudi Arabia is the protection and promotion of Islam. The tenets of the Islamic faith affect personal conduct, such as the prohibition on alcoholic beverages; conduct toward others, such as the relationships between men and women; and elements of business transactions, such as the prohibition on interest. The study of contract law that follows illustrates the way Islamic law applies to business practices.

FOCUS ON CONTRACTS

Contract Formation

In common law systems such as that in the United States, parties form a contract with an offer, acceptance, and consideration. In some cases, a contract will need to be in writing to be enforceable. The rules for contract formation in Saudi Arabia will not seem unfamiliar to students of the common law.

In Saudi Arabia, a valid legal contract requires an offer, acceptance, and consideration. The offer must be a definite expression of an intent to enter into a contract, and the acceptance must correspond to the offer. Generally, the contract comes into existence at an actual meeting of the parties, but if the parties do not meet, an acceptance is effective when pronounced, rather than upon communication to the offeror.

With a few exceptions, contracts don't have to be in writing to be enforceable, even though the Quran strongly advocates reducing all contracts to writing:

> When ye contract a debt for a fixed term, record it in writing. Let a scribe record it in writing between you in (terms of) equity. . . . [L]et him who incurreth the debt dictate. . . . Be not averse to writing down (the contract) whether it be small or great, with record of the term thereof. That is more equitable in the sight of Allah and more sure of testimony, and the best way of avoiding doubt between you. . . . (Quran 2:282).

In keeping with the general Islamic reliance upon witnesses, the Quran urges parties to written contracts to have the signing witnessed by two males, or by at least one male and one female (Quran 2:282).

To be valid, a contract must leave no doubt about the obligations the parties incur. The subject of the contract must be certain, and quantities, price, and consideration must be specified. Similarly, employment contracts of agents are for a specified job or term, rather than at will.

Saudi Arabian contract law also requires consideration for most contracts. Islamic law, however, forbids the unjustified enrichment of one party to a contract. One who receives monetary value without giving countervalue in return must give away his profits as a charitable gift.

Contract Enforceability

Islamic law has several restrictions on the validity of contracts. Saudi Arabia, however, recognizes wide latitude in freedom of contract, as long as the contract is within the bounds of the law.

A contract concerning activities forbidden in the Quran is void. Thus, a contract to sell pork or wine would be unenforceable. Perhaps most significant for business activity, the Quran forbids the charging of interest: "Surely, they say, usury is like sale. But God has made sale lawful and usury unlawful" (Quran 2:282). Islamic businessmen have devised many ways to bypass the prohibition on charging interest, including service or management fees, profit-sharing arrangements, and offsetting sales.

Islamic law also forbids entering into contracts in which the obligations of the parties are uncertain or at risk. The prohibition of what Islamic law calls "risk" in contracts was originally designed to end gambling contracts. Today, the only legal gambling contracts concern horse racing and contests of knowledge of Islamic principles. However, the prohibition of risk may void contracts such as those for property insurance, where payment by an insurance company would be contingent on the occurrence of an event that might not happen.

Contracts may be unenforceable for other reasons familiar to students of Western legal traditions. Duress, fraud, and mistake are all defenses to contracts, as is lack of capacity. Slavery, minority, insanity, mortal illness, and financial irresponsibility all reduce or eliminate the capacity to enter into agreements. Although not all religious scholars agree, women generally have the capacity to enter into contracts.

Dispute Resolution

Contract disputes may go before a *shari'a* court or before an administrative tribunal, depending on whether the contract falls into an area regulated by administrative decree or into a traditional area of obligation. As a practical matter, many contracts involving foreign firms are with the Saudi government, so they are heard by the Board of Grievances. In 1983, Saudi Arabia issued rules allowing for the arbitration of commercial disputes.

The two primary remedies for breach of contract are damages and rescission. Rescission is available for deficiencies in the quantity and quality of goods. Damages are a more difficult issue for a party used to the Western concept of using damages to make an injured party whole. Consequential damages are not generally recognized under *shari'a* law, nor are damages for lost profits awarded because they are too uncertain. In the case of personal injury caused by defective products, the amount of damages an injured person can recover is established by the reference to the *diyah,* or "blood money," established by Muhammad. As of 1988, the amount payable was roughly $32,000 for the death of a Moslim male, $16,000 for the death of a Muslim female or non-Muslim male, and $8000 for the death of a non-Muslim female. Injuries not resulting in death are compensated by a partial payment of the *diyah.*[1]

---

[1]P. Sloane, "The Status of Islamic Law in a Modern Commercial World," 22 *International Lawyer* 743, 750 (1988).

CONCLUSION

The Saudi Arabian legal system presents many hazards for foreigners accustomed to secular, Western legal traditions. The legal environment changes and grows only within the limits of the word of God revealed in the Quran and the traditions of men who lived more than 1300 years ago. Yet within those boundaries, Saudi Arabian law has grown to accommodate rapid economic and technological development.

The Islamic legal tradition is becoming more important in countries from the Pacific Rim to southern Africa. The revival of Islam in the 1970s gave new voice to Islamic law in countries with secular, "modern" legal systems. Even where Islam is not explicitly the law of the land, it can provide a cultural framework for business activity. Any firm seeking to do business in an Islamic nation should take the time first to become familiar with Islamic legal, religious, and social customs.

4.3 JAPAN

Most business students and executives are familiar with the rise of Japan from a war-ravaged, impoverished nation to an economic superpower. Many are also familiar with Japan's reputation as a society that shuns litigation and lawyers in favor of informal means of regulation and dispute resolution. The legal environment of business in Japan has been an important factor in the nation's economic growth. However, that legal environment is far more complex and dynamic than the stereotype familiar to Westerners.

The foreign executive doing business in Japan should expect to encounter a mix of Japanese and Western business and social customs. Similarly, the Japanese legal tradition mixes elements of Chinese, Japanese, and Western outlooks on law and legal institutions. Japan has long looked to other nations as well as to its own traditions to develop legal institutions and methods. As early as the 7th century, Japan adapted the Chinese legal system to meet its own political and social needs. Many modern Japanese attitudes toward law and business have their roots in centuries-old traditions. We will first examine the major sources of the Japanese legal tradition, then the institutions and attitudes that determine the legal environment of business in contemporary Japan.

THE TOKUGAWA PERIOD

Perhaps the most significant historical era for the development of contemporary Japanese attitudes toward law was the Tokugawa era, from roughly 1600 to 1868. Despite significant later legal reforms, the values of the Tokugawa era, especially the importance of harmony, consensus, and hierarchy, remain at the core of current business and legal relationships.

PAUL LANSING AND MARLENE WECHSELBLATT, "DOING BUSINESS IN JAPAN: THE IMPORTANCE OF THE UNWRITTEN LAW"

17 International Lawyer 647 (1983)

A. THE TOKUGAWA PERIOD

The legal and psychological basis of society in Japan became the group, not the individual, during this feudal period. This concept is based on the Confucian ideal of the importance of the family within society. Taken a step further, the daimyo [feudal lord] is like a father to his *samurai* (warriors) and they are like his sons. The samurai, in turn, protect the commoners, who respect and pay allegiance to him. As the father is responsible for his family, the village head is responsible for the well-being of his people etc. The individual per se is unimportant; it is the group to which he belongs and his position in the hierarchy that must be recognized. Thus the law focused on the maintenance and preservation of the group, not on the establishment of individual rights.

This need for group harmony was not just based on the Confucian ideal of the family and the father/son model of relationships as the basis of social order, but on a yet more fundamental need. Unlike western farming, wet rice cultivation requires cooperation and group effort to plant and harvest. Therefore, group maintenance was not merely an abstract social or ethical ideal; it was an economic necessity since rice was the monetary unit of the times. Maintaining order was the duty of the village head; failure to do so resulted in strict punishment, for failure to keep order meant a loss of revenue for his lord.

In order to preserve social order, the individual had to recognize and accept his place within society. According to Neo-Confucian theory, society could be divided into four classes: the *samurai*, the *hyakuhsho* (farmers), the *shokunin* (the merchanges (sic) and artisans), and the *eta* (outcasts, usually animal tanners or undertakers). These classes were hereditary and clearly delineated. Interestingly, the farmers ranked before the merchants because tradition maintained that farmers contributed something to society while merchants were essentially parasites who contributed little but gained a lot. This class stratification had to be legally maintained since it was the underlying structure that held Japanese society together. The legal ramifications of this view that men were essentially unequal are clear enough: the law can be applied unequally to different classes. For example, only the *samurai* were allowed to bear arms.

Most striking in such a system is the individual's lack of recourse to the law. In feudal Japan there was no mechanism for appeal if you disagreed with a superior's decision. The individual as such had no legal existence; he was only part of a group, family, *kumi* (village group), or class. Connected with this lack of individual rights, perhaps paradoxically, is the Confucian sense of duty and loyalty to one's superiors. To question their decisions is to question the entire social order. Therefore conciliation was preferred to litigation, and disagreements were settled by superiors, preferably in a manner that would maintain group harmony. Maintenance of the class structure, not the delineation of individual rights was of value; duty, not vindication was expected. Since the moral force of filial loyalty inhibited the development of litigation, "dispensing justice was regarded as a matter of grace from the lord to the commoners and a good commoner was expected not to disturb the lord or use his time litigating. Thus a case must have real merit before a commoner would have the courage to impose upon his governor for justice."

Because of the pervasive Confucian code, ethics and law were synonymous. "One of the most notable aspects of Tokugawa legislation is that it usually takes the form of guides to moral administration rather than precise unbending rules purporting to be exact measures of specific behavior. If action is ethical and moral, it is legal; the law is ipso facto ethical and moral." Thus the law was not generalized principles of behavior but moral precepts which might alter given differing circumstances. The law is not an objective measurement of society's values, but a subjective morality applied by one's lord. Law was a matter of right relations based on the moral tenets of Confucian thought; it did not develop as a separate institution.

Not only did law and ethics merge, but private and public law combined through personal oblig-ations. The contractual relationship between the shogun and his vassals, the daimyo and his samu-rai were based on personal obligations of the lord to his samurai in exchange for their loyalty. This essential private contract was the basis of all pub-lic functions and behavior. It was maintained through custom for (sic) generation to generation. Contractual relationships were not just legal re-sponsibilities, but moral claims to one's family and descendants.

Civil Law Influences

Japan's isolation from the West came to an abrupt end with the appear-ance of Commodore Perry's ships in 1853. As the country began the process of industrialization, it turned to Western legal systems for institu-tions and legal methods. Japan began training its legal scholars in Western legal traditions as early as 1870 and began codifying its law in the 1870s.

The Japanese looked for a legal system with certainty and method. The somewhat chaotic, highly individualistic, and evolutionary approach of the common law was not suitable for a society valuing group harmony and hi-erarchy. The Japanese scholars turned to the civil law tradition to system-atize their own legal order. The Japanese Civil Code, drawn from the German Civil Code, went into effect in 1898, for the first time recognizing and encouraging the merchant class. The Japanese Commercial Code, again heavily influenced by German law, became effective in 1899.

By 1900, the Japanese legal system had found expression in five compre-hensive codes and a constitution. However, the codes expressed the au-thoritarian and paternalistic nature of the Japanese government, where legal rules were bestowed by the emperor and were not the creation of the people. The Confucian ideals of the group and of family remained an im-portant assumption of the Western-style codes adapted by Japan.

The U.S. Influence

The most radical change in the Japanese legal system came at the end of World War II. The victorious United States changed the underlying as-sumptions of the Japanese legal system as well as the legal institutions and the codes. The Japanese constitution of 1947 separated church and state, created an independent judiciary, declared the people, not the emperor, to be the source of authority for law, and established new government insti-tutions on a parliamentary model. The new constitution introduced the U.S. concepts of individual rights and of due process to Japan.

The occupation authorities also forced the reform of all five of Japan's codes. The most significant changes occurred in the codes of Criminal Law and Criminal Procedure, but the Civil and Commercial codes were also rewritten. The portions of the Commercial codes dealing with business organizations underwent substantial revision.

Finally, the U.S. occupying forces changed the legal environment of business in Japan by establishing laws based on U.S. business regulation. New income tax, securities, and antitrust laws and the establishment of the Fair Trade Commission *(Kosei torihiki iinikai)* resulted from the U.S. reforms.

CONTEMPORARY SOURCES OF LAW

Modern Japanese lawyers, when confronted with a legal problem, take an essentially civil law approach to its solution. They turn first to the codes as sources of law, then to the regulations of the appropriate ministry. If the codes and regulations are inconclusive, the lawyer will often turn to the commentaries on the code written by prominent law professors. Finally, the lawyer may turn to court decisions for guidance in interpreting the law.

In the sources for positive law, the Japanese legal system operates in much the same way as most civil law systems. However, the values of Tokugawa Japan still influence the ways in which Japanese lawyers and businessmen choose to use and respond to the legal system. Rights granted by the constitution and the codes may seem antithetical to the duties one business owes to another or to the government. Japan has largely Western legal institutions operating within a framework of Eastern traditional values.

Government Institutions

Modern Japan has a parliamentary system of government, with a popularly elected bicameral legislature, called the Diet. The Diet elects from its members a prime minister, who in turn appoints a cabinet. Japan has several important political parties. The Liberal Democratic Party has controlled the Diet for decades, but other parties have made significant gains on local levels.

Much of the real regulatory power over business is wielded by the various ministries. The ministries are staffed by highly respected career bureaucrats who, upon retirement in their fifties, generally go to work for the businesses they had regulated. Many of the best students at Japan's most prestigious universities aspire to positions in Japan's bureaucracy.

The bureaucracy is the main government actor in the relationship between law and business. Business and government maintain extremely close working relationships, aided by the personal contacts of those leaving the ministries to work in business. Ministries draft many of the laws for the Diet and regulations for business. Finally, the ministries often act informally, using a regulatory device known as administrative guidance.

The Japanese constitution created a judiciary independent of the legislature, and gave it the express power to review all legislative and administrative acts, as well as to hear cases and make rules. The Supreme Court administers the entire judicial system, including the one law school, the Legal Training and Research Institute.

Litigation and Lawyers

The popular perception of Japan includes a vision of a society with few lawyers and little litigation. On the surface, this perception may appear to be correct. The Legal Training and Research Institute, which trains all lawyers, judges, and procurators (government attorneys), runs the most competitive graduate program in the country. It admits only a few hundred of the thousands of students taking the entrance exam each year, and operates as an extremely effective entry barrier to the profession of law.

Similarly, Japanese law erects barriers to litigation. One barrier is the rule requiring the losing party to pay the costs and fees of the winning party. Another effective barrier is the entrustment of controversial matters to the ministries. For example, in the 1960s and 1970s, women won several significant court victories in legal challenges to overtly discriminatory employment practices. In 1986, the Diet passed the Equal Employment Opportunity Act, which affirmed the principle of equal employment opportunity, but provided no penalties for discrimination. Instead, the act gave the Ministry of Labor the power to mediate disputes between women and their employers and the power to recommend settlements.[2]

The lack of lawyers *(bengoshi)* and litigation does not indicate a freewheeling interaction between business and law. The study of law is one of Japan's most popular undergraduate majors in the universities, and it is widely perceived as an ideal preparation for higher management positions. Most students with bachelor's level degrees in law work in corporate law departments, specializing in narrow areas of business law. Their expertise can be formidable, and these trained specialists often serve as part of the negotiating teams on international business contracts. Similarly, litigation can be important in effecting change and in acting as a check on the bureaucracy. When business and the ministries are not responsive to the needs of a group of people—for example, working women or pollution victims—litigation can force change.

The Regulatory Environment

On a day-to-day basis, the most important legal restrictions on business activity come from the ministries. Sometimes the restrictions may take the form of formal regulation. More often, restrictions on business activity re-

---

[2]F. Upham, *Law and Social Change in Postwar Japan,* 152–53 (1987).

sult from the informal regulatory process of administrative guidance. Agencies use administrative guidance to avoid formal regulation, to create national policies on business issues, and to work with industry to solve problems without invoking adversarial processes.

The most important administrative agency in Japan is the Ministry of International Trade and Industry (MITI). The excerpt below illustrates the ways in which MITI uses informal processes to regulate Japanese business activities. Note how different the relationship between MITI and the businesses it regulates is from similar situations in the United States.

FRANK UPHAM, *LAW AND SOCIAL CHANGE IN POSTWAR JAPAN*

Harvard University Press, Cambridge, 1987, pp. 169–174 (footnotes omitted)

The legal framework within which the *shingikai* process [informal discussions between regulators and business leaders in affected industries] and administrative guidance operate consists of the statutory basis of MITI's authority and the administrative law doctrines that define its limits. The former delineates the areas in which MITI can exercise its discretion; the latter determine by whom, when, and in what forum that exercise can be challenged.

At the foundation of MITI's authority is the MITI Establishment Act, which defines MITI's jurisdiction, goals, and structure. On the next level are statutes like the Foreign Exchange and Foreign Trade Control Law (FECL) that give MITI responsibility for broad areas of economic policy. At a third level of specificity are statutes like the Petroleum Industry Law (PIL) that give MITI general authority to promote particular industries, and statutes like the Depressed Industries Law (DIL) that give MITI specific authority to deal with economic conditions affecting a number of industries.

Overriding characteristics of all statutes are the wide scope of authority delegated to MITI and the vagueness of the standards by which MITI is to exercise that authority. Statutory provisions do not provide clear guidelines for the Ministry to use in carrying out the legislative intent of the Diet. As with the EEOA [Equal Employment Opportunity Act] in the employment discrimination area, economic statutes are better viewed as

identifying an area (such as the promotion of industry and international trade) or a problem (for example, the decline in competitiveness of Japanese industries after the oil shocks of the 1970s) and delegating legal authority to MITI to deal with it as it sees fit. When it comes to how, when, or toward what end that legal power should be used, most economic statutes are so broad as to be virtually meaningless. . . .

Plaintiffs seeking judicial review of administrative action face the initial problem of whether the challenged agency behavior constitutes an "administrative disposition [*shobun*] or other exercise of public power" as required by Article 3 of the Administrative Case Litigation Law (ACLL). If so, the action is justiciable, and the inquiry shifts to whether the plaintiff is an appropriate person to challenge it. If not, the case is dismissed. The Japanese Supreme Court has limited Article 3 to administrative acts that immediately and directly create or delimit private rights and duties.

Under this definition, most of industrial policy is beyond judicial review. MITI almost invariably acts informally in a legal sense, and only a final and legally formal act directly creates legal rights and duties. Thus in allocating quotas for the elimination of capacity in declining industries, MITI does not issue legally binding orders prohibiting production above a certain level. Instead, informal discussion among the members of the industry is encouraged until consensus is reached, with forceful arm twisting by the bureaucrats if necessary. Nothing in the process has immediate legal effect; it is only when the process breaks down that MITI relies on its statutory authority, and then often by way of a threat of collateral future action, such as the decline of required approvals for plant expansion or foreign exchange transactions. Such threats remain informal and thus are not administrative dispositions.

It is not just informal actions that escape judicial scrutiny. Supervisory orders, permissions, approvals, or regulations within an agency or even among agencies and public bodies like *shingikai*, no matter how formal or final, are not reviewable because they are considered internal government behavior that does not directly affect the legal rights or duties of private citizens. Furthermore, administrative acts with general effect, such as agency plans or regulations, are not judicially recognizable unless they immediately and concretely affect a specific person's legal rights or obligations.

. . . While the formulation of industrial policy is invariably legally informal, its implementation cannot always be successful without recourse to formal powers under specific statutory provisions. If, for example, a petroleum company resists MITI's recommendations concerning production quotas during a period of oversupply, MITI need only remind the company of its powers in other areas, whether this involves controlling import of petroleum under the Foreign Exchange Control Law or approving plant expansion under the Petroleum Industry Law. If the company does not accede to the Ministry's demands, it faces the prospect of being rejected the next time it needs approval for an entirely different matter. Even when MITI does not have direct statutory power over the relevant industry, a recalcitrant company can be reminded of indirect sanctions such as the denial of government benefits or retaliation against allied companies in industries over which MITI has direct control.

FOCUS ON CONTRACTS

The sources of law governing Japanese contracts are the Civil and Commercial codes. Generally, the contract rules are familiar to students of Western law, as they are derived from the civil law tradition. Mutual consent is the basic requirement to form a contract, although writings and consideration are not required for enforceability. Most international transactions, though, will involve written, carefully negotiated contracts with consideration.

The real change for Westerners entering into contracts with Japanese businesses, though, is a different perception of what the contract means and of its purpose. Westerners often view a contract as a document memorializing the details of a transaction, whereas Japanese executives see a contract as a document establishing a relationship. To Westerners, contracts define rights and duties of the parties; to Japanese, contracts express the nature of the business relationship. From this fundamental difference flow several consequences for managers.

First, the substance and style of contract negotiations will differ. The Western negotiator will look to define terms, obligations, and the details of the transaction. The Japanese negotiating team will use the dialogue to establish personal ties, trust, and a sense of how the parties will treat each other before settling terms.

Second, the contract terms will differ. Westerners tend to want to spell out all the rights and obligations of the parties, while Japanese executives look for flexibility and openness in terms. Typical of Japanese contracts are "good faith" or "amicability" clauses, which obligate the parties to work together to resolve any differences of opinion arising from the fulfilling of the contract. Western executives and their attorneys tend to feel uncomfortable with such open-ended contract provisions.

Third, Japanese and Western managers will have different expectations about the extent of their obligations. Westerners generally look to the specific terms of the contract to determine the extent of required performance, and will take the letter of the contract seriously. Japanese managers see the contract as a starting point, with the flexibility to change in case of altered circumstances. Thus, a Westerner tends to see the need for contract modification as a serious problem requiring renegotiation of contract terms, whereas a Japanese may see the same need to modification without renegotiating the terms of the original agreement.

Finally, Western and Japanese managers have quite different perceptions of the nature of breach of contract and of the ways to resolve disputes. The Civil Code may have some provision for what Westerners would know as the doctrine of frustration or commercial impracticability, but the Japanese business expectation is that the parties will work out their differences in order to maintain the business relationship. Although the contract may call for arbitration in the event of conflict, Japanese executives are extremely reluctant to invoke the aid of formal legal processes and are much more likely to try to assess blame to both parties, in accordance with traditional beliefs.

CONCLUSION

The legal environment for business in Japan is far more complex than most Western managers would expect. The popular perception of Japanese law is of a society without disputes and without lawyers; yet the reality shows a highly developed but different way of resolving legal problems, and different sources for legal advice for business.

A student looking at the constitution and the laws of Japan would come away with a perception of law that is quite different from the popular image, but just as erroneous. Japan does have a formal legal structure in place, and a heritage of Western-style legal institutions. Yet these formal institutions of the law are invoked primarily after informal means fail to obtain harmonious resolutions of problems.

The lesson that Western managers can draw from an examination of the Japanese legal tradition applies in many countries borrowing legal institutions from the West. Managers must look beyond popular perceptions and beyond the existence of legal institutions. Even though Japan has adopted much Western law, its own traditional values have a great influence on the way the Western law is used. A manager ignorant of the social and business culture of Japan simply will not be able to do business effectively with the Japanese. The Western influence exists only through a filter of Eastern values.

4.4 THE PEOPLE'S REPUBLIC OF CHINA

China, like Japan, exemplifies a legal environment in which Western-style institutions clash with underlying non-Western social values. Unlike Japan, though, China looked to socialism for its formal legal institutions and methods. Also unlike Japan, China is still experimenting with both its economic and its legal system, resulting in a highly unstable legal environment for foreign businesses. China's legal tradition is not yet fully developed, despite China's long history.

China has long fascinated foreign traders both as a source for goods unobtainable in home countries and as a large and diverse market. Today, China has well over one billion people, and stands on the edge of emergence as a major world economic power. U.S. businesses alone have invested and spent billions of dollars in China, with European and other Asian businesses also investing billions of dollars. In 1997, when Hong Kong returns to Chinese control, China's economic importance will increase dramatically.

Since Mao Zedong's death in 1976, China has made a major commitment to the rule of law and the development of legal institutions. The foreign executive doing business in China should be aware both of the new structures for business and of the pitfalls of relying on formal, written law.

SOURCES OF THE CHINESE LEGAL TRADITION

Even though China has officially rejected religion, religious traditions still heavily influence Chinese attitudes toward law. In particular, like Japan, Confucian attitudes toward law and obligation play a large role in attitudes toward law and lawyers in China.

In the Confucian tradition, invoking formal law, or *fa,* is a step of last resort and a sign of the breakdown of order in society. Instead, honorable people strive to conform their behavior in honorable, ethical ways known as *li.* Confucian standards of honor in large measure involve the respect of hierarchy and relationships: The son honors the father; the wife honors the husband; and the inferior honors the superior.

China built thousands of years of legal tradition on these principles. In the process, it invented the bureaucracy, a merit-based group of officials who, in keeping with their superiority over commoners, wielded unchecked and sometimes arbitrary power over the populace.

CHINA AFTER THE REVOLUTION

In 1949, the Chinese Communists took power and dismantled the country's law and legal institutions. They began the process of writing all new laws and creating entirely new legal institutions consistent with a

Marxist–Leninist state. However, as the bureaucrats and scholars began writing new laws, the political winds changed. Activities seen as needed reforms in 1949 became reactionary and bourgeois. From 1957 to 1966, the process of creating a new legal tradition halted.

The beginning of the Cultural Revolution in 1966 marked the beginning of what many legal scholars call the "Dark Ages" of Chinese law. Law schools and courts were closed. Lawyers and judges, like many other groups of people, such as students and scientists, were exiled to rural areas for reeducation, criticism, and manual labor. Law, lawyers, and legal institutions were labeled reactionary or rightist. The leaders of the Cultural Revolution openly encouraged lawlessness, and urged the Red Guards to "smash the police organs, procuracies, and courts."[3] By the early 1970s, China was effectively a nation without law.

THE SECOND REVOLUTION

Mao Zedong's death in 1976 started a new, economic revolution in China. The new leadership pledged to modernize the country's industry, agriculture, defense, and technology. To modernize, it opened China to Western trade, and committed the nation to the rule of law. Once again, China began to create all-new laws and legal institutions, this time to promote China's development, under socialism, to the status of a world economic power. China's new constitution, passed in 1982, commits the government and the Communist party to operation within the law.

CONTEMPORARY SOURCES OF LAW

Virtually all of the formal Chinese law a foreigner will encounter is in the form of statutes and regulations. China is working toward a civil law framework, with legislation as the primary source of law, and no real recognition of judge-made law or precedent. The seventh 5-year plan (1986–1990) counts among its goals the systematic codification of law.

Since 1979, China has enacted significant legislation in many areas affecting business. Among those laws are statutes regulating joint ventures between Chinese and foreign businesses, contract laws, intellectual property laws, statutes establishing special economic zones for export-related businesses, tax laws, and products liability law. The Foreign Economic Contract Law will be the subject of the Focus on Contract section later in this chapter.

As part of China's commitment to the rule of law, it has joined the international community of nations on several issues important to trade. In

---

[3]"In Praise of Lawlessness," *Renmin Ribao (People's Daily)*, Jan. 31, 1967, at 6, quoted in Hsia and Zeldin, "Recent Legal Developments in the People's Republic of China," 28 *Harvard International Law Journal* 240, 253–254 (1987).

1980, China opened relations with the GATT. China has also ratified the United Nations Convention on the International Sale of Goods.

Government Institutions

China, like most Socialist nations, has a dual structure of government, involving the Communist party and a legislature. The party sets the policies for the government to follow, while the legislature enacts the laws to carry out party policy.

The National People's Congress is China's main legislative body. It approves and amends the constitution and deals with major legislative initiatives. The Standing Committee of the National People's Congress decides what legislation the Congress will consider, and drafts that legislation. It has been responsible for the content of China's new laws on foreign trade.

The executive powers of the government are concentrated in the State Council, which consists of the heads of ministries and commissions, the premier, and the vice premiers. As a practical matter, the members of the State Council are high officials of the Communist party.

Courts and Lawyers

The judicial branch of government in China is organized within the Ministry of Justice. The People's Courts, which are the trial courts in China, have begun to hear increasing numbers of cases involving economic matters, foreigners, and the government. The courts are only available to foreigners who do not have arbitration clauses in their contracts. If a foreign party has an arbitration clause, contract disputes must go to arbitration. Reports of case decisions are still not widely available, although the Supreme People's Court has begun to publish some of its decisions. The decisions are meant to give guidance to local courts, but do not have precedential value.

China still has mixed feelings about lawyers and their role in business. Although the leadership has, since 1979, encouraged the rule of law, Chinese tradition denigrates law as a profession. In a Marxist–Leninist analysis, law has traditionally been used as a tool to oppress the working classes. As a result of law's checkered past in Chinese history, China has very few legally trained professionals.

Chinese lawyers work as state employees in legal advisory offices, at set salaries. They act as legal advisors to the government or to businesses, sometimes represent individuals in criminal and civil litigation, and help draft and explain legal documents. In contrast to Western lawyers, whose primary focus is on the client's interests, Chinese lawyers have the obligation to further the interests of the government. The government regulation on lawyers states:

> Lawyers are the State's legal workers and function to give legal assistance to the state organs, enterprises, establishments, mass organizations, the people's com-

munes and the citizens in order to ensure the correct implementation of law and protect the interests of the state and the collectives as well as the legitimate rights and interests of the citizens.[4]

China also does not favor litigation as a means of resolving civil disputes. In part, the disfavor stems from the traditional view of litigation as an event bringing dishonor to its participants. In the Chinese tradition, negotiation and mediation are always preferable to the adversarial solutions of litigation and even arbitration. In Marxist–Leninist thought, the litigation process is a means of oppressing the working class.

Since the 1949 revolution, both litigation and arbitration have sometimes yielded to political movements. One notorious example of the bending of law to politics occurred in the early days of the Cultural Revolution. The Vickers-Zimmer Company had a contract to build a petrochemical plant in China. When the Red Guards prevented the company from completing the project, Vickers-Zimmer invoked the arbitration clause in its contract with the government. In response, the government arrested two company employees as spies. The Chinese courts then rendered judgment against Vickers-Zimmer for £650,000, a sum that happened to match the amount the company was seeking in damages.[5]

As a result of China's aversion to adversarial dispute resolution, most business dealings with China call for resolving disputes by good faith negotiation, then conciliation, then arbitration or litigation. Successful arbitration tends to use the arbitrators to bring the parties to a mutually satisfactory result, rather than ruling entirely in favor of one party.

The Regulatory Environment

China has a large, complex system of agencies, bureaus, and commissions drafting legislation, writing regulations, and making written and unwritten policy. Because China's economic system is a centrally controlled command economy, Chinese bureaucrats reach into almost all aspects of economic life in the nation. Although the government has taken many recent steps to reduce the central government's role in business decisions, a foreign trader doing business with China should expect to encounter the Chinese regulatory system in every business transaction.

In foreign trade, the most important government agency is the Ministry of Foreign Economic Relations and Trade (MOFERT). MOFERT sets policy for most of China's foreign trade corporations, which are the businesses that conduct the bulk of China's international trade. Foreign trade corporations represent Chinese companies that want to buy or sell products.

---

[4]1 *China Law Reporter*, 217–221 (1981).
[5]Reported in Jerome Alan Cohen and Hungdah Chiu, *People's China and International Law*, Princeton University Press, Princeton, N.J., 1974, pp. 656–668.

Under the guidance of MOFERT, the foreign trade corporation plans transactions, finds the foreign party, and negotiates and signs contracts. For example, the China National Light Industrial Products Import and Export Corporation is the foreign trade corporation for the purchase and sale of radios, paper goods, electrical appliances, leather products, and several other light industrial products. Suppose that a factory in Beijing was making radios for export. Rather than sending its own sales force out to find overseas buyers, the factory managers would turn to the relevant foreign trade corporation. Representatives from the industry trade corporation would find the buyer, negotiate, and sign the contract for the goods.

Since 1979, China has decentralized some controls over foreign trade. Branch offices of MOFERT now may negotiate some contracts without central office approval. Other ministries have established foreign trading corporations for products within their jurisdiction. Some individual factory managers now have the authority to negotiate contracts for their businesses. In some areas, local or regional officials now may negotiate or give approvals for contracts.

For foreign businesses, China's reforms to encourage foreign trade present both new opportunities and new pitfalls. Decentralization creates new opportunities to reach the end users of products and open new markets. However, the structure of the Chinese bureaucracy is changing rapidly. Lines of authority are no longer as certain as they were when China's economy was completely centrally planned.

Furthermore, China's bureaucracy issues new regulations at a rapid rate, but China still has no mechanism for systematic publication of new regulations. Some regulations may be published in newspapers, but others are given only to the officials of the factory or foreign trade corporation involved. A foreign business trying to negotiate a deal may have to do so in a regulatory environment to which it has limited access.

FOCUS ON CONTRACTS

Like most Socialist legal systems, Chinese contract law finds its sources in statutes and regulations, rather than in case law. The statutes governing contracts are all quite new, and some areas of law and regulation are still in the formative stages.

China has four main statutes governing contracts. The Civil Code, enacted in 1986, sets out the general principles of law governing all civil legal obligation. Included in the Civil Code are provisions on contract formation, legality, breach, and remedy. The Economic Contract Law governs contracts between Chinese nationals. The Foreign Economic Contract Law, enacted in 1985, governs contracts between Chinese businesses, organizations, and government agencies and foreigners. Finally, China is a party to the United Nations Convention on the International Sale of Goods (CISG).

For traders, the most important statute governing contracts is the Foreign Economic Contract Law (FECL). FECL governs the entire range of commercial relationships between Chinese and foreign businesses, except for contracts under the CISG. It controls sales of services and technology, leasing, licenses, joint venture contracts, insurance agency relationships, and other cooperative ventures.

ZHANG YUQING AND JAMES S. MCLEAN, "CHINA'S FOREIGN ECONOMIC CONTRACT LAW: ITS SIGNIFICANCE AND ANALYSIS"

8 Northwestern Journal of International Law & Business, 120, 126–129 (1987)

Four principles provide the actual basis for the FECL: equality and mutual benefit; the primacy of international treaties to which China is a party; honoring the contract and maintaining good faith in business activities; and national laws and regulations protect national sovereignty and social welfare. The first principle, that of equality and mutual benefit, has been instrumental in promoting and developing China's foreign economic relations. It is also observed by Chinese economic entities in their international economic activities. Thus, it is not surprising to find this principle incorporated in Article 3 of the FECL: "contracts should be made in conformity with the principles of equality and mutual benefit, and of achieving unanimity through consultations." The first component of the principle—equality—requires that parties, regardless of their size and strength, should be on an equal footing in negotiating their contract. The contractual agreement should reflect the parties' interests, needs, and understanding of the contract terms. No party has the right to use its economic power to impose or force the other party to accept unfair or unreasonable conditions. The second component of the principle—mutual benefit—means that the interests of both parties to a contract should be reasonably considered and realized, so that a party enjoys benefits only after fulfilling its obligations under the contract. Under Chinese commercial practice, the concepts of equality and mutual benefit are so closely linked that there is to be no mutual benefits unless the parties are on an equal footing. . . .

A second major principle incorporated in the FECL is the primacy of international treaties to which China is a party, influenced by China's open door policy and its desire to further its economic contacts with foreign countries. In recent years, China has participated in the discussion and conclusion of various international treaties and conventions, which greatly influenced the drafting of the FECL. . . . It is evident that the drafters intended the FECL to be consistent with international commercial practice. . . .

In order for treaty law to take precedent over Chinese law, the following conditions must be met, as deduced from the FECL: 1) the provisions of the treaty must relate to the particular issue or issues resulting from the relevant contract; 2) a conflict must exist between the provisions of the treaty and Chinese domestic law; 3) China is a party to the treaty; and 4) China has not declared reservations under the treaty provisions invoked by one party. . . .

The FECL's third principle requires that the contract be honored and that good faith be maintained in business activities. These linked concepts require that Chinese corporations consciously consider whether they are capable of performing the contractual obligations before signing it. It is customary in China that, once a contract is signed, it should be performed exactly and fully according to its terms, except for events of force majeure. Parties are not to take advantage of market changes to breach a contract intentionally. These principles of Chinese commercial practice are firmly embedded in the FECL.

The fourth and last FECL principle underscores that national laws and regulations are to protect national sovereignty and social welfare. One of the tasks of China's foreign trade laws is to serve the country's economic construction and to promote China's four modernizations. It is of paramount importance for China to keep its foreign economic activities in line with these goals. Consequently, it is not surprising that several articles of the FECL are designed to preserve China's sovereignty and social interest. For example, contracts may be invalidated on public policy grounds. In addition, the FECL provides that certain contracts be approved by the government. This approval guards against Chinese enterprises entering into contracts that would contravene Chinese sovereignty or public policy. Consequently, Western lawyers and business executives must be aware that the contracts may be invalidated for public policy reasons.

Contract Formation

The FECL does not have many specific provisions on contract formation, but the Civil Code contains provisions generally governing contract obligations. Article 55 of the Civil Code provides for three conditions to form a contract: the parties must have legal capacity; the agreement must express the real intent of the parties; and the agreement must not violate the law or the public interest. Although in general contracts may be oral or written, all contracts under the FECL must be in writing.

Enforceability

Chinese contract law provides for several defenses to contracts, including duress, mistake, and fraud. Because China has a centrally planned economy, three other possible defenses may create problems for foreign traders. First, a contract that violates a state plan is invalid. Second, a contract is void when one party is an enterprise or individual who does not have the legal authority to enter into the transaction. Finally, some contracts, such as joint ventures and imports of technology, require provincial or central government approvals as well as authorized signatures. Contracts without those approvals are void.

Dispute Resolution

Chinese law and business practice both support informal means of resolving contract disputes as preferable to arbitration or litigation. Parties to contract disputes will generally take a series of steps to resolve problems out of court.

The first step is consultation, or, as it is sometimes called, "friendly consultation." The parties will meet to clarify the facts of the dispute, explore and resolve misunderstandings, and negotiate a mutually acceptable resolution of the problem.

If consultation fails, the next step often involves calling in an outsider to mediate the dispute. The function of the mediator is to help the parties understand the dimensions of the problem and possible solutions, and to help them reach conclusions that leave both parties satisfied and the business relationship intact.

Contracts with Chinese businesses generally include arbitration clauses. Often, the arbitration will take place in conjunction with further mediation to resolve the dispute. In recent years, China has shown an increasing willingness to agree to neutral-country arbitrations applying Chinese or the neutral country's law. In particular, Chinese contracts have invoked Sweden as a neutral site for arbitration of contract disputes. China does not recognize the International Chamber of Commerce arbitral forum in Paris or the ICC rules, because Taiwan is a member of the ICC.

Practical Considerations

Because Chinese law is still in formation, and because China has very few legal professionals, many Chinese negotiators rely on form contracts prepared by MOFERT in negotiating agreements with foreigners. Although the form contracts need many additions and alterations, they provide a framework for negotiation and the major terms of the agreement.

ZHANG YUQING AND JAMES S. MCLEAN, "CHINA'S FOREIGN ECONOMIC CONTRACT LAW: ITS SIGNIFICANCE AND ANALYSIS"

8 Northwestern Journal of International Law & Business 120 (1987)

As China's FECL is still relatively new, its interpretation by domestic courts and domestic and foreign arbitration tribunals presents both uncertainties and opportunities for the international transactions practitioner. Within the context of the FECL, as well as other general considerations involved in doing business with China, the following practice recommendations should be considered when negotiating contracts with Chinese enterprises.

First, a prudent practitioner should realize that it may be the exception to the rule to have a body of law other than Chinese law to apply to a transaction. Consequently, familiarity with applicable principles of Chinese law is strongly advised when structuring a transaction. Second, when a contract with Chinese parties is concluded, the practitioner should consider consulting lawyers in MOFERT or lawyers working for Chinese law offices. These individuals will be able to review a

transaction for possible conflicts with Chinese rules or regulations. On a related point, the practitioner should have MOFERT also review the transaction to determine whether government approval is necessary. Third, during the negotiation stage, the practitioner should consult MOFERT or other government agencies to verify the authority of the Chinese enterprise and its officers to enter into a contract.

A fourth suggestion is that the practitioner must be patient when negotiating with Chinese parties and remember that China is a developing country. Its nonmarket economy possesses different values and cultural traits than Western trading partners. Fifth, the practitioner should obtain the various form contracts which are currently used by Chinese enterprises and available in English. Sixth, the practitioner must remember that China is still in the process of codifying new laws and regulations, that English translations may be inexact or unavailable, and that care must be taken to understand the true meaning of the laws and regulations. Finally, in negotiating a commercial transaction in China, an attorney should be prepared to assume a secondary role, allowing the business parties to negotiate face-to-face as is customary in Asian countries.

CONCLUSION

The Chinese legal system is still a system in transition. The heady westernization of the mid-1980s has given way to more conservative modernization. The democracy movement and the riots at Tiananmen Square in 1989 provoked a political backlash that has, at times, spread to the economic reforms, but has left much of the new legal structure intact, at least formally. The leaders of China are now in their eighties. When they are gone, the new leaders may decide to move the Chinese legal system in new directions. Businesses contemplating trade and investment with China need to keep a constant awareness of the changing political and legal environment. Business strategies must retain enough flexibility to allow for surprising changes in laws and government policies.

4.5 CONCLUSION

Many countries around the world, including some of the most significant world trading nations, have legal systems based on non-Western ways of thinking. Each country's system is unique, and traders doing business in non-Western countries need to explore several issues before they do business. They should inquire into the cultural traditions of each country and the significant historical events that shaped the legal system. They should look at the function of law in each society, and the role of its legal institutions and its lawyers. Last, they should look to see under what circumstances traditional Western ways of thinking about business and legal issues will be inadequate for resolving trade and investment problems. Equipped with this knowledge, the Western businessperson can improve the prospects for success in dealings with non-Western cultures.

4.6 QUESTIONS FOR DISCUSSION

1. Western judges have sometimes viewed Islamic courts as less than fair to participants in the legal process, and have sometimes used the term "*qadi* court" as a synonym for irrationality. For example, in his dissent in *Terminiello v. City of Chicago*, 337 U.S. 1, 11 (1949), Justice Frankfurter said, "This is a court of review, not a tribunal unbounded by rules. We do

not sit like a kadi under a tree dispensing justice according to considerations of individual expediency." What is your response to Justice Frankfurter's statement?

2. Japan and China both draw upon Confucian sources for parts of their legal traditions. What role do you see for Confucian values in their contemporary legal systems? Explain.

3. If China were to decide to move to a free market economic system, what changes would it need to make in its legal system? If you were to recommend a legal tradition for China to follow, what tradition would that be? Explain.

4. Would a Japanese-style system of informal consultation and administrative guidance be an effective way to regulate business in your country? Why is it successful in Japan? Explain.

4.7 FURTHER READINGS

ISLAMIC LAW

Joseph L. Brand, "Aspects of Saudi Arabian Law and Practice," 9 *Boston College International & Comparative Law Review* 1 (1986) (contains an extensive bibliography).

Gali Hagel, "A Practitioner's Introduction to Saudi Arabian Law," 16 *Vanderbilt Journal of Transnational Law* 113 (1983).

Joseph Schacht, *An Introduction to Islamic Law,* Clarendon Press, Oxford, 2d ed., 1982.

Bryant W. Seaman, "Islamic Law and Modern Government: Saudi Arabia Supplements the Shari'a to Regulate Development," 18 *Columbia Journal of Transnational Law* 411 (1979).

JAPANESE LAW

Dan F. Henderson, *Foreign Enterprise in Japan,* University of North Carolina Press, Chapel Hill, 1973.

Paul Lansing and Marlene Wechselblatt, "Doing Business in Japan: The Importance of the Unwritten Law," 17 *International Lawyer* 647 (1983).

Hideo Tanaka, *The Japanese Legal System: Introductory Cases and Materials,* University of Tokyo Press, Tokyo, 1976.

Hideo Tanaka, "The Role of Law in Japanese Society: Comparisons with the West," 19 *University of British Columbia Law Review* 375 (1983).

Frank K. Upham, *Law and Social Change in Postwar Japan,* Harvard University Press, Cambridge, 1987.

Mark Zimmerman, *How to Do Business with the Japanese*, Random House, New York, 1985.

CHINESE LAW

Thomas Haney, "The Trial of a Contract Dispute in China," 22 *International Lawyer* 475 (1988).

Harry Harding, *China's Second Revolution: Reform after Mao*, Brookings, Washington, D.C., 1987.

Chan Kim, "The Modern Chinese Legal System," 61 *Tulane Law Review* 1413 (1987).

Roderick Mackleod, *China, Inc.,* Bantam, New York, 1988.

SUPRANATIONAL LAW: THE EUROPEAN COMMUNITY

5.1 INTRODUCTION

World War II left many of Europe's cities and industrial regions in ruins. The Allied nations, remembering the aftermath of World War I, feared the consequences of a rebuilt Germany, yet a weakened Germany invited the occupation of Soviet troops already occupying East Germany. If each country in Europe restored its industrial economy to its prewar state, the inefficiencies of production caused by numerous small markets would set up the conditions for another protectionist trade war. Just as the protectionism of the 1930s set the stage for World War II, the Allies thought, another bout of protectionism could lead to the next world war.

Cooperation seemed the only way to rebuild Europe, yet French–German and French–British cooperation seemed almost unthinkable. The countries of Europe had hundreds of years of belligerence toward each other to overcome. Fortunately, the same kind of political leadership that saw the Allies through World War II was able to start the nations of Western Europe toward economic and political cooperation. Winston Churchill, in a speech at Zurich University on September 19, 1946, laid down the challenge to cooperate. He said, "We must build a United States of Europe." Elaborating on his premise, he said:

> I am now going to say something that will astonish you. The first step in the re-creation of the European family must be a partnership between France and Germany. In this way only can France recover the moral leadership of Europe. There can be no revival of Europe without a spiritually great France and a spiritually great Germany. The structure of the United States of Europe, if well and truly built, will be such as to make the material strength of a single state less important. Small nations will count as much as large ones and gain their honour by their contribution to the common cause. . . .

The European Community grew from these postwar foundations: Currently twelve nations totaling more than 300 million people strive for a unified economic market and compatible political and legal institutions. To achieve their economic alliance, the European nations ceded some of their own sovereign authority to the institutions of the Community, allowing Community law to prevail over conflicting national law. The result was an international organization with more legal power than other multilateral organizations, and a new kind of law: not international, but supranational.

The nations of the European Community are now formidable competitors in the global marketplace. Any business competing with European companies in the United States or in Europe should be familiar with the functions of the European Community, its legal and political institutions, and most important, with its substantive law. Over the coming decades, the power of the European Community is likely to expand, as more countries become members, and the institutions grow more powerful. This chapter explores the rapidly developing supranational legal environment of Europe.

5.2 DEVELOPMENT

The first step in the economic integration of Europe was the formation of the European Coal and Steel Community (ECSC). The French government proposed a common market between France and Germany in coal and steel, with decision-making ceded to a multinational High Authority. For the French, the ECSC allowed some control over the redevelopment of the industrial heart of Germany, while for the Germans, the ECSC represented a large step toward redevelopment and healing with former enemies.

In 1951, France, Germany, Italy, Belgium, the Netherlands, and Luxembourg signed the Paris Treaty establishing the ECSC. The treaty eliminated protectionist measures in the member countries; established a common market for coal, steel, coke, iron ore, steel, and scrap; harmonized freight rates; and through taxes on freight, paid for some of the human costs associated with the restructuring of the market.

The success of the ECSC in its limited sphere led the Benelux countries (Belgium, the Netherlands, and Luxembourg) to call for integration of all areas of the economy across Europe. A lengthy series of conferences and negotiations led to the establishment of two more communities in 1957. The first treaty, signed in Rome in 1957, established EURATOM, a European agency regulating nuclear energy. The second, more important treaty, established the European Economic Community (EEC). This agreement among the six countries is known as the Treaty of Rome, and is the operating constitution for the economic integration of Western Europe.

THE TREATY OF ROME

The treaty is a complex, lengthy document that sets out the fundamental principles of the Community, establishes its institutions, and creates a substantive Community law in agriculture, transport, and competition. Articles 2 and 3 affirm the purposes and goals of the EC.

TREATY ESTABLISHING THE EUROPEAN ECONOMIC COMMUNITY

(Treaty of Rome, 1957)

ARTICLE 2

The Community shall have as its task, by establishing a common market and progressively approximating the economic policies of Member States, to promote throughout the Community a harmonious development of economic activities, a continuous and balanced expansion, an increase in stability, an accelerated raising of the standard of living and closer relations between the States belonging to it.

ARTICLE 3

For the purposes set out in Article 2, the activities of the Community shall include, as provided in this Treaty and in accordance with the timetable set out therein

(a) the elimination, as between Member States, of customs duties and of quantitative restrictions on the import and export of goods, and of all other measures having equivalent effect;

(b) the establishment of a common customs tariff and of a common commercial policy towards third countries;

(c) the abolition, as between Member States, of obstacles to freedom of movement for persons, services and capital;

(d) the adoption of a common policy in the sphere of agriculture;

(e) the adoption of a common policy in the sphere of transport;

(f) the institution of a system ensuring that competition in the common market is not distorted;

(g) the application of procedures by which the economic policies of Member States can be coordinated and disequilibria in their balance of payments remedied;

(h) the approximation of the laws of Member States to the extent required for the proper functioning of the common market;

(i) the creation of a European Social Fund in order to improve employment opportunities for workers and to contribute to the raising of their standard of living;

(j) the establishment of a European Investment Bank to facilitate the economic expansion of the Community by opening up fresh resources;

(k) the association of the overseas countries and territories in order to increase trade and to promote jointly economic and social development.

Initially, only six nations signed the Treaty of Rome: France, West Germany, Italy, Belgium, Luxembourg, and the Netherlands. In 1973, Denmark, Ireland, and the United Kingdom entered the European Community. This first expansion was followed in 1981 by Greece, and in 1986 by Spain and Portugal. Turkey, Austria, and Sweden have applied for membership in the European Community, but have not yet been accepted as members.

The road to a truly unified European market has not been smooth. Twice, President Charles de Gaulle of France blocked British attempts to join the EC. Norway was invited to join, but by popular referendum rejected membership. For a time in 1965, the French refused to send a minister to the EC, objecting to majority votes on the EC Council of Ministers. The addition of Greece, Spain, and Portugal, with their far less developed economies, has created new strains on the economies of the remaining member countries, as has the absorption of the former East Germany into the member country of Germany.

THE SINGLE EUROPEAN ACT

The EC entered a new phase of market unification with the signing of the Single European Act in 1986. The Act, which was really a treaty among the member countries of the EC, amended the Treaty of Rome to make decision-making less cumbersome. Perhaps more important, the Act set a deadline of December 31, 1992, for the completion of the internal market. The Act mandates the removal of physical, technical, and tax barriers to the free movement of persons, goods, services, and capital.

THE MAASTRICHT AGREEMENT (TREATY ON EUROPEAN UNION)

In February 1992, the leaders of the EC member nations signed a far-reaching agreement designed to create political and economic union in the EC. The treaty, known as the Maastricht Agreement because it was signed in the city of Maastricht in the Netherlands, contains several provisions designed to create a federal system of government in some ways similar to that of the United States or of Germany.

To achieve political union, the Maastricht Agreement commits the member countries to work toward a common foreign policy and toward a common defense. On a more tangible level, Maastricht establishes EC citizenship and allows EC citizens to vote in municipal elections wherever they reside, Thus, a French person living in Ireland would be entitled to vote in Irish local elections.

The Maastricht Agreement also takes major steps toward establishing economic union. It establishes a European Central Bank and a European System of Central Banks to manage monetary policy and maintain price

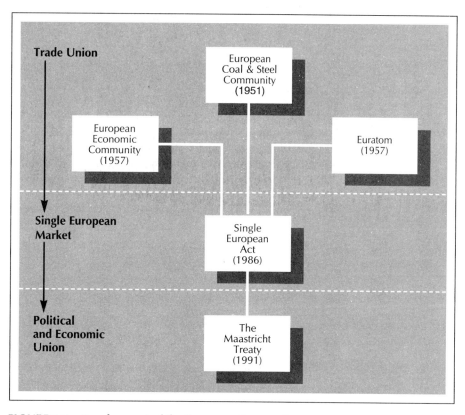

FIGURE 5-1   Development of the European Community

stability, similar in form and function to the U.S. Federal Reserve system. It also establishes a European currency, the ECU, to come into gradual use during the 1990s. Maastricht also commits the member countries to reducing excessive government deficits.

As this book went to press, the Maastricht Agreement had run into some difficulties. It requires ratification by all the member countries of the EC. In June 1992, Danish voters narrowly defeated the treaty in a national referendum. EC leaders have vowed to press on, but it is possible that some of the provisions of Maastricht that are most controversial will be diluted or delayed in order to obtain ratification.

5.3 LEGAL AND POLITICAL INSTITUTIONS

Each of the European Community treaties (ECSC, Euratom, and EEC) provided for separate political institutions. In 1965, the original six EC members signed a Merger Treaty, streamlining the multiple institutions of the three communities into a unified set of legal and political institutions. The major institutions of the EC are the Council of Ministers, the Commission, the Parliament, and the Court of Justice. The EC also has a Court of Auditors, which audits the financial records of the EC, and an advisory Economic and Social Committee.

THE COUNCIL OF MINISTERS

The main decision-making body of the EC is the Council of Ministers. The Council consists of a representative from each member country. Generally that representative is the country's foreign minister, but may be a different minister, depending on the issue before the Council. For example, when agricultural matters are before the Council, the ministers of agriculture from each member country are likely to attend the Council meeting.

The Council acts on the recommendations made by the Commission. Its role in originating legislation is limited to instructing the Commission to investigate problems and recommend solutions. The Council may amend a Commission proposal, but only by a unanimous vote.

Council decisions sometimes require unanimity, or the vote of a "qualified majority." If these margins are not specified, the Council acts by majority vote. For example, the decision to admit a new member requires unanimity. Thus, France was able to block the admission of the United Kingdom to EC membership until 1973. As a practical matter, the Council strives to make its decisions unanimous, because it helps to pressure member nations to comply.

A qualified majority is a weighted vote, designed to keep the larger nations from setting policy for the entire community. Germany, France, Italy, and the United Kingdom get ten votes apiece; Spain eight votes; Belgium, Greece, the Netherlands, and Portugal five votes apiece; Denmark and Ireland three votes apiece; and Luxembourg two votes. To carry, the decision must get 54 votes. Decisions requiring a qualified majority include the measures necessary to implement common policies among member nations.

Much of the work of the Council goes on prior to the Council meetings. Each member country sends an ambassador to the Community who sits on the Committee of Permanent Representatives (best known by its French abbreviation COREPER). This committee prepares the Council meetings, negotiates, compromises, and works out details. When the ministers from each country arrive for Council meetings, the COREPER representative generally has done all the preparation and instructs the minister on the issue before the Council.

THE COMMISSION

Whereas the Council represents national interests, the European Commission represents the interests of the Community as a whole. The Commission's main functions are to propose legislation to the Council and to act as an executive branch, carrying out Community law.

The Commission has seventeen commissioners appointed by the Council to four-year terms. At least one national of each member country must be on the Commission, although no country may have more than two commissioners. Although national governments nominate individuals to the Council, commissioners act independently of their national governments. The Treaty of Rome forbids them from seeking or taking instructions from any national government and forbids member countries from attempting to influence the members of the Commission. Commissioners tend to be prominent political figures in their home countries who, upon completion of their service on the Commission, often return to national political life.

The Commission acts by majority vote. As part of its task of administering Community law, each commissioner has at least one portfolio, or area of responsibility, such as agriculture, competition policy, or external relations.

The actual administration of Community law is carried out by a bureaucracy of nearly 20,000 EC civil servants, known in some circles as Eurocrats. These civil servants enjoy a limited diplomatic status and their salaries are exempt from any national taxation. Like the commissioners, Eurocrats are forbidden from seeking or taking instructions from national governments. Entry is by competitive examination in higher-level positions. Most of the civil servants work for the Commission, in a bureaucratic structure patterned after the French government.

Areas of administration are organized into directorates general (DG), by tradition headed by a civil servant director general of a different nationality than the commissioner overseeing the DG. DGs are further divided into directorates and divisions. The size of these organizations ranges from the DG in charge of agriculture, with eight directorates and 91 divisions, to the DGs in charge of transport and of regional policy, which act primarily as coordinating boards.

THE PARLIAMENT

Of all the institutions of the EC, the European Parliament has had the most difficulty finding a meaningful role in the Community processes. Despite its name, it is not a supranational legislature. It is a directly elected body, with members paid by their national governments, in the same amount as a member of the country's parliamentary body. Each country is represented according to its population, but the Parliament has organized by European political parties rather than nationality. The 518 seats in Parliament are split among eight major parties, with other minor affiliations. Delegates are elected every five years, with the dates of elections set by the Council.

Until the Single European Act, the Parliament's role in creating policy was almost nonexistent. It could, if unhappy with the Commission, take a vote of no confidence, after which the Council would have to appoint a new Commission. The Parliament could not vote to reject the entire Community budget, but could set budget amounts on a limited number of individual budget items. The Single European Act gave Parliament a small amount of authority. The Parliament can now veto treaties between the EC and other countries. It also now has a formal consultative role in the process of legislation. Although the Parliament is still not a legislative body, it does have a role in the review, amendment, and formation of legislation.

THE EUROPEAN JUDICIARY

The Treaty of Rome also established a judicial branch for the Community, consisting of two courts: the European Court of Justice, and, as of 1988, a Court of First Instance of the European Communities. Both courts have similar functions, although they have the power to hear different kinds of cases.

The EC judiciary is charged with the interpretation of Community law. It has an explicit right to review the legality of acts of the Council, Commission, and Parliament, as well as acts of member countries. Much of its activity takes the form of advisory opinions on the interpretation of EC law. Often, a court in a member country will seek a preliminary ruling from the EC courts when a national case touches on EC law.

Several different kinds of parties may bring cases before the courts of the EC. Sometimes the parties are two different branches of the EC, seeking a determination of what authority each branch has. The Commission may also bring suit against a member country for failing to comply with EC law. The EC may also hear suits brought by individuals and businesses charging other persons or their national government with violations of EC law.

Enforcement of EC court decisions generally rests with the courts of the member countries. At this time, there is no Community-wide criminal law, so the EC courts cannot order criminal sanctions. Court decisions tend to be cease-and-desist orders, and occasionally fines, with issues of damages left largely to national courts.

The European Court of Justice is the EC's highest court. It consists of 13 judges, appointed by the Council to renewable six-year terms. Six advocates-general assist the judges by making independent presentations to the Court on cases of interest. The European Court of Justice hears appeals on issues of law from the Court of the First Instance, and in all other matters sits as a trial court.

The Council established the Court of First Instance of the European Communities in 1988 in order to lighten the case load of the European Court of Justice. The Court of First Instance has twelve judges who hear cases concerning the ECSC Treaty, disputes between the Community and members of its staff, and, most important, disputes concerning the enforcement of the rules on competition. This court may, in the future, obtain the jurisdiction to hear some unfair trade disputes.

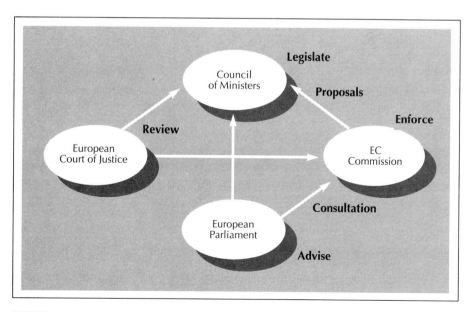

FIGURE 5-2 European Community Institutions

5.4 COMMUNITY LAW

In the areas in which the Treaty of Rome mandates common policies among the member nations of the EC, the Community institutions have developed substantive law. The law takes the form of treaty provisions, regulations, directives, and decisions. Each form of law has a different function.

The treaty sets out the principles of law common to the entire Community. For example, Articles 85 and 86 of the Treaty of Rome, the basic antitrust provisions of the European Community, forbid practices that restrict or distort business competition among the member countries. In areas covered by the treaty, the member nations have ceded some of their sovereign authority to legislate contrary practices.

Commission regulations, approved by the Council, are a second source of law. Regulations apply to nations, people, and businesses, displacing any contrary national law. For example, in 1990 the EC enacted Merger Control Regulations, requiring Commissions approval of certain mergers that might affect competition in the EC. These new regulations supersede any individual nation's law to the contrary. We will discuss those regulations further in Chapter 13.

Directives, again formulated by the Commission and approved by the Council, bind the governments of member countries to results, but leave to those governments the means of achieving the results. The idea that laws need not be uniform among countries so long as they are harmonized has been important to the success of the EC in changing the legal systems of different cultures and traditions.

Decisions of the EC courts and of the Commission are binding on the parties to the particular dispute. They also serve as precedent for the courts and agencies of member nations, and as persuasive for future decisions of the Commission and the EC courts.

As Community law has evolved, two important legal principles have emerged. First is the principle of supranationality; that is, that Community law prevails over conflicting national law. The second is the principle of direct effect; that is, that Community law creates rights in individuals and businesses that national courts are required to protect. Thus, a French citizen, for example, now has both the rights afforded by French law and the rights afforded by Community law.

A closer look at one of the common areas of policy shows the ways in which Community law affects nations and individuals.

CASE STUDIES: COMPARABLE WORTH AND THE UNITED KINGDOM

When the six original members of the European Economic Community negotiated the Treaty of Rome in 1957, among the provisions on Community social policy was Article 119, mandating that "Each Member State shall during the first stage ensure and subsequently maintain the application of the principle that men and women should receive equal pay for equal work." In 1975, the EC enacted an Equal Pay Directive [75/117], providing, in part, as follows:

Article 1
The principle of equal pay for men and women outlined in Article 119 of the Treaty . . . means, for the same work or for work to which equal value is attributed, the elimination of all discrimination on grounds of sex with regard to all aspects and conditions of remuneration.

Article 2
Member-States shall introduce into their national legal systems such measures as are necessary to enable all employees who consider themselves wronged by failure to apply the principle of equal pay to pursue their claims by judicial process after possible recourse to other competent authorities. . . .

Thus, by Council Directive, the EC adopted the principle known in the United States as "comparable worth." Each member nation was required by treaty and directive to enact whatever national laws were necessary to implement equal pay for work of equal value within its borders.

RE EQUAL PAY FOR EQUAL WORK: *E.C. COMMISSION v. UNITED KINGDOM*

[1982] 3 C.M.L.R. 284
European Court of Justice of the European Communities

FACTS:
In 1970, the United Kingdom passed an Equal Pay Act, which it amended in 1975 in response to the Equal Pay Directive from the EC. The U.K. law required equal pay for men and women performing "like work" or work "rated as equivalent." With respect to work rated as equivalent, the law provided that equivalency would be determined by a job classification study rating various jobs for the same employer in terms of attributes such as skill, effort, and judgment required.

While the Commission was not troubled by the evaluation of comparable worth using a job evaluation system, the U.K. law made the performance of job classification studies a voluntary undertaking, requiring the employer's consent. Because an employee could not force an employer to evaluate jobs for comparable value, the Commission believed that the law did not comply with Article 119 of the Treaty.

In 1979, the Commission wrote the government of the United Kingdom a letter stating that it did not believe that United Kingdom equal pay legislation complied with EC law. Unsatisfied with the United Kingdom's response to its letter, the Commission issued a formal opinion requesting the amendment of the law to conform to the Directive. When the United Kingdom failed to act, the Commission filed suit against it in the European Court of Justice.

ISSUE:
Does the law in the United Kingdom conform to the EC requirement of equal pay for work of comparable value?

RESULT:
No. The United Kingdom has failed to fulfill its obligations under the Treaty of Rome.

REASONS:

[5] . . . [A]s the United Kingdom concedes, British legislation does not permit the introduction of a job classification system without the employer's consent. Workers in the United Kingdom are therefore unable to have their work rated as being of equal value if their employer refuses to introduce a classification system.

[6] The United Kingdom attempts to justify that state of affairs by pointing out that Article 1 of the directive says nothing about the right of an employee to insist on having pay determined by a job classification system. On that basis it concludes that the worker may not insist on a comparative evaluation of different work by the job classification method, introduction of which is at the employer's discretion.

[7] The United Kingdom's interpretation amounts to a denial of the very existence of a right to equal pay for work of equal value where no classification has been made. Such a position is not consonant with the general scheme and provisions of the Equal Pay Directive 75/117. The recitals of the preamble to that directive indicate that this essential purpose is to implement the principle that men and women should receive equal pay contained in Article 119 of the Treaty and that it is primarily the responsibility of the member-States to ensure the application of this principle by means of appropriate laws, regulations and administrative provisions in such a way that all employees in the Community can be protected in these matters.

[8] To achieve that end the principle is defined in the first paragraph of Article 1 so as to include under the term 'the same work,' the case of 'work to which equal value is attributed', and the second paragraph emphasises merely that where a job classification system is used for determining pay it is necessary to ensure that it is based on the same criteria for both men and women and so drawn up as to exclude discrimination on the grounds of sex.

[9] It follows that where there is disagreement as to the application of that concept a worker must be entitled to claim before an appropriate authority that his work has the same value as other work and, if that is found to be the case, to have his rights under the Treaty and the directive acknowledged by a binding decision. Any method which excludes that option prevents the aims of the directive from being achieved.

[10] That is borne out by the terms of Article 6 of the directive which provides that member-States are, in accordance with their national circumstances and legal systems, to take the measures necessary to ensure that the principle of equal pay is applied. They are to see that effective means are available to take care that this principle is observed.

[11] In this instance, however, the United Kingdom has not adopted the necessary measures and there is at present no means adopted by which a worker who considers that his post is of equal value to another may pursue his claims if the employer refuses to introduce a job classification system.

[12] The United Kingdom has emphasised (particularly in its letter to the Commission dated 19 June 1979) the practical difficulties which would stand in the way of implementing the concept of work to which equal value has been attributed if the use of a system laid down by consensus were abandoned. The United Kingdom believes that the criterion of work of equal value is too abstract to be applied by the courts.

[13] The Court cannot endorse that view. The implementation of the directive implies that the assessment of the 'equal value' to be attributed to particular work, may be effected notwithstanding the employer's wishes, if necessary in the context of adversary proceedings. The member-States must endow an authority with the requisite jurisdiction to decide whether work has the same value as other work, after obtaining such information as may be required.

[14] Accordingly, by failing to introduce into its national legal system in implementation of the provisions of Council Directive 75/117 of 10 February 1975 such measures as are necessary to enable all employees who consider themselves wronged by failure to apply the principle of equal pay for men and women for work to which equal value is attributed and for which no system of job classification exists to obtain recognition of such equivalence, the United Kingdom has failed to fulfil its obligations under the Treaty.

The *EC Commission v. U.K.* case illustrates the process by which the Community enforces its law, as well as the obligations imposed on member nations by treaties and directives. Note that in this case, the process started with a Commission inquiry, with an opportunity for the member nation to respond. The Commission then issued a reasoned opinion, advising the British government on compliance with EC law. When these less formal means failed, the Commission commenced a legal action in the European Court of Justice.

The British government acted quickly to comply with the decision of the European Court of Justice. The secretary of state for employment drafted amendments to British law, which were passed by Parliament without amendment. The new procedure allowed an employee to claim equal pay for work of comparable value with that of an employee of the opposite sex. The first step to resolve the claim would be conciliation. If conciliation failed, an industrial tribunal would evaluate equivalency, by looking at existing job classification studies, or, if needed, by appointing an independent expert to evaluate the equivalency of the jobs.

The next case follows the story of comparable worth claims to its next logical step: an employee–employer dispute requiring interpretation of the new British law within the framework of EC law.

PICKSTONE v. FREEMANS PLC

[1988] 2 All E.R. 803
House of Lords

FACTS:

Freemans was a mail order business, for whom Mrs. Pickstone worked as a "warehouse operative" at a weekly wage of £77.66. She sued, along with several other female warehouse operatives, alleging that her work was equal in value to the work of a Mr. Phillips, who was one of ten men paid £81.88 per week as a "checker warehouse operative," and that the different pay for the two jobs was sex discrimination. Freemans argued that there could be no sex discrimination because one of the fifteen warehouse operatives was male. The industrial tribunal accepted Freemans' position, but the Court of Appeal ruled in favor of Mrs. Pickstone. Freemans appealed to the highest court of the United Kingdom, the House of Lords.

ISSUE:

Does the fact that a woman and a man hold the same job title at the same pay prevent the woman from claiming that her job should be equal in pay to another job of comparable value?

RESULT:

No. Appeal of Freemans dismissed.

REASONS:

Lord Keith of Kinkel: . . . [This case raises the question of whether a woman loses her right to claim for work of equivalent value] whenever the employers are able to point to some man who is employed by them on like work with the woman claimant . . . or whether [she loses her right to claim] only where the particular man with whom she seeks comparison is employed on such work. In my opinion the latter is the correct answer. The opposite result would leave a large gap in the equal work provision, enabling an employer to evade it by employing one token man on the same work as a group of potential women claimants who were deliberately paid less than a group of men employed on work of equal value with that of the women. This would mean that the United Kingdom had failed yet again fully to implement its obligations under Article 119 of the Treaty and the Equal Pay Directive, and had not given full effect to the decision of the European Court in E.C. Commission v. United Kingdom. It is plain that Parliament cannot possibly have intended such a failure.

Lord Templeman: Under Community law, a woman is entitled to equal pay for work of equal value to that of a man in the same employment. That right is not dependent on there being no man who is employed on the same work as the woman. Under British law, namely the Equal Pay Act 1970 as amended in 1975, a woman was entitled to equal pay for work rated equivalent with that of a man in the same employment. That right was not dependent on there being no man who was employed on the same work as the woman. Under the ruling of the European Court of Justice in E.C. Commission v. United Kingdom (61/81), the Equal Pay Act as amended in 1975 was held to be defective because the Act did not entitle every woman to claim before a competent authority that her work had the same value as other work, but only allowed a claim by a woman who succeeded in persuading her employer to consent to a job evaluation scheme. The Regulations of 1983 were intended to give full effect to Community law and to the ruling of the European Court of Justice which directed the United Kingdom Government to introduce legislation entitling any woman to equal pay with any man for work of equal value if the difference in pay is due to the difference in sex and is therefore discriminatory. I am of the opinion that the Regulations of 1983, upon their true construction, achieve the required result of affording a remedy to any woman who is not in receipt of equal pay for work equal in value to the work of a man in the same employment.

. . . In Von Colson and Kamann v. Land Nordrhein-Westfalen (Case 14/83) the European Court of Justice advised that in dealing with national legislation designed to give effect to a directive:

> 3. . . It is for the national court to interpret and apply the legislation adopted for the implementation of the directive in conformity with the requirements of Community law, in so far as it is given discretion to do so under national law.

In Duke v. G.E.C. Reliance Systems Ltd. this House declined to distort the construction of an Act of Parliament which was not drafted to give effect to a directive and which was not capable of complying with the directive as subsequently construed by the European Court of Justice. In the present case I can see no difficulty in construing the Regulations of 1983 in a way which gives effect to the declared intention of the Government of the United Kingdom responsible for drafting the Regulations and is consistent with the objects of the European Community Treaty, the provisions of the Equal Pay Directive and the rulings of the European Court of Justice. I would dismiss the appeal.

Pickstone is significant in that it shows that the House of Lords will attempt to implement the rights afforded individuals by Community law, and will interpret British legislation wherever possible in a manner consistent with Community law. The case also features the highest court in Britain looking to the European Court of Justice for precedents, and giving the decisions of the ECJ at least persuasive value.

5.5 THE EUROPEAN COMMUNITY: A UNITED STATES OF EUROPE?

While Winston Churchill's exhortation to create a United States of Europe has not come to full fruition, the nations of the European Community are moving rapidly toward a political and economic association that is unlike anything Europe has ever known. The Single European Act, with its timetable for full market integration, has accelerated the unification process dramatically. Mergers and takeovers are now the norm in Europe as businesses build European, rather than national, structures. Even within nations, smaller businesses are combining to create businesses large enough to tackle competitors from other countries.

In the attempt to create a Europe without internal frontiers, the institutions of the Community have used three main strategies to reshape the law. First, the EC has created new European law, applicable uniformly in all member nations. Second, the EC has called for the harmonization of law, with common objectives and national implementation. Finally, the EC has mandated reciprocity, or the acceptance of each country's standards in other countries.

EUROPEAN LAW

In some areas, the European Community has replaced a multiplicity of laws with a single law covering all member nations. As an example, a truck driver traveling across Europe used to have to carry as many as seventy documents to gain entry to the member nations. The EC created a Single Administrative Document for transport, replacing all those forms. Goods imported to member countries are now also subject to a uniform customs classification procedure.

In the area of company law, the EC created new forms of doing business for companies spanning more than one country. The European Company was in the process of enactment as this book was written, and the EC has created a new form of business association, the European Economic Interest Group.

HARMONIZATION

One of the methods the EC has used to achieve its objectives in a politically acceptable manner is to specify harmonization, rather than unification of law. The equal pay case is one prominent example of principle of harmonization. The EC is seeking harmonization of law in many other areas; two in particular will affect the unification of the market.

In company law, the EC has proposed a series of directives on topics ranging from management structure to disclosure of information to shareholders and the public. Some of the more controversial directives pertain to the role of workers in the management of business; the EC is moving toward a German-style system of having workers represented on the governing boards of business enterprises.

In tax law, the EC has begun to harmonize both the levels of taxation and the kinds of goods taxed. Europe relies heavily on value-added taxes (VAT) to raise revenue, yet differences in tax rates and applicability make some products significantly more expensive in some countries than in others.

RECIPROCITY

Reciprocal treatment plays a large role in the elimination of internal barriers in Europe. The concept of reciprocity has been important in the EC for some time, as the following case indicates.

REWE-ZENTRAL AG v. BUNDESMONOPOLVERWALTUNG FÜR BRANNTWEIN [CASSIS DE DIJON]

[1979] 3 C.M.L.R. 494
European Court of Justice

FACTS:
Rewe was an importer of goods into West Germany. When it applied to the Bundesmonopolverwaltung für Branntwein (Federal Monopoly Administration for Spirits) for permission to import Cassis de Dijon, a liqueur, Rewe was informed that importation was prohibited. German law required an alcoholic content for liqueurs of at least 25 percent, and Cassis de Dijon had an alcohol content of only 15 to 20 percent.

Rewe brought suit to overturn the minimum alcohol content regulation in the German courts, who referred issues of Community law to the European Court of Justice for a preliminary ruling.

ISSUE:
Does the German regulation act as a limit on the import of goods from other States in violation of Articles 30 and 37 of the Treaty?

RESULT:
Yes.

REASONS:
[4] The plaintiff takes the view that the fixing by

the German rules of a minimum alcohol content leads to the result that well-known spirit products from other member-States of the Community cannot be sold in the Federal Republic of Germany and that the said provision therefore constitutes a restriction on the free movement of goods between member-States which exceeds the bounds of the trade rules reserved to the latter. . . . Since, furthermore, it is a measure adopted within the context of the management of the spirits monopoly, the plaintiff considers that there is also an infringement of Article 37, according to which the member-States shall progressively adjust any State monopolies of a commercial character so as to ensure that when the transitional period has ended no discrimination regarding the conditions under which goods are procured or marketed exists between nationals of member-States. . . .

[8] In the absence of common rules relating to the production and marketing of alcohol—a proposal for regulation submitted to the Council by the Commission on 7 December 1976 not having yet having received the Council's approval—it is for the member-States to regulate all matters relating to the production and marketing of alcohol

and alcoholic beverages on their own territory. Obstacles to movement within the Community resulting from disparities between the national laws relating to the marketing of the products in question must be accepted in so far as those provisions may be recognised as being necessary in order to satisfy mandatory requirements relating in particular to the effectiveness of fiscal supervision, the protection of public health, the fairness of commercial transactions and the defence of the consumer.

[9] The Government of the Federal Republic of Germany, intervening in the proceedings, put forward various arguments which, in its view, justify the application of provisions relating to the minimum alcohol content of alcoholic beverages, adducing considerations relating on the one hand to the protection of public health and on the other to the protection of the consumer against unfair commercial practices.

[10] As regards the protection of public health the German Government states that the purpose of the fixing of minimum alcohol contents by national legislation is to avoid the proliferation of alcoholic beverages on the national market, in particular alcoholic beverages with a low alcoholic content, since, in its view, such products may more easily induce a tolerance toward alcohol than more highly alcoholic beverages.

[11] Such considerations are not decisive since the consumer can obtain on the market an extremely wide range of weakly or moderately alcoholic products and furthermore a large proportion of alcoholic beverages with a high alcohol content freely sold on the German market is generally consumed in a diluted form.

[12] The German Government also claims that the fixing of a lower limit for the alcohol content of certain liqueurs is designed to protect the consumer against unfair practices on the part of producers and distributors of alcoholic beverages. This argument is based on the consideration that the lowering of the alcohol content secures a competitive advantage in relation to beverages with a higher alcohol content, since alcohol constitutes by far the most expensive constituent of beverages by reason of the high rate of tax to which it is subject. Furthermore, according to the German Government, to allow alcoholic products into free circulation wherever, as regards their alcohol con-

tent, they comply with the rules laid down in the country of production would have the effect of imposing as a common standard within the Community the lowest alcohol content permitted in any of the member-States, and even of rendering any requirements in this field inoperative since a lower limit of this nature is foreign to the rules of several member-States.

[13] As the Commission rightly observed, the fixing of limits in relation to the alcohol content of beverages may lead to the standardisation of products placed on the market and their designations, in the interests of a greater transparency of commercial transactions and offers for sale to the public. However, this line of argument cannot be taken so far as to regard the mandatory fixing of minimum alcohol contents as being an essential guarantee of the fairness of commercial transactions since it is a simple matter to assure that suitable information is conveyed to the purchaser by requiring the display of an indication of origin and of the alcohol content on the packaging of products.

[14] It is clear from the foregoing that the requirements relating to the minimum alcohol content of alcoholic beverages do not serve a purpose which is in the general interest and such as to take precedence over the requirements of the free movement of goods, which constitutes one of the fundamental rules of the Community. In practice, the principle effect of requirements of this nature is to promote alcoholic beverages having a high alcohol content by excluding from the national market products of other member-States which do not answer that description. It therefore appears that the unilateral requirement imposed by the rules of a member-State of a minimum alcohol content for the purposes of the sale of alcoholic beverages constitutes an obstacle to trade which is incompatible with the provisions of Article 30 of the Treaty. There is therefore no valid reason why, provided that they have been lawfully produced and marketed in one of the member-States, alcoholic beverages should not be introduced into any other member-State; the sale of such products may not be subject to a legal prohibition on the marketing of beverages with an alcohol content lower than the limit set by the national rules.

The principle that goods meeting the standards of one member nation are acceptable for import into other member nations is increasingly a part of the EC's attempt to remove technical barriers to trade. It has also been expanded into nongoods areas of the economy. For example, in the banking sector, a license to operate in one country now constitutes a license to operate in all member nations. Similarly, the Community is enacting reciprocal treatment for educational, vocational, and professional training. An architect licensed to practice in Italy may now also practice throughout the Community.

A LOOK TO THE FUTURE

As recently as the mid-1980s, eminent commentators were predicting the collapse of the European Community. It now appears, with apologies to Mark Twain, that reports of the EC's death were greatly exaggerated. The Single European Act provided the inspiration to new attempts to remove the remaining barriers to trade within the European Community.

Since the Single European Act, the debate on the future of the EC has centered on the issue of "widening" versus "deepening" the EC. "Wideners" favor the expansion of the Community by the admission of more member states. First on their list for membership would be the prosperous countries of the European Free Trade Association (EFTA), most of which are in the process of asking for membership in the EC. The "wideners" would then look to add some kind of membership status for the more developed countries of Central Europe and some of the countries that were formerly part of the Soviet Union. In contrast, the "deepeners" favor strengthening the power of the EC institutions, to create a real federal Europe.

At the moment, both sides seem to be achieving some success. The "wideners" won a victory when, in October 1991, the seven EFTA countries (Austria, Finland, Iceland, Liechtenstein, Norway, Sweden, and Switzerland) agreed to join the single European market, accepting EC law and regulation of economic activity. The "deepeners" won a victory with the Maastricht Agreement, which, if accepted, will create a common currency and monetary policy and lead toward common foreign and defense policies.

What no one can yet know, however, is whether Europe really will evolve into a federal system. In the early years of the United States, people thought of themselves as Virginians or Georgians rather than as Americans. Although today a resident of Paris considers his primary identity to be as a Frenchman, perhaps in the future he will consider himself a European who happens to be from France.

Working against the federation of Europe are the strong cultural and political differences among the member nations. As European legislation moves from the strictly economic sphere to social and cultural issues, some nations are likely to resist the erosion of national identity. Some resistance is already apparent in the Danish vote against the Maastricht Agreement, as well as in the resistance of the conservative British government to the proposals spearheaded by the Socialist French government. The member nations are also likely to be wary of ceding foreign policy powers to Community institutions.

Another unknown is the way a more unified Europe will treat other competitors, like Japan and the United States. It appears that reciprocity will be the guide to the treatment of outsiders, but what that means in specific cases is not clear. For example, the principle of reciprocity would indicate that an American bank may operate in the EC on the same terms as a bank from an EC country is allowed to operate in the United States. However, banks in the United States are prohibited from engaging in the securities and insurance businesses, while banks in Europe have no such restrictions. The way the EC and its competitors resolve these difficult issues will dictate whether the unified European market helps create a truly global economy or whether it becomes what some politicians already call "Fortress Europe."

Finally, political developments in Eastern Europe have added another layer of uncertainty to the future of the EC. The former East Germany is now a part of the Community. Several of the former Communist nations have undertaken negotiations with the EC, and even the former Soviet republics are looking to become players in the European market.

5.6 CONCLUSION

The success of the European Community may rival the economic growth of Japan in its significance to the post-World War II world. The EC set an objective of removing barriers to the movement of goods, services, capital, and labor among its members, and now stands on the threshold of achieving its objective. In the process, the EC has created new political institutions, including the powerful Commission. It has also developed a new form of supranational law, binding on the member countries. It seems to have found ways to bring disparate political, cultural, and legal systems together, using harmonization of laws and reciprocity. The EC, as it has developed after the Single European Act, has become a model for other regional trading groups and a forceful voice in world affairs. In years to come it may become a home for many other European nations and regulate an even larger market.

5.7 QUESTIONS FOR DISCUSSION

1. Compare the functions of the four main EC institutions with those of your own country. What similarities and differences do you see?

2. Some critics of the EC claim that the EC does not allow enough participation by ordinary citizens. In your opinion, does the EC have what its critics call a "democracy deficit" in its main institutions?

3. Your company makes small electric appliances for consumers and is considering locating a factory in Greece to take advantage of low wage rates and a favorable regulatory environment. You have heard that the EC Commission is considering regulating the quality and safety of small electric appliances. What form of regulation would be the best for your business: regulation or directive? Would your business benefit more from reciprocity or from harmonization of standards?

4. The Danish government, concerned about solid waste, mandated that bottlers use approved, recyclable containers. Several bottlers from other EC countries challenged the law, alleging that the Danish restriction requiring approval and requiring recyclability prevented them from using containers they would use in other countries. Where would the bottlers bring their challenge? What are the arguments the bottlers would use in support of their attempt to overturn the Danish law? What arguments would the Danish government use in support of its law? Who should prevail? Explain.

5.8 FURTHER READINGS

Rob Dixon, *Banking in Europe: The Single Market,* Routledge, London, 1991.

Ralph H. Folsom, *European Community Law,* West Publishing Co., St. Paul, Minn., 1992.

E. G. Friberg, "1992: Moves Europeans Are Making," *Harvard Business Review,* May–June 1989, pp. 85–89.

J. F. Magee, "1992: Moves Americans Are Making," *Harvard Business Review,* May–June 1989, pp. 78–84.

PART TWO

INTERNATIONAL COMMERCIAL TRANSACTIONS

119

INTERNATIONAL CONTRACTS: NEGOTIATION AND FORMATION

6.1 INTRODUCTION

Contract law lies at the heart of international business transactions. Whether the business activity is a joint venture, license, or sale of goods or services, the contract establishes the major boundaries of the relationship between the parties. Although different kinds of contractual relationships use different negotiating and drafting criteria, the underlying principles of contract relationships are relatively common to all contracts. This chapter, along with Chapters 7 to 9, explores the basic principles of international contracting, with particular reference to the most basic kind of transaction: the sale of goods.

APPLICABLE LAW

One of the most significant questions negotiators should ask in the course of contract negotiations is "What law applies to this transaction?" As Chapter 2 discusses, the answers are not always obvious. Some courts will apply their own law, while others may apply the law of the place in which the contract was negotiated, signed, or performed. Others may look to the place of payment or the place where a defect became apparent.

The law governing the contract may determine the outcome of a dispute arising from the contract. For example, consider the problem of the effectiveness of an acceptance. The traditional common law rule, known as "the mailbox rule," provides that an acceptance is effective when it is dispatched to the offeror. By contrast, the traditional civil law rule indicates that an acceptance is effective upon its receipt by the offeror. Thus, if the offeror attempted to revoke its offer while an acceptance was in transit, the courts of a common law system would probably recognize the existence of a contract, whereas the courts of a civil law system would not.

THE LAW MERCHANT

Fortunately for managers trading goods across national borders, international transactions around the world share a common legal heritage. The common basis, known as *Lex Mercatoria*, or the law merchant, has its source in the trading fairs and merchant communities of medieval Europe and the Middle East. As Chapter 1 discussed, medieval and Renaissance merchants created a set of relatively uniform rules for international commercial transactions, existing outside the reach of local legal systems and enforced through merchant courts. Although many of the specific rules were modified by later national courts, the law merchant still affected the development of modern law in the areas of sales of goods, financing instruments, and transportation.

In the 20th century, the principles of the law merchant have found expression in treaties regulating the international sale of goods, treaties governing shipping conditions, and, most notably, in a widely followed body of business practices. Many of the international trading community's practices have been codified and published by the International Chamber of Commerce (ICC), a private organization headquartered in Paris. Among the publications of the ICC of importance to managers trading internationally are the *International Commercial Terms (INCOTERMS)*, the Uniform Customs and Practices (UCP) for letters of credit, and the ICC rules for arbitration. The ICC maintains a Court of Arbitration in Paris that businesses regularly use to resolve international contract disputes.

THE CISG

For most of the 20th century, legal scholars and practitioners have been trying to revive the law merchant as a body of internationally uniform law. One of the main efforts, taking place over the last 60 years, has been an attempt to develop a uniform international law for contracts. The latest attempt was in the United Nations Commission on International Trade Law (UNCITRAL). In 1980, UNCITRAL produced a treaty, the United Nations Convention on Contracts for the International Sale of Goods (CISG). The treaty went into force on January 1, 1988, when ten nations signed it. As of this writing, twenty-six nations have ratified the treaty, including Socialist countries such as China, civil law countries, such as France and Argentina, and common law countries, such as the United States. Excerpts from the CISG can be found in Appendix A to this book.

In the United States, the treaty became federal law on January 1, 1988. It replaces Article 2 of the Uniform Commercial Code for contracts for the sale of goods when the buyer and seller are from countries that have ratified the CISG. So, for example, a contract for a U.S. seller like Apple Computer to sell computers to a French distributor would be governed by the CISG, since it is a contract between two businesses from countries that have ratified the convention. Some of the countries that have ratified the CISG do not require the other party to a deal to come from a CISG country. In that case, the CISG would apply to all international sales contracts originating in that country. As increasing numbers of countries that are major trading partners of the United States ratify the CISG, it will become more significant in international commercial transactions.

The CISG provides uniform rules governing the formation, performance, and breach of contracts for the sale of goods. It is a careful compromise among civil law, common law, and Socialist law principles. For example, Article 12 of the CISG essentially abolishes the Statute of Frauds, yet allows countries to exclude the Article from their laws. Countries with planned economies, such as China, thus can still require a contract to be in writing in order to be enforceable.

The CISG does not provide answers for all questions of contract law in international business. By its terms, it applies only to contracts for the sale of goods. Thus, contracts for services and technology and contracts for leases and licenses are not subject to the CISG. Joint ventures and investment agreements are not covered either. Those contracts would be governed by the more general principles of contract law that will be covered in the next two chapters. Article 2 of the CISG excludes from coverage several other kinds of contracts—most notably contracts for goods bought for personal, family, or household use—unless the seller knows of the intended consumer use. Therefore, virtually all contracts subject to the CISG are about sales between two merchants.

The CISG leaves two major areas of contract law to individual national laws. First, it leaves to national law questions of the validity of a contract. Issues of the capacity of parties to contract, fraud, duress, illegality, and unconscionability will have different results in different countries, even when the CISG applies to the transaction. Second, Article 5 of the CISG leaves to each nation the laws on products liability. The responsibility of a seller for death or personal injury caused by its goods will vary from country to country, even when the contract for the sale of goods is governed by the CISG.

What the CISG does provide is a set of uniform rules for the formation of contracts between merchants and a set of uniform rules establishing the obligations of the buyer and the seller in a transaction for the sale of goods. The contract formation rules will be discussed in more detail later in this chapter; the performance and breach rules are discussed in Chapter 7.

6.2 CONTRACT FORMATION

Managers from common law legal systems know the concepts of offer, acceptance, and consideration as the foundation of contract obligations. As Chapters 3 and 4 reveal, much of the rest of the world views these concepts differently from the way common law systems do. For example, recall that civil law systems generally do not require consideration to create legally binding obligations.

The elements of a contract will vary among different countries, as will typical contract defenses, issues of capacity, and requirements of form. For example, in China many contracts are void without appropriate government approvals, even when they have been signed by the highest-level managers of the Chinese business. A manager operating in the legal environment of another country needs to obtain specific legal advice about the contract law of that country before negotiating contractual obligations. However, the different approaches to contract law create traps for unwary negotiators, creating legal obligations when American law might not and avoiding obligations that American law would uphold.

PRELIMINARY AGREEMENTS

A common law contract generally requires an offer, acceptance, and consideration to be valid. But before these elements of a contract fall into place, the parties to an international deal may spend months or even years negotiating the terms of the transaction. While it is well beyond the scope of this book to discuss the mechanics or the psychology of international negotiations, there are certain aspects of the negotiations that can create legal pitfalls for the negotiators.

The negotiations for international transactions can range from quite simple to quite complex. On the simple end of the spectrum, the parties may exchange order forms or fax offer and acceptance letters to each other. On the complex end of the spectrum are deals for joint ventures, transfers of technology, and investment agreements. In these cases, the negotiations may take months or even years. The two (or sometimes more) sides to the deal may bring teams of bargainers to the table, with each person having an area of expertise. Executives may shake hands on some issues while others are still the subject of intense bargaining. In these instances, the negotiators need to be extremely watchful for situations that create unintended legal obligations. For example, what happens to the partial agreements if the parties ultimately fail to achieve total agreement on all issues?

Because many legal systems do not require consideration to bind a contract, questions of offer and acceptance may be more complex than a manager might expect. One particular area of concern is that of agreements to negotiate, letters of intent, and other agreements preliminary to a contract. As the reading below illustrates, common negotiating practices may create binding legal obligations.

JOANNA SCHMIDT, "PRELIMINARY AGREEMENTS IN INTERNATIONAL CONTRACT NEGOTIATION"

Houston Journal of International Law 37 (1983).

The existence and consequences of preliminary agreements are of particular interest in the course of negotiating an international contract. Various legal systems accord differing legal consequences to the different stages of negotiation. It is therefore important to know which law is applicable to particular negotiations, especially when there could be a question of the existence of a preliminary contract. It may well happen that the negotiators have entered into a preliminary contract without being conscious of it. Such will be the case, for instance, under French law, where the principle of consensualism implies that a contract is concluded when a party demonstrates the existence of a meeting of minds, without any further condition being required. This rule applies to any contract including preliminary agreements, and may thus lead to the imposition of contractually binding obligations upon the negotiators simply because, in the course of discussion, they have expressed an agreement on certain points. . . .

I. Preliminary Agreements Relating to the Negotiation of the Definitive Contract

Persons contemplating the conclusion of a future contract may seek to define the conditions of the negotiations itself in a preparatory agreement. The object of a preliminary agreement may be to address two kinds of concerns: either the parties wish to obligate themselves to undertake negotiations; or they wish to organize their mutual obligations during the negotiation. . . .

Typical practices in the negotiation of industrial contracts provide for numerous examples of such agreements relating to the conditions of the negotiation itself: "[C]onsidering the urgency of this project . . . the contract will be signed as soon as possible after the initial discussions and every effort will be made to make this possible. . . ."

. . . The legal consequences of such agreements may vary according to the legal system under which they are interpreted. The contractual nature of such an agreement is recognized by the principal continental European systems.

For instance, French law and French legal writers know this type of preliminary agreement under the name of "agreement of principle," which is a contract obligating the parties to make an offer or to continue an already existing negotiation relating to a contract, the object of which is only partially determined. This form of preliminary agreement was recognized as positive law in a decision of the French *Cour de Cassation* (Supreme Court). At the end of World War II, the management of Renault wrote to one Mr. Marchal, a former employee who was seeking to be rehired: "We will consider with you the possibility of employment as soon as the resumption of automobile activity allows." This they did not do. At the request of Mr. Marchal, the courts found that a contract existed, the object of which was not an obligation to conclude the labor contract, but to negotiate it. Mr. Marchal was allocated damages for Renault's failure to perform. . . .

The contractual nature of such preliminary agreements is also recognized under Belgian and Italian law. Such a contractual obligation to negotiate must be performed in good faith. . . .

The admission by some legal systems of the existence of a contract to negotiate might, however, be dangerous for the negotiators, in view of the breadth of interpretation which judges might give it. Think of the many cases where the classic expression appears: "leave your address, we'll be in touch." Such an expression is a means, without saying it expressly, of getting rid of someone who wants to negotiate and ultimately concludes a contract. It certainly does not mean that the party wishes to bind himself, anymore than that he undertakes to negotiate. Indeed, a party should express his real intentions in order to avoid double meanings and the dangers just mentioned. Statements limiting liability "without obligation on a part" are thus advisable.

The parties' intention not to create legally binding relations does not produce, however, the same consequences under all legal systems. English courts assume that the parties meant to create legally enforceable rights and obligations under their agreement, but will take into account a contrary intention expressed or necessarily implied. Under English law, the crucial element in determining the enforceability is the analysis of the parties' real intention. English law gives full significance to the notion that a contract is understood to be an agreement designed to produce legal consequences.

Although the classical continental doctrine incorporates the same definition, more recent legal writers show that the parties' intentions are not the sole criteria of contract. An agreement only creates an objective situation for which the law recognizes certain consequences. Thus, an agreement may produce legal effects independently of the parties' intention. French case law, for example, recognizes the existence of a contract even when an agreement is expressly said to be binding "in honor" and meant not to produce any legal consequences. . . .

If there is a moral to the negotiation story, it is that managers need to be extremely careful of the commitments they make to the other parties to the transaction. It may be helpful in complex deals to create a road map of the structure of the negotiations that all parties can agree to, so that there are no misunderstandings about the intent of any party during the course of negotiating.

OFFER–ACCEPTANCE VARIATIONS

Another point of practical consequence for managers operating in varying legal systems is the legal effect of variations between an offer and an acceptance. Suppose, for example, that Acme Office Supply Co. sent a purchase order for 1000 file cabinets to Beta Manufacturing Co. Beta responded by shipping the goods, then sending an invoice. The invoice, in addition to specifying goods and price, also provided that 18 percent annual interest would be charged on balances due longer than 30 days from the date of the invoice. Do the parties have a contract? If so, does Acme owe interest on past-due balances?

In the United States, the legal effect of this contract would be governed by Section 2-207 of the Uniform Commercial Code. That section allows an acceptance to have legal effect, even if it contains additional or different terms than the offer [UCC 2-207(1)]. Between merchants, such additional terms become part of the contract unless the terms materially alter the agreement or the other party objects within a reasonable time [UCC 2-207(2)]. The Code rules have been criticized because they do not define the nature of material alterations. They also tend to encourage merchants to engage in a "battle of the forms," each hoping to have the document that will be the last shot and thus control the terms of the contract.

Under the Code, Acme and Beta have a contract. Although the Code does not provide a categorical answer to the question of which terms govern the agreement, in this case the addition of interest on overdue accounts is probably a common enough commercial practice not to be deemed to "materially alter" the agreement. Beta's terms control the agreement.

Adding an international dimension to the Acme–Beta example raises new legal issues. The variation issue won't appear when the parties successfully complete a contract despite the differing forms. Rather, the issue appears when the deal goes sour and one party looks for a means to escape contract obligations. As the article below indicates, other legal systems have different approaches to the problem of the battle of the forms.

FRANCOIS VERGNE, "THE BATTLE OF THE FORMS" UNDER THE 1980 UNITED NATIONS CONVENTION ON CONTRACTS FOR THE INTERNATIONAL SALE OF GOODS (MOST FOOTNOTES OMITTED)"

33 American Journal of Comparative Law, 233 (1985)

THE CIVIL LAW APPROACH: THE FRENCH EXAMPLE

A. *Law of Formation*

In French law, there are no statutes dealing explicitly with offer and acceptance. The only requirement set forth by Article 1108 of the Civil Code is that there must be an agreement between the parties. This is the only broad rule for the validity of the formation of a contract. With respect to the law of sales, Article 1583 of the Civil Code requires for the conclusion of the contract that an agreement as to the subject-matter and the price has been reached by the parties.

The question whether there is an agreement and where and how it was reached is a question of fact which is left to the decision of the regular courts (*juge du fond*) and escapes the control of the *Cour de Cassation*.

Because of this paucity and imprecision of the Civil Code on offer and acceptance, the point is ruled by case law and considered by scholarly writings (*doctrine*). But even under these two rubrics, the question of the battle of the forms has not been considered. The French doctrine has not coined any expression to denominate the particular situation of a difference between the offer and the acceptance in contracts negotiated on standard forms. Therefore, one must consider the main trends expressed by court decisions and doctrinal writings and attempt to derive a general rule as to the law applicable in cases of battle of the forms.

1. The Traditional Approach:

Traditionally, it is considered that the acceptance must be pure, simple and totally conform to the offer. Following this approach, similar to the mirror image rule, an acceptance with reservations or a counter-offer is considered as a rejection paired with a new offer. This view was early expressed by the first commentators of the Civil

Code and the subsequent trend of case law is firmly settled in that direction. A good example may be found in a decision of July 1967:[1]

> At the end of a negotiation, a broker sent to the parties a draft contract for the sale of a commercial property. The seller signed the document. The buyer added a clause: "expressly subject to the obtaining of a loan of 120,000 Francs by the Credit Hotelier." Some time after the due date for payment, the buyer sued the seller to enforce the sale. The *Cour de Cassation* cancelled the lower court decision in favor of the buyer on the ground that this decision recognized the formation of a contract "[w]ithout having ascertained that there was an agreement of the parties on all the conditions of the contract."

Under this approach, only very minor differences will not change the character of the response and will not preclude the formation of the contract. In a 1961 case the *Cour de Cassation* held that an acceptance which differs from the offer merely because it includes some details about the property subject-matter of the sale is valid and does not affect the formation of the contract. In the same manner, if the acceptance includes new terms which are implied by law, the contract is considered formed by the application of Article 1135 of the Civil Code. Thus a decision in 1885 established the rule that the silence of the parties as to the modalities of performance of a contract is construed as an implied reference to the supplementary provisions of the Civil Code. . . .

2. Modification by Modern Decisions:

A more detailed analysis of recent case law reveals some evolution of these basic principles. In effect, a second trend of opinion considers that the nature of the discrepancy between the offer

---

[1] Cass, Civ. 3ème, 17 juillet 1967, Bull. Civ. III, 29.

and the acceptance must be taken into consideration. This leads to the establishment of a distinction between essential (or substantial) and subsidiary elements of the contract. If the discrepancy bears on an essential element the contract will never be formed, whereas if it bears on a subsidiary element the formation will not necessarily be precluded. . . .

B. *Consistency with the Modern Civil Law Approach*

The French law of formation reflects the fact that problems arising out of the battle of the forms are not frequent. Nevertheless, the solution outlined by case law and doctrinal analysis is consistent with the trends of civil law systems which expressly deal with this question.

The German Civil Code (B.G.B.) in articles 150, 154 and 155 provides:

> B.G.B. Article 150(2): "An acceptance with amplifications, limitations, or other alterations is deemed to be a refusal coupled with a new offer."
>
> B.G.B. Article 154: "So long as the parties have not agreed upon all points of a contract upon which agreement is essential, according to the declaration of even one party, the contract is, in case of doubt, not concluded. An understanding concerning particular points is not binding, even if they have been noted down.
>
> If authentication of the contemplated contract has been agreed upon, in case of doubt the contract is not concluded until the authentication has taken place."
>
> B.G.B. Article 155: "If the parties to a contract that they regard as concluded have not agreed upon a point which they should have settled, their agreement is valid if it appears they would have contracted even without agreement on that point."

Swiss law follows the same approach. The Swiss Code of Obligations contains the following provisions:

> Article 1: "The contract is perfect when the parties have mutually and in similar terms manifested their intention.
>
> This manifestation can be express or implied."
>
> Article 2: "If the parties have agreed upon all the essential points, the contract is deemed concluded even if subsidiary points have been reserved."

The law of most of the Scandinavian countries reflects the same analysis. When a purported acceptance contains terms which differ from those of the offer, it is deemed to be a rejection of the offer and to constitute a counter-offer unless the offeree considers his response to conform to the offer and the offeror is aware of it. In that case, if the offeror does not want to be bound, he must give notice.

In Japanese law, the solution is also similar. Under Article 528 of the Japanese Civil Code, if the offeree has accepted an offer conditionally or with modifications, he is deemed to have rejected the original offer and made a new offer himself. However, literal and precise compliance of an acceptance with the terms of the offer is usually not required. Generally an acceptance with minor modifications will not invoke the application of Article 528. Despite the possibility that this article may lead to a practical or theoretical confrontation, as seen in the battle of the forms, it has not been the subject of either scholarly concern or actual dispute.

The CISG undertakes to solve some of the problems created by inconsistencies between offers and acceptances. In response to the concerns raised by countries that strictly follow the mirror image rule, the CISG takes a more restrictive view of variations between offer and acceptance. Article 17(1) of the CISG states the premise that a reply to an offer containing "additions, limitations or other modifications" is a rejection and counteroffer. However, Article 17(2) allows additional or different terms that do not "materially alter" the offer to be part of the contract, unless the offeror objects to their inclusion "without undue delay." So far, the CISG takes an approach similar to the merchants' provisions of UCC 2-207. Article 17(3) defines kinds of terms that *would* materially alter an agreement, including "price, payment, quality and quantity of the goods, place and time of delivery, extent of one party's liability to the other or the settlement of disputes. . . ."

In the problem posed at the beginning of this section, the UCC and the CISG might well end up with different results. The reply adds a payment term, which probably falls within the list of material alterations. Other common terms found in form contract documents state the law that will govern a contract or provide for arbitration. These would constitute counteroffers under the CISG, even if the offeror failed to object immediately to their inclusion.

LANGUAGE PROBLEMS

A third issue that takes on added significance in the context of international contracts is the problem of having a meeting of the minds in two or more languages. The words of a contract create legal obligations. Often, those words are difficult to interpret even when both parties to the contract speak the same language. The words easily can take on or lose shades of meaning when the parties speak different languages and come from different cultures.

Choosing a language for a written contract may itself be a subject of negotiation. Some of the factors that influence the choice of a language include the relative economic power of the parties to a contract, the place of performance, the familiarities of the negotiators with other languages, and nationalistic pride of the parties.

Ideally, a final contract will contain terms that both parties understand to mean the same thing. In a multilingual setting, one option the parties have is to have one official contract, with or without an unofficial translation. A translation may help resolve the meaning of terms in the official version of an agreement. Another option parties sometimes employ is to have an original contract in more than one language, each officially binding. This solution to language problems is widely used in treaty negotiations among governments. It eliminates the negotiating over which language is official contract language, but leaves the problem of equivalency between words in different languages.

The problem of translation becomes more difficult when a word may have both an ordinary meaning and a technical meaning. The case below illustrates the perils of casual language usage in negotiating international commercial transactions.

FRIGALIMENT IMPORTING CO., LTD v. B.N.S. INTERNATIONAL SALES CORP.

190 F. Supp. 116 (S.D.N.Y. 1960)

FACTS:

Plaintiff, a Swiss corporation, contracted to buy 175,000 pounds of frozen chicken in two shipments from the defendant, a New York corporation. Some of the chickens were to be 1.5–2 lbs, while others were to be 2.5–3 lbs. When the first shipment of frozen chickens arrived in Switzerland, plaintiff discovered that the larger chickens were stewing chickens, or "fowl," unsuitable for broiling and frying. Plaintiff stopped the next shipment of chickens in transit and brought suit for breach of contract in federal district court in New York.

ISSUE:

What is chicken? What kind of chicken does the contract require?

RESULT:

Plaintiff was unable to show that "chicken" in the contract had a special meaning. Therefore, defendant's interpretation of the term, including fowl, will control the contract. Judgment for defendant.

REASONS:

The issue is, what is chicken? Plaintiff says "chicken" means a young chicken, suitable for broiling and frying. Defendant says "chicken" means any bird of that genus that meets contract specifications on weight and quality, including what it calls "stewing chicken" and plaintiff pejoratively terms "fowl". Dictionaries give both meanings, as well as some others not relevant here. To support its [case], plaintiff sends a number of volleys over the net; defendants essays to return them and adds a few serves of its own. . . . I have concluded that plaintiff has not sustained its burden of persuasion that the contract used "chicken" in the narrower sense. . . .

Since the word "chicken" standing alone is ambiguous, I turn first to see whether the contract itself offers any aid to interpretation. . . . Defendant notes that the contract called not simply for chicken but for "US Fresh Frozen Chicken, Grade A, Government Inspected." It says the contract thereby incorporated by reference the Department of Agriculture's regulations which favor its interpretation; I shall return to this after reviewing plaintiff's other contentions.

The first hinges on an exchange of cablegrams which preceded execution of the formal contracts. The negotiations leading up to the contracts were conducted in New York between defendant's secretary, Ernest R. Bauer, and a Mr. Stovicek, who was in New York for the Czechoslovak government at the World Trade Fair. A few days after meeting Bauer at the fair, Stovicek telephoned and inquired whether defendant would be interested in exporting poultry to Switzerland. Bauer then met with Stovicek, who showed him a cable from plaintiff . . . [indicating plaintiff's readiness to purchase large quantities of frozen chicken]. After testing the market for price, Bauer accepted, and Stovicek sent a confirmation that evening. Plaintiff stresses that although these and subsequent cables between plaintiff and defendant . . . were predominantly in German, they used the English word "chicken"; it claims this was done because it understood "chicken" meant young chicken whereas the German word "Huhn," included both "Brathuhn" (broilers) and "Suppenhuhn" (stewing chicken), and that defendant, whose officers were thoroughly conversant with German, should have realized this. Whatever force this argument might otherwise have is largely drained away by Bauer's testimony that he asked Stovicek what kind of chickens were wanted, received the answer "any kind of chickens," and then, in German, asked whether the cable meant "Huhn" and received an affirmative response. . . .

Defendant advances several other points which it claims affirmatively support its construction. Primary among these is the regulation of the Department of Agriculture, 7 C.F.R. S 70.300–70.370, entitled, "Grading and Inspection of

Poultry and Edible Products Thereof." and in particular S 70.301 which recited:

> *"Chickens.* The following are the various classes of chickens:
> (a) Broiler or fryer . . .
> (b) Roaster . . .
> (c) Capon . . .
> (d) Stag . . .
> (e) Hen or stewing chicken or fowl . . .
> (f) Cock or old rooster . . ."

Defendant argues, as previously noted, that the contract incorporated these regulations by reference. Plaintiff answers that the contract provision related simply to grade and Government inspection and did not incorporate the Government definition of "chicken," and also that the definition in

the regulations is ignored in the trade. However, the latter contention was contradicted by [witnesses at trial] . . . and there is force in defendant's argument that the contract made the regulations a dictionary. . . .

When all the evidence is reviewed, it is clear that defendant believed it could comply with the contracts by delivering stewing chicken in the 2½–3 lbs. size. Defendant's subjective intent would not be significant if this did not coincide with an objective meaning of "chicken." Here it did coincide with one of the dictionary meanings, with the definition in the Department of Agriculture Regulations to which the contract made at least oblique reference, with at least some usage in the trade, with the realities of the market, and with what plaintiff's spokesman had said. . . .

6.3 COMMERCIAL TERMS

An international commercial contract functions not only to set out what the parties intend to do, but also allocates risks between the parties. For example, if Acme Office Supply Co. buys file cabinets from Beta Manufacturing Co., what happens when the ship carrying the cabinets to Acme hits an uncharted rock and sinks? Does Acme have to pay anyway, or does Beta have to reship the order? Over the years, merchants have developed shorthand terminology to express the obligations of the parties and the risks of the transaction. Some of the most common contract usages pertain to shorthand terms for price, delivery, title, and the risk of loss during shipment. FOB, FAS, CIF, C&F are just a few of the more common expressions used in international contracting. Merchants sometimes use the expressions in a casual manner as part of a price term, but each term carries with it delivery obligations, title implications, and allocation of the risk of loss.

SOURCES

Commercial terms for shipment are at the heart of the law merchant. They are, therefore, relatively consistent from nation to nation and port to port. However, there are some variations, so contracting parties often indicate which set of definitions will govern their contract.

American merchants will be familiar with the definitions of commercial terms contained in the UCC. These terms are widely used in domestic transactions, and were drafted to reflect the needs of American commerce. However, most international transactions will refer to a document known as *INCOTERMS*, published by the International Chamber of Commerce. The definitions in *INCOTERMS* are not law, but are often adopted by contracting parties. The definitions of commercial terms will vary between *INCOTERMS* and the UCC, so parties should specify which set of definitions they wish to have govern their contract.[2]

The most recent version of *INCOTERMS*, which became effective in 1990, contains thirteen commercial terms, each of which is a shorthand phrase for a set of obligations and rights of a buyer and seller, spanning a range of duties benefiting the seller at one end and the buyer at the other.

The seller has the fewest obligations by using the term "Ex-Works" (EXW) in a contract. EXW requires the seller simply to make the goods available at the named factory or warehouse. If Acme's contract specified EXW-Osaka, all that Beta would have to do is make the goods available to Acme at its factory or warehouse in Osaka. Acme would take ownership of the goods at that point and be responsible for their transport and any risk of loss after that point.

In contrast, the seller takes on the most responsibility by using the term "delivered duty paid" (DDP). DDP requires the seller to arrange the shipping, obtain any import or export permits required, pass the goods through customs, and deliver them to the named point. If Acme's contract specified DDP-Houston, Beta would have to arrange to get the goods to Acme in Houston, paying all charges to that point and taking the risk of loss. Obviously the price of goods in a DDP contract will be higher than the price of goods in an EXW contract, since the seller has to pay several additional charges.

Most international contracts for goods use commercial terms that allocate some risks to each party. The terms fall into two groups. The first, all beginning with the letter "F," requires the seller to get the goods to a shipment point. FOB (free on board) and FAS (free alongside ship) have both been used widely for sending goods by ship, while FCA (free carrier) is a new term designed to be used in any mode of transport.

The second group of terms begins with the letter "C", and requires the seller to get the goods to a named place and pay some additional costs. These terms include CFR (cost and freight), known in the United States as C&F, and CIF (cost, insurance, and freight). The next two sections will explore the legal implications of using the "F" terms and the "C" terms as shorthand in contracts.

---

[2] There is a third set of definitions to which American traders sometimes refer in contracting. The *Revised American Foreign Trade Definitions* (1941) contain definitions of the commercial shorthand terms discussed in this chapter. As *INCOTERMS* has gained wider acceptance, the *Foreign Trade Definitions*, at least with respect to shipment terms, have fallen into disuse.

FOB CONTRACTS

FOB (free on board) is perhaps the most common delivery term in both domestic and international transactions. The term will always be used in connection with a place. For example, a contract for the sale of machinery between a Texas seller and a Korean buyer may specify that the goods will be sold FOB Galveston, or FOB Seoul. If the contract specifies the seller's location as the FOB point, it is known as a shipment contract. If the contract specifies the buyer's location, it is a destination contract. In both domestic and international commerce, the shipment contract is the normal delivery term.

The way in which the parties use the FOB term determines the seller's contractual delivery obligation, the place at which title to the goods passes to the buyer, and the party who bears the risk of loss while the goods are in transit. The FOB term has different meanings and imposes different legal obligations, depending on whether the parties use the UCC definition, some other national law, or the *INCOTERMS* definition.

If the parties use the UCC to govern their contract, a contract that is FOB seller's place of shipment requires the seller to put the goods into the possession of the carrier. When the carrier takes possession, its delivery obligation is complete [UCC Sec. 2-319 (1)(a)]. If the contract is FOB destination, the seller must transport the goods to the destination place and make them available to the buyer. At that point, the seller's delivery obligation is complete. Unless the parties specify otherwise in their contract, the risk of loss and the title to the goods pass to the buyer at the FOB point. As the case below illustrates, that point of complete delivery is not always apparent.

A.M. KNITWEAR CORP. v. ALL AMERICA EXPORT-IMPORT CORP.

41 N.Y.2d 14, 390 N.Y.S.2d 832 (1976)
New York Court of Appeals

FACTS:
All-America placed an order to purchase several thousand pounds of yarn from A.M. Knitwear. Using its own purchase order form, All-America specified that the buyer would "Pick up from your Plant to Moore-McCormak Pier [sic] for shipment to Santos, Brazil." In the blank space on the form for the price, the buyer typed: "FOB PLANT PER LB. $1.35." A place in the contract for the FOB term was left blank.

The buyer hired a freight forwarding company to make transport arrangements for the yarn. The freight forwarder arranged for a local trucking firm to pick up the goods at the seller's plant and deliver them to the carrier, Moore-McCormack, at its pier. As part of its service, the trucker picked up an empty container from Moore-McCormack and delivered the container to the seller's plant in Brooklyn.

The seller loaded the yarn into the shipping

container, then notified the buyer that loading was complete. The buyer had the freight forwarder arrange with the trucker to pick up the loaded container. Later that evening, a truck arrived to pick up the goods. The truck driver signed a bill of lading (illegibly), then drove off with the yarn. Subsequently, the trucker engaged by the freight forwarder arrived, thus revealing that the yarn had been stolen by an imposter.

The buyer stopped payment on its check for payment of the goods and the seller brought suit, claiming that its delivery obligations were complete before the goods were stolen. The seller sued the buyer for its failure to pay the contract price. The trial court ruled in favor of the seller, whereas the appellate court reversed, holding in favor of the buyer.

ISSUE:

Did the seller complete delivery under the terms of the contract?

RESULT:

No. Judgment in favor of the buyer affirmed.

REASONS:

With respect to shipment by the seller, the Code provides that where the seller is "required or authorized" to send the goods, but not required to deliver them to a particular destination, then "unless otherwise agreed" the seller must "put the goods into the possession of . . . a carrier" [U.C.C.2-504(a)]. . . .

Despite the provisions of the Code which place the risk of loss on the seller in the FOB place of shipment contract until the goods are delivered to the carrier, here the seller contends that the parties "otherwise agreed" so that pursuant to its agreement, the risk of loss passed from the seller to the buyer at the time and place at which the seller completed physical delivery of the subject goods into the container supplied by the buyer for that purpose. In support of this contention, the seller alleges that the language of the purchase order "Pick Up from your Plant" is a specific delivery instruction and that the language "FOB

PLANT PER LB. $1.35," which appears in the price column, is a price term and not a delivery term. Further support for the seller's contention is taken from the fact that the space provided in the buyer's own purchase order form for an FOB delivery instruction was left blank by the buyer. Thus, the seller contends its agreement with the buyer imposed no obligation on it to make delivery of the loaded container to the carrier.

As often happens in commercial transactions, the parties to this action did not prepare an extensive written agreement, but merely made an arrangement that, under normal circumstances, would have been entirely satisfactory. The intervention of a wrongdoer who stole the goods that were the subject of the agreement forces the court to determine who should bear the loss resulting from the theft.

The seller's contention, that the parties intended the FOB term as a price term and not a delivery term, conflicts with the Code provision that states that the FOB term is a delivery term "even though used only in connection with the stated price". . . .

. . . [T]he seller has a formidable task in trying to prove that the parties did not intend the ordinary meaning of the term "FOB PLANT," i.e. delivery to the carrier. Although the only written expression in the transaction was the buyer's purchase order form on which the buyer typed the FOB term, if the seller did not agree to this term, the seller should have expressed its disagreement after it received the purchase order form. For example, the seller should have indicated that the term "FOB PLANT" was merely a price term and not a delivery term . . . or that the risk of loss was on the buyer after loading. . . . The Code anticipates that a written confirmation by a party may state terms additional to, or even different from, those offered and agreed upon, which terms, depending on certain factors, may become part of the contract. . . . Yet here the seller did not seek to modify the FOB term typed on the buyer's purchase order, but apparently relied on its own understanding of the agreement.

The UCC definition of the term FOB (place) requires the seller to put the goods into the possession of the carrier at the named place, but the *IN-COTERMS* definition of FOB carries slightly different obligations. Under *INCOTERMS*, the seller is responsible for the goods until they are on board the carrier's vessel. For example, suppose that Acme Widgets, Inc., is to ship one ton of widgets under a contract term of FOB San Francisco. Acme takes the widgets to a shipping company at the port of San Francisco. The shipper issues a dock receipt showing that it has received the goods. While the shipper is loading the goods aboard a ship they slip off their pallet, fall into the water, and are lost. Under the UCC, the risk of this loss passed to the buyer when the carrier took possession of the widgets. Under *INCOTERMS*, the seller bears the risk of loss until the goods pass the ship's rail. The slight difference between the UCC and *IN-COTERMS* may pose a major trap for unwary traders thinking that FOB has the same meaning worldwide.

Traders concerned about the different meanings of commercial terms have several options for avoiding problems. First, they can choose not to use the abbreviations, but specify in detail each party's obligations under the contract. This solution is not always practical, especially in an age of form contracts and computerized shipping practices. Second, instead of using the term FOB (place), they could use the term FOB (vessel). When the parties to a contract name the ship, rather than the place, the UCC puts the risk of loss on the seller until the goods are loaded aboard. Under the UCC, the term FOB (vessel) is equivalent to *INCOTERMS'* FOB (place). Finally, the parties could avoid problems by specifying which rules will govern the contract. *INCOTERMS* is widely respected around the world, and courts will generally honor the choices merchants make in their contracts.

The other "F" terms are similar to FOB in their application. FAS (free alongside ship) requires the seller to get the goods to the dock alongside a named ship. Note that the goods don't have to pass the ship's rail, but just be ready to load. The new term FCA (free carrier) obligates the seller to deliver goods into the custody of a carrier at a named point.

CIF CONTRACTS

The second kind of commercial term commonly found in international contracts is CIF, which is an abbreviation for cost, insurance, and freight. Like the FOB term, it is often used to set a price for goods, but has implications for delivery and risk of loss. When a seller sells goods at a price that is CIF, the seller agrees that the price of the goods includes the selling cost, the cost of insurance for transit, and the cost of freight. The seller undertakes to arrange and pay for transportation and purchase insurance to cover the risk of loss during transport. A variation on this term is a C&F term, which imposes the same obligations on the seller, except that the buyer must arrange its own insurance. Under *INCOTERMS*, C&F is abbreviated CFR (cost and freight). A CIF or C&F contract is generally a shipment contract with respect to the seller's delivery obligations.

The CIF term in a contract is a fundamental piece of a documentary transaction for the sale of goods. In a CIF contract, the seller arranges transportation, gets the goods to the carrier (or, under *INCOTERMS*, loaded aboard the vessel), and obtains appropriate documents from the carrier. Once the seller presents the documents to the buyer, it is entitled to payment. The CIF contract is a contract for the sale of goods that is performed by presenting the appropriate documents. The *Tradax* case illustrates the obligations of buyers and sellers using CIF or C&F terms.

PHILLIPS PUERTO RICO CORE, INC.
v. TRADAX PETROLEUM, LTD.

41 UCC Rep. 1678
Second Circuit Court of Appeals, 1985

FACTS:

Phillips contracted to buy 20,000 to 30,000 metric tons of naphtha, located in Algeria, from Tradax, to be shipped to Puerto Rico. The sale was to be C&F, and the parties incorporated *INCOTERMS* in their contract. The agreement was made by telephone and confirmed by telex.

Tradax hired the integrated tub barge Oxy Trader to transport the naphtha from Algeria to Puerto Rico. On September 24, 1981, the Oxy Trader left port.

At roughly the same time Phillips and Tradax were negotiating, the admiralty press reported an accident on the Oxy Trader's sister ship, the Oxy Producer. On September 17, the press reported that the accident was caused by defective cushioning between the tug and the barge parts of the vessel. On September 20, the Oxy Producer sank.

The Oxy Trader approached Gibraltar, where the Coast Guard stopped the ship for an inspection. On October 7, Tradax found out that the Coast Guard would not let the ship proceed, because it apparently had the same defect that caused the Oxy Producer to sink.

On October 9, Phillips telexed Tradax, declaring that it considered its performance excused under the contract due to acts beyond its control, and that it would instruct its representatives not to pay Tradax for the naphtha. When Tradax presented documents for payment in Puerto Rico, the Phillips representative stated that although the documents looked all right, he had been instructed not to pay Tradax.

Tradax ultimately sold the cargo of naphtha at a loss of more than $1 million. It sued Phillips for the loss, claiming that it was entitled to payment as soon as the naphtha went aboard the Oxy Trader in Algeria. The district court ruled in favor of Tradax, and Phillips appealed.

ISSUE:

At what point does the risk of loss pass to the buyer in a C&F contract?

RESULT:

In a C&F contract, the risk of loss passes to the buyer when the goods pass the ship's rail. Judgment in favor of Tradax affirmed.

REASONS:

The 1980 Incoterms define a "C & F" contract as one in which:

> "[t]he seller must pay the costs and freight necessary to bring the goods to the named destination but the risk of loss or of damage to the goods, as well as of any cost increases, is transferred from the seller to the buyer when the goods pass the ship's rail in the port of shipment." . . .

As a "C & F" seller Tradax had two duties that are relevant here: to deliver the naphtha to an appropriate carrier with which it had contracted for shipment and to tender proper documents to Phillips. Phillips in return was contractually obliged to pay for the naphtha when presented with the shipping documents by Tradax. It is undisputed that after Tradax loaded the naphtha on the Oxy Trader and presented Phillips with the shipping documents on October 13, 1981, Phillips refused to pay for the cargo. If Tradax had adequately performed its contractual duties, Phillips' refusal to pay constituted a breach of the contract. . . .

. . . Phillips' proposed interpretation is clearly inconsistent with the "C & F" terms of sale in the contract itself, which were confirmed by the pre-shipment telex from Phillips, stating that "title and risk of loss to products shall pass to buyer at the time product reaches the vessel[']s flange at the load port." This conclusion is further bolstered by Tradax's cross-examination of Kurt Goehman, one of the persons who originally negotiated the contract for Phillips. Goehman gave his commercial opinion that under "C & F" terms, such as those agreed on, the risk of loss passes to the buyer upon the cargo's being loaded and that if the goods should thereafter be destroyed or if the ship should be delayed, the buyer would not be excused from paying the seller; the buyer would, however, have a claim against the carrier if the loss or delay were the fault of the ship. In sum, Tradax's only obligation regarding delivery of the goods was to deliver them to the carrier; events occurring thereafter were not its concern.

The new *INCOTERMS* adds a new term, designed to be used in contracts that will involve different forms of transport. The term CPT (carriage paid to) requires the seller to pay the cost of transport to the named point. However, in a manner similar to CIF and CFR, the risk of loss passes to the buyer once the first carrier takes possession of the goods. This term can be useful if the goods will travel via several different carriers, like goods that travel by truck to reach a train that takes the goods to a ship.

6.4 CURRENCY ISSUES

A contract among traders from more than one nation generally involves a choice of more than one currency. Most often, the currency the parties use to pay for the goods is a reflection of the relative bargaining strength of the traders and of the relative strength of their respective currencies.

Suppose that an American seller is negotiating a contract to sell 1000 sets of golf clubs to a Japanese buyer. The usual selling price is $500 per set of clubs. If this price is payable in dollars, the buyer will bear the risk that the dollar will strengthen against the yen by the time payment is due. It would then cost the buyer more in Japanese currency to purchase the clubs. On the other hand, the Japanese buyer may benefit if the dollar weakens against the yen. The buyer would then need fewer yen to obtain the purchase price in dollars. In this example, a small change in the relative value of the two currencies, such as 1 yen per dollar, yields a difference of 500,000 yen in the price of the clubs to the Japanese buyer. If the purchase price of the contract is denominated in yen, the American seller bears the same risk of currency fluctuation (and the same possible savings or loss).

The risk of currency fluctuation is allocated between the parties as soon as they make a choice of currency. Many businesses will protect against this risk by making complementary investments in currency markets, as a hedge against fluctuation. Multinational corporations make a practice of trading different currencies to maximize the value of company assets. Occasionally, especially in a long-term supply relationship, the contract will contain a clause allowing the revaluation of the purchase price of the goods in the event of a substantial relative change in the value of the parties' own currencies.

A different problem arises when doing business with countries that regulate the flow of currency out of the country. Historically, both Socialist nations and developing nations have prevented the flow of dollars and other stable currencies out of their countries. A seller encountering such currency restrictions may have to resort to any of a series of measures known as countertrade. The problems of countertrade will be discussed in more detail later; let us note, however, that the need to engage in countertrade usually first appears in contract negotiations.

One form of countertrade is barter. Barter was a common form of trade in ancient times, before systems of exchanging currencies developed. Barter is an exchange of one kind of goods for another, with no money changing hands. For example, a seller may agree to trade 10,000 tons of fertilizer for 100 tractors. Obviously, barter works best when the goods satisfy the needs of both parties and are of good quality. If the seller doesn't need the goods or if the goods are of inferior quality, the seller will have to resell them, probably taking a loss on the transaction.

A second form of countertrade is to offset purchases. For example, in the 1980s Pepsico sold its soft drinks in the former U.S.S.R., obtaining rubles, which were not convertible to dollars. It used its Soviet currency to buy vodka, which it exported to the United States. The benefit of this arrangement to the U.S.S.R. was in helping it build an export economy. Pepsi measured its profits on the arrangement by the money it made in the United States on the sales of Stolichnaya vodka.

A final form of countertrade is more complex. In return for capital investment in a country, a trader will agree to make purchases from that country. For example, Occidental Petroleum contracted to sell phosphate fertilizers to the former U.S.S.R.. In return, it agreed to help finance and construct plants to produce ammonia in the former U.S.S.R., and agreed to purchase ammonia from those plants for sale in the West. The payments on each side of this $20 billion package will roughly balance over a 20-year period. This form of countertrade can be very useful to a company, but may create concern in the home country over the jobs lost to manufacturing abroad.

6.5 CONCLUSION

At the heart of almost all international transactions are the principles of contract law. These contract principles are important whether the transaction is a simple sale of inexpensive goods or a complicated joint venture, a patent license, or even the acquisition of another firm. In an international context, contract negotiations raise many issues not apparent in domestic contracts. Those issues include when parties become obligated to each other, what terms are included in a contract, language barriers, the use of shorthand commercial terms, and currency issues. In goods contracts, there are some formal and informal international rules, such as the CISG and *INCOTERMS*, that can help parties by providing ground rules for their transactions. In other kinds of contracts, such as those for services, technology, and investment, the parties have to set out a more complete structure for their deals.

The most important ability a trader can bring to contract negotiations is the ability to anticipate possible problem areas, so that the negotiating process brings potential misunderstandings into the open. Once buyer and seller are aware of problems, they can negotiate solutions before entering into the contractual relationship. If the parties set out what they intend to do carefully and clearly, they are far more likely to create a successful working relationship and end up with positive results for each side.

6.6 QUESTIONS FOR DISCUSSION

1. Jean-Pierre has a job interview with a French company. At the end of the interview, the interviewer thanks him, tells him he has enjoyed the interview, and that he will be in touch with Jean-Pierre to talk further about his filling the job opening. Three weeks have passed, but Jean-Pierre has heard nothing. Has the French company breached a contract? If so, for what? Would your answer be different if the company were based in Toronto, Canada?

2. Silks Unlimited, a California company, sent an order by fax to Fleur-De-Lis Scarves, a French company, for "300 assorted silk ladies' scarves at a price of 200F each, FCA Paris." Fleur-De-Lis returned a confirmation, stating: "300 ladies' scarves, 50 each of blue, red, and green paisley pattern, and 50 each of yellow, orange, and red lily pattern, to be shipped via Air France at 200F each FCA Paris." Do the parties have a contract? If so, what are the terms? What law governs this transaction? Would your answer be different if the seller were in Germany?

3. As a seller, why wouldn't you always insist on using the EXW term? As a buyer, why wouldn't you insist on using DDP? Explain.

4. As a short research project, go to the library and find an article on a company operating in one of the countries that used to make up the Soviet Union. Find out how it set up its operation to get its profits home.

6.7 FURTHER READINGS

J. Gornall, "Negotiating and Drafting the International Sales Contract and Related Agreements," 14 *Georgia Journal of International and Comparative Law* 491–503 (1984).

J. Graham, "Brazilian, Japanese and American Business Negotiations," *Journal of International Business Studies,* Spring/Summer 1983, pp. 47–61.

"Guide to Incoterms 1990," International Chamber of Commerce No. 461/90, New York, 1990.

Robert Marsh, *The Japanese Negotiator,* Kodansha International, Tokyo and New York, 1988.

P. Winship, "A Bibliography of Commentaries on the United Nations International Sales Convention," 21 *The International Lawyer* 585–601 (1987).

INTERNATIONAL CONTRACT DISPUTES

143

7.1 INTRODUCTION

Chapter 6 explored the process of negotiating the international business transaction. This chapter has two main purposes: first, to explore the kinds of events that may lead to a breach of contract, and second, how, as an international trader, to resolve disputes that may result from contractual relationships.

Litigation over a breach of contract costs time and money and disrupts ongoing business relationships. The costs and disruptions caused by the breach of an international contract may be many times worse than those resulting from the breach of a domestic contract. Suppose, for example, that Acme Widgets, Inc., ships 10,000 widgets from Seattle to Los Angeles. When the widgets arrive, Acme's buyer wrongfully refuses to accept them. Acme's options in response to its customer's breach of contract are relatively sure. It could have the goods returned or "cover" its losses by selling the goods in what should be a relatively familiar market. If it must sue its customer for damages, the suit will take place in federal or state courts in California or Washington, using the familiar rules of the Uniform Commercial Code and the relatively familiar procedural rules of litigation in the United States.

Now suppose that Acme shipped its widgets to Shanghai rather than Los Angeles, and Acme's Chinese customer wrongfully rejected the shipment. Acme could try to ship the goods back to the United States, but that option is expensive and time-consuming. Acme could attempt to resell the goods, but may have to work with unfamiliar markets. If Acme sues its customer, what court would hear the case? Could Acme expect a fair trial in the People's Republic of China? What procedures would the courts follow? What substantive rules would govern the contract? What remedies would be available?

As the example shows, the framework for contract disputes is very different in an international setting. Fortunately, managers can take some steps to reduce the risks of breach of contract and to manage the dispute resolution process.

7.2 PERFORMANCE AND BREACH

As a general rule, both parties to any contract have the obligation to follow the terms they have negotiated. Different legal systems will have somewhat different substantive rules governing contract performance. For example, in contracts for the sale of goods, the Uniform Commercial Code requires the seller to "transfer and deliver" the goods, and requires the buyer to "accept and pay" for the goods (U.C.C. 2-301). The CISG, by contrast, recognizes the documentary nature of many international transactions. It requires the seller to "deliver the goods, hand over any documents relating to them, and transfer the property in the goods" in order to perform (CISG Art. 30). The buyer must "pay the price" for the goods and take delivery of them.

The differences in the two codes may seem small, but reflect a real difference in the legal treatment of performance and breach. Under the U.C.C., the term "acceptance" has a special meaning (U.C.C. 2-606). Acceptance is an act or a failure to reject, signifying to the seller that the goods conform to the contract or that the buyer will take them despite their defects. Until a buyer accepts goods, it may reject the shipment for any nonconformity to the contract terms. Once a buyer accepts goods, it loses the right to reject them, must pay the contract price, and bears the burden of proving that any breach was the seller's fault (U.C.C. 2-607).

The CISG, by contrast, takes an approach to the problems of performance and breach that is much closer to the civil law approach. First, it defines a "fundamental breach" of contract, an event that triggers a variety of remedies for each party. A belief that the other party is about to commit a fundamental breach also triggers the right to avoid a contract or suspend performance (similar to anticipatory repudiation). A breach is "fundamental" if it "results in such detriment to the other party as substantially to deprive him of what he is entitled to expect under the contract" (Art. 25).

The CISG also incorporates in the seller's obligations of performance provisions quite similar to the U.C.C.'s warranty provisions. Article 35 requires the seller to deliver goods that are of the "quantity, quality and description" packaged in the manner required by the contract (similar to express warranties), are fit for the ordinary purposes of such goods (merchantability), are fit for any particular purpose made known to the seller (fitness for a particular purpose), conform to samples or models (express warranties), and are adequately packaged (merchantability). The CISG, unlike the U.C.C., allows the free disclaimer of these obligations.

7.3 REMEDIES FOR BREACH

In common law legal systems, the traditional remedy for breach of contract has been compensatory money damages. A court order of specific performance has been the exception to the usual rule. The U.C.C. liberalized the use of the remedy of specific performance by allowing the remedy "where the goods are unique or in other proper circumstances" (U.C.C. 2-716). The common law approach, however, is different from that of other legal traditions. Most other legal traditions recognize a right to compel contract performance as a standard remedy, not requiring any special circumstances. Therefore, a trader who breaks a contract may be forced to deliver goods, rather than just paying damages. This remedy can be particularly useful in times when goods are in short supply.

The CISG provides many remedies for breach of contract that would be familiar to managers in common law systems, and adds remedies that would be more familiar to managers in civil law countries. Under the CISG, in the event of a breach of contract, the damaged party may seek damages equal to the loss, including lost profits (Art. 74), or may cover, by buying substitute goods or selling the goods to another buyer, then seek damages for the difference between the contract price and the cover price (Art. 75).

As an alternative to damages, the CISG gives the buyer and seller other possible actions. The buyer may require performance by the seller [Art. 46(1)], require the delivery of substitute goods [Art. 46(2)], extend the time for performance (Art. 47), or reduce the price of the goods "in the same proportion as the value that the goods actually delivered had at the time of the delivery bears to the value that conforming goods would have had . . . (Art. 50). The seller may compel the buyer to take delivery or pay the contract price (Art. 62) or extend the time for the buyer's performance (Art. 63).

The CISG's approach makes an action for specific performance a standard remedy. This approach was not acceptable to the representatives of common law countries who took part in drafting the CISG. As a compromise, the CISG provides that, in an action for specific performance, a court need not enter a judgment for specific performance unless it would do so in a domestic (non-CISG) contract case (Art. 28). Some commentators have criticized this provision, saying that it allows a nonuniform law and encourages parties to look for a litigation forum that will grant the best remedies.

The use as a legal remedy of a price reduction in defective goods is also new to American managers, although it is a standard remedy in civil law and Socialist legal systems. The U.C.C. requires payment of the contract price after acceptance. This CISG remedy, however, reflects common commercial practice in virtually all trading countries, including the United States. Merchants often make price adjustments for defects as a way of avoiding the costs of reshipment, storage, resale, or litigation. The CISG's adoption of the remedy of price reduction heeds the legal and business realities of most trading nations.

7.4 SURPRISE AND FRUSTRATION

Even though an international contract may be the product of careful, thorough negotiation, unexpected events will occur before the contract is fully performed. On some occasions, the unexpected events may make performance onerous or even impossible. When one party cannot or will not perform the contract under the changed circumstances, the other party is likely to charge a breach of contract. The issue in the ensuing litigation will be whether the performance under the contract is excused by virtue of the legal doctrines of impossibility, commercial impracticability, or frustration.

The kinds of unforeseen problems that may arise in an international transaction are broader than those that might appear in a domestic transaction. The subject matter of the contract might be destroyed, by natural calamity, such as fire or earthquake, or by war or insurrection. One or more of the governments regulating the activities of the parties to the contract could change its regulations governing the subject of the agreement. A revolution or a coup d'état could lead a country to abrogate its existing contracts with foreign firms. Shortages or rationing of raw materials may affect a firm's ability to fulfill its obligations.

In addition, a whole set of monetary issues may create hardship for one of the parties to a contract. Hyperinflation or currency devaluations may make contract prices meaningless. A country may decide to impose restrictions on the outflow of funds or may decide to make its currency nonconvertible. Conversely, a contract made under the assumption that a currency cannot be converted may change dramatically if a country adopts a free-market economy and a fully convertible currency.

Many contract provisions are designed to reduce or allocate the risks of unforeseen events. The most common provisions allocate the risk of loss for goods during transport. Recall from Chapter 6 the discussion of commercial terms such as FOB and CIF. In addition to being a convenient shorthand reference, one of the primary functions of those commercial terms is to allocate the risk that the goods will be lost, delayed, or destroyed in transit.

Another common set of risk-allocating terms relates to the price of the contract goods or services. The choice of a currency, such as dollars or yen, automatically allocates the risk of fluctuations of value in that currency. Contracting parties often negotiate price escalator clauses, allowing the price of goods or services to increase or decrease in conjunction with changes in inflation or the cost of raw materials basic to the contract. In general, managers should be able to foresee market and economic changes. A court or a panel of arbitrators will be very reluctant to release a party from a contract simply because performance has become considerably more expensive.

CONTRACT CLAUSES

Political risks, such as regulation, wars, insurrections, and embargoes, are often left unallocated, but are sometimes covered by a contract provision known as a *force majeure* clause. Translated literally from the French as "superior force," *force majeure* clauses allow a party to delay or terminate contract performance in the event of unexpected, disruptive events. These events may have human or governmental causes, such as strikes or embargoes, or may be "Acts of God," natural events such as earthquakes or storms.

Some *force majeure* clauses will be quite simple. For example, a contract might specify that "in the event of a *force majeure*, the affected party may terminate its obligations under the contract." Obviously, a general clause like this leaves room for interpretation, and thus a lot of room for breach of contract litigation. Different legal systems will interpret the range of this general concept quite differently. Some, for example, might include a labor strike as a qualifying event, while others would not.

Another approach to the problem of unforeseen events has been to try a generalist approach to *force majeure.* For example, a contract may specify that "any event beyond the control of the parties that impedes performance gives the burdened party the right to relief." This approach, too, tends to create interpretive difficulties, giving rise to breach of contract litigation.

A more useful approach to the problem of unforeseen events, particularly among sophisticated traders, is to list the kinds of events that will allow a party to suspend or terminate contract performance. Such a contract clause might include "fire, flood, earthquake, war, rebellion, blockade, or government restrictions on imports or exports." The advantage of the specific approach is that the contract retains its character as a negotiated risk allocation device, with the parties deciding on what will or will not be on the list of excuses for performance. The disadvantage of this approach is that rarely do the parties think of all the events that could occur. In the example above, suppose that a tornado blew the roof off the seller's plant, preventing timely performance of the contract. Tornadoes are not on the list of events excusing performance, so the seller might have to pay damages for breach of contract.

A solution to the problems caused by a specific approach to *force majeure* is to list the most common kinds of events, including some general language. For example, the clause in the last paragraph might read in part, "fire, flood, earthquake, or other natural disaster, war, rebellion, blockade, or other military action. . . ." The contract language might also use the list of events as a list of examples ("events such as fire, flood, etc.) With some care, negotiators can cover the most likely surprises, yet leave room for truly unforeseen events.

LITIGATION

When the parties have not successfully negotiated a clear *force majeure* provision, a court may have to decide whether a party has breached a contract or is excused from performance. Different legal systems take very different approaches to the problems of excuse.

A prominent example of a strict approach to the problem of unforeseen events is the French legal system. For private contracts, an unforeseen event must make performance physically impossible in order to provide an excuse for performance. French legal scholars and the administrative courts have tried to widen the scope of excuses to include commercial impracticability, but have been unsuccessful. Under the French system, then, the parties to a contract must be extremely careful to include contract provisions specifying events that will excuse contract performance, especially when performance is burdensome or futile, but not impossible.

The United States and most other common law countries have moved away from a strict approach to contract excuses. Physical impossibility, commercial impracticability, and frustration all may allow a party to terminate its contractual obligations. Recall, for example, the *Petrogas Processing* case in Chapter 3, which involved the impact of new government regulations on an existing contract. The American approach is contained in U.C.C. 2-615, which states:

> Except so far as a seller may have assumed a greater obligation . . .
>
> (a) Delay in delivery or non-delivery in whole or in part by a seller . . . is not a breach of his duty under a contract for sale if performance as agreed has been made impracticable by the occurrence of a contingency the nonoccurrence of which was a basic assumption on which the contract was made or by compliance in good faith with any applicable foreign or domestic governmental regulation or order whether or not it later proves to be invalid.

The expansion of the concept of excuse to include impossibility, impracticability, and frustration does not necessarily mean that courts will easily release parties from their negotiated promises. On the contrary, as the following case illustrates, a party seeking to be excused from its contractual obligations bears a heavy burden of persuasion in an American court.

TRANSATLANTIC FINANCING CORP. v. UNITED STATES

363 F.2d 312 (D.C. Cir. 1966)

FACTS:

In July 1956, the Egyptian government nationalized the operations of the Suez Canal, angering the British and French governments, and creating an international crisis. In early October 1956, the United States Department of Agriculture (USDA) chartered the SS *Christos*, operated by Transatlantic Financing, to carry a full cargo of wheat from Galveston, Texas, to Bandur Shapur, Iran. On October 27, 1956, the SS *Christos* left Galveston for Bandur Shapur, on a course leading her through Gibraltar and the Suez Canal.

On October 29, Israel invaded Egypt, followed two days later by British and French troops invading the Suez Canal Zone. Egypt sank ships at both ends of the canal and closed it to all traffic. With its ship already at sea, Transatlantic called the USDA to find out what it should do, and to try to get an agreement for additional compensation to take the cargo on a route around the Cape of Good Hope. The USDA representative informed Transatlantic that it expected full performance for the contract price, but that Transatlantic could file a claim for additional compensation.

After this conversation, the SS *Christos* changed course, sailing around the Cape of Good Hope and arriving in Bandar Shapur on December 30. Transatlantic then sued the United States for its extra expenses. The lower court ruled in favor of the United States, and Transatlantic appealed.

ISSUE:

Did the closing of the Suez Canal excuse Transatlantic from performing its original contract obligations?

RESULT:

No. The contract was not commercially impracticable. Judgment in favor of the United States affirmed.

REASONS:

The doctrine of impossibility of performance has gradually been freed from the earlier fictional and unrealistic strictures of such tests as the "implied term" and the "parties' contemplation."

It is now recognized that "A thing is impossible in legal contemplation when it is not practicable; and a thing is impracticable when it can only be done at an excessive and unreasonable cost." The doctrine ultimately represents the ever-shifting line, drawn by courts hopefully responsive to commercial practices and mores, at which the community's interest in having contracts enforced according to their terms is outweighed by the commercial senselessness of requiring performance. When the issue is raised, the court is asked to construct a condition of performance based on the changed circumstances, a process which involves at least three reasonably definable steps. First, a contingency—something unexpected—must have occurred. Second, the risk of the unexpected occurrence must not have been allocated either by agreement or by custom. Finally, occurrence of the contingency must have rendered performance commercially impracticable. Unless the court finds these three requirements satisfied, the plea of impossibility must fail.

The first requirement was met here. It seems reasonable, where no route is mentioned in a contract, to assume the parties expected performance by the usual and customary route at the time of contract. Since the usual and customary route from Texas to Iran at the time of contract was through the Suez, closure of the Canal made impossible the expected method of performance, but this unexpected development raises rather than resolves the impossibility issue, which turns additionally on whether the risk of the contingency's occurrence had been allocated and, if not,

whether performance by alternative routes was rendered impracticable.

Proof that the risk of a contingency's occurrence has been allocated may be expressed in or implied from the agreement. Such proof may also be found in the surrounding circumstances, including custom and usage of the trade. The contract in this case does not expressly condition performance upon availability of the Suez route. Nor does it specify "via Suez" or, on the other hand, "via Suez or Cape of Good Hope." Nor are there provisions in the contract from which we may properly imply that the continued availability of Suez was a condition of performance. Nor is there anything in custom or trade usage, or in the surrounding circumstances generally, which would support our constructing a condition of performance. The numerous cases requiring performance around the Cape when Suez was closed, indicate that the Cape route is generally regarded as an alternative means of performance. So the implied expectation the route would be via Suez is hardly adequate proof of an allocation of the promises of the risk of closure. In some cases, even an express expectation may not amount to a condition of performance. . . .

If anything, the circumstances surrounding this contract indicate that the risk of the Canal's closure may be deemed to have been allocated to Transatlantic. We know or may safely assume that the parties were aware, as were most commercial men with interests affected by the Suez situation, that the Canal might become a dangerous area. No doubt the tension affected freight rates, and it is arguable that the risk of closure became part of the dickered terms.

We do not deem the risk of closure so allocated, however. Foreseeability or even recognition of a risk does not necessarily prove its allocation. Parties to a contract are not always able to provide for all the possibilities of which they are aware, sometimes because they cannot agree, often simply because they are too busy. Moreover, that some abnormal risk was contemplated is probative but does not necessarily establish an allocation of the risk of the contingency which actually occurs. In this case, for example, nationalization by Egypt of the Suez Canal Corporation and formation of the Suez Users Group did not necessarily indicate that the Canal would be blocked even if a confrontation resulted. The surrounding circumstances do indicate, however, a willingness by Transatlantic to assume abnormal risks, and this fact should legitimately cause us to judge the impracticability of performance by an alternative route in stricter terms than we would were the contingency unforeseen.

We turn then to the question whether occurrence of the contingency rendered performance commercially impracticable under the circumstances of this case. The goods shipped were not subject to harm from the longer, less temperate Southern route. The vessel and crew were fit to proceed around the Cape. Transatlantic was no less able than the United States to purchase insurance to cover the contingency's occurrence. If anything, it is more reasonable to expect [the] owner-operator of vessels to insure against the hazards of war. They are in the best position to calculate the cost of performance by alternative routes (and therefore to estimate the amount of insurance required), and are undoubtedly sensitive to international troubles which uniquely affect the demand for and cost of their services. The only factor operating here in appellant's favor is the added expense, allegedly $43,972.00 above and beyond the contract price of $305,842.92, of extending a 10,000 mile voyage by approximately 3,000 miles. While it may be an overstatement to say that increased cost and difficulty of performance never constitute impracticability, to justify relief there must be more of a variation between expected costs and the cost of performing by an available alternative than is present in this case, where the promisor can legitimately be presumed to have accepted some degree of abnormal risk, and where impracticability is urged on the basis of added expense alone.

We conclude, therefore, as have most other courts considering related issues arising out of the Suez closure, that performance of this contract was not rendered legally impossible.

The CISG takes a different approach to unforeseen events than either the strict approach of the French or the more commercially oriented American approach. Article 79 (1) states that:

> A party to a contract is not liable for a failure to perform any of his obligations if he proves that the failure was due to an impediment beyond his control and that he could not reasonably be expected to have taken the impediment into account at the time of the conclusion of the contract or to have avoided or overcome it or its consequences.

The CISG language takes into account the problem of fault, in that the impediment must be beyond the party's control. It also accounts for the problem of allocation of risk, in requiring that the intervening event essentially be unforeseeable. The CISG provision, in contrast to the provisions of the U.C.C., also envisions a remedy both for the buyer and for the seller.

On the whole, the CISG provision recognizes the primary approach of civil law and common law systems. It recognizes that performance need not be physically impossible to justify some relief from contract obligations. Yet the CISG still places a heavy burden of persuasion on a buyer or seller wishing to escape its contract obligations.

7.5 DISPUTE RESOLUTION

Sometimes, despite the most careful contract negotiations, a breach of contract still occurs. In that event, the parties to the contract face some difficult decisions in obtaining a resolution of their dispute.

In a domestic contract dispute, decisions of when and where to litigate are fairly straightforward. A manager should ask a series of questions before proceeding. What would the firm get if we won? What is the likelihood that we will win? Is there a risk of countersuit? What are the estimated legal fees? How long will the suit take? Is there a principle involved that is more important than the cost of proceeding? What will a lawsuit do to the business relationship with the defendant? How much negative publicity will the suit generate?

The manager facing a breach of contract suit in an international context has several additional questions to ask. What court will hear this case? What law will apply, and will it recognize my breach of contract claims? Will we have to hire additional, foreign lawyers, and if so, what will their fees be? Will we get a fair trial? How do we make witnesses attend the trial, and can we collect evidence from other countries? Will we be able to collect a judgment we might win?

Chapter 2 discusses many of the issues posed by the prospect of international litigation. The material that follows discusses the steps a manager can take in order to manage and control the process of dispute resolution in an international setting. They include choosing the site of a lawsuit, choosing alternative dispute resolution procedures, and choosing an applicable law.

CHOICE OF FORUM

Suppose that a South Carolina business orders goods from the Czech Republic. The goods will be taken by truck from Prague to Rotterdam, where they will be loaded on board a ship bound for Charleston. If something goes wrong with this transaction, many different courts could take jurisdiction of the dispute, using the principles discussed in Chapter 2. South Carolina courts and Czech courts are two obvious possibilities, but consider the courts of West Germany and the Netherlands, who might be involved in the event of an accident involving the truck. Consider too the possible involvement of the courts of England, Belgium, or France, as the ship passes through their coastal waters.

It is easy to see, even from this brief example, why managers might want to reduce the number of locations that might hear a lawsuit involving their international transactions. In order to control the site of any lawsuits regarding the transaction, the parties to a contract will often negotiate a contractual choice-of-forum clause. A typical choice-of-forum clause might state:

The parties agree that all disputes arising out of this contract be tried in the courts of Prague, the Czech Republic, to the exclusion of all other courts that might otherwise have jurisdiction apart from this contract provision.

A choice-of-forum clause is only as good as a nonchosen court's willingness to enforce it. In the above example, if the buyer sued the seller in court in South Carolina, the effectiveness of the contract clause would rest on the willingness of the South Carolina court to dismiss the case. Traditionally, most American courts, as well as those of other nations, were reluctant to divest themselves of jurisdiction. Jurisdiction was a public policy matter, not to be undermined by private agreements. Gradually, though, more and more nations have recognized the merits of allowing the parties to a contract to decide where to resolve their disputes. In the United States, the real recognition of choice-of-forum clauses came in the case below, known as *The Bremen*.

M/S BREMEN v. ZAPATA OFF-SHORE COMPANY

407 U.S. 1 (1972)

FACTS:

Zapata, a Houston-based company, contracted with Unterweser, a German company, to tow a Zapata offshore oil rig, the Chaparral, from Louisiana to a point off Ravenna, Italy. The contract contained a clause reading: "Any dispute arising must be treated before the London Court of Justice."

Unterweser's seagoing tug *Bremen* left Louisiana with the drilling rig in tow on January 5, 1968. On January 9, while the tug and rig were in international waters, a severe storm damaged the oil rig. Zapata instructed the *Bremen* to head for Tampa, Florida, the nearest port.

On January 12, Zapata sued Unterweser in federal district court in Tampa, charging negligent towage and breach of contract. Unterweser responded by seeking dismissal of the suit in Florida, based on the terms of the contract and other grounds. Unterweser also began a suit for breach of contract in the High Court of Justice in London. The British court accepted jurisdiction. The federal district court also accepted jurisdiction, holding that choice-of-forum clauses violated public policy. Unterweser appealed to the Fifth

Circuit court of appeals, which affirmed the district court decision *en banc* (all of the judges in the circuit made the decision, rather than a panel of three judges). Unterweser appealed to the Supreme Court.

ISSUE:

Do forum selection clauses in private contracts violate public policy?

RESULT:

No. The decision of the court of appeals is reversed, and remanded to the district court to allow Zapata to attempt to prove that the clause deprives it of "a meaningful day in court."

REASONS:

We hold, with the six dissenting members of the Court of Appeals, that far too little weight and effect was given to the forum clause in resolving this controversy. For at least two decades we have witnessed an expansion of overseas commercial activities by business enterprises based in the United States. The barrier of distance that once tended to confine a business concern to a modest territory no longer does so. Here we see an American company with special expertise contracting with a foreign company to tow a complex machine thousands of miles across seas and oceans. The expansion of American business and industry will hardly be encouraged if, notwithstanding solemn contracts, we insist on a parochial concept that all disputes must be resolved under our laws and in our courts. . . . We cannot have trade and commerce in world markets and international waters exclusively on our terms, governed by our laws and resolved in our courts. . . .

The argument that such clauses are improper because they tend to "oust" a court of jurisdiction is hardly more than a vestigial legal fiction. It appears to rest at core on historical judicial resistance to any attempt to reduce the power and business of a particular court and has little place in an era when all courts are overloaded and when businesses once essentially local now operate in world markets. It reflects something of a provincial attitude regarding the fairness of other tribunals. No one seriously contends in this case that the forum-selection clause "ousted" the District Court of jurisdiction over Zapata's action. The threshold question is whether that court should have exercised its jurisdiction to do more than give effect to the legitimate expectations of the parties manifested in their freely negotiated agreement, by specifically enforcing the forum clause.

There are compelling reasons why a freely negotiated private international agreement, unaffected by fraud, undue influence, or overweening bargaining power, such as that involved here, should be given full effect. In this case, for example, we are concerned with a far from routine transaction between companies of two different nations contemplating the tow of an extremely costly piece of equipment from Louisiana across the Gulf of Mexico, and the Atlantic Ocean, through the Mediterranean Sea to its final destination in the Adriatic Sea. In the course of its voyage, it was to traverse the waters of many jurisdictions. The Chaparral could have been damaged at any point along the route, and there were countless possible ports of refuge. That the accident occurred in the Gulf of Mexico and the barge was towed to Tampa in an emergency were mere fortuities. It cannot be doubted for a moment that the parties sought to provide for a neutral forum for the resolution of any disputes arising during the tow. Manifestly much uncertainty and possibly great inconvenience to both parties could arise if a suit could be maintained in any jurisdiction in which an accident might occur or if jurisdiction were left to any place where the *Bremen* or Unterweser might happen to be found. . . .

Thus, in the light of present day commercial realities and expanding international trade we conclude that the forum clause should control absent a strong showing that it should be set aside. Although their opinions are not altogether explicit, it seems reasonably clear that the District Court and the Court of Appeals placed the burden on Unterweser to show that London would be a more convenient forum than Tampa, although the contract expressly resolved that issue. The correct approach would have been to enforce the forum clause specifically unless Zapata could clearly show that enforcement would be unreasonable and unjust, or that the clause was invalid for such reasons as fraud or overreaching. Accordingly, the case must be remanded for reconsideration.

CHOICE OF LAW

In addition to choosing a place for litigation, many contracts now include a choice-of-law clause, specifying which state or country's law will govern the obligations of the parties. Choice-of-law clauses have achieved wide recognition both in domestic and in international contracts. The U.C.C., for example, provides in part in Section 1-105 (1) that: ". . . when a transaction bears a reasonable relation to this state and also to another state or nation the parties may agree that the law either of this state or of such other state or nation shall govern their rights and duties." The CISG recognizes the autonomy of contracting parties by allowing the parties to "opt out" of the application of the CISG to their contracts (Art. 6).

To some extent, the recognition of choice-of-law clauses may go farther in international contracts than in domestic contracts. In some instances, such as *The Bremen*, the parties to a contract may seek a neutral forum to resolve disputes. That forum will often apply its own law to the contract problem, reasoning that the substantive law of the forum may have been one reason for the choice the parties made. Thus, courts will recognize choices of substantive law that bear no relation to the contract.

The ability of parties to a contract to choose applicable law does have some limitations. As the Supreme Court discussed in *The Bremen*, a choice resulting from fraud, undue influence, or a contract of adhesion need not be given effect. A contract choice-of-law provision applies only to the parties directly involved in the contract. If, for example, the conditions created by the contract violated American antitrust laws, an injured third party could bring a civil suit in the United States and the government could bring criminal actions in the United States, despite a contrary choice-of-law provision.

Another limitation on the parties' choice of law is that the provision cannot violate the public policy of a forum that would otherwise apply its own law to the contract. The most notable American example of a public policy issue pertains to the Carriage of Goods by Sea Act (46 U.S.C. 1300 *et seq.*), also known as COGSA. As its name indicates, COGSA regulates the shipment of goods in and out of American ports. Chapter 9 will discuss COGSA in more detail, but one of its main provisions regulates attempts on the part of ocean carriers to limit liability for damage to goods on board their ships. COGSA invalidates any attempt by a carrier to avoid liability beyond that allowed by the statute. A number of American courts have interpreted choice-of-law and choice-of-forum clauses to be the kind of provision that could allow a shipper to escape statutory liability. These courts have invalidated the contract clauses in favor of allowing the jurisdiction of American courts.

ARBITRATION

Perhaps the most widely used form of dispute resolution in international contracting is arbitration. When the parties to a contract choose a forum, a popular choice is that of an arbitral forum rather than a litigation forum.

The advantages of arbitrating an international contract dispute are many. The arbitrators may or may not be lawyers: For example, a construction contract dispute may have engineers as arbitrators. The arbitration process is likely to be faster than some litigation, especially in the United States. It may have a more streamlined process of getting to a hearing, especially when compared to the expensive and cumbersome discovery process in the United States. A major factor in favor of arbitration is its lack of publicity. Unlike court proceedings, which are open to the public and often result in published decisions, arbitration is a private process. The ultimate decision goes only to the involved parties. A business concerned about the public disclosure of confidential information will tend to try to resolve disputes through arbitration.

Several organizations provide arbitration services for international commercial disputes. The best-known is the International Chamber of Commerce (ICC), headquartered in Paris. In addition, a substantial number of commercial arbitrations are heard by the London Court of International Arbitration, in England, and the American Arbitration Association, in New York. The Stockholm Chamber of Commerce, in Sweden, has been a popular choice for arbitrating disputes between Socialist traders and their Western counterparts. The International Center for the Settlement of Investment Disputes arbitrates many cases involving governments and foreign investors. These organizations may use their own rules of proceeding, or may use a set of rules developed by the United Nations Committee on International Trade Law (UNCITRAL). The UNCITRAL rules are widely recognized in arbitrations around the world.

In order to arbitrate a dispute, the parties must agree to do so, usually in their initial contract. For example, a typical arbitration clause would have the parties agree to arbitrate any dispute "arising from or related to" the contract before a specific group, such as the ICC; would designate a substantive law to govern the contract; would contain language allowing the enforcement of an arbitral award in court; could specify the number of arbitrators; and could choose a place and a language for the arbitration proceedings.

Like a choice-of-forum clause, an arbitration provision is only as good as a court's willingness to enforce it. Historically, courts were reluctant to enforce the removal of disputes to arbitration, in part because of a reluctance to have nonlawyers judge disputes. Special problems have arisen when the contract dispute involved more than just a breach of contract claim. Particularly in complex commercial disputes, the arbitrator may have to decide claims related to patent and trademark rights, antitrust violations, securities fraud, or even a civil claim under RICO (Racketeer Influenced Corrupt Organizations Act). In the *Mitsubishi* case below, the Supreme Court strengthened the ability of parties to choose alternative methods of dispute resolution for international commercial disputes.

MITSUBISHI MOTORS CORP. v. SOLER CHRYSLER-PLYMOUTH, INC.

473 U.S. 614 (1985)

FACTS:

Mitsubishi was a Japanese manufacturer of automobiles. It was the product of a joint venture between Mitsubishi Heavy Industries, a Japanese corporation, and Chrysler International, S.A. (CISA), a Swiss corporation owned by Chrysler Corporation. Mitsubishi's purpose was to manufacture cars bearing Mitsubishi and Chrysler name trademarks for distribution through Chrysler dealers outside the continental United States. Soler was a Chrysler dealer located in Puerto Rico.

On October 31, 1979, Soler entered into a distribution agreement with CISA, covering sales of cars within Puerto Rico, and a sales agreement with Mitsubishi and CISA. The sales agreement contained an arbitration clause providing that all disputes between Mitsubishi and Soler "shall be finally settled by arbitration in Japan in accordance with the rules and regulations of the Japan Commercial Arbitration Association."

Initially, Soler had great success in selling Mitsubishi cars. The parties renegotiated their sales agreement, requiring Soler to take a higher minimum number of cars. In 1981, however, the market slowed and Soler had difficulty meeting its annual sales volume. It asked Mitsubishi to delay or cancel several orders, and attempted to arrange for the transshipment of some of its allotment of cars for sale in the continental United States and Latin America. Mitsubishi and CISA refused, citing several reasons.

In March 1982, Mitsubishi filed suit in federal district court in Puerto Rico, seeking an order compelling arbitration in Japan. It also filed a request for arbitration with the Japan Commercial Arbitration Association. Soler counterclaimed against Mitsubishi and CISA in federal court, alleging breach of contract, defamation, and violations of several statutes, including the Sherman Act. Soler's Sherman Act claim alleged that Mitsubishi and CISA tried to divide markets in restraint of trade, by refusing to allow Soler to ship vehicles to North, Central, or South America, by refusing to ship cars with parts such as heaters and defoggers that would make the cars suitable for sale outside Puerto Rico, and by wrongfully trying to replace Soler as a distributor.

The district court ordered the parties to arbitrate all claims, including the antitrust claims. Soler appealed to the First Circuit Court of Appeals, which ruled that all claims but the antitrust claims should proceed to arbitration. Mitsubishi then petitioned the Supreme Court for review.

ISSUE:

In an international transaction, are all claims arbitrable, including statutory claims of antitrust violations?

RESULT:

Yes. Judgment in favor of Mitsubishi.

REASONS:

We now turn to consider whether Soler's antitrust claims are nonarbitrable even though it has agreed to arbitrate them. In holding that they are not, the Court of Appeals followed the decision of the Second Circuit in *American Safety Equipment Corp. v. J.P. Maguire & Co.*, 391 F.2d 821 (1968). Notwithstanding the absence of any explicit support for such an exception in either the Sherman Act or the Federal Arbitration Act, the Second Circuit there reasoned that "the pervasive public interest in enforcement of the antitrust laws, and the nature of the claims that arise in such cases, combine to make . . . antitrust claims . . . inappropriate for arbitration." *Id.*, at 827–828. We find it unnecessary to assess the legitimacy of the *American Safety* doctrine as applied to agreements to arbitrate arising from domestic transactions. As in *Scherk v. Alberto-Culver Co.*, 417 U.S. 506 (1974), we conclude that concerns of international comity, respect for the capacities of foreign and transnational tribunals, and sensitivity to the need of the international commercial system for predictability in the resolution of disputes require that we enforce the parties' agreement, even assuming that a contrary result would be forthcoming in a domestic context. . . .

At the outset, we confess to some skepticism of certain aspects of the *American Safety* doctrine. As distilled by the First Circuit . . . , the doctrine comprises four ingredients. First, private parties play a pivotal role in aiding government enforcement of the antitrust laws by means of the private action for treble damages. Second, "the strong possibility that contracts which generate antitrust disputes may be contracts of adhesion militates against automatic forum determination by contract." Third, antitrust issues, prone to complication, require sophisticated legal and economic analysis, and thus are "ill-adapted to strengths of the arbitral process, *i.e.*, expedition, minimal requirements of written rationale, simplicity, resort to basic concepts of common sense and simple equity." Finally, just as "issues of war and peace are too important to be vested in the generals, . . . decisions as to antitrust regulation of business are too important to be lodged in arbitrators chosen from the business community—particularly those from a foreign community that has had no experience with or exposure to our law and values. . . .

Initially, we find the second concern unjustified. The mere appearance of an antitrust dispute does not alone warrant invalidation of the selected forum on the undemonstrated assumption that the arbitration clause is tainted. A party resisting arbitration of course may attack directly the validity of the agreement to arbitrate. . . .

Next, potential complexity should not suffice to ward off arbitration. . . . The anticipated subject matter of the dispute may be taken into account when the arbitrators are appointed, and arbitral rules typically provide for the participation of experts either employed by the parties or appointed by the tribunal. Moreover, it is often a judgment that streamlined proceedings and expeditious results will often best serve their needs that causes parties to agree to arbitrate their disputes; it is typically a desire to keep the effort and expense required to resolve a dispute within manageable bounds that prompts them mutually to forgo access to judicial remedies. . . .

For similar reasons, we also reject the proposition that an arbitration panel will pose too great a danger of innate hostility to the constraints on business conduct that antitrust law imposes. International arbitrators frequently are drawn from the legal as well as the business community; where the dispute has an important legal component, the parties and the arbitral body with whose assistance they have agreed to settle their dispute can be expected to select arbitrators accordingly. We decline to indulge the presumption that the parties and arbitral body conducting the proceeding will be unable or unwilling to retain competent, conscientious, and impartial arbitrators.

We are left, then, with the core of the *American Safety* doctrine—the fundamental importance to American democratic capitalism of the regime of the antitrust laws. . . .

The treble damages provision wielded by the private litigant is a chief tool in the antitrust enforcement scheme, posing a crucial deterrent to potential violators. . . .

The importance of the private damages remedy, however, does not compel the conclusion that it may not be sought outside an American court. Notwithstanding its important incidental policing function, the treble-damages cause of action conferred on private parties by 4 of the Clayton Act, 15 U.S.C. 15, and pursued by Soler here by way of its third counterclaim, seeks primarily to enable an injured competitor to gain compensation for that injury. . . .

. . . And, of course, the antitrust cause of action remains at all times under the control of the individual litigant; no citizen is under an obligation to bring an antitrust suit . . . and the private antitrust plaintiff needs no executive or judicial approval before settling one. It follows that, at least where the international cast of a transaction would otherwise add an element of uncertainty to dispute resolution, the prospective litigant may provide in advance for a mutually agreeable procedure whereby he would seek his antitrust recovery as well as settle the other controversies.

There is no reason to assume at the outset of the dispute that international arbitration will not provide an adequate mechanism. To be sure, the international arbitral tribunal owes no prior allegiance to the legal norms of particular states; hence, it has no direct obligation to vindicate their statutory dictates. The tribunal, however, is bound to effectuate the intentions of the parties. Where the parties have agreed that the arbitral body is to decide a defined set of claims which includes, as in these cases, those arising from the application of American antitrust law, the tribunal therefore should be bound to decide that dispute in accord with the national law giving rise to the claim. . . . And so long as the prospective litigant effectively may vindicate its statutory cause of action in the arbitral forum, the statute will continue to serve both its remedial and deterrent function.

In the United States, the trend toward enforceability of the choices that parties make about dispute resolution in their contracts seems very clear. In the *Mitsubishi* case, Soler should have objected during negotiations. Because it didn't, it had to use a Japanese forum to resolve its dispute with Mitsubishi and CISA.

The trend toward enforcement of dispute resolution clauses in contracts is also noticeable among most of the developed countries of the world. A manager dealing with a business in Europe or in the more developed nations of the Pacific Rim should have little trouble designating arbitration as a method of resolving a dispute. Historically, less-developed countries in Latin America, Africa, and Asia have not been as receptive to commercial arbitration or choice-of-law provisions. There has been some reluctance to believe that commercial arbitrators in Paris, London, New York, or Stockholm can be sympathetic to the special needs of developing nations. The UNCITRAL arbitration rules, developed with the full participation of developing nations, may help reduce the reluctance of those countries to allow alternative methods of dispute resolution.

OTHER FORMS OF DISPUTE RESOLUTION

Courts and arbitrators are not the only ways of resolving disputes. Over the years, businesses have resorted to a variety of alternative means of settling problems. Some methods, like mediation or conciliation, have been in use for many years and are particularly popular in non-Western legal systems. Others, like minitrials, have emerged more recently. The minitrial, in particular, has found some use in complex commercial litigation. It involves an abbreviated presentation of each party's evidence, usually before senior executives from each party and a neutral facilitator. Depending on the agreement of the parties, the recommendations of the facilitator may be "off the record," or may be admissible at a later trial. The minitrial may be very helpful at getting executives to see the true merits of the dispute, so as to reach a settlement without need for a trial or arbitration.

The enforceability of agreements to use forms of dispute resolution other than litigation or arbitration is still an open question, and will probably vary greatly among different nations. Thus, managers using these forms of dispute resolution should draft their contracts carefully, and perhaps have contingency plans in case the first-choice method is not enforceable.

ENFORCEMENT OF JUDGMENTS AND AWARDS

Of course, a court judgment or an arbitral award is useless if the relevant judicial systems choose not to enforce it. Chapter 2 discussed some of the legal problems associated with the enforcement of foreign judgments in American courts. Recall that although there is no widely uniform law among the states, most states will not reexamine the substance of a foreign judgment. They will choose not to enforce judgments that violate fundamental notions of due process, but will begin their analysis with a strong presumption of the validity of the foreign judgment.

The same approach is generally true of most developed nations. The EC, for example, has a Convention on Jurisdiction and Enforcement of Judgments in Civil and Commercial Matters, providing for the enforcement of judgments rendered in member states. There will be some variation in approach even among the developed nations, but the overall trend is toward the recognition and enforcement of foreign judgments.

The enforcement of foreign arbitral awards has had a somewhat different history than that of court judgments. In 1958, the United Nations opened the Convention of the Recognition and Enforcement of Foreign Arbitral Awards, known as the New York Convention. The Convention allows a party to apply for enforcement of an award in any relevant judicial system. The grounds for refusing to enforce the award are set forth in Article V of the Convention.

CONVENTION OF THE RECOGNITION AND ENFORCEMENT OF FOREIGN ARBITRAL AWARDS (1958)

9 U.S.C. 201-208 (1970)

ARTICLE V

1. Recognition and enforcement of the award may be refused, at the request of the party against whom it is invoked, only if that party furnishes to the competent authority where the recognition and enforcement is sought, proof that:

(a) The parties to the agreement referred to in article II were, under the law applicable to them, under some incapacity, or the said agreement is not valid under the law to which the parties have subjected it or, failing any indication thereon, under the law of the country where the award was made; or

(b) The party against whom the award is invoked was not given proper notice of the appointment of the arbitrator or of the arbitration proceedings or was otherwise unable to present his case; or

(c) The award . . . contains decisions on matters beyond the scope of the submission to arbitration . . . ; or

(d) The composition of the arbitral authority or the arbitral procedure was not in accordance with the agreement of the parties . . . ; or

(e) The award has not yet become binding on the parties, or has been set aside or suspended by a competent authority of the country in which, or under the law of which, that award was made.

2. Recognition and enforcement of an arbitral award may also be refused if the competent authority in the country where recognition and enforcement is sought finds that:

(a) The subject matter of the difference is not capable of settlement by arbitration under the law of that country; or

(b) The recognition or enforcement of the award would be contrary to the public policy of that country.

As of 1989, eighty countries had enacted the New York Convention into law. While there are some differences in the ways different countries interpret the New York Convention, an arbitral award rendered by one of the major arbitration organizations should be enforceable in a New York Convention country. An arbitral award is less likely to be enforced in countries that have not ratified the New York Convention. Those countries include much of Latin America as well as other less-developed nations.

7.6 CONCLUSION

When managers negotiate international contracts, the final agreement should serve three main functions. First, it should set out with some precision the obligations each party undertakes. Second, the agreement should allocate the risks of the transaction between the parties to the contract. Finally, the agreement should contain a mechanism for resolving disputes relating to the contract.

This chapter explored the general obligations that parties undertake, some of the things that can go wrong, and what managers may do about breaches of contract. The emphasis of this chapter was on preventive law: what managers can do to anticipate problems and control the course of events.

As the world moves toward one interdependent economy, managers should be able to dictate their own contractual destinies with increasing success. Freedom of contract is one of the central features of the new law merchant. With this freedom comes an ability to operate in a business-oriented manner within the various national legal systems touching upon international transactions.

7.7 QUESTIONS FOR DISCUSSION

1. Wildcat, Inc., an Oklahoma corporation, recently heard of an opportunity to provide several hundred thousand dollars worth of oil field equipment over 5 years to a firm in Siberia. Make a list of the kinds of circumstances Wildcat's chief negotiator should consider before beginning negotiations, and suggest some general ideas of ways to deal with these issues.

2. Neal-Cooper contracted to purchase potash from Texas Gulf Sulfur (TGS). TGS planned to fill the order from its Canadian mines. A new Canadian regulation fixed minimum prices for the sale of potash at a level above the contract price. TGS could fill the order from U.S. mines, but at a loss. If TGS claims to be excused from performance on this contract, how would a court rule? Would it make a difference if the court applied U.S. law, Canadian law, or the CISG? Explain.

3. Discuss the reasons a business in the United Kingdom or in Japan might choose to have its contract disputes tried in the United States.

4. Compare the New York Convention with the Uniform Enforcement of Foreign Money Judgments Act found in Chapter 2. What are the similarities or differences? Should it be more difficult to enforce arbitration awards than court judgments?

7.8 FURTHER READINGS

E. Alley, "International Arbitration: The Alternative of the Stockholm Chamber of Commerce," 22 *The International Lawyer*, 837–844 (1988).

O. Gonzalez, "Remedies under the U.N. Convention for the International Sale of Goods," 2 *International Tax and Business Lawyer*, 79–100 (1984).

Charles Norberg, *Inter-American Commercial Arbitration*, International Chamber of Commerce/Oceana Publications, New York, 1992.

M. Rapsomanikas, "Frustration of Contract in International and Comparative Law," 18 *Duquesne Law Review*, 551–605 (1980).

LETTERS OF CREDIT

8.1 INTRODUCTION

When businesspeople negotiate contracts for the sale of goods, services, or technology, one of the major topics for discussion will always be the method of payment. One choice would be for the buyer to pay cash on delivery, but distance generally doesn't make this practical. Another option is for the seller to grant credit terms to a buyer. Obviously, sellers don't tend to see this as a desirable option, particularly with buyers they don't know well, or from whom the seller might have trouble collecting the money. As the last chapter discussed, a third option, found where currency can't be used easily, would be countertrade. The most widespread choice, however, is the use of letters of credit. Because they are so important in international commerce, managers in every field of international business need a thorough understanding of the way letters of credit work.

Merchants and traders have used various forms of letters of credit since the 12th century. There is even some evidence that traders in ancient Greece, Rome, Phoenicia, and Egypt may have used letters of credit to conduct trade. For nearly 3000 years, letters of credit have provided businesses with a convenient, flexible, and reliable way of financing international trade. More recently, banks have developed new uses for letters of credit, as ways to provide guarantees of contract performance. Today, both buyers and sellers of goods and services use letters of credit to reduce the risks of nonpayment and nonperformance in international transactions.

This chapter examines the two primary forms of letters of credit: documentary letters of credit and standby letters of credit. The documentary letter of credit reduces the seller's risk that the buyer will not pay for goods. In contrast, buyers of goods and services use standby letters of credit essentially like insurance policies, to reduce the risk that a seller will not perform under a contract. Both kinds of letters of credit are ways that parties to a contract negotiate who will bear the risks of breach of contract.

8.2 GOVERNING LAW

In the United States, Article 5 of the Uniform Commercial Code governs both documentary and standby letters of credit. However, many letters of credit refer to a document known as the Uniform Customs and Practices (UCP). The UCP is a compilation of international banking practices with respect to letters of credit, published by the International Chamber of Commerce in Paris. Although it has not been enacted as law anywhere, bankers in all countries regularly use the UCP to govern letters of credit. In the United States, New York, Alabama, Arizona, and Missouri have all amended the UCC to provide that where the parties to a letter of credit designate the UCP as governing, the UCP will supersede the UCC. In most cases, the UCC and the UCP are very similar in substance.

8.3 DOCUMENTARY LETTERS OF CREDIT

Suppose that a buyer and a seller stand face-to-face to transact business. The seller has the opportunity to discover the buyer's ability to pay before delivery. The buyer, in turn, can inspect the goods before making payment. Most domestic transactions don't take place face-to-face, but the seller can still learn about the buyer's ability to pay from several different credit bureaus, banks, or other businesses that have dealt with the buyer. The buyer usually still has the opportunity to inspect the goods before making payment.

In an international transaction, the distance between buyer and seller, as well as the different dynamics of the foreign market, increases the risk to the seller. What if the seller ships the goods but the buyer never pays? The seller may have to engage a lawyer abroad to sue for payment in an unfamiliar (and in some cases unfriendly) legal system. What if the buyer rejects the goods? The seller may be forced to try to find another buyer in an unfamiliar market or pay expensive shipping costs to bring the goods home for resale.

One method of reducing the seller's risk would be to demand payment before shipment, but few buyers would agree to pay without some indication that the goods will conform to the contract. The documentary letter of credit is a compromise between payment on delivery and total prepayment. It allows the seller to be paid as soon as the goods are shipped, yet gives the buyer some assurance that the goods are en route and will conform to the contract. A letter of credit acts as a substitute for cash. As such, its requirements need to be carefully and clearly defined, so all parties to a contract know whether or not it is effective.

ELEMENTS

Initially, a letter of credit may look like a very complex way of making a contract payment. It generally involves four parties: the buyer and the seller and two banks. It requires the flow of many different documents among the parties. It also requires attention to detail by all the parties, and what may initially seem like harsh legal doctrines. If you dissect the transaction, however, you will see that all of the pieces contribute to the whole, and that the seemingly harsh legal rules provide valuable protections for everyone involved. Figure 8-1 illustrates the relationship of the parties to a typical documentary letter of credit. As you read the materials that follow, trace the actions of the parties, using the diagram.

The letter of credit begins in the contract between the buyer and the seller. The seller agrees to deliver goods in return for a proper document, known as the letter of credit. The top of the diagram shows the contract between the buyer and the seller.

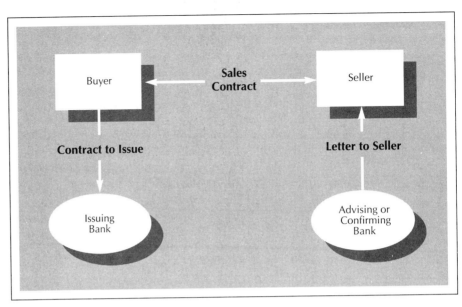

FIGURE 8-1   The Parties to a Letter of Credit

The buyer's next step is to go to its bank, usually in its own country, to obtain a letter of credit. Technically, a letter of credit is a contract between an issuer—usually a bank—and its customer—the buyer. The bank promises to pay the amount of the credit to the seller when the seller presents certain specified documents. The documents generally include a negotiable bill of lading showing that the goods have been shipped, invoices, and packing lists. The required documents also often include insurance certificates, export licenses, and inspection certificates, showing that an independent inspection company has determined that the goods shipped conform to the contract description. The buyer and seller generally negotiate what documents will be necessary when they negotiate their original contract. The documents are extremely important, as they provide the only real protection for the buyer from the seller's mistakes or fraud. The original letter of credit contract is shown on the left side of Figure 8-1.

A letter of credit can be revocable, but in most cases it is irrevocable once issued. The UCC does not address what happens if the letter of credit is silent as to its revocability, but the UCP states that credits will be deemed revocable unless they clearly indicate their irrevocability [UCP Art. 7(c)]. Since the seller generally doesn't want the buyer to be able to revoke a letter of credit once issued, it should specify in the contract for the sale of goods that the buyer must obtain an irrevocable letter of credit.

The third part of the letter of credit transaction, noted at the bottom of Figure 8-1, is getting another bank to advise or confirm the letter of credit. In international transactions, the buyer's bank will probably be located in a different country than that of the seller. The seller usually asks the buyer to get a second bank, close to the seller, to advise or confirm the issued letter. There is a legal difference in the two terms. An advising bank will help the seller collect on the credit by acting as a conduit to the issuing bank. In contrast, a confirming bank undertakes an independent obligation to pay on the letter of credit upon the seller's presentation of the appropriate documents. It is easier for the seller to collect on the letter of credit when the seller's local bank is a confirming bank. The legal differences are noted below.

> UCC Sec. 5-107 *Advice of Credit; Confirmation; Error in Statement of Terms.*
> (1) Unless otherwise specified an advising bank by advising a credit issued by another bank does not assume any obligation to honor drafts drawn or demands for payment made under the credit but it does assume obligation for the accuracy of its own statement.
> (2) A confirming bank by confirming a credit becomes directly obligated on the credit to the extent of its confirmation as though it were its issuer and acquires the rights of an issuer. . . .

The advising or confirming bank issues a letter to the seller restating the terms of the original letter of credit and indicating that it has advised or confirmed the issuing bank's terms. That relationship is illustrated on the right of Figure 8-1.

Once the seller has a letter of credit in hand, it will proceed to ship the goods. In the process, the seller will obtain all the documents required by the terms of the letter. To obtain payment, the seller brings the specified documents to the confirming bank, along with a draft for the amount of the credit.[1] The bank has three banking days to examine the documents and decide whether to honor the demand for payment (UCC §5-112). Under the UCP, a bank has a reasonable time to make the same decision [UCP Art. 16(c)]. Many courts interpreting the UCP have held that three banking days is the "reasonable time" under the UCP.

The banker examines the documents carefully to ensure that they conform to the requirements of the letter of credit. If the documents conform, the confirming bank pays the draft, as shown on the right side of Figure 8-2. It then sends the documents to the issuing bank. The issuing bank examines the documents, reimburses the confirming bank, and debits the account or bills its customer, the buyer, as shown along the bottom of Figure 8-2. Upon the buyer's payment, the bank releases the documents to the buyer, who uses the bill of lading to take possession of the goods. The left side and the top of Figure 8-2 illustrate the flow of paper and goods.

---

[1] A draft is an order to a bank or to someone who owes money to pay it. One form of a draft is a check, which is a writing by a depositor to a bank, ordering the bank to pay money to a named person or business or to its order. (See the front of a check for the words "Pay to the Order of. . . .")

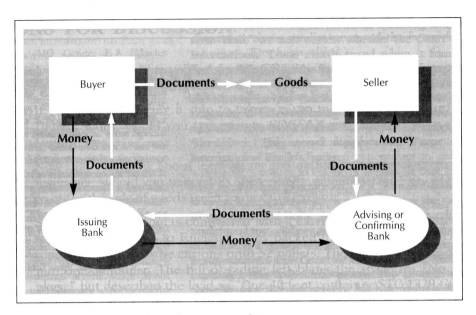

FIGURE 8-2   **The Flow of Goods, Money, and Documents**

THE INDEPENDENCE PRINCIPLE

The key feature of the documentary letter of credit is that payment for goods is made against documents, not against delivery. The letter of credit is a separate contract, independent of the underlying contract for the sale of goods. A seller can comply with the terms of a letter of credit and still breach the contract for the sale of goods. The banker's sole obligation is to use care in examining the documents "so as to ascertain that on their face they appear to comply with the terms of the credit" (UCC §5-109). As long as the documents conform to those the letter of credit calls for, the seller will be paid. Whether the goods actually conform to the contract is irrelevant to the banker's inquiry.

UNIFORM CUSTOMS AND PRACTICES (1983 REV.)

ARTICLE 3

Credits, by their nature, are separate transactions from the sales or other contract(s) on which they may be based and banks are in no way concerned with or bound by such contract(s) even if any reference whatsoever to such contract is included in the credit.

ARTICLE 4

In credit operations all parties concerned deal in documents, and not in goods, services, and/or other performances to which the documents may relate.

The documentary nature of the letter of credit raises several questions. How strictly do the documents need to conform to the letter of credit? What happens when the instructions in the letter of credit are unclear? What happens when the seller tries to use a letter of credit to defraud the buyer?

STRICT COMPLIANCE

The traditional approach to the law of letters of credit has been to require documents to conform exactly to the letter of credit. Bankers may reject claims for payment for virtually any variation from the words of the credit. Lord Sumner of Great Britain stated the rule and its rationale:

> There is no room for documents which are almost the same, or which will do just as well. Business could not proceed securely on any other lines. The bank's branch abroad, which knows nothing officially of the details of the transaction thus financed, cannot take upon itself to decide what will do well enough and what will not. If it does as it is told, it is safe; if it declines to do anything else, it is safe; if it departs from the conditions laid down, it acts at its own risk.[2]

A banker examining letter of credit documents is not expected to know abbreviations or equivalencies commonly used in different industries. Nor does the banker need to make any investigation into seemingly innocent discrepancies between the presented documents and the letter of credit. The following case illustrates the trouble that follows even a single typographical error in the seller's documents.

BEYENE v. IRVING TRUST CO.

762 F.2d 4 (2d Cir. 1985)

FACTS:
Beyene contracted to sell two prefabricated houses to Mohammed Sofan, a resident of the Yemen Arab Republic. Sofan financed the purchases with a letter of credit issued by the Yemen Bank for Reconstruction and Development (YBRD). YBRD designated Irving Trust as the confirming bank. When Irving received the documents called for by the letter of credit, it noticed that the bill of lading listed the party for the shipping company to notify

upon arrival of the houses as Mohammed Soran, not Mohammed Sofan. Irving refused to pay Beyene, citing the discrepancy between the bill of lading and the letter of credit. The district court ruled in favor of Irving and Beyene appealed.

ISSUE:
Does the misspelling of Sofan's name in the bill of lading give Irving the right to refuse to pay the letter of credit?

---

[2]*Equitable Trust Co. of New York v. Dawson Partners, Ltd.,* (1927) 27 Ll. L. Rep. 49, 52.

RESULT:

Yes. Judgment in favor of Irving affirmed.

REASONS:

. . . The terms of a letter of credit generally require the beneficiary of the letter to submit to the issuing bank documents such as an invoice and a bill of lading to provide "the accredited buyer [with] some assurance that he will receive the goods for which he bargained and arranged payment." H. Harfield, *Bank Credits and Acceptances* 57 (5th ed. 1974). The issuing bank, or a bank that acts as a confirming bank for the issuer, takes on an absolute duty to pay the amount of the credit to the beneficiary, so long as the beneficiary complies with the terms of the letter. In order to protect the issuing or confirming bank, this absolute duty does not arise unless the terms of the letter have been complied with strictly. Literal compliance is generally "essential so as not to impose an obligation upon the bank that it did not undertake and so as not to jeopardize the bank's right to indemnity from its customer." *Voest-Alpine International Corp. v. Chase Manhattan Bank,* 707 F.2d at 683; *see* H. Harfield, *Letters of Credit* 57–59

(1979). While some variations in a bill of lading might be so insignificant as not to relieve the issuing or confirming bank of its obligations to pay . . . we agree with the district court that the misspelling in the bill of lading of Sofan's name as "Soran" was a material discrepancy that entitled Irving to refuse to honor the letter of credit. First, this is not a case where the name intended is unmistakably clear despite what is obviously a typographical error, as might be the case if, for example, "Smith" were misspelled "Smithh." Nor have appellants claimed that in the Middle East "Soran" would obviously be recognized as an inadvertent misspelling of the surname "Sofan." Second, "Sofan" was not a name that was inconsequential to the document, for Sofan was the person to whom the shipper was to give notice of the arrival of the goods, and the misspelling of his name could well have resulted in his nonreceipt of the goods and his justifiable refusal to reimburse Irving for the credit. (Indeed, the record includes a telex from Beyene, stating that Sofan had not been notified when the goods arrived in YAR . . . .) In these circumstances, the district court was entirely correct . . . .

BUYER'S INSPECTION

The buyer authorizing payment before receiving the goods could be understandably nervous about the quality of the goods and whether they will conform to the contract description. In some cases, buyers will negotiate into their contracts with the seller a provision calling for an inspection by an independent inspection firm. A certificate from the inspection company is then one of the documents the seller must present in order to obtain payment on the letter of credit.

An inspection certificate from a reputable inspection firm substantially reduces the buyer's risk that the goods it has already paid for will not conform to the contract. However, the buyer must state exactly what it wishes the inspection firm to certify, and must spell out the precise terms of the certification in the letter of credit. As with all other documents, the banker has no obligation to look beyond the face of the documents to the facts of the transaction. The *Banco Español* case illustrates the wrong way to handle the inspection process and the perils of leaving loose ends in the contract and the letter of credit. Note that the issue in this case is not whether the seller shipped the right goods, but whether the documents were those called for by the letter of credit.

BANCO ESPAÑOL DE CREDITO v. STATE STREET BANK AND TRUST CO.

385 F.2d 230 (2d Cir. 1967)

FACTS:

Lawrence, an American clothing dealer, contracted to buy raincoats, beach jackets, knit shirts, and cardigans from two Spanish sellers. State Street Bank issued two letters of credit to pay for the goods. Banco Español was the advising bank on the letters of credit. The letters of credit required signed invoices, customs invoices, full sets of on-board clean bills of lading, and inspection certificates. At the time of issuance, the contract and letter of credit did not name an inspector.

After several months of negotiations, the buyer and seller amended the letters of credit to require a certificate from the inspection firm of Supervigilancia Sociedad General de Control S.A. (Supervigilancia), certifying that "the goods are in conformity with the order." The parties did not specify what documents constituted the order, although the buyer sent documents entitled "order" and "stock sheets" to the seller. On the "stock sheets" the buyer noted, "Coats [and jackets] to be as sample inspected in Spain." The parties then engaged in several weeks of telexed communications concerning the goods and the inspection.

Faced with a deadline under the letter of credit, Supervigilancia inspected the goods and issued certificates. The first part of each certificate stated that the goods conformed with the conditions stipulated in the "order-stock-sheets," based upon the sworn statement of the seller that the samples it provided to Supervigilancia corresponded to those seen by the buyer in Spain. The second part of each certificate stated that the seller required Supervigilancia to issue each certificate "under reserves," not as to the quality of the goods, but as to the underlying contract dispute between the buyer and the seller. Banco Español examined the documents and paid the Spanish sellers. State Street refused to reimburse Banco Español, stating that the inspection certificates did not conform to the letters of credit.

The district court ruled in favor of State Street, finding three defects in the certificates: (1) that

they certified that the goods conformed to "conditions," not to the order; (2) that the "order-stock-sheet" might have been different than the order; and (3) that the certificate was based on samples provided by the seller.

ISSUE:

Did the inspection certificate conform to the requirements of the letter of credit?

RESULT:

Yes. District court decision reversed.

REASONS:

What we face here is a matter of procedure which can in the first instance be structured by the purchasing party. How may a buyer in the international market place be assured before payment that his purchase as delivered is of the quality agreed upon by the parties? As buyers become more concerned about quality, this issue is likely to become more important. . . .

. . . [T]he buyer here—Lawrence—was striving to assure the delivery of quality goods. To be sure, it deliberately postponed the problem when it caused the letters of credit to be issued without resolving the question of the inspecting agent. Then it naively sought to have the sellers accept one of its own representatives. It had long since sown the seeds of dispute by sending to the sellers both "stock sheets" which were really orders and "orders" which were merely preliminary papers. When it finally reached agreement with the seller as to an inspecting agency, it neglected to specify precisely how it would conduct the inspection operation, leaving only the bland instruction that the goods must conform to orders. And, so far as the inspecting agency was concerned, the orders merely referred to samples that might very well have been inspected in Spain at some past time.

Consequently, when faced on the eve of the shipping deadline both with a barrage of contradictory telegrams from the buyer and with samples which the sellers under oath stated "corresponded" with samples approved earlier by the buyer's representative in Barcelona, Supervigilancia had to act to the dissatisfaction of one of the parties to the basic contract. That it took the word, under oath, of the seller as to the appropriateness of the sample is no more than any inspector must ordinarily do. Unless the buyer is physically present (and Lawrence presumably could have arranged this during the frenetic two week period of cable traffic), the inspector must take someone's word that he is judging by the proper samples. . . . We see no significant difference in Supervigilancia being told by the manufacturers that the samples were those approved by the buyer and being told that they "corresponded" to such samples. Webster's Dictionary (3d Int'l ed.) gives such meanings of "correspond" as "in agreement," "conformity," "equivalent," "match," "equal." . . .

To hold otherwise—that a buyer could frustrate an international transaction on the eve of fulfillment by a challenge to authenticity of sample—would make vulnerable many such arrangements where third parties are vested by buyers with inspection responsibilities but where, apart from their own competence and integrity, there is no iron clad guarantee of the sample itself. As for the argument that Supervigilancia's finding that the goods conform "to the conditions stipulated [sic] on the Order-Stock-sheets" is a meaningful variance from the terms of the letters of credit, we confess to semantic myopia. "The conditions" mean, as we read the certificates, all the conditions, hence the order itself. As for the dual use by the agency of the words "Order-Stock-sheets," we have already indicated both the nature and cause of the confusion and conclude that Supervigilancia acted solomonically in borrowing the substance of the stock sheets and the label of the "orders." We do not see how it could have been done otherwise.

The remaining contention that "under reserves" has some mysterious meaning which infects the entire certificate is not borne out by the inapposite cases cited to us and is directly refuted by the limiting language immediately following— "not as far as the goods are concerned." Further reading of the document indicates clearly that the phrase was directed to the underlying dispute between buyer and seller, which could not be the concern of the advising bank.

Banco Español holds two lessons for managers who use letters of credit to facilitate their international transactions. The first is that dealing with the details of a transaction is important. The problems of this case might not have appeared had the parties taken the time while they were still getting along well to specify the inspector and what would be inspected. Secondly, the case should tell managers that they will probably have to pay a letter of credit even when there are serious problems with the underlying contract. Like cash, once the letter of credit gets to the seller, it will be difficult to retrieve it.

FRAUD

A buyer, particularly one who is dealing with an unfamiliar seller, may be worried about paying money but receiving no goods or worthless goods. Because the letter of credit calls for payment against documents and because bankers examining documents have no obligation to examine the underlying transaction, an unscrupulous seller can defraud a buyer relatively easily. A seller might fill cartons with worthless material, then forge shipping documents showing shipment of the contract goods. Or it might simply forge shipping documents, but send no goods. The seller might also persuade a shipper to back-date documents to make a transaction meet a shipment deadline. Or a thief could steal valid documents from a seller, then present them to a bank for payment. In each of these instances, a bank could be faced with a demand for payment in the face of a notification of fraud from its customer.

UNIFORM COMMERCIAL CODE §5-114.
ISSUER'S DUTY AND PRIVILEGE TO HONOR; RIGHT
TO REIMBURSEMENT

(1) An issuer must honor a draft or demand for payment which complies with the terms of the relevant credit regardless of whether the goods or documents conform to the underlying contract for sale or other contract between the customer and the beneficiary. The issuer is not excused from honor of such a draft or demand by reason of an additional general term that all documents must be satisfactory to the issuer, but an issuer may require that specified documents must be satisfactory to it.

(2) Unless otherwise agreed when documents appear on their face to comply with the terms of a credit but a required document does not in fact conform to the warranties made on negotiation or transfer of a document of title (Section 7-507) or is forged or fraudulent or there is fraud in the transaction:

(a) the issuer must honor the draft or demand for payment if honor is demanded by a negotiating bank or other holder of the draft or demand which has taken the draft or demand under the credit and under circumstances which would make it a holder in due course (Section 3-302) and in an appropriate case would make it a person to whom a document of title has been duly negotiated (Section 7-502) or a bona fide purchaser of a certificated security (Section 8-302); and

(b) in all other cases as against its customer, an issuer acting in good faith may honor the draft or demand for payment despite notification from the customer of fraud, forgery or other defect not apparent on the face of the documents but a court of appropriate jurisdiction may enjoin such honor.

Under the UCC, the bank has the option to honor or to dishonor a draft on a letter of credit where its customer informs it of fraud in the transaction. Note, however, that the law does not require the bank to dishonor the draft, even if it gets prior notice of fraud. The only means a customer has to force the bank to stop payment on the letter of credit is to seek an injunction in court.

Under some circumstances, a seller may create a draft to use to obtain payment, then negotiate the draft or a shipping document to a third party who may become a holder in due course.[3] When a bank is faced with a

---

[3]A draft is one kind of negotiable instrument, which can be negotiated to a third party. If the third party takes the instrument for value, in good faith, and without notice of any claims against the instrument or defenses to the instrument, it will get the status of holder in due course. Holders in due course take negotiable instruments free of virtually all defenses, including most forms of fraud.

payment demand from a holder in due course, it must pay, even if the underlying transaction is tainted by fraud. The following case illustrates the way courts will examine claims of fraud in the transaction.

UNITED BANK, LTD. v. CAMBRIDGE SPORTING GOODS CORP.

41 N.Y.2d 254, 392 N.Y.S.2d 265, 360 N.E.2d 943
Court of Appeals of New York, 1976

FACTS:

Cambridge Sporting Goods contracted with Duke Sports, a Pakistani corporation, to purchase 27,936 pairs of boxing gloves for $42,576.80. To finance the sale, Cambridge opened an irrevocable letter of credit for the purchase price with Manufacturers Hanover Trust Company in New York. Duke's banks in Pakistan, United Bank and the Muslim Commercial Bank, confirmed the letters of credit.

Duke later told Cambridge that it could not meet the delivery deadline under the contract. It sought an extension of the date for delivery of the gloves, which Cambridge denied because it had resale commitments. Cambridge then cancelled the contract and requested the return of the letter of credit. Cambridge also informed United of the cancellation.

Nearly a month later, Cambridge was informed that Manufacturers had received documents and drafts drawing on the letters of credit. Duke had presented the drafts to United and Muslim, who had paid, then sent them to Manufacturers. An inspection of the goods showed that Duke had shipped "old unpadded, ripped and mildewed gloves," rather than the new gloves called for by the contract. Cambridge sued Duke and Manufacturers in state court, obtaining an injunction against payment.

The two Pakistani banks sued to obtain payment on the drafts, asserting that they were holders in due course and thus were entitled to payment despite any defenses Cambridge might have against Duke. The trial court ruled in favor of the banks.

ISSUE:

Were the Pakistani banks holders in due course?

RESULT:

No. Judgment reversed.

REASONS:

The history of the dispute between the various parties involved in this case reveals that Cambridge has in a prior, separate proceeding successfully enjoined Manufacturers from paying the drafts and has attached the proceeds of the drafts. . . . The petitioning banks do not dispute the validity of the prior injunction nor do they dispute the delivery of worthless merchandise. Rather, on this appeal they contend that as holders in due course they are entitled to the proceeds of the drafts irrespective of any fraud on the part of Duke. Although precisely speaking there was no specific finding of fraud in the transaction by either of the courts below, their determinations were based on that assumption. The evidentiary facts are not disputed and we hold upon the facts as established, that the shipment of old, unpadded, ripped and mildewed gloves rather than the new boxing gloves as ordered by Cambridge constituted fraud in the transaction within the meaning of subdivision (2) of section 5-114. . . .

If the petitioning banks are holders in due course they are entitled to recover the proceeds of the drafts but if such status cannot be demonstrated their petition must fail. The parties are in agreement that section 3-307 of the code governs the pleading and proof of holder in due course status. . . . Thus, a presenter of drafts drawn under a letter of credit must prove that it took the drafts for value, in good faith and without notice of the underlying fraud in the transaction. . . .

The courts below erroneously concluded that Cambridge was required to show that the banks had participated in or were themselves guilty of the seller's fraud in order to establish a defense to payment. But, it was not necessary that Cambridge prove that United and Muslim actually participated in the fraud, since merely notice of the fraud would have deprived the Pakistani banks of holder in due course status.

. . . [W]e conclude that the banks have not satisfied the burden of proving that they qualified in all respects as holders in due course, by any affirmative proof.

The *United Bank* case raises some interesting problems for managers. Here, the buyer was successful in stopping payment on the letter of credit. However, the circumstances under which a buyer can succeed are very limited. If the seller sells its right to receive the money due from the letter of credit to an innocent third party, the buyer will have to pay even if it receives worthless trash. Cambridge was wise to notify the confirming banks so that they could not take the documents in innocence, and lucky in that Duke presented the documents to a bank that already had notice of the fraud.

The UCP is silent on the problem of fraud in the transaction, but courts in other countries have followed the lead of the UCC. One interesting question pertains to notice of fraud committed by a party other than the seller. In a recent English case, *The American Accord*,[4] the House of Lords decided that fraud in the transaction did not extend to third party actions. Here, a loading broker back-dated documents to show that goods were loaded before a shipping deadline, when in fact the goods were loaded past the deadline. However, the seller had no knowledge of the fraudulent act. The British view has been criticized as inviting sharp sellers to involve third parties for the purpose of committing fraud.

8.4 STANDBY LETTERS OF CREDIT

Standby letters of credit are a relatively new use for letters of credit. They exist in large part because American (and Japanese) banks cannot legally engage in insurance activities. In most other countries, banks will issue guarantees on behalf of their customers. Standby letters of credit look much more like insurance policies, performance bonds, or repayment guarantees than like true letters of credit.

Standby letters of credit generally take the form of a bank's promise to pay a beneficiary in the event of a contract default by the bank's customer. Suppose that a French company is purchasing a new computer system

---

[4]*United City Merchants (Investments) v. Royal Bank of Canada (The American Accord)*, [1982] 2 All. E.R. 720.

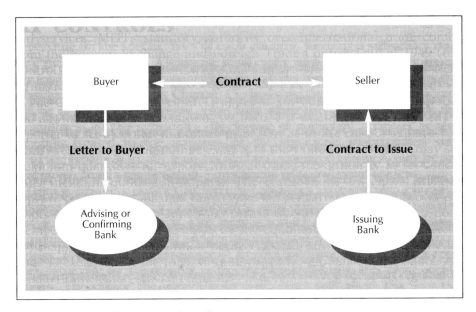

FIGURE 8-3   Standby Letters of Credit

from   an
American company. The buyer may want some assurance that it really will
get what it is paying for, especially when sophisticated installation is part
of the package. It may ask the American company to provide a standby letter of credit. If the Americans don't fulfill their contract, the French buyer
will draw on the letter of credit to prevent loss. The standby letter of credit,
like a regular letter of credit, can be confirmed; in this case, probably by a
French bank. Figure 8-3 shows the way standby letters of credit work.

DIFFERENCES FROM DOCUMENTARY LETTERS OF CREDIT

Standby letters of credit differ from regular letters of credit in three significant ways. First, regular letters of credit are payment methods. In contrast,
standby letters of credit carry the assumption that if all goes well, they will
not be used by the parties. Under ordinary circumstances, a bank does not
pay a standby letter of credit.

Second, regular letters of credit involve only financial obligations, usually for the purchase of goods. The standby letter of credit, however, is used
to secure both financial and nonfinancial obligations, including, for example, construction contracts, activity in the commercial paper market, commodity futures contracts, and contracts for services.

Third, the two kinds of letters of credit differ in the kinds of documents
that trigger payment by a bank. A beneficiary of a regular letter of credit
demands payment by presenting relatively standard commercial documents, such as bills of lading, invoices, packing lists, or inspection certifi-

cates. The documentation required for payment on standby letters, though, is very broad, ranging from a simple statement by the buyer that the seller is in default (sometimes called a "suicide credit") to elaborate certifications by third parties or arbitrators.

The international banking community spent several years discussing whether to treat standby letters of credit as letters of credit or as contract guarantees. Both the UCC and the UCP now treat standby letters of credit as one form of a letter of credit. Thus, like regular letters of credit, a beneficiary must be in strict compliance with the terms of the letter in order to demand payment. Also like regular letters of credit, the credit is documentary in nature. The banker has no obligation to look behind the certification to find out whether its customer has in fact breached its contract. If the beneficiary presents documents conforming to the terms of the letter of credit, the issuing bank must pay and the bank's customer must reimburse the bank. Banks need not, and should not, look beyond the terms of the letter of credit. A standby letter of credit is independent of the underlying contract in the same way that a regular letter of credit is independent.

FRAUD IN THE TRANSACTION

The biggest problem courts have faced in examining standby letters of credit is fraud in the transaction. Although the same rules that apply to regular letters of credit apply to standby letters of credit, standby letters of credit are found in such a broad range of circumstances that courts may have some difficulty applying the rules. When a beneficiary of a standby letter of credit (usually a buyer) demands payment, it is certifying that the bank's customer is in breach of contract. The banker has no obligation to look behind the certification to see if its customer really has breached the contract. However, in some cases the bank's customer may claim that the buyer is fraudulently stating that a breach has occurred and may seek to stop payment on the letter of credit. Courts are generally unsympathetic to such claims of fraud, although in unusual circumstances they may enjoin payment on the standby letter of credit. Compare the following two cases arising out of the Iranian revolution in 1979.

AMERICAN BELL INTERNATIONAL, INC. v. ISLAMIC REPUBLIC OF IRAN

474 F. Supp. 420 (S.D.N.Y. 1979)

FACTS:

In 1978, American Bell International (Bell) contracted to provide consulting services and telecommunications equipment to the Imperial Government of Iran. Iran made a substantial down payment, which it secured by requiring Bell to obtain a standby letter of credit for $38,800,000 from Manufacturers Hanover Bank, confirmed by

Bank Iranshahr. The letter of credit provided for payment upon receipt of a Tested Telex, signed by an officer of Bank Iranshahr, stating that the War Ministry of the government of Iran had requested payment under the letter of credit, and that Bank Iranshahr had made such payment.

The contract between Bell and Iran provided that the down payment would be refundable according to a formula specified in the contract, and that Iran had the right to demand the return of the down payment at any time. The contract further provided that all disputes arising under it were to be resolved in Iranian courts, under Iranian law.

When the Iranian revolution occurred in 1978–1979, the government stopped payments on the contract. Bell, left with mounting unpaid bills, stopped performance. The new government then attempted to draw down the remaining $30,200,000 on the standby letter of credit. Bell sought an injunction against payment in the federal district court.

ISSUES:

Has Bell shown fraud in the transaction? Is Bell entitled to enjoin payment on the standby letter of credit?

RESULT:

No. No. Bell's motion for an injunction denied.

REASONS:

. . . Plaintiff contends that the alleged repudiation, viewed in connection with its demand for payment of the Letter of Credit, supplies that basis from which only one inference—fraud—can be drawn. Again, we remain unpersuaded.

Plaintiff's argument requires us to presume bad faith on the part of the Iranian government. It requires us further to hold that that government may not rely on the plain terms of the consulting contract and the Letter of Credit arrangements with Bank Iranshahr and Manufacturers providing for immediate repayment of the down payment upon demand, without regard to cause. On the evidence before us, fraud is no more inferable than an economically rational decision by the government to recoup its down payment, as it is entitled to do under the consulting contract

and still dispute its liabilities under that Contract. . . .

To be sure, Bell faces substantial hardships upon denial of its motion. Should Manufacturers pay the demand, Bell will immediately become liable to Manufacturers for $30.2 million, with no assurance of recouping those funds from Iran for the the services performed. . . .

But Manufacturers would face at least as great a loss, and perhaps a greater one, were we to grant relief. Upon Manufacturers' failure to pay, Bank Iranshahr could initiate a suit on the Letter of Credit and attach $30.2 million of Manufacturers' assets in Iran. In addition, it could seek to hold Manufacturers liable for consequential damages beyond that sum resulting from the failure to make timely payment. Finally, there is not [sic] guarantee that Bank Iranshahr or the government, in retaliation for Manufacturers' recalcitrance, will not nationalize additional Manufacturers' assets in Iran in amounts which counsel, at oral argument, represented to be far in excess of the amount in controversy here. Apart from a greater monetary exposure flowing from an adverse decision, Manufacturers faces a loss of credibility in the international banking community that could result from its failure to make good on a letter of credit. . . .

. . . Bell, a sophisticated multinational enterprise well advised by competent counsel, entered into these arrangements with its corporate eyes open. It knowingly and voluntarily signed a contract allowing the Iranian government to recoup its down payment on demand, without regard to cause. . . . One who reaps the rewards of commercial arrangements must also accept their burdens. One such burden in this case, voluntarily accepted by Bell, was the risk that demand might be made without cause on the funds constituting the down payment. To be sure, the sequence of events that led up to that demand may well have been unforeseeable when the contracts were signed. To this extent, both Bell and Manufacturers have been made the unwitting and innocent victims of tumultuous events beyond their control. But, as between two innocents, the party who undertakes by contract the risk of political uncertainty and governmental caprice must bear the consequences when the risk comes home to roost.

ITEK CORPORATION v. FIRST NATIONAL BANK OF BOSTON

730 F.2d 19 (1st Cir. 1984)

FACTS:

Itek entered into a contract in 1977 to provide high-technology optical equipment to the War Ministry of the government of Iran. Among the contract provisions was a *force majeure* clause stating that in the event of war or natural disaster, or if the United States cancelled necessary export licenses for the equipment, either party could cancel the contract. The contract also provided that all disputes would be settled in Iranian courts, using Iranian law.

Iran required Itek to obtain two kinds of guarantees from Bank Melli in Iran. The first guaranteed Iran's down payment of $4.5 million, while the second guaranteed Itek's satisfactory performance in the amount of $2.25 million (10 percent of the total contract price). Iran could demand payment on the guarantees simply by submitting a written request for payment to Bank Melli. The guarantees were secured by standby letters of credit issued by the First National Bank of Boston (FNBB).

In April 1979, the U.S. government revoked Itek's licenses to export the contract goods. Itek informed Iran of the *force majeure* situation and negotiated with Iran over the summer. In November 1979, Iranian militants seized the U.S. embassy, taking the embassy staff as hostages. Although Itek continued to apply for licenses to export the contract goods, the applications were denied.

Finally, Itek fully invoked the *force majeure* provisions, notifying Iran that it was cancelling the contract because it could not get export licenses. Shortly thereafter, Bank Melli notified FNBB that Iran had requested payment on the guarantees. It demanded payment on the standby letters of credit, based on its payment to the government of Iran. Bank Melli lost in the district court, then appealed.

ISSUE:

Should the court enjoin payment on the letters of credit due to fraud in the transaction?

RESULT:

Yes. The district court's judgment is affirmed.

REASONS:

The basic legal question in this case is whether the circumstances surrounding Melli's calls on FNBB's letters of credit establish "fraud in the transaction" within the meaning of this U.C.C. provision [5-114(2)]. We answer this question fully aware of the need to interpret the "fraud" provision narrowly. The very object of a letter of credit is to provide a near foolproof method of placing money in the beneficiary's hands when he complies with the terms contained in the letter itself—when he presents, for example, a shipping document that the letter calls for or (as here) a simple written demand for payment. Parties to a contract may use a letter of credit in order to make certain that contractual disputes wend their way toward resolution with money in the beneficiary's pocket rather than in the pocket of the contracting party. Thus, courts typically have asserted that such letters of credit are "independent" of the underlying contract. . . .

Despite these reasons for hesitating to enjoin payment of a letter of credit, the need for an exception is apparent. . . . Thus, courts have stated that the "fraud in the transaction" exception is available only where the beneficiary's conduct has "so vitiated the entire transaction that the legitimate purposes of the independence of the issuer's obligation would no longer be served." . . .

We conclude that the issue before us is whether, given the terms of the contract, the Ministry and in turn Melli have a colorable right to call the "guarantees". . . . If Melli has no plausible or colorable basis under the contract to call for payment of the letters, its effort to obtain the money is fraudulent and payment can be enjoined. The district court found that Itek had met this standard and shown fraud. . . . We agree.

American Bell represents the more typical approach to fraud claims on standby letters of credits. Because the range of documentation and causes for demands is so broad, courts tend to hold the parties to the terms they negotiated. As *American Bell* shows, courts are also concerned about the effect an injunction will have on the certainty of commercial transactions and on the reputation of American banks in the international banking community. The *Recon/Optical* decision may be the best illustration that the judicial response to the commercial problems caused by the Iranian revolution is still not the typical result a seller should expect in standby letter of credit litigation.

RECON/OPTICAL, INC. v. GOVERNMENT OF ISRAEL

816 F.2d 854 (2d Cir. 1987)

FACTS:

Recon/Optical contracted to provide a high-technology aerial reconnaissance system for the Israeli Air Force. The contract provided that all disputes would be settled by arbitration, and that work on the contract would continue pending the arbitrator's decision. The contract also allowed either party to terminate performance in the event of a material breach of contract. In order to receive advance payments from Israel, the contract required Recon to obtain a standby letter of credit. Israel could draw against the letter of credit in amounts not exceeding its advance payment when it certified to the bank "that it was 'entitled' to such amount because of: (i) non-delivery by Seller of a deliverable item hereunder in accordance herewith or (ii) other material breach by Seller of its obligations hereunder."

As work progressed, it became clear that the contract specifications were inadequate. Recon proposed contract modifications, which the Israeli Air Force representative orally accepted. Israel denied the authority of the representative to make changes and refused to pay.

Recon submitted its dispute to arbitration, but also terminated performance, claiming a material breach of the contract. Israel, claiming a material breach by Recon because of the termination of performance, demanded payment of $21.5 million on Recon's standby letter of credit. Recon sued in

federal district court to enjoin payment, lost its suit, and appealed.

ISSUE:

Was the Israeli demand for payment fraudulent?

RESULT:

No. Judgment of the district court affirmed.

REASONS:

In its final argument on the merits, Recon claims that the drawdown must be enjoined as a matter of law under New York's "fraud in the transaction" doctrine. . . . This doctrine is an exception to the general rule that a letter of credit is independent of the underlying obligation it secures . . . and allows a court to enjoin payment under a letter of credit where a drawdown would amount to an "outright fraudulent practice" by the beneficiary. . . .

In *Rockwell*, we stated that "the 'fraud' inheres in first causing the default and then attempting to reap the benefit of the guarantee." . . . In that case, the government of Iran had prevented Rockwell from performing under the contract and then sought to draw against a letter of credit based on that non-performance. No such circumstances exist here. Although the parties dispute the responsibility for the original specifications and increased costs due to modifications, Israel has sought only to have these disputes resolved by the arbitrators as provided in the contract. Whether or not its view of the merits of these disputes is correct, there is no evidence that Israel has acted in bad faith or impeded Recon's continued performance. Far from constituting fraud, a drawdown by Israel under the circumstances is entirely consistent with the parties' contractual intent.

8.5 CONCLUSION

Letters of credit are a useful way for buyers and sellers to shift the risks of nonpayment and nonperformance in contracts. The usual use of a documentary letter of credit is as a means for a buyer to finance the purchase of goods. In international business, the usual use of a standby letter of credit is for a buyer to secure refunds of advance payments for goods or services or to secure the performance of the contract by the seller.

One of the major purposes of letters of credit is to act as a substitute for cash. Thus, if the beneficiary presents documents that conform to the terms of the letter of credit, it will receive payment. Bankers have no obligation to interpret documents or supply missing terms. The only circumstances under which a beneficiary will not receive payment are: (1) if the documents it presents do not conform to the terms of the letter of credit, and (2) if there is fraud in the transaction.

8.6 QUESTIONS FOR DISCUSSION

1. What are the major differences between regular letters of credit and standby letters of credit?

2. Should standby letters of credit be subject to the UCC and UCP, or should they be regulated differently?

3. Suppose you were the bank officer at State Street Bank and Trust when Lawrence approached you about obtaining a letter of credit. Would you have issued the letter of credit on the terms in the case? What advice would you have given Lawrence?

4. Under what circumstances would you recommend that a company agree to a standby letter of credit that is a "suicide credit"? What alternatives would you recommend to avoid the problems of American Bell, Itek, and Recon/Optical?

8.7 FURTHER READINGS

John F. Dolan, *The Law of Letters of Credit*, Warren, Gorham & Lamont, New York, 1984.

"Guide to Documentary Credit Operations," International Chamber of Commerce No. 415, New York, 1985.

M. Zimmett, "Standby Letters of Credit in the Iran Litigation: Two Hundred Problems in Search of a Solution," 16 *Law and Policy in International Business*, 927–962 (1984).

TRANSPORT AND INSURANCE

9.1 INTRODUCTION

In addition to negotiations over price, quantity, specifications, and financing, the parties to an international contract for the sale of goods will also have to arrange transportation and insurance for the goods. The degree of interest each party shows in the issues of transport and insurance generally depends on which party has agreed to bear the risk of loss or delay. As you might suspect after reading Chapter 6, a buyer will be more interested in these arrangements on a shipment contract, and a seller on a destination contract.

Historically, ocean shipping has provided the basis for the legal treatment of most shipping issues in international commerce. However, the technological changes of the last 50 years have revolutionized the entire shipping industry. The development of air freight systems, the containerization of cargo, and computerization have led to what is known as multimodal transportation. For example, a manufacturer in Denver, Colorado, agrees to sell 1000 small electric motors to a buyer in Berlin. The journey begins when a trucker leaves a container at the seller's plant. The seller packs and loads the goods into the container, then seals it. The trucker then takes the container to a rail yard, where a crane lifts the container onto a "piggy-back" flat car. The freight train may then take the goods directly to the port of Galveston, Texas, where a crane will take the container from the railcar and stack it in the hold of a ship. When the ship arrives in the port of Hamburg, Germany, a crane will transfer the container to a waiting railcar or truck, which will take the container directly to the buyer. Because the goods are only packed and unpacked once, there is a far lower risk of damage in transit and of theft or pilferage.

Even in the era of containerization, the laws of ocean shipping still provide much of the framework to resolve transportation disputes. This chapter will look at the structure and laws of ocean shipping, then at the laws governing air cargo transport and multimodal transport, and, finally, will provide an introduction to insurance issues. Most managers do not need to become experts on the intricacies of shipping law, but shipping terms are an important part of every contract negotiation.

9.2 OCEAN SHIPPING

Although a few large companies, like Exxon, have their own in-house shipping businesses to carry company cargo, most international traders find it more cost-effective to arrange for transportation on an as-needed basis. The two most common arrangements are chartering a ship and hiring a common carrier. With a charter, the ship's owner agrees to carry a particular company's goods or allow another company to operate its ship. A common carrier, by contrast, will carry anyone's goods, usually by regularly scheduled vessels.

CHARTER PARTIES

A shipper with large cargoes of goods or commodities may decide to charter an entire ship to take goods to overseas markets. The contract between the shipper and the owner is known as a "charter party." The three main types of charters are voyage charters, time charters, and bareboat charters.

A *voyage charter* involves hiring the ship for a specific voyage. The vessel's owner provides the captain and crew and is responsible for the safe navigation of the vessel.

A *time charter,* as its name indicates, is the hire of a vessel for a specific period of time. The owner again provides the captain and crew, but the ship travels by direction of the charterer. Voyages could be worldwide or the charter could limit voyages to a specific geographic area. The ship may make as many voyages as the charterer directs during the contract time period.

A *bareboat charter,* sometimes known as a demise charter, is also a charter for a specific period of time. However, it operates as a true lease of the ship in that possession and control of the ship pass to the charterer for the duration of the contract. The charterer provides the captain and crew and decides where and when the ship travels. The owner's obligation is to provide a seaworthy vessel at the beginning of the contract period, while the charterer's obligation is to return the vessel in good condition, less normal wear and tear, at the end of the time period.

For all three types of charters, the contract between the charterer and the owner is the subject of relatively free negotiation between the parties, without the regulatory framework affecting common carriers. Voyage charter contracts typically begin by identifying the parties and the vessel, naming the cargo, and setting the voyage and the price. They will contain a specified port of loading, but may give some discretion as to the destination port. The contract may contain a "safe ports" clause, obligating the charterer to unload only at safe ports within a certain specified area. Under a "safe ports" clause, the destination is determined by the bill of lading issued at the time the cargo is loaded. Voyage and time charter contracts also contain provisions covering frustration and impossibility, a provision allowing the owner a lien against the cargo until the freight is paid, and provisions governing loading, unloading, and liability for the costs associated with delay in port (demurrage). These provisions recognize that in both voyage and time charters, the contract covers a complex, ongoing business relationship between the owner, who physically controls the ship's movements, and the charterer, who directs the ship's voyages.

Liability for Damage to Goods

Parties to a charter contract may adjust liability in any way they see fit. Many charter contracts adopt the provisions of the Carriage of Goods by Sea Act (COGSA), which we will discuss later in this chapter. In contracts that do not adopt COGSA, the shipowner has a general duty to provide a seaworthy ship. The concept of seaworthiness includes both a general fitness for ocean travel and a specific fitness to carry the designated cargo. For example, if the cargo is perishable goods, a seaworthy ship might need to have refrigerated holds. A ship that has recently carried one type of chemical would need to be completely cleaned before carrying another, possibly reactive chemical on a later charter. The warranty of seaworthiness applies to all three kinds of charters.

A shipowner is also held liable for loss or damage to cargo under a voyage charter if the ship "deviates" from the scope of the voyage. The doctrine of deviation has a long history in admiralty law. A deviation will be found where the goods are improperly stowed aboard ship or where the ship makes additional interim stops not anticipated by the parties or takes an unusual route.

General Average

One twist on the responsibility of the shipowner for loss or damage involves the ancient admiralty concept of "general average." Suppose that a ship at sea faces an imminent peril, and the only way to save the ship is to jettison some portion of the cargo. When that portion of the cargo is tossed overboard, the ship is saved. Under these circumstances, the shipowner should not have to bear the entire liability for the loss of the goods. Rather, everyone whose cargo was saved and the shipowner contribute proportionately to the owner of the lost cargo, until everyone bears the loss equally. The law of general average has existed since the times of ancient Greece and is common to all maritime nations. While relatively simple in principle, it is quite complex in application. It applies both to charter parties and common carriers.

COMMON CARRIERS

In contrast to a charter party, common carriers are ships that will carry anyone's cargo. The term is not restricted to ships; common carriers exist in all modes of transport. In the United States, well-known common carriers include UPS, Federal Express, North American Van Lines, Conrail, and Sea-Land. A shipper will contract with a common carrier to have a specific load of goods carried to a specific place, usually within a specified time. The ship, train, truck, or plane may be filled by the one shipment, but more likely it will be one of several different orders pooled together for transport. In contrast to charters, the conduct of common carriers is heavily regulated.

THE OCEAN BILL OF LADING

The bill of lading is the contract between the carrier and the shipper. Its terms determine the obligations of the parties. You should also remember that the bill of lading serves two other functions. It is a receipt for the goods, showing that the carrier has taken possession of the cargo, and, if in proper form, it is a negotiable document of title. If the bill of lading is negotiable, the document allows the owner to sell the cargo while it is in transit. Recall that a bill of lading is one of the documents that a seller must present to the bank in order to obtain payment under a letter of credit.

The letter of credit documents in a transaction generally call for a "clean, on-board bill of lading." A bill of lading is clean when it shows language from the carrier that the goods shipped are in "apparent good order and condition." Such language indicates that from all external appearances, the goods are not damaged. When the carrier's employees notice damage such as wet or crushed packaging or visible rust on metal goods, such damage should be noted on the bill of lading, and the bill then is said to be "claused." A bill of lading qualifies as "on board" when it is issued after the goods are loaded onto the vessel. Requiring a clean on-board bill of lading is an important protection for the buyer in international transactions.

Once the carrier issues a bill of lading, its chief legal obligation becomes delivery to the correct party. The carrier must deliver the cargo to the person who holds a properly endorsed negotiable bill of lading or, if the bill is nonnegotiable (a "straight bill"), to the identified party in the bill (usually referred to as the consignee). If the carrier delivers the goods to the wrong party, it is strictly liable to the rightful owner of the goods. The following case demonstrates that even in difficult circumstances, the carrier faces a strict duty to deliver the goods only to an authorized party.

WABCO TRADE CO. v. S.S. INGER SKOU

482 F. Supp. 444 (S.D.N.Y. 1979)

FACTS:

Wabco contracted with a common carrier, GCC, to ship four motor graders from Charleston, South Carolina, to Beirut, Lebanon, aboard the S.S. *Inger Skou*. Constellation, an agent for GCC, prepared a negotiable bill of lading. Due to political fighting in Beirut, the *Inger Skou* unloaded its freight in Piraeus, Greece, in late October 1975. Constellation then sent the following letter to Wabco:

"Dear Sirs:

We very much regret to advise that because of the current state of affairs in Beirut we have been compelled to discharge the above captioned cargo at Piraeus, Greece. While we have taken this step pursuant to our rights under clauses 5 and 6 of the bill of lading, and reserve all of our rights under said bill of lading and those clauses, it is our intention for the time being to bear the expense of storage at the Piraeus Free Zone in the hope that the situation in Beirut will stabilize in the reasonably near future and the cargo can be reloaded onto one of our vessels and transshipped to Beirut. Although we shall pay the cost of storage, all risk during this storage is and will continue to be for the account of cargo.

If there is any change in this arrangement, or if final delivery will in fact have to be made at Piraeus, we shall notify you."

In December Wabco instructed Constellation to hold the cargo in Greece until further notice. Constellation orally agreed and forwarded a copy of Wabco's instructions to GCC. GCC did not reply, but did hold the goods in Greece until March.

In March 1976, without notifying Wabco or the consignee listed on the bill, GCC shipped the graders to Beirut. GCC's Beirut agent stored the graders in a warehouse, from which they were "liberated" by one of the factions involved in the fighting there. They were never recovered.

ISSUE:

Was GCC justified in shipping the goods to Beirut against the shipper's instructions?

RESULT:

No. Whether or not the parties terminated the bill of lading's effect with new instructions, GCC should not have delivered the goods to Beirut.

REASONS:

GCC relies on clauses 6(a) and 7 of the original bill of lading. These clauses permit the carrier to divert cargo to an unscheduled port to avoid risk of damage to the ship, to store the goods at shipper's expense, and to act as forwarding agent in transshipping the goods by any means. GCC urges that it did no more than fulfill its duties under its contract of carriage by discharging the goods in Piraeus, holding them for four months, and then transshipping to Beirut without further notice to Wabco.

[Under the circumstances of this case] the parties agreed to terminate the original bill of lading as of December, 1975. There was a mutual assent to the new arrangement proposed by Wabco whereby GCC would hold the goods in Piraeus until Wabco advised it of further plans. GCC's onshipment of the graders represented not an attempt to comply with its original contract of car-

riage, but rather an inadvertent error in violation of its new agreement.

GCC has further contended that under the Federal Bills of Lading Act, 49 U.S.C. Secs. 81-124, it had no choice but to deliver the goods in accordance with the terms of the bill and that as long as the negotiable bill of lading remained outstanding, it acted at its peril in complying with the instructions of the shipper, Wabco. While GCC had the right to demand the surrender of the bill of lading from Wabco in order to protect itself from liability to a good faith purchaser of the bill, GCC chose not to do so and never questioned Wabco's ownership of the goods or possession of the bill of lading.

Furthermore, Section 90 of the Bills of Lading Act provides:

> Where a carrier delivers goods to one who is not lawfully entitled to the possession of them, the carrier shall be liable to anyone having a right of property or possession in the goods if he delivered the goods [other than to a person in possession of an order bill from the goods indorsed to him] and, though he delivered the goods [to such a person], he shall be so liable if prior to such delivery he—(a) Had been requested by or on behalf of a person having a right of property or possession in the goods, not to make such a delivery. . . .

The Act permits a person having a right of possession in goods to exercise a right of stoppage in transit. If the Carrier delivers goods—even to the holder of a negotiable bill of lading—in violation of the owner's request, it is liable for loss of the goods. Accordingly, even if GCC's contention that the bill of lading was not terminated prior to transshipment were accepted, GCC would still not have been justified in delivering the goods to Beirut, in contravention of Wabco's instructions.

Limiting Liability

The central problem in the law of bills of lading has been attempts by carriers to limit their liability for lost or damaged cargo. In the 19th century, carriers regularly used the fine print of bills of lading to totally remove any liability, even for their own negligent conduct. Protests from shippers resulted in congressional legislation designed to strike a balance between carriers and shippers.

Ocean bills of lading in the United States are regulated by three federal statutes. The first is the Harter Act of 1893 (46 U.S.C. Secs. 190–193). The Harter Act applies to shipments between American ports (coastal shipping) and shipments from American ports to foreign ports. It prohibits carriers from disclaiming liability for their own negligence, but allows them to indicate in a bill of lading that any description of the goods is based on the shipper's representation.

The Harter Act also requires a carrier to issue a bill of lading containing descriptive information, such as identifying marks, number of packages, or quantity, and the apparent condition of the goods. A carrier may use language in a bill of lading such as "shipper's load and count" to avoid liability for goods it never received.

The second law regulating ocean bills of lading is the Pomerene Act of 1916, also known as the Federal Bill of Lading Act (49 U.S.C. Secs. 81–124). The Pomerene Act allows a carrier to avoid liability by using a bill of lading stating that the goods are "said to be" of a certain kind, quality, or condition. The language in the bill of lading controls the liability of the carrier.

The third and most important statute regulating ocean bills of lading is the Carriage of Goods by Sea Act of 1936, or COGSA (46 U.S.C. Secs. 1300–1315). COGSA is the U.S. enactment of a multilateral convention, known as the Hague Convention. Many maritime nations have adopted the Hague rules, so there is some degree of uniformity concerning the law of ocean shipping. Yet, changes in the shipping industry have brought about two efforts to update the Hague Convention that have made some differences in the rules. In 1968, a marine conference amended the Hague rules, in some measure to deal with the rise of containerized shipping. Some nations adopted the new rules, known as the Hague-Visby rules, but the United States did not. In 1978, representatives of seventy-eight nations met at Hamburg, Germany, to create a new uniform law regarding limitations of liability. The Hamburg rules, which went into effect in 1992, have been adopted by many developing countries. The United States, although it signed the treaty creating the Hamburg rules, has not yet enacted them as law.

Today, businesses shipping goods by sea will find that one of the three sets of rules governs their agreements with carriers. COGSA, which is still the law in the United States, applies to all shipments between U.S. and foreign ports. As Chapter 7 noted, parties to a contract to ship goods cannot choose a different law to govern that agreement: if COGSA applies, it is mandatory.

COGSA requires carriers to issue a bill of lading containing two significant pieces of information. The first is that the bill must indicate the quantity of goods, in packages, pieces, number, or weight. The shipper generally furnishes this information, and is liable to the carrier for inaccurate information it provides.

The second kind of information the bill must show is the condition of the goods. Here, usually all the carrier can do is examine the external appearance of the goods. If there appears to be nothing wrong, the carrier notes on the bill that the goods were in "apparent good order and condition." Such a bill of lading is called a "clean bill of lading." If the goods are damaged or the packaging is torn, crushed, water-stained, or otherwise defective, the carrier should note that condition on the bill. Bills of lading with notations of damage are said to be "claused."

The difference in the language of the bill of lading is important. Most sales contracts using letters of credit call for clean bills of lading. That language protects the buyer's interests by indicating that the goods were, as far as one could tell by examining the packaging, undamaged at the time of shipment. A seller who gets a claused bill of lading from a carrier will probably not be able to collect on its letter of credit. The language also helps to fix the blame, and thus the risk of loss, if the goods arrive damaged.

The core of COGSA's regulatory scheme allows a carrier to limit its liability for loss or damage to goods if it meets two obligations. First, the vessel must be seaworthy. A carrier must use *due diligence* to make a vessel seaworthy, including having a proper crew, equipment, and supplies and making the holds safe for the carriage of cargo. The second obligation is for cargo stowage. A carrier must "properly and carefully load, handle, stow, carry, keep, care for, and discharge the goods carried."

Once the carrier has met its obligations under COGSA, the statute provides several areas in which the carrier bears no liability for lost or damaged cargo:

1. Navigation and Management. The carrier is not liable for losses or damage caused by "act, neglect, or default of the master, mariner, pilot, or the servants [employees] of the carrier in the navigation or in the management of the ship."

2. Fire. The carrier is not liable for losses caused by fire, unless the fire is actually the fault of the carrier.

3. Perils of the Sea.

4. Acts of God.

5. Overwhelming Human Force, including wars, restraints of princes (governments), seizure by legal process, quarantines, riots, and strikes.

As a practical matter, suits against carriers come down to a disagreement between the shipper, arguing that a loss was caused by unseaworthiness or unsafe carriage, and the carrier, citing one of the causes. For example, cargo damage might be the result of fire, but could also be caused by the carrier's failure to carry proper fire-fighting equipment or to train a crew properly in fire-fighting procedures. If the latter is the case, the vessel was unseaworthy, and the shipper will recover its loss.

For losses due to all other causes, COGSA allows a carrier to limit its liability to $500 per package or per customary freight unit if the goods are not carried in packages. The definition of a package has caused courts many problems, especially as containerized shipping becomes the norm. Some of the dimensions of this problem are described in the *Croft & Scully* case that follows. Although the judge is lighthearted, the issues are not.

CROFT & SCULLY CO. v. M/V SKULPTOR VUCHETICH

664 F. 2d 1277 (5th Cir. 1982)

FACTS:

Croft & Scully contracted to ship soda from Houston to Kuwait. The soda was packaged in six-packs, into cases, then into a container. While the soda was being loaded by stevedores onto the ship, an employee of the stevedore company negligently dropped the container, damaging the cans. The District Court gave summary judgment to the defendants, ruling that as a matter of law, the container was the package, so that Croft & Scully's recovery was limited to $500. Croft & Scully appealed.

ISSUE:

Was the container the package contracted for carriage, or should the lower court make a factual determination about what constituted the package for purposes of this shipment?

RESULT:

The container is not the package. The case is remanded to the District Court to determine what the stevedores knew about the contents of the container.

REASONS:

Croft & Scully contracted to ship 1755 cases of soft drinks from Houston, Texas to the middle eastern country of Kuwait. Apparently Kuwaitis would like to be Peppers, too. Croft & Scully arranged to ship the soft drinks on board M/V SKULPTOR VUCHETICH, which would arrive in Houston on December 8, 1977. Baltic Shipping Co., owner of SKULPTOR, dispatched a 20-foot steel container to Croft & Scully's supplier in Wharton, Texas. Employees of the supplier loaded

the 1755 cases, each containing 4 "6 packs" or 24 cans, into the container, closed and sealed it—a real Teem effort. The supplier then trucked the container to Goodpasture's yard, near the Houston Ship Channel, which Baltic had selected as a convenient storage facility pending arrival of the SKULPTOR.

During the Refreshing Pause between the arrival of the container and arrival of SKULPTOR, the vessel's agent prepared a Bill of Lading[1] and hired Shippers Stevedoring, Inc., to load the soft drink container on board SKULPTOR.

Pepsi Cola Hits the Spot—On the Pavement

As one of the Stevedore's employees was lifting the container, with the use of a forklift, he negligently dropped it. By our calculations, 42,120 cans of soft drinks crashed to the ground, never a thirst to quench. In the Crush, the cans were damaged. The stevedore, no doubt, was in no mood to have a Coke and a smile.

Don't Judge the Package by its Appearance

Even if liability is limited to $500 per package, Croft & Scully argues, the cardboard cases of soft drinks rather than the 20-foot container should constitute the relevant "package." Shippers Stevedoring responds with equal fervor that the container is the "package." Their argument, we think, given the recent decision in *Allstate Insurance Co. v. Inversiones Navieras Imparcas* . . . holds no water, carbonated or otherwise.

We begin by pointing out that COGSA does not apply by its own force and effect, since the incident occurred in the yard and not on the vessel.

---

[1]The bill of lading described the container's contents as follows: "20' CONTAINER STC [said to contain] 1755 CASES DELAWARE PUNCH."

Rather, the Bill of Lading incorporates COGSA. Thus, its provisions are merely terms of the contract of carriage which, like any other contractual terms, call out for judicial interpretation in case of dispute. . . .

Allstate involved the loss of 341 cartons of stereo equipment. The shipper loaded the cartons inside a container, sealed it, and had its agent deliver it to the carrier. The carrier issued a Bill of Lading which described the contents both in number and in kind. When the container arrived in Venezuela, it was as empty as a can of soda on a hot summer day. The shipper sought recovery for its full damages, but the carrier, relying on COGSA, sought shelter in the $500 limitation. Although the District Court concluded that the container was the COGSA package, the winds of judicial change Schwepped away the $500 shelter and exposed the carrier to full liability.

Judge Anderson . . . found that each stereo carton was a discrete "package." He based his decision on a case in the Second Circuit, *Mitsui & Co. v. American Export Lines*. . . . There, Judge Friendly . . . looked to see whether the carrier had clear, unequivocal notice of the container's contents. . . .

We find nothing in the Bill of Lading to indicate that the contracting parties intended some special meaning of the term "package." Since Croft & Scully included information about the contents of the package and their number, *Allstate* governs. Therefore, the District Court erred in granting summary judgment on the "package" issue.

As a result of cases like *Croft & Scully,* carriers have started including language in their bills of lading defining the container as the package and requiring the shipper to declare otherwise quite specifically. Litigation over this new language has not yet resolved packaging problems. An example of a recent case upholding the new limitations of liability follows.

SENTINEL ENTERPRISES, INC. v. M/V SIMO MATAVULJ

1990 A.M.C. 177 (S.D.N.Y 1990)

FACTS:
Mitsubishi Corporation packed, sealed, and shipped three containers of glass aboard the M/V *Simo Matavulj*, a ship controlled by Barber Lines. Upon the ship's arrival in New York, the glass was badly damaged by exposure to water. The insurer paid the full loss ($38,442.05), and on its behalf, Sentinel sued to recover from the carrier. Barber claimed that the bills of lading defined the container as the package, so that its losses were limited to $1500. The back of the bill of lading contained the following information:

Clause 11: "Package Limitation. Neither the carrier nor the vessel shall in any event be or become liable for any loss or damage to or in connection with the transportation of goods in an amount exceeding U.S. $500 per package, or in case of goods not shipped in packages, per customary freight unit, unless the nature and value of such goods have been declared by the Shipper before shipment and inserted in the Bill of Lading (Box 27) and the Shipper has paid the additional charges on such declared value (Box 23). Where container(s) is stuffed by Shipper or on his behalf, and the container is sealed when received by Carrier for shipment, the Carrier's liability will be limited to U.S. $500 with respect to the contents of each container, except when the Shipper declares value on the face hereof (Box 27) and pays additional charges on such declared value (Box 23). The freight charged on sealed containers when no higher valuation is declared by the Shipper is based on a value of U.S. $500 per container. . . ."

Both boxes 23 and 27 on the front of the bill of lading were blank, and Mitsubishi did not pay the extra value charge of 5.3 percent of FOB value (in this case, $1,919.48). However, the front of the bill of lading, in the section labeled "Description of Goods," showed for each bill "1 Container" containing 12, 11, and 17 cases, respectively.

ISSUE:

Can the carrier limit its liability to $500 per container based on its language on the back of the bill of lading, even when it has knowledge of the number of packages in each container from the remainder of the bill?

RESULT:

Yes. The shipper needs to be sure the bill of lading is filled out correctly.

REASONS:

The carrier is not obliged to open a container sealed by a shipper so as to verify the contents. . . . It cannot be expected to assume the risk that the shipper might overstate the number of cases, cartons, etc. being shipped, thus writing its own "limitation ticket."

. . . Barber established a special rate for sealed containers and gave the shipper an opportunity to declare the value if it wanted to exceed the $500 limitation. Such a declared value of the goods (upon which premium is paid) presumably would be a more precise measure of risk of carriage undertaken than the alleged number of "packages" that a shipper may be claiming are inside a sealed container.

The shipper elected to leave blank the space in which to declare the value (Box 27) and the bills of lading show no declared value charge was paid (bottom of Box 23). Both of these spaces on the lading called attention to Clause 11 which clearly set forth that the $500 limitation applied with respect to containers pre-packaged and pre-sealed by the shipper and just as clearly provided for declarations of excess value in such instance, if a shipper wished to recover for damages in excess of that limitation. The shipper and plaintiff's underwriter, which insured that cargo for full value, therefore should not complain now that it can recover only a limited amount from the carrier.

Rather than pay additional freight, the shipper declared full value to its cargo underwriter who collected a full premium, and in due course paid the claimed loss in this case. The $500 per container limitation was not imposed by the carrier. It was selected by the shipper when it chose not to declare full value to the carrier.

Deviation

Under COGSA, the carrier's ability to limit its liability for loss or damage applies only if it has not deviated from the contract of carriage. If it has, the shipper is entitled to recover its full loss. So, for example, a ship that went several hundred miles out of its way to take advantage of lower refueling costs might be held to have deviated from the contract of carriage. If the cargo were subsequently lost, the carrier would be liable for the entire loss. Also note that the shipper has the right to declare a higher value for its cargo than $500 per package.

For managers, the technical aspects of COGSA may be difficult to follow. They do, however, lead to two important lessons. The first is that insurance is a very important part of any contract that involves sending goods from one place to another. The popularity of CIF contracts, as

Chapter 6 discussed, may result in part from the pro-carrier bias of COGSA. The second lesson for managers is that the documentation that accompanies the goods is very important. Bills of lading need to describe the cargo in a way that protects both the buyer and the seller. One way to make sure the bills of lading are specific is to specify the description of goods in the initial contract between the buyer and the seller. An ounce of preventive management in ocean shipping is far better than the inadequate pound of cure after the goods are damaged or lost.

9.3 AIR TRANSPORT

International transport of goods by air is governed by a different international treaty, known as the Warsaw Convention. Negotiated in 1929, the Warsaw Convention covers liability for freight and for checked luggage. It also limits the liability of carriers for death or personal injury to passengers. Unlike COGSA, the Warsaw Convention requires the shipper to prepare the shipping documentation. Here, that documentation is called an *air waybill.* It looks much like a bill of lading and performs many of the same functions, except that it generally is not negotiable. Air waybills must include information about the nature of the goods, the number of packages and their packing, the weight, quantity, and volume of the goods, and their apparent condition.

Like COGSA, the Warsaw Convention provides limits on the liability of the air carrier for lost or damaged cargo. When the air carrier meets the requirements of the convention, its liability is limited to $20 per kilogram, or $9.07 per pound. Of course, shippers or airline passengers may declare a higher value (and pay a fee) for their cargo or luggage. The *Exim Industries* case that follows explains what a carrier has to do in order to limit its liability successfully.

EXIM INDUSTRIES, INC. v. PAN AMERICAN WORLD AIRWAYS, INC.

754 F.2d 106 (2d Cir. 1985)

FACTS:
Pan Am lost two shipments of silk blouses en route from India to New York. Exim sued to recover the market value of the goods, which exceeded $80,000, claiming that the air waybills failed to comply with the requirements of the Warsaw Convention. The District Court ruled in favor of Pan Am, limiting Exim's recovery to $8,740. Exim appealed.

ISSUE:
Can a carrier effectively limit its liability for lost or damaged goods even when it doesn't perfectly comply with the requirements of the Warsaw Convention?

RESULT:
Yes. Judgment in favor of Pan Am affirmed.

REASONS:

Exim contends that Pan Am's waybills for the lost shipments fail to comply with subsections (h), (i), and (q) of article 8 of the Convention, which require the following particulars:

(h) The number of packages, the method of packing, and the particular marks or numbers upon them;
(i) The weight, the quantity, the volume, or dimensions of the goods;
(q) A statement that the transportation is subject to the rules relating to liability established by this convention.

The district court found that several of these particulars were missing from the waybills covering the two shipments. The first waybill gave the number of packages and their weight and dimensions but did not describe the method of packing or indicate that the packages were numbered 1 through 7. The second waybill, the court said, omitted the volume and dimensions of the cargo. Finally, rather than stating categorically that the transportation "is" subject to the Warsaw Convention, each waybill stated that it "may be" so subject. . . .

Depending upon the nature of the shipment, some of the particulars set forth in subsections (h) and (i) may have practical significance, and some may not. It is possible, for example, that the statement of a cargo's weight may assist the shipper, not only in checking the rate, but also in calculating the carrier's liability for loss. . . . In the instant case, however, the particulars missing from the first waybill—the method of packing and the numerical markings—were technical and insubstantial omissions that did not prejudice the shipper and were of little commercial significance. Their omission did not preclude limitation of liability. . . .

The second waybill contained information as to the weight and the number of packages, but said nothing about their volume and dimensions or the number of blouses in each package. Appellant contends that subsection (i), properly translated from the original French version, requires that the waybill state the weight *and* the quantity *and* the volume or dimensions of the goods. . . . In the instant case, because the rate was based on weight, figures showing the volume and dimension of each carton and the quantity of blouses contained therein would be of no practical significance with respect to either the identity of the shipment or the rate to be charged. Their omission, therefore, is not a ground for denying limitation of liability.

Like the district court, we are not persuaded by appellant's argument concerning the alleged inadequacy of the "Notice Concerning Carriers Limitations of Liability". . . . Although the Convention prescribes the use of the word "is," not the words "may be," we believe the framers' intent was that the shipper be given reasonable notice of the likelihood that the Convention would be applicable, not that the carrier be treated as a didactic arbiter of the law. The phrase "may be" is consistent with this intent. . . .

The judgment of the district court is affirmed.

The Warsaw Convention applies to passengers' checked baggage as well as to cargo. Although for many of us, lost or damaged luggage is mostly an inconvenience, for business travelers carrying models, samples, or even valuable goods as checked luggage, the limitation of liability provisions of the Warsaw Convention can cause considerable practical and financial loss. Passengers should consider declaring a higher value for their luggage than $20 per kilogram and paying the extra fee when they carry goods of high value. The *Republic National Bank* case explores the parameters of the Warsaw Convention for checked luggage.

REPUBLIC NATIONAL BANK OF NEW YORK v. EASTERN AIRLINES, INC.

815 F.2d 232 (2d Cir. 1987)

FACTS:

On December 13, 1982, Renzo Baronti, an international courier, accompanied two bags of currency on a flight from New York to South America. One bag contained $2 million and was bound for Lima, Peru, while the other contained $4.5 million bound for Santiago, Chile. The courier checked the luggage in New York, receiving a standard claim check for the $4.5 million bag and a substitute claim check, or limited release form, for the $2 million bag (the agent could not find a standard Lima baggage claim check). The substitute claim check did not contain all of the information that would be found on a standard claim check.

Both bags were present at an intermediate stop in Miami, but when the plane reached Lima, the $2 million bag was missing. Six weeks later, five persons were arrested in Atlantic City, New Jersey, with $150,000 of the missing currency in their possession.

Republic sued to recover its full $2 million loss. Eastern claimed that, pursuant to the Warsaw Convention, Republic's recovery should be limited to $9.07 per pound. The District Court granted summary judgment to Eastern for $634.90 ($9.07/16. × 70 lbs., the maximum weight allowed) and Republic appealed.

ISSUE:

Can Eastern effectively limit its liability for lost luggage even when it does not perfectly comply with the Warsaw Convention?

RESULT:

Yes. Judgment for Eastern affirmed.

REASONS:

[Article 4 of the Warsaw Convention, which applies to checked baggage, requires disclosures similar to Article 8, the section discussed in *Exim* above.]

On the facts of this case, we see no reason for refusing out of hand to apply *Exim* to Article 4 baggage checks. The requirements of Article 4 essentially parallel those of Article 8. Both articles require that basic information of notice, identification and weight appear on cargo documents. . . . Moreover, both articles contain requirements which, if not satisfied, may result in prejudice to the airline customer. For these reasons, therefore, we hold that where, as here, the traveler is more like a commercial shipper than the typical airline passenger, our analysis in *Exim* applies to claims brought under Article 4 of the Warsaw Convention.

Turning to the facts before us, we note that none of the required information appeared on the limited release form used to identify Republic's baggage. We agree, however, . . . that the absence of the printed notice and weight of the bag did not prejudice Republic. First, with respect to notice of the Convention's applicability, the district court found that Baronti was an experienced courier, having made over 250 flights in his career with Republic. Republic cannot reasonably contend that Baronti was unaware of the Warsaw Convention's application to his two hundred fifty-first such flight. In fact, a proper notice was printed both on Baronti's passenger ticket and on his baggage claim check for the Santiago bag. As an experienced courier, it would be incredible for Baronti to be unaware of the applicability of the Warsaw Convention and its attendant limited liability. The district court, therefore, committed no error in finding this element of Article 4 satisfied.

Second, under the facts of this particular case, the failure of Eastern to record the weight of Republic's baggage on the limited release was not prejudicial. As the district court noted, the purpose of the weight requirement is to enable passengers to calculate the amount recoverable under the Warsaw Convention for lost or damaged baggage. . . . A passenger need only multiply the amount recoverable per pound under the

Convention ($9.07) by the weight of his baggage to arrive at this figure. Once having made this calculation, a passenger has enough information to decide whether to purchase insurance.

In the case at bar, Republic must have known that it could not obtain recovery for $2 million under the Convention, even if Baronti could not make the calculation because he did not know the precise weight of his bag. In order to recover $2 million at $9.07 per pound, Republic's currency bag would need to weigh 22,507 pounds. Obviously, Republic was on notice that insurance coverage would be necessary to adequately protect its shipment. Moreover, Republic stated in its export declaration that its bag weighed fifty-two pounds. . . . Therefore, the absence of weight information, under the facts of this case, did not prejudice Republic.

The absence of a baggage identification number on the limited release is more troubling. Obviously, the purpose of the baggage identification number is to assure the proper recovery of a passenger's baggage at the point of destination. Several factors peculiar to this case, however, indicate that Republic was not prejudiced by the absence of an identification number. First, the Republic courier did not present his baggage to Eastern's attendant at the baggage check counter. Instead, Republic's currency bags were located in an armored truck parked on the airport tarmac. Eastern, therefore, had no opportunity to assure that Republic's baggage was properly identified. Second, Republic's courier personally supervised the handling of the currency bags at each point in the journey. This supervision virtually eliminated the possibility that Eastern mishandled Republic's bag as a result of the missing identification number. Eastern personnel, in fact, easily located Republic's currency bag in Miami. After carefully viewing the bag, Baronti identified it as belonging to Republic. For these reasons, Republic cannot claim that the absence of an identification number was prejudicial.

Under *Exim*, it is apparent here that "the particulars missing from [the baggage check] . . . were technical and insubstantial omissions that did not prejudice the shipper and were of little commercial significance." . . . [T]heir omission will not preclude Eastern's assertion of liability limitations.

9.4 MULTIMODAL TRANSPORTATION

As you learned from the example at the beginning of this chapter, much of the international transport of goods involves more than one method of carriage. This multimodal transport relies on the containerization of goods in relatively standard-sized containers, and on computerized routing and tracking of containers as the goods are in transit. The move toward multimodal transport has had both practical and legal effects.

On the practical side, containerization has required enormous capital investments in the ship, rail, and trucking industries, and a redevelopment of port facilities to handle containers. Shipping lines, in particular, had to build new ships suitable for containers, while rail and truck lines had to change their methods of doing business. Port authorities had to build new facilities, with rail lines extending onto the docks and giant cranes for loading and unloading containers. As a result of the restructuring of shipping, some ports that do not have good road and rail access have suffered, while new ports have thrived. Shipping lines without the capital to build new ships have gone out of business, and new lines have picked up business.

The next two decades will see the further consolidation of transportation, using computers and satellite technology to create land–sea bridges. For example, a Japanese firm shipping to Tampa, Florida, may send its goods via ship to San Diego, where a waiting train will take the goods to their destination. Regular schedules coordinated among the different forms of transport, and computerized tracking of cargo will minimize the time in port. Today, the goods in this example might well go entirely by ship to Tampa. By building the land–sea link, the shipping line will only have to operate its ships in the Pacific Ocean, rather than around the world. Thus, its voyage time will be shorter and it will be able to carry more cargo.

The legal world has not yet caught up with the changes in the transportation industry. As you learned in Chapter 7, the 1990 version of *IN-COTERMS* has started to address the contractual issues of defining risk of loss in a multimodal setting. Up to now, few carriers have created single bills of lading or waybills good for the several different stages of a journey. The next two decades will see the development of such integrated transport documentation and the creation of electronic bills of lading and other documents of transit.

9.5 INSURANCE

Generally, the parties to a contract for the sale of goods insure those goods against the risk of loss during transit. Often, the obligation to obtain insurance is one of the responsibilities the parties negotiate. Recall that the commercial term CIF obligates the seller to obtain insurance on behalf of the buyer, while the commercial term C&F (or, under *INCOTERMS*, CFR) means that the price includes the cost of the goods and the freight cost, but not insurance.

PRACTICES

Cargo insurance is usually handled through an insurance broker, who knows all the companies writing policies. Rates will vary depending on the risk involved in the shipment. The largest variable in rates is the political risk in the transit areas. During the Gulf Crisis in 1991, for example, insurance rates to Persian Gulf destinations were extremely volatile, changing weekly to reflect the political developments in the region.

The most well-known insurer of cargo risks is Lloyd's of London. Lloyd's began in the 17th century as a group of traders and shipowners who met at Edward Lloyd's coffeehouse to discuss matters of common concern. An act of Parliament incorporated Lloyd's in 1834. The corporation provides services and facilities, but the actual underwriting of risks is done by the individual members of Lloyd's. Each member has unlimited personal liability for the risks he insures against. If a risk is too large for one underwriter, she may assemble a group of members, called a syndicate, to carry the risk. Although many companies in many countries now write insurance on cargo, Lloyd's still has a preeminent role in the industry.

TERMS

Historically, marine cargo insurance covered two separate categories of underwriting risks: marine risks and war risks. Marine risks included, among others, perils of the sea, piracy, fire, thieves, and barratry (the serious misconduct of the captain or crew). War risks included the risk of aerial bombardment, mines, torpedoes, and takings or seizures by governments, factions, or belligerents in wars, civil wars, and rebellions. Today, it is common to obtain insurance to cover all risks, including war risks, rather than to rely on a listing of specific risks covered. Buyers negotiating CIF contracts should ask for such coverage.

Some insurance policies may still contain the term "free of particular average" (FPA). This clause means that the underwriter will not pay for any partial loss unless the loss is general to the entire cargo. Recall the materials on general average discussed earlier in this chapter. If a ship jettisons some cargo in order to save the ship, all shippers and the shipowner suffer proportionately. If a shipper is shipping wool that is partially destroyed and other shippers did not also suffer loss, her loss would be "particular," and thus not payable under an FPA clause. Some policies state "FPA unless 10 percent." In this situation, the insurer will pay partial losses exceeding 10 percent of the valuation of the cargo.

9.6 CONCLUSION

The transportation of goods from the seller to the buyer is a critical part of the transaction for the sale of goods. The law, largely founded on ocean shipping as the method of choice for transport, has a long and specialized history. As buyers or sellers in an international transaction, your actions in negotiating the contract should reflect concern over the contents of the bill of lading or waybill, the valuation of the shipment, and the terms of the insurance covering possible losses in transit. Anticipating problems before they arise will enable both parties to a transaction to get satisfaction, even if something unexpected occurs in the shipping process.

9.7 QUESTIONS FOR DISCUSSION

1. Are there any benefits you can see in COGSA's provisions allowing carriers to limit their liability effectively?

2. If you were chartering a ship to take a cargo to or from a port in the United States, would you incorporate COGSA's terms or negotiate different terms?

3. Now that you know about legal rights and obligations in transport and insurance, would you negotiate different commercial terms into a contract for the sale of goods (see Chapter 6)? Explain.

4. Sony Magnetic Products contracted with a carrier to ship videocassette tapes from Alabama to England. Sony packed the tapes into 1320 cartons, then strapped the cartons onto 52 pallets. The pallets were loaded into one container. The bill of lading left blank the space for "No. of pkgs.," but described the load as "One 40 foot container STC 1320 Ctns Magnetic Tape (blank)." The bill of lading declared no value for the load, but an attached export certificate showed a value of $424,765.44.

   While the tapes were being loaded aboard the ship, the crane holding the container exploded, causing the container to fall 60 feet onto a concrete dock. The tapes were damaged beyond repair or resale. Assuming that the carrier was negligent, how much should Sony recover: $500, $26,000, $424,765.44, or $660,000? Explain.

5. As a project, collect some shipping documents from carriers in your area. You can find them at airports, seaports, rail terminals, and from trucking firms, freight forwarders, and air express companies. Examine the documents for the provisions that limit the liability of the carrier.

9.7 FURTHER READINGS

Alan Branch, *Elements of Shipping*, 6th ed., Chapman and Hall, London and New York, 1989.

W. Hawkland, "Documentary Transactions: New Solutions to Old Problems," 18 *Uniform Commercial Code Law Journal* 291–310 (1986).

D. Murray, "History and Development of the Bill of Lading," 37 *University of Miami Law Review* 689–732 (1983).

PART THREE

THE REGULATION OF INTERNATIONAL TRADE

THE LEGAL STRUCTURE OF INTERNATIONAL TRADE

REGULATING IMPORTS AND EXPORTS

THE LEGAL STRUCTURE OF INTERNATIONAL TRADE

10.1 INTRODUCTION

Analyzing the conceptual foundation of international trade is somewhat similar to analyzing a complex musical composition. The trade composition has many themes: protecting or developing domestic industries; improving consumer standards of living; protecting national security; maximizing economic efficiency; and even xenophobia and personal animosity between national leaders. The instruments of international trade policy are the tools of law, economics, politics, ethics, and human relations, and the players come from local, national, and international settings.

At different times in history some themes become more prominent than others. In Great Britain, the early 19th century saw high barriers to imports, while the mid–19th century saw the repeal of most protectionist legislation. In the United States, the Smoot-Hawley Tariff of 1930 was a high-water mark of protectionism, while the Canada–U.S. Free Trade Agreement in 1988 marked the ascendance of free-trade principles. Like many modern compositions, the themes of world trade often conflict, and their apparent dissonance makes underlying trends difficult to discern.

The rise of principles of free trade as viable economic and political objectives can be traced to the work of early economists. Among the most prominent exponents of free trade was Adam Smith, who articulated the economic rationale for free trade in *The Wealth of Nations*.

ADAM SMITH, *THE WEALTH OF NATIONS*, 1776.

To give the monopoly of the home-market to the produce of domestic industry, in any particular art or manufacture, is in some measure to direct private people in what manner they ought to employ their capitals, and must, in almost all cases, be either a useless or a hurtful regulation. If the produce of domestic industry can be brought there as cheap as foreign industry, the regulation is evidently useless. If it cannot, it must generally be hurtful. It is the maxim of every prudent master of a family, never to attempt to make at home what it will cost him more to make than to buy. The taylor does not attempt to make his own shoes, but buys them of the shoemaker. The shoemaker does not attempt to make his own clothes, but employs a taylor. The farmer attempts to make neither the one nor the other, but employs those different artificers. All of them find it worth their interest to employ their whole industry in a way in which they have some advantage over their neighbours, and to purchase with a part of its produce, or what is the same thing, with the price of a part of it, whatever else they have occasion for.

What is prudence in the conduct of every private family, can scarcely be folly in that of a great kingdom. If a foreign country can supply us with a commodity cheaper than we ourselves can make it, better buy it of them with some part of the produce of our own industry, employed in a way in which we have some advantage. The general industry of the country, being always in proportion to the capital which employs it, will not thereby be diminished, no more than that of the above-mentioned artificers; but only left to find out the way in which it can be employed with the greatest advantage. It is certainly not employed to the greatest advantage, when it is thus directed towards an object which it can buy cheaper than it can make. The value of its annual produce is certainly more or less diminished, when it is thus turned away from producing commodities evidently of more value than the commodity which it is directed to produce. . . .

The natural advantages which one country has over another in producing particular commodities are sometimes so great, that it is acknowledged by all the world to be in vain to struggle with them. By means of glasses, hotbeds, and hotwalls, very good grapes can be raised in Scotland, and very good wine too can be made of them at about thirty times the expence for which at least equally good can be brought from foreign countries. Would it be a reasonable law to prohibit the importation of all foreign wines, merely to encourage the making of claret and burgundy in Scotland? But if there would be a manifest absurd-

ity in turning towards any employment, thirty times more of the capital and industry of the country, than would be necessary to purchase from foreign countries an equal quantity of the commodities wanted, there must be an absurdity, though not altogether so glaring, yet exactly of the same kind, in turning towards any such employment a thirtieth, or even a three hundredth part more of either. Whether the advantages which one country has over another, be natural or acquired, is in this respect of no consequence. As long as the one country has those advantages, and the other wants them, it will always be more advantageous for the latter, rather to buy of the former than to make. It is an acquired advantage only, which one artificer has over his neighbour, who exercises another trade; and yet they both find it more advantageous to buy of one another, than to make what does not belong to their particular trades.

Very few nations completely follow Adam Smith's theory, although many nations have treaties and agreements that attempt to reduce barriers to free trade. The purpose of this chapter is to examine the structural framework for the regulation of international trade. Through the institutions and agencies of trade regulation, nations create law reflecting their economic, political, and social objectives.

10.2 NATIONAL STRUCTURES

U.S. TRADE REGULATION

Chapter 2 discussed the constitutional allocation between the legislative and executive branches of the power to regulate international trade. That chapter took the larger perspective on trade regulation; the day-to-day implementation of trade policy is the responsibility of many different federal agencies. At times, these federal agencies have conflicting policy objectives that hinder American businesses in their dealings abroad. The federal agencies that have major responsibility for international trade include the office of the U.S. Trade Representative, the Departments of State, Commerce, and the Treasury, and the International Trade Commission. In addition, other agencies, such as the Departments of Agriculture and Defense, have more specialized roles in regulating international trade.

The U.S. Trade Representative (USTR) is a cabinet-level position reporting directly to the President. The USTR is the chief negotiator on behalf of the President on trade issues, serves as an advisor to the President, coordinates trade agreement programs, advises the President on trade relief actions, and coordinates administrative actions dealing with unfair competition and the protection of American intellectual property rights by foreign countries. These last responsibilities will be discussed in greater detail in Chapter 14.

The Department of Commerce carries the conflicting functions of controlling exports and promoting exports. The Export Administration unit is responsible for restricting exports by licensing, for reasons of national security, short supply, and foreign policy. The Department of Commerce is also responsible for promoting exports. Among its export promotion programs is the U.S. & Foreign Commercial Service, a network of commercial specialists assigned to embassies around the world. Both the export control and export promotion functions of the Department of Commerce will be discussed in Chapter 11. In addition, the Department of Commerce houses the International Trade Administration, which makes determinations of dumping and of unfair subsidies, and of the amount of countervailing and antidumping duties. These topics will be discussed later in this chapter.

The Department of the Treasury plays an important role in regulating international trade. The U.S. Customs Service, which regulates imports, is part of the department. The Department of the Treasury also administers foreign trade zones and has an important role in negotiating tax treaties and setting monetary policy. The department is often used to enforce restrictions on trade with other countries.

The Department of State has a role in formulating trade policy as part of its function in formulating and carrying out overall foreign policy. Other executive branch agencies, such as the Departments of Defense and Agriculture, carry out trade policies in specific areas. Additionally, government agencies such as the Small Business Administration, the Export-Import Bank, and the Overseas Private Investment Corporation provide technical assistance to U.S. businesses.

The International Trade Commission (ITC) is an independent agency, with commissioners appointed by the President and confirmed by the Senate. The ITC is primarily a research agency, providing economic research for Congress and the President. The ITC also conducts investigations of the impact of unfair foreign trade practices on domestic industry.

All civil court actions arising from import questions, such as tariff or other customs revenue disputes, questions of embargoes, or appeals from International Trade Commission findings, must be brought to the Court of International Trade rather than to the regular federal district courts. The Court of International Trade sits in New York. Appeals from the court go to the Federal Circuit Court of Appeals in Washington.

Although Congress and the President have made several attempts to streamline the administration of U.S. trade policy, the structure still leaves room for inconsistency and delay. Critics charge that American businesses are less competitive than their foreign counterparts because of the large amount of bureaucratic involvement in the import/export processes. Some of the criticism may not be justified, but a brief comparison with the trade policy and structure of Japan might lend credence to the view that the American regulatory environment impedes international business activity.

JAPANESE TRADE STRUCTURES

Japanese trade regulation occurs within the framework of a national industrial policy. The main aspects of the national industrial policy have been formulated by the Ministry of International Trade and Industry (MITI) in a series of policy papers. They include:

1. Achieving an appropriate industrial structure maximizing Japan's comparative advantage;

2. Ensuring adequate and economically efficient supplies of natural resources and energy;

3. Promoting research and development;

4. Developing small and medium-sized businesses;

5. Promoting international trade; and

6. Encouraging sensible industrial location decisions within Japan.[1]

The way in which MITI carries out each of these policy objectives will change over time. For example, the appropriate industrial structure in the 1960s involved the development of heavy industry, whereas the 1980s saw MITI phase out heavy manufacturing in favor of knowledge-based, high-technology industry. MITI's articulated energy policies formulated in response to the Arab oil embargo of the 1970s allowed Japanese business to reduce dependence on imported oil. In 1990, MITI announced plans to reduce that dependency even more, by promoting the construction of thirty new nuclear power plants in Japan.

As Chapter 4 discussed, Japan has a parliamentary system of government. The cabinet ministers are appointed by the Prime Minister, who in turn is elected by the Diet. A majority of cabinet ministers must be members of the Diet. Thus, unlike in the United States, the government institutions carrying out trade policy must be from the same political party that controls the institution making trade policy.

Although several ministries have authority over some trade-related issues, the main agencies influencing trade policy are MITI, the Ministry of Finance (MOF), and the Ministry of Foreign Affairs (MOFA). Of those,

---

[1]Takashi Wakiyama, "The Nature and Tools of Japan's Industrial Policy," 27 *Harvard International Law Journal* 467 (1986).

MITI has the broadest and most direct authority over trading in goods and services. MITI's statutory authority over international trade comes from the Foreign Exchange and Foreign Trade Control Law of 1949 (the Control law) and from the Export and Import Transactions Law of 1952 (Transactions law).

The Control law requires MITI approval for both exports and imports, and allows MITI to set conditions on both. For example, MITI may tell an exporter to set a certain minimum price. Or, as in the case of Japan's voluntary restraints on automobile exports to the United States, MITI may set maximum quantities for export. MITI also has the authority to set conditions, including quotas, on imports. The Transactions law allows MITI to approve privately established import and export cartels. MITI approval exempts such cartels from Japan's antitrust law. MITI may also force non-members of such cartels to abide by the conditions it sets for the cartels. As Chapter 4 discussed, much of MITI's real power over international trade is exercised in the form of administrative guidance suggestions for conduct rather than official regulatory action.

10.3 MULTILATERAL TRADE STRUCTURES

As long ago as the Middle Ages, governments realized that trade across borders could benefit from treaties and understandings among many nations. In the early 1600s, a group of cities across northern Europe formed the Hanseatic League for the purpose of granting each other trade advantages. This multilateral trade organization provided a foundation for many subsequent attempts to regulate international trade on a multilateral basis.

Today, many different kinds of groups attempt to regulate different forms of international trade on a multilateral basis. The United Nations has several agencies and commissions working on trade-related problems. The most prominent, the United Nations Conference on Trade and Development (UNCTAD), has played a significant role in bringing the concerns of developing nations to the attention of the industrialized nations. The industrialized nations have their own group working on trade problems, the Organization for Economic Cooperation and Development (OECD). Regional trade groups have also contributed to the multilateral regulation of trade. The European Community is the most prominent example of such a regional structure. Finally, some multilateral organizations concentrate on specific trade-related problems. The World Intellectual Property Organization (WIPO) is one such group.

At the core of all the international organizations working on trade across boundaries are three organizations founded in the 1940s: the International Monetary Fund, the International Bank for Reconstruction and Development (the World Bank), and the General Agreement on Tariffs and Trade (GATT). Of these, the GATT is most directly relevant to trading in goods and services across national borders. It will be the focus of the materials that follow.

HISTORY OF GATT

As the tide of World War II turned in favor of the Allies, the political leadership of the Allied nations turned their attention to the causes of war and the prevention of future wars. One manifestation of this discussion took the form of the conference in 1945 establishing the United Nations as a political organization. Another manifestation of this discussion was the Bretton Woods conference in Bretton Woods, New Hampshire, in 1944. The Allies, believing that the trade wars following the Smoot-Hawley Tariff of 1930 led not only to the Great Depression but also to World War II, planned to put into place a system of worldwide economic and financial cooperation. The Bretton Woods conference succeeded in establishing the International Monetary Fund and the World Bank. It also saw the beginning of discussions about the formation of a worldwide organization to regulate tariffs and trade practices.

After Bretton Woods, the United States, and then the United Nations, pushed other nations toward an international treaty to reduce tariffs and regulate trade. At a series of four international conferences between 1945 and 1948, the charter for the International Trade Organization (ITO) was drafted. The ITO was to administer two agreements: one a multilateral agreement to reduce tariffs and the other a multilateral statement of general obligations of nations with respect to orderly world trade.

Unfortunately, the U.S. Senate never confirmed the treaty establishing the ITO. Without the cooperation of what was then the world's strongest economy, the ITO had no chance of becoming an effective international organization. The two multilateral trade agreements, however, were adopted by many nations around the world, and were accepted in the United States by executive agreement. These two agreements for tariff reduction and regulating trading practices are the General Agreements on Tariffs and Trade: the GATT.

Since the initial conferences creating the GATT, the members of the GATT have held seven rounds of discussions designed to lower tariff and trade barriers worldwide. These discussions, known as "rounds," have resulted in significant expansion of the scope of the GATT. The three most recent rounds were the Kennedy Round, lasting from 1962 to 1967, the Tokyo Round, from 1973 to 1979, and the Uruguay Round, which began in 1986. These rounds have added agreements on technical barriers to trade, government procurement, agriculture, technology, and services, and have substantially reduced the levels of tariffs worldwide.

STRUCTURE OF GATT

Since the ITO never came into being, the GATT began its existence with a somewhat haphazard institutional structure. But an administrative structure has evolved. The members of the GATT, also known more formally as the contracting parties, have found it cumbersome to meet as a group on all issues. Over time, therefore, the contracting parties have created a Council to be a smaller working group, and a host of committees, subcommittees, working groups, panels, and other groups. The host of GATT institutions is administered by a director general, who oversees a Secretariat of administrators.

DISPUTE RESOLUTION MECHANISMS

One of the functions of the GATT has been to provide a mechanism for resolving disputes among nations regarding tariffs and trade practices. The GATT has established a dispute resolution procedure, using impartial panels. The panels have successfully resolved several significant trade issues that if they had remained unresolved, could have led to retaliatory trade wars.

The lack of a formal constitution for the GATT has meant that the GATT is slow in making substantive changes. It also has no real enforcement power, but must rely on the ability of its members to persuade an offending nation to change laws or policies that violate the GATT. GATT dispute resolution is also limited in its ability to consider all the factors that might be relevant to a national decision that affects trade. For example, in 1991, a GATT panel considered a U.S. law intended to protect dolphins from slaughter by banning imports of tuna caught using certain fishing methods. At the request of Mexico and several other countries, the GATT panel ruled that the U.S. law operated as a nontariff barrier to trade, and violated the GATT even though the intent was not to restrict trade but to preserve marine mammals.[2] This decision would seem to indicate that GATT panels cannot consider environmental factors.

OPERATING PRINCIPLES

The GATT has two major functions. The first is to reduce barriers to trade and the second is to promote fair trade. Each of these functions has several means of implementation. Using the methods outlined by the GATT, individual nations will enact their own trade regulation. This section will introduce the operating principles of the GATT, and Chapters 11 and 12 will discuss more specifically their legislative basis, particularly in the United States.

Promotion of Free Trade

The primary means of reducing trade barriers is through multilateral discussions, or *rounds*. Table 10–1 gives some idea of the extent to which the various rounds have affected world trade.

---

[2]General Agreement on Tariffs and Trade: Dispute Settlement Panel Report on United States Restrictions on Imports of Tuna, 30 I.L.M. 1594 (1991).

TABLE 10–1.   Summary of GATT Rounds[3]

Round	Dates	No. of Countries	Value of Trade Covered (billions)	Avg. Tariff Cut, %	Avg. Tariffs Afterward, %
Geneva	1947	23	$ 10	35	n/a
Annecy	1949	33	n/a	n/a	n/a
Torquay	1950	34	n/a	n/a	n/a
Geneva	1956	22	$ 2.5	n/a	n/a
Dillon	1960–1961	45	$ 4.9	n/a	n/a
Kennedy	1962–1967	48	$ 40	35	8.7
Tokyo	1973–1979	99	$155	34	4.7

[3]John H. Jackson, *The World Trading System,* MIT Press, Cambridge, Mass., 1989, p. 53.

The Uruguay Round, which began in 1986, technically ended in 1990 without agreement, although talks continued well after that point. Starting with the Kennedy Round, but continuing with more effectiveness in the Tokyo Round, GATT talks also took up the problems of nontariff barriers to trade. These might include problems such as technical specifications for products, government procurement policies (known in the United States as "buy American" laws), and safety or environmental standards. The Uruguay Round took up the problem of extending GATT agreements to service industries, capital movement, and the protection of technology.

Reduction of Trade Barriers

Within the structure provided by the agreements reached at the conclusion of the GATT rounds, two major principles operate to reduce barriers to trade. Both principles have been in use for many centuries, in bilateral treaties. The GATT, however, gives these principles a far broader reach.

The first operating principle of the GATT is that of *most favored nation* status (MFN). When one nation grants MFN status to another nation, it agrees to charge that nation the lowest generally applicable tariff rate on goods from that nation. If, subsequent to the grant of MFN status, the granting nation negotiates a lower tariff rate with another country, the lower tariff rate will apply to the MFN country as well. Suppose, for example, that Singapore imports children's clothing from South Korea. If Singapore grants MFN status to South Korea, imports from South Korea will be charged the lowest applicable tariff rate when they enter Singapore. If, subsequent to the grant of MFN status, Singapore grants a lower tariff rate on children's clothes to India, imports from South Korea automatically receive the new, lower tariff rate. Singapore would not need to renegotiate its tariff rates with South Korea, but would just adjust its tariff schedules. Any nation having MFN status would be entitled to the lower rate.

The GATT's provisions on MFN status are found in Article I of the treaty and require members to grant MFN status to other members.

GENERAL AGREEMENT ON TARIFFS AND TRADE

55 U.N.T.S. 194 (1947)

ARTICLE I. GENERAL MOST-FAVOURED-NATION TREATMENT

1. With respect to customs duties and charges of any kind imposed on or in connection with importation or exportation or imposed on the international transfer of payments for imports or exports, and with respect to the method of levying such duties and charges, and with respect to all rules and formalities in connection with the importation and exportation, and with respect to all matters referred to in paragraphs 2 and 4 of Article III, any advantage, favour, privilege or immunity granted by any contracting party to any product originating in or destined for any other country shall be accorded immediately and unconditionally to the like product originating in or destined for the territories of all other contracting parties.

Despite the blanket language of Article I, the practice under the GATT has been to allow a variety of exceptions. Some, like the tariff concessions for countries formerly part of the British Commonwealth, were "grandfathered" because they existed before the GATT. Others, like concessions involving the EC or the Canadian–American Automotive Products Agreement, recognize specific regional needs. Still others, like the Caribbean Basin Initiative and the Generalized System of Preferences, recognize the special situation of developing nations. Late materials in this chapter will discuss some of the larger exceptions to MFN obligations.

The United States' position on MFN status has varied from the principles of the GATT. For some time, the United States has hesitated to grant MFN status to nonmarket economies, notably those controlled by Communist governments. The Trade Act of 1974 provided that the President could recommend such a country for congressional approval of MFN status under two conditions. The first, known as the Jackson–Vanik requirement, is that the country allow free emigration. If the country restricted emigration, the President could still request MFN status, under a waiver of Jackson–Vanik. If Congress granted MFN status under this second method, the status would be subject to yearly review. In 1990, 1991, and 1992, the renewal of MFN status for China under the waiver of Jackson–Vanik was the subject of heated congressional debate and in 1992, of a presidential veto of a congressional act removing that status.

The second operating principle for the reduction of trade barriers is that of *national treatment*. Essentially, national treatment mandates that once imported goods clear customs, they are treated no differently from domestic goods. A nation may not use its legal or tax structure to treat imports differently from domestic goods once the imports are in the country. For example, suppose that the United States charges a tariff on imported cars. It also requires that imported vehicles, in order to qualify for sale in the United States, must meet emission requirements some 50 percent more stringent than those required for domestic cars. Such a requirement might have many motives, but it looks like an attempt to protect a domestic industry from foreign competition. This requirement, because it treats domestic products differently from imported products once those products are in the country, would violate the national treatment obligation of the GATT.

The obligation of national treatment is found in Article III of the GATT.

GENERAL AGREEMENT ON TARIFFS AND TRADE

55 U.N.T.S. 194 (1947)

ARTICLE III. NATIONAL TREATMENT ON INTERNAL TAXATION AND REGULATION

1. The contracting parties recognize that internal taxes and other internal charges, and laws, regulation and requirements affecting the internal sale, offering for sale, purchase, transportation, distribution or use of products, and internal quantitative regulations requiring the mixture, processing or use of products in specified amounts or proportions, should not be applied to imported or domestic products so as to afford protection to domestic production.

2. The products of the territory of any contracting party imported into the territory of any other contracting party shall not be subject, directly or indirectly, to internal taxes or other internal charges of any kind in excess of those applied, directly or indirectly, to like domestic products. Moreover, no contracting party shall otherwise apply internal taxes or other internal charges to imported or domestic products in a manner contrary to the principles set forth in paragraph 1. . . .

4. The products of the territory of any contracting party imported into the territory of any other contracting party shall be accorded treatment no less favourable than that accorded to like products of national origin in respect of all laws, regulations and requirements affecting their internal sale, offering for sale, purchase, transportation, distribution or use. The provisions of this paragraph shall not prevent the application of differential internal transportation charges which are based exclusively on the economic operation of the means of transport and not on the nationality of the product.

Promotion of Fair Trade

In addition to promoting free trade, the GATT has developed two principles that encourage fair international trade. Both of these principles have been very controversial since 1947.

The first and clearer principle is that prohibiting *dumping*. The general antidumping provisions are found in Article VI of the GATT.

GENERAL AGREEMENT ON TARIFFS AND TRADE

55 U.N.T.S. 194 (1947)

ARTICLE VI. ANTI-DUMPING AND COUNTERVAILING DUTIES

1. The contracting parties recognize that dumping, by which products of one country are introduced into the commerce of another country at less than the normal value of the products, is to be condemned if it causes or threatens material injury to an established industry in the territory of a contracting party or materially retards the establishment of a domestic industry. For the purposes of this Article, a product is to be considered as being introduced into the commerce of an importing country at less than its normal value, if the price of the product exported from one country to another

(a) is less than the comparable price, in the ordinary course of trade, for the like product when destined for consumption in the exporting country, or

(b) in the absence of such domestic price, is less than either

   (i) the highest comparable price for the like product for export to any third country in the ordinary course of trade, or

   (ii) the cost of production of the product in the country of origin plus a reasonable addition for selling cost and profit.

Due allowance shall be made in each case for differences in conditions and terms of sale, for differences in taxation, and for other differences affecting price comparability.

A second practice prohibited under the GATT is the payment of *unfair subsidies,* bounties, or grants. The principle opposes attempts by governments to distort the world market by specifically subsidizing exports. As more governments assist industry to promote economic growth, the issue of what an unfair subsidy is has become considerably more complex. Many governments use subsidies in a variety of forms, such as grants, tax forgiveness or deferral, or low-interest loans, in order to encourage businesses to train workers, locate in depressed areas of a country, develop needed products, or restructure industries. When those subsidies are aimed at export-generating businesses, there is the risk that the lowered cost of producing products for export will distort world markets. In the Tokyo Round, the United States led an effort to create a GATT subsidies code. The Subsidies Code adopted as part of the Tokyo Round and enacted into U.S. law takes aim at export subsidies, as opposed to those designed to achieve domestic objectives. If an importer is found to have received unfair subsidies, the Department of Commerce will assess a *countervailing duty* in an amount to offset the amount of the subsidy.

MULTILATERAL TRADE NEGOTIATIONS SUBSIDIES CODE (1979)

ARTICLE 11—SUBSIDIES OTHER THAN EXPORT SUBSIDIES

1. Signatories recognize that subsidies other than export subsidies are widely used as important instruments for the promotion of social and economic policy objectives and do not intend to restrict the right of signatories to use such subsidies to achieve these and other important policy objectives which they consider desirable. Signatories note that among such objectives are:

—the elimination of industrial, economic and social disadvantages of specific regions;

—to facilitate the restructuring, under socially acceptable conditions, of certain sectors, especially where this has become necessary by reason of changes in trade and economic policies, including international agreements resulting in lower barriers to trade;

—generally to sustain employment and to encourage re-training and change in employment;

—to encourage research and development programs, especially in the field of high-technology industries;

—the implementation of economic programs and policies to promote the economic and social development of developing countries;

—redeployment of industry in order to avoid congestion and environmental problems.

2. Signatories recognize, however, that subsidies other than export subsidies, certain objectives and possible forms of which are described, respectively, in paragraphs 1 and 3 of this Article, may cause or threaten to cause injury to a domestic industry of another signatory or serious prejudice to the interests of another signatory or may nullify or impair benefits accruing to another signatory under the General Agreement, in particular where such subsidies would adversely affect the conditions of normal competition. Signatories shall therefore seek to avoid causing such effects through the use of subsidies. . . .

3. Signatories recognize that the objectives mentioned in paragraph 1 above may be achieved, inter alia, by means of subsidies granted with the aim of giving an advantage to certain enterprises.

Examples of possible forms of such subsidies are: government financing of commercial enterprises, including grants, loans or guarantees; government provision or governmental financed provision of utility, supply distribution and other operational or support services or facilities; government financing of research and development programs; fiscal incentives; and government subscription to, or provision of, equity capital.

The signatories note that the above forms of subsidy are normally granted either regionally or by sector. The enumeration of forms of subsidy set out above is illustrative and non-exhaustive, and reflects those currently granted by a number of signatories to this Agreement.

ANNEX

Illustrative List of Export Subsidies

(a) The provision by governments of direct subsidies to a firm or an industry contingent on export performance.

(b) Currency retention schemes or any similar practices which involve a bonus on exports.

(c) Internal transport and freight charges on export shipments, provided or mandated by governments, on terms more favourable than for domestic shipments.

(d) The delivery by governments or their agencies of imported or domestic products or services for use in the production of exported goods, on terms or conditions more favourable than for delivery of like or directly competitive products or services for use on the production of goods for domestic consumption, if (in the case of products) such terms or conditions are more favourable than those commercially available on world markets to its exporters.

(e) The full or partial exemption, remission, or deferral specifically related to exports, of direct taxes or social welfare charges paid or payable by industrial or commercial enterprises.

(f) The allowance of special deductions directly related to exports or export performance, over and above those granted in respect to production for domestic consumption, in the calculation of the base on which direct taxes are charged.

(g) The exemption or remission in respect of the production and distribution of exported products, of indirect taxes in excess of those levied in respect of the production and distribution of like products when sold for domestic consumption. . . .

(j) The provision by governments (or special institutions controlled by governments) of export credit guarantee or insurance programs, of insurance or guarantee programs against increases in the costs of exported products or of exchange risk programmes, at premium rates, which are manifestly inadequate to cover the long-term operating costs and losses of the programmes.

(k) The grant by governments (or special institutions controlled by governments) of export credits at rates below those which they actually have to pay for the funds so employed (or would have to pay if they borrowed on international capital markets in order to obtain funds of the same maturity and denominated in the same currency as the export credit), or the payment by them of all or part of the costs incurred by exporters or financial institutions in obtaining credits, in so far as they are used to secure a material advantage in the field of export credit terms. . . .

(l) Any other charge on the public account constituting an export subsidy. . . .

Each member of the GATT adheres to the basic principles on dumping and unfair subsidies, but each country enforces them differently. In the United States, many industries leveled charges of dumping and unfair subsidies against foreign competitors in the 1980s. In both instances, the process for a U.S. manufacturer to obtain relief is long and complex, and can be political in part. Both dumping and unfair subsidy complaints may originate with a U.S. business, a group of businesses, or the International Trade Commission (ITC).

The ITC determines whether U.S. business is suffering injury or the threat of injury from the foreign competitors. The International Trade Administration, which is part of the Department of Commerce, then determines to what extent dumping or unfair subsidies are occurring and calculates the amount of offsetting duty. A party unhappy with the result may appeal the agency decisions to the Court of International Trade. The following case illustrates the process and some of the considerations in determining the amount of a countervailing duty.

PPG INDUSTRIES, INC. v. UNITED STATES

746 F. Supp. 119 (Court of International Trade, 1990)[4]

FACTS:

PPG brought a complaint against two Mexican exporters of automotive glass, alleging that they were receiving unfair export subsidies from the Mexican government. In January 1985, the Commerce Department published a determination that the companies had been unfairly subsidized, and assessed a countervailing duty of 4.68 percent. The defendants lost on appeal to the Court of International Trade in 1989.

In August 1985, the defendants renounced any further participation in the export programs that had been found to be unfair. In January 1986, the Commerce Department agreed to review its determination of countervailing duty rates. It published its results in July 1986, setting a countervailing duty rate of 6.51 percent for 1984 and 0.12 percent for 1985. After public comment and a hearing, the rates were adjusted to 2.45 percent for 1984 and 0.17 percent for 1985. The latter rate was found to be *de minimis*, so exempt from countervailing duties.

PPG appealed, alleging that the ITA: (1) failed to properly compute the benefits of the defendants' participation in FOMEX (Fund for the Promotion of Exports of Mexican Manufacture) a government trust providing low-interest loans to Mexican exporters; (2) wrongly found that Mexico's FICORCA program (Fund for the Coverage of Exchange Risks) was not an unfair subsidy; (3) wrongly found that Mexico's natural gas pricing system was not an unfair subsidy; and (4) failed to investigate whether the CEDI program (Certificado de Devolution del Impuesto), an export tax rebate program, was countervailable.

ISSUE:

Was the ITA's analysis of the various subsidy programs supported by substantial evidence?

RESULT:

The calculation of benefits received from the FOMEX program was incorrect. The three other determinations were supported by substantial evidence. The court sent the case back to the ITA for recalculation.

REASONS:

I. FOMEX Program. PPG contends that Commerce failed to calculate the full benefit provided to Mexican autoglass producers by FOMEX loans and improperly allocated the benefits over an arbitrarily chosen time period.

In determining whether a countervailable subsidy had been conferred by FOMEX pre-export loans at preferential rates, and the amount of any such subsidy, Commerce compared the FOMEX loan interest rate with a benchmark national average interest rate. The benchmark rate purportedly reflected the loan interest rate a Mexican company could have obtained through private channels. In determining the benchmark rate for 1984, Commerce used the effective interest rates published by the Bank of Mexico in the publication *Indicadores Economicos* (I.E.) for that year. . . .

. . . PPG does not object to Commerce's methodology per se, but contends that Commerce understated the benefit conferred by pre-export peso denominated loans by assuming that compensating balances [funds held by a bank as security for a loan] were accounted for in the I.E. interest rates, upon which Commerce based its benchmark rates. . . .

. . . The Court holds there is substantial evidence on the record to support Commerce's determination that the I.E. rates included an accommodation for the effect of compensating balances. The record reflects that the I.E. rates measured *average* effective interest rates on short term loans, and were compiled through a survey of a cross-section of Mexican loan transactions. . . . Loan terms varied from bank to bank and loan to loan. Compensating balances were not required for all loans; they were merely one of many charges that might have been added to the nomi-

[4]This decision was upheld after PPG's appeal, *PPG Industries, Inc. v. United States*, 928 F.2d 1568 (Fed. Cir. 1991).

nal interest rate to increase the total cost of the loan. . . .

PPG also claims Commerce incorrectly calculated the benefit arising from FOMEX export loans denominated in United States dollars.

In its final administrative review determination, Commerce stated that it lacked sufficient information to calculate an effective interest rate benchmark of 1984, and was compelled to rely upon the nominal interest rate for short-term loans in the United States. . . . PPG argues that Commerce had enough evidence in the record to calculate the effective 1984 interest rate for its FOMEX export loan benchmark, and that it was error for Commerce to use nominal rates.

For calculations concerning 1985 FOMEX export loans, Commerce used the quarterly weighted average effective interest rates published by the Federal Reserve as its benchmark. Commerce noted that the effective interest rates reflected the terms of the loans plus the nominal interest rates.

PPG argues that Commerce failed to include anything in the record that would explain how the Federal Reserve effective rates for 1985 had been compiled. In particular, PPG questions whether the Federal Reserve effective rates, utilized by Commerce in constructing its benchmark rate, accounted for compensating balances.

In its response, Commerce originally agreed with both of PPG's arguments and requested a remand so that it could "ascertain which finance charges, if any, are included in the benchmark dollar interest rates for the years 1984 and 1985." . . . Commerce agreed that within the context of a remand it could ascertain the effective interest

rates for the 1984 export loan benchmark and that utilizing effective rates over nominal rates would be desirable. . . .

In support of its request for a remand to reexamine the 1985 benchmark rate, Commerce indicated it harbored some uncertainty as to which finance charges were included in the quarterly average interest rates published in the Federal Reserve Bulletin. However, at oral argument, Commerce took the position that a remand was only appropriate on the issue of the 1984 FOMEX export benchmark rates. Commerce contended that the 1985 benchmark rate did indeed account for the effect of compensating balances and was supported by substantial evidence on the record.

The Court agrees that a remand is appropriate to allow Commerce to determine an effective interest rate for its benchmark for 1984 FOMEX export loans, and to recalculate the actual amount of the benefit conferred upon the defendant-intervenors [the glass exporters].

Additionally, the Court directs that on remand Commerce reexamine the 1985 benchmark rate to ascertain which finance charges, if any, were included in the quarterly average interest rates Commerce relied upon in compiling its benchmark. Further, Commerce is directed to examine whether or not the Federal Reserve effective rates used by Commerce in constructing its benchmark rate, accounted for compensating balances and what effect that factor had upon its determination.

[The court then held that all of the remaining decisions of the ITA were supported by substantial evidence, so could not be overturned on appeal.]

As the *PPG* case shows, the process for a U.S. business to obtain relief from unfair subsidies can be extremely long and complicated. Six years after the import of unfairly subsidized auto glass, PPG still had no final determination of the remedy. As a tool that a U.S. business might want to use against an unfairly competing foreign business, the proceedings are not always very helpful.

One significant area of difficulty with both dumping and subsidy cases during the 1980s was with imports from nonmarket economies. In dumping cases, the issue became one of determining fair value in a home market that did not set prices based on supply and demand. In subsidy cases, one of the main arguments from U.S. businesses is that a command economy's artificial pricing of both finished products and component parts of products operated as an unfair export subsidy. With the nations of Eastern Europe rapidly moving toward market economies, these problems should diminish considerably in the 1990s, although imports from China will continue to be problematic.

10.4 BILATERAL AND REGIONAL TRADE STRUCTURES

The GATT has not proven a sufficiently adaptable structure to regulate world trade. Even before the difficulties of the Uruguay Round, many nations found the need to look outside the framework of the GATT for structures for trading relationships. In some cases, two countries will negotiate trade agreements directly, either for limited purposes or for more general regulation. In other cases, such as the European Community, a region may establish a trade regime comprehensive enough perhaps to replace the GATT.

TRADING TREATIES

Long before the GATT, nations negotiated trade agreements on a one-on-one basis. Historically, the most widely used form of treaty was known as a Treaty of Friendship, Commerce and Navigation (FCN). Such treaties were comprehensive agreements providing for MFN status, national treatment for trade, investment, property ownership and transfer, access to courts, intellectual property rights, and employment rights. Additionally, FCN treaties opened ports to the ships of each signatory country, and provided for navigation rights in each country's territorial waters. Although they have been used for centuries, FCN treaties can have surprising effects in the current era of multinational business.

MACNAMARA v. KOREAN AIR LINES

863 F.2d 1135 (3d Cir. 1988)

FACTS:
MacNamara worked as a district sales manager for Korean Air Lines (KAL) in New Jersey. As part of a reorganization, he was one of six American managers discharged and replaced by four Korean citizens. MacNamara charged that he was terminated on the basis of race, national origin, and age, in violation of Title VII of the Civil Rights Act of 1964, the Age Discrimination in Employment Act, and the Employee Retirement Income Security Act of 1974 (ERISA). KAL argued that it was exempt from the reach of these statutes under

Article VIII of Korea's FCN treaty with the United States. That article reads, in part:

> Nationals and companies of either Party shall be permitted to engage, within the territories of the other Party, accountants and other technical experts, executive personnel, attorneys, agents and other specialists of their choice.

KAL's motion to dismiss was granted by the district court. MacNamara appealed to the court of appeals.

ISSUE:

Does the FCN treaty exempt KAL from complying with U.S. employment discrimination laws?

RESULT:

Not entirely. The FCN does not conflict with the prohibitions against intentional discrimination. However, the FCN does prevail against claims that employment practices have a disparate impact on a group based on race, national origin or age.

REASONS:

[The court first held that both MacNamara and his successors were executives, so that the treaty language applied.]

Article VIII(1) of the Korean FCN Treaty on its face is absolute and ostensibly self-defining. Neither KAL nor MacNamara, however, suggest that a literal interpretation of the provision is an appropriate one. Both parties agree, for example, that the right to "executive personnel . . . of their choice" does not entitle a foreign company operating in the United States to select among American citizens on the basis of their age, race, sex, religion, or national origin, although Article VIII(1) on its face would permit such discrimination. . . .

The parties also agree that Article VIII(1) goes beyond assuring national treatment. Whatever the rules governing the selection of executive personnel by host country companies, foreign businesses are granted the right to engage "executive personnel . . . of their choice." Moreover, the parties further agree that this right include the right to discriminate on the basis of citizenship; thus foreign businesses clearly have the right to choose

citizens of their own nation as executives because they are such citizens. . . .

MacNamara contends that the only right granted by Article VIII(1) is the right to choose one's own citizens because of their citizenship. As a result, according to MacNamara, Article VIII(1) does not confer the right to choose one's own citizen over a citizen of the host country because of race, sex, or age. KAL, on the other hand, reads Article VIII(1) to confirm more than the right to choose one's citizens because of their citizenship; it finds in the provision an immunity from Title VII and the ADEA for any decision on executive personnel that favors a citizen of one's own nation. The KAL argues in effect that it has the right under Article VIII(1) to choose a citizen of Korea for an executive position for any reason and a concomitant right to be free from judicial scrutiny of its subjective motivation in choosing the Korean citizen. . . .

While we find some merit in KAL's position, we conclude that it paints with far too broad a brush. The target of Article VIII(1) was legislation that forced foreign employers to hire host country personnel. Because its objective was thus limited, the text and the relevant history indicate that the negotiators understood that employment decisions regarding the personnel described in Article VIII(1) would be free of domestic laws utilizing citizenship as a criterion, but would be subject generally to other legally imposed criteria.

. . . Having concluded that KAL cannot purposefully discriminate on the basis of age, race or national origin, we now turn to the most difficult aspect of this case. To this point, we have confined our analysis to liability for intentional discrimination. The reach of Title VII and the ADEA, however, extends beyond intentionally discriminatory employment policies to those practices fair in form, but discriminatory in impact. . . . Accordingly, Title VII and ADEA liability can be found where facially neutral employment practices have a discriminatory effect or "disparate impact" on protected groups, without proof that the employer adopted these practices with a discriminatory motive. . . . In establishing this kind of disparate impact liability, parties generally rely exclusively on statistical evidence of disproportionate effect. . . .

The fact that empirical evidence can satisfy the

substantive standard of liability would pose a substantial problem in disparate impact litigation for corporations hailing from countries, including perhaps Korea, whose populations are largely homogeneous. Because a company's requirement that its employees be citizens of the homogeneous country from which it hails means that almost all of its employees will be of the same national origin and race, the statistical disparity between otherwise qualified non-citizens of a particular race and national origin, and citizens of the foreign country's race and national origin is likely to be substantial. As a result, a foreign business from a country with a homogeneous population, by merely exercising its protected Treaty right to prefer its own citizens for management positions, could be held in violation of Title VII. . . .

For this reason, we conclude that disparate impact liability under Title VII and the ADEA for a foreign employer based on its practice of engaging its own nationals as managers cannot be reconciled with Article VIII(1). Accordingly, we hold that such liability may not be imposed.

[The court remanded the case to the district court, in order to allow MacNamara to allege and prove intentional discrimination.]

Another kind of bilateral treaty currently in use is simply called a Trade Agreement. One recent example of such an agreement establishing trade relations is the Czechoslovakia–United States Agreement on Trade Relations, signed in 1990. Different in scope from the traditional FCN treaty, the Czech–U.S. agreement affirms that each country will participate in the GATT, extends MFN status to each, reaffirms commitments to multilateral intellectual property treaties, affirms that each country will encourage trade in goods and services, and agrees not to encourage barter and countertrade. As the excerpt below indicates, the tone of the trade agreement is one of encouragement rather than legalities.

AGREEMENT ON TRADE RELATIONS BETWEEN THE GOVERNMENT OF THE UNITED STATES OF AMERICA AND THE GOVERNMENT OF THE CZECHOSLOVAK FEDERATIVE REPUBLIC

29 I.L.M. 902 (1990)

ARTICLE IV. *EXPANSION AND PROMOTION OF TRADE*

1. The Parties affirm their desire to expand trade in products and services consistent with the terms of this Agreement. They shall take appropriate measures to encourage and facilitate the exchange of products and services and to secure favorable conditions for the long term development of trade relations within their respective nationals and companies. The Parties shall promote the development and diversification of their commercial exchanges to the fullest extent possible.

2. The Parties shall take appropriate measures to encourage the expansion of commercial contacts with a view to increasing trade. In this regard, the Government of Czechoslovakia shall, consistent with commercial considerations, increase their purchases of products and services from the United States, while the Government of the United States expects that the effect of this Agreement will be to encourage increased pur-

chases by nationals and companies of the United States of products and services from Czechoslovakia. Toward this end, the Parties shall publi-

cize this Agreement and ensure that it is made available to all interested parties.

The agreement goes on to allow the removal of profits earned in convertible currencies, encourage the establishment of trade fairs, encourage the use of arbitration to resolve commercial disputes, and allow companies to employ nationals of each country.

THE CANADA–U.S. FREE TRADE AGREEMENT

One of the most significant bilateral treaties negotiated in recent years is the Canada–U.S. Free Trade Agreement (FTA). Canada–U.S. trade is already the largest exchange in the world, and this agreement will create the largest free trade structure between two nations in the world. The agreement also served as a model for negotiations with Mexico to create a North American Free Trade Agreement, with a regional free trade zone including Mexico, Canada, and the United States. That agreement, reached in August 1992, had not been ratified by any of the countries as this book went to press. As the authority of the GATT wanes, the EC and the North American free trade zone are good examples of the kinds of regional trading blocs that are likely to replace the GATT.

The FTA begins with a schedule for removing tariffs from all goods shipped between the two countries. The parties agree not to increase any current tariffs and to eliminate all tariffs in three stages. Category A goods, including automated data processing equipment, leather, telephones, motorcycles, modems, whiskey and rum, furs, animal feeds, and unwrought aluminum, had their tariffs eliminated on January 1, 1989. Category B goods, which include, for example, paper products, furniture, some auto parts, machines and chemicals, and petroleum, had their tariffs lowered annually, then eliminated by January 1, 1993. Category C goods, which include, for example, steel, rubber, most agricultural products, and textiles, will gradually eliminate tariffs over a period ending on January 1, 1998.

In addition to the usual area of trading in goods, the FTA covers several areas of special interest to both countries. It provides that the two nations will work together to eliminate the global subsidies that distort world trade in agriculture. The FTA also specifically targets some bilateral agriculture issues, such as import quotas on meat and sugar and import licensing schemes. The FTA removed most restrictions on the bilateral trade in energy, of significance because Canada presently supplies all of the U.S. imports of natural gas and electricity, as well as large quantities of oil and uranium.

A substantial component of all exports from Canada to the United States and vice versa is trade in automobiles and parts. Both countries have operated under a special Automotive Agreement for many years. The FTA preserves that Agreement, providing for special tariff treatment for automobiles manufactured in Canada or the United States.

What is most revolutionary about the FTA is that it deals with many areas not usually a part of trade agreements. Some of these areas are the very topics that are dividing the GATT. For example, the FTA agrees that the parties will end "buy national" restrictions for the government procurement of a wide variety of goods. The FTA also commits to changing immigration procedures to make it easier for Canadian firms to assign Canadian executives to American offices, and vice versa. Most importantly, the FTA provides a regime for trading in services and for investment, two issues that were serious stumbling blocks in the Uruguay Round of the GATT talks.

In services, the FTA agrees to provide national treatment for many commercial service providers (exemptions include transportation, some telecommunications, doctors and dentists, lawyers, and child-care services). Professional licensing requirements may not discriminate between American and Canadian nationals, and neither country may introduce new regulations requiring the other's nationals to establish a commercial presence in order to provide services. This services agreement should allow for the binational provision of services by accounting firms, management consultants, computer service providers, and many other business services.

The FTA's investment regime makes significant changes in the Investment Canada Act, which the United States has regarded as an impediment to investment. The FTA provides for national treatment in the commencement of new businesses, the conduct of existing businesses, and the acquisition of businesses. As of 1992, an American's acquisition of a Canadian business will be subject to government review if it exceeds $150 million for a direct investment, with no review of indirect investments.

Finally, the FTA created dispute resolution mechanisms that will give binding decisions on trade issues within a reasonable period of time. In dumping and subsidy cases, the FTA replaces judicial review of determinations of dumping and unfair subsidies with binding review by a binational panel. The binational panels are made up of five persons drawn from a list of fifty candidates. There is functionally no appeal from the decision of the panel. Thus, rather than consuming years in the court systems, dumping and subsidy cases may take only months.

For other trade-related issues, the FTA uses a different procedure. Suppose that the Canadian lobster industry believes that U.S. regulations requiring lobsters to measure 3^{1}/4 inches from claw to claw operate as a nontariff barrier to trade. Under the FTA, the first step toward resolving the dispute would be a consultation between the governments. If that contact did not resolve the dispute to the satisfaction of the governments, either one could request a meeting of the Canada–U.S. Trade Commission, which would have to meet within 10 days. If the Commission could not resolve the dispute within 30 days, the dispute would go either to binding arbitration or to a panel of experts that would provide recommendations to the Commission, which would then have to come to an agreement.

The Free Trade Agreement has gotten off to a somewhat rocky start. Popular opinion in Canada is negative, as the agreement has, in the short term, cost Canada many jobs. The United States and Canada have been able to resolve many trade issues using the binational panels, but the United States, in particular, continues to pressure Canada on trade issues for reasons that many Canadians believe are political rather than real. In 1991, the United States went so far as to request the convening of an Extraordinary Challenge Committee, ordinarily reserved for instances of abuse of process or gross misconduct, to review a panel decision it had lost. The Committee convened and rejected the U.S. appeal.[5]

10.5 THE SPECIAL ROLE OF DEVELOPING NATIONS

From the start of the GATT talks, many of the less-developed countries (LDCs) of the world did not share the GATT's favorable view of the tariff reduction system. The LDCs argued that the state of their economies was in some measure due to the history of colonialism by the developed nations, and that they needed special tariff incentives to develop their economies. They contended that the tariff reductions negotiated in each round tended to favor the manufactured and more complex products exported by developed countries, rather than the raw materials, commodities, and goods like shoes and textiles often exported from LDCs.

In recognition of these positions, the developed nations have established several preferential trading regimes. Britain and France both developed trade preference schemes for their former colonies. In 1964, the United Nations Commission on Trade and Development (UNCTAD), which tends to represent the interests of developing nations, proposed that the developed nations should work up a system of tariff preferences for exports from developing nations. Most of the developed countries, including the United States, responded.

THE GENERALIZED SYSTEM OF PREFERENCES (GSP)

First enacted in 1976, the United States' GSP program allows duty-free imports for roughly 3000 different items from about 140 countries. It is de-

---

[5]*In the Matter of Fresh, Chilled or Frozen Pork from Canada*, 30 I.L.M. 1155 (1991).

signed to be a temporary program to help LDCs develop the business infrastructure necessary to compete in world trade. To get duty-free treatment, the import must be an eligible product from an eligible country.

The U.S. Trade Representative maintains the list of eligible products, from which certain kinds of goods have been excluded as "import sensitive"; that is, likely to harm U.S. domestic industries. Among those items are textiles and textile products, many leather goods, some electronics goods, some steel products, watches, some footwear, and some glass products. Items may be added to the list, but may also be deleted as they become import sensitive. Items may also be deleted for a specific country if imports of that item from one country exceed 50 percent of the total imports from all countries, or a specific dollar value (approximately $60 million) in any one year.

Most of the LDCs are eligible to become beneficiary countries under the GSP, but some restrictions do apply. For example, Communist-dominated countries and members of OPEC that participated in oil embargoes are ineligible. So are countries that do not cooperate with U.S. drug suppression efforts or expropriate U.S. property. In 1984, Congress added a provision requiring beneficiary countries to recognize workers' rights. Chile was suspended from beneficiary status using this provision in 1987.

In 1984, Congress added a graduation program to the GSP. Countries whose per-capita gross national product exceeds $8500 (indexed for inflation) must be phased out of GSP participation. The graduation program also allowed for the removal of countries from the program when they were no longer serving the interests of the GSP. In 1989, South Korea, Hong Kong, Taiwan, and Singapore were graduated from the GSP program, based in part on their status as advanced developing countries and in part on their large trade surpluses with the United States. The rationale for their removal was that the four countries were enjoying a disproportionate share of GSP benefits, and that their removal might help other LDCs in gaining benefits from the GSP program.

THE CARIBBEAN BASIN INITIATIVE

This tariff program began in 1983 as a way to encourage economic development in the Caribbean, including Central America. To qualify for duty-free entry of a wide variety of goods to the United States, a country must meet extensive eligibility requirements, including agreeing to assist in U.S. drug control efforts, agreeing to follow GATT principles and maintain markets open to U.S. goods, maintaining basic workers' rights, recognizing arbitration awards, and agreeing to protect U.S. intellectual property rights.

An eligible country may import its products into the United States duty-free. Unlike the GSP, the product is automatically eligible unless it is on a specific exclusion list. That list includes textiles and apparel, footwear, leather goods, tuna, petroleum and its products, and watches. The CBI also does not have a maximum level of imports allowed, except for sugar.

Thus, the nations of the Caribbean enjoy broader tariff preferences than the nations in the GSP program.

THE LOMÉ CONVENTION

The EEC has taken a different approach to the problem of trading regimes to aid LDC development. The current treaty, Lomé IV, is between the EC and sixty-nine LDCs in Africa, the Caribbean, and the Pacific (ACP nations). Lomé IV provides for duty-free imports of a variety of industrial products from ACP nations and tariff preferences on many agricultural products.

Beyond the standard tariff benefits, Lomé IV contains provisions designed to stabilize the economies of LDCs'. Because many LDCs economies are dependent on commodity or mineral exports, fluctuations in commodity or mineral prices, often a product of events in other nations, can be destructive to economic development. Lomé adopts two systems, Stabex and Minex, designed to make payments to ACP nations when commodity or mineral prices fall. Under Stabex, a country that is highly dependent on export earnings from one of the eligible products such as cocoa, coffee, vanilla, leather products, cotton, bananas, or tea may receive payment from the EC to stabilize export earnings when the price of those commodities falls too far in a given period. Minex works on a similar basis.

10.6 CONCLUSION

The world trading system in place since the end of World War II is at a crossroads today. Either the GATT will expand to cover successfully a wider variety of issues, such as intellectual property, services, investment, and agriculture, or it will disintegrate. If it fails, and even if pieces of the GATT remain useful, regional trading blocs such as the EC and the proposed North American Free Trade Area will provide much of the structure for world trade well into the next century. Bilateral agreements will also have an important role in areas in which no regional agreement is in place, or where governments are in transition, such as the nations of Eastern Europe and of the Pacific Rim.

Through all of this change, tariff preference programs will remain in place, although they will be subject to political pressure based on job losses to LDCs. Eligibility for tariff preference programs, already an important basis for strategic business decisions on location of maufacturing facilities, may become more important as the regional associations gain strength. For example, a plant located in Jamaica may be eligible for duty-free treatment in the EC, as part of Lomé, and in the United States, as part of the Carribean Basin Initiative.

10.7 QUESTIONS FOR DISCUSSION

1. An EC directive mandates that 50 percent of all television broadcasts within EC member countries should be "European" in origin. Does that rule violate the GATT? Explain.

2. Health issues are also prominent in GATT problems. The EC banned imports of beef from cattle routinely fed hormones. The ban primarily affected U.S. beef exporters, who claim that Americans eat this beef regularly with no ill effects. Similarly, the United States bans imports of cheeses, such as authentic French Camembert, made from unpasteurized milk. The French have eaten this cheese for hundreds of years with no ill effects. Do either of these bans violate the GATT?

3. In the late 1960s Compagnie Générale de Etablissements Michelin, a French tire maker, decided to establish a North American manufacturing facility. After lengthy negotiation, it decided to locate a large truck tire plant in New Brunswick, Canada. Since the Canadian market for truck tires would not use the plant's capacity, one of the specific purposes of the plant was to make tires for export. The Canadian federal and provincial authorities offered incentives to get Michelin to locate in New Brunswick. Among the incentives were a land donation, tax reductions, cash grants for capital costs and employee training, and below-market interest rate loans. If U.S. tire makers challenged the imports of truck tires produced at Michelin's Canadian plant, would they be entitled to a countervailing duty?

4. One idea that U.S. politicians regularly float is that the United States should adopt a Japanese-style system of managed trade. Do you think this would be a good idea? If so, what do you think should be the strategic industries in a U.S. industrial plan?

5. As a project, go to a local, state, or provincial economic development office. Find out what incentives it offers businesses to locate in your area. Could any of these incentives be considered unfair subsidies?

10.8 FURTHER READINGS

S. Battram, "Canada–United States Trade Negotiations: Continental Accord or a Continent Apart?," 22 *International Lawyer* 345–391 (1988).

John H. Jackson, *The World Trading System*, MIT Press, Cambridge, Mass., 1989.

J. Newman, "Korea and the American Generalized System of Preferences: Was Graduation a Proper Response?," 11 *University of Pennsylvania Journal of International Business Law* 687–708 (1990).

B. Zagaris, "A Caribbean Perspective of the Caribbean Basin Initiative," 18 *International Lawyer* 563–581 (1984).

REGULATING IMPORTS AND EXPORTS

11.1 INTRODUCTION

The import and export of goods are subject to extensive regulation in virtually all countries. As you learned in Chapter 10, the regulatory framework starts with the GATT, and is supplemented by regional and bilateral trade treaties. Within this framework, each country has laws and regulations implementing its agreements and protecting its perceived national interests.

Import regulations affect both financial and nonfinancial issues. On the financial side, import regulations take the form of a tax known as a tariff. On the nonfinancial side are restrictions on quantities, in the form of licenses or quotas, and such other nontariff barriers as safety standards, environmental requirements, and technical standards. Import restrictions are the subject of much of the GATT and of other treaties.

Export regulations affect both export promotion and control. Export promotions have as their outer legal boundary the unfair subsidy–countervailing duty provisions of the GATT. By contrast, export controls tend to reflect national interests, although export controls do address issues relating to the collective national security of NATO and the Allied nations.

This chapter examines import and export regulation primarily in the context of the U.S. experience and legal system. Many of the issues raised in U.S. law are similar to those raised by the laws of other nations and of the EC.

11.2 TARIFFS AND CUSTOMS

As you learned in Chapter 1, governments have always looked to the traffic in goods across their borders as an important source of revenue. The tax charged on incoming goods is known as a tariff or a duty. In the United States, the program of monitoring goods at the border and collecting applicable tariffs is run by the U.S. Customs Service, a branch of the Treasury Department.

As the worldwide legal environment for trade has become more complex, the application of customs laws has also become more complex. When goods are imported into the United States, three main issues need to be resolved in order to determine the appropriate tariff: the classification of the product, its value, and its place of origin. In U.S. law, the importer has the primary responsibility for resolving these issues within the framework of the law.

PRODUCT CLASSIFICATION

As of January 1, 1989, the United States has adopted the Harmonized Tariff Schedule, an international system of tariff classification, to determine the proper classification and duty for goods entering the country. The Harmonized Schedule contains more than 9000 product listings, organized into sections of broad product descriptions, and within each section, chapters. Each chapter contains headings and subheadings, which are labeled with a four-, six-, or eight-digit code. The code numbers apply across all the countries using the Harmonized System, which speeds the entry of goods, the use of electronic documentation, and the statistical reporting of imports.

Despite the multitude of available product listings, some products fit more than one category or, in the case of new technologies, do not neatly fit any category. In that case, the Harmonized Schedule provides several rules of interpretation designed to help the importer and the Customs Service choose the proper designation. The difficulties of choosing the proper category may be apparent from the following relatively simple case. Although this case was about transactions that preceded the date on which the Harmonized Schedule went into effect, the court's method of interpretation still applied.

HASBRO INDUSTRIES, INC. v. UNITED STATES

879 F.2d 838 (Fed. Cir. 1989)

FACTS:

Hasbro imported G.I. Joe Action Figures from Hong Kong during 1982–1983. It sought to have the toys classified under Item 737.40 of the then Tariff Schedule of the United States (TSUS) as "Toy Figures of animate objects (except dolls): Not having a spring mechanism: Not stuffed: Other." The Customs office classified the toys under Item 737.24, "other dolls," which subjected them to various rates of duty, depending on the date of import. Hasbro appealed the designation to the Court of International Trade, which ruled in favor of the Customs Service. Hasbro appealed.

ISSUE:

Is G.I. Joe a doll?

RESULT:

Yes. The Customs Service designation is correct.

REASONS:

The articles in dispute are fully described in the opinion below:

All the figures are made of plastic, are approximately 3 ½ inches tall, and have the appearance of human beings dressed and equipped in a manner associated with actual or fictional warfare. They are noticeably *lifelike* and constructed in a manner which permits an impressive range of movement. The head turns from side to side, the arms are jointed at the shoulder and elbow and also have a rotational joint above the elbow and a rotational joint capacity in the shoulder. They can turn at the waist and also bend slightly in all directions from the waist. The legs have a wide range of movement at the hip and sufficient bending action in the knees to allow the figure to kneel or sit. The articulated joints maintain the position in which they are placed by manipulation. (Emphasis added). . . .

Each figure is packaged singly in a large plastic blister mounted on a large card which contains specific biographical information for each figure. For example, First Sergeant, Code Name: Duke, has the following personnel card:

File Name: Hauser, Conrad S.
SN: RA213757793
Primary Military Specialty: Airborne Infantryman

Secondary Military Specialty: Artillery, Small-arms armorer

Birthplace: St. Louis, MO Grade: E-8 (Master Sergeant)

Duke was fluent in French, German and English when he enlisted in 1967. Graduated top of his class at airborne school, Fort Benning. Opted for U.S. Army Special Language School. Specialized in Han Chinese and South East Asian dialects. Went Special Forces in 1969. Worked with tribesmen in the boonies of South Vietnam. Ran four different Special Forces schools. Turned down a commission in 1971. Commands by winning respect. Current assignment: Acting First Sergeant, G.I. Joe team. Statement after declining commission. "They tell me that an officer's job is to impel others to take risks—so that the officer survives to take the blame in the event of total catastrophe. With all due respect, sir . . . if that's what an officer does, I don't want any part of it."

In addition, each figure comes with its own specialized accessories. For example, First Sergeant comes with plastic pieces representing binoculars, a helmet, an assault pack, and an M-32 sub-machine gun.

. . . To determine the common meaning of a tariff term like "doll," it is well established that the court "may consult dictionaries, scientific authorities, and other reliable information sources to ascertain that common meaning." . . . The Court of International Trade referred to a general dictionary defining the word "doll" as a representation of a human being used as a child's plaything. While we conclude that this summary definition is not an all inclusive definition for the term "doll," we determine that it is suitable for this case.

. . . Given this broad common meaning of the term "doll," we next review whether the Court of International Trade clearly erred when it found that the G.I. Joe action figure fit within that term. We determine it did not. The evidence of record includes testimony (including expert testimony), magazine articles referring to G.I. Joe as a doll, doll collector books, and the imported articles themselves. The record supports the Court of International Trade's finding.

Finally, we turn to Hasbro's argument that the long established practice of the Customs Service is to exclude traditional toy soldiers from the tariff provision for dolls. Assuming, arguendo, that traditional toy soldiers are treated differently than dolls for tariff purposes, Hasbro's argument is not persuasive. As the Court of International Trade explained, the individual personality of each of these figures, as evidenced by his biographical file cards and physical characteristics inviting "intimate and manipulative" play, . . . indicates that these figures are not comparable to the identical, immobile faceless toy soldiers of yesteryear that were sold in groups of a dozen or so in bags. The G.I. Joe action figures do come within the common meaning of the term "doll" as set forth in lexicographic authorities and earlier judicial decisions.

Accordingly, although Hasbro has fought valiantly that these figures are not dolls, we are unable to agree. Even though G.I. Joe has lost this battle, hopefully he will not lose his courage for combat, despite being officially designated by the United States Customs Service as a "doll."

CUSTOMS VALUATION

Most customs duties are ad valorem taxes; that is, the tax is a percentage of the value of the goods. Thus, determining the value of the goods is an important part of the customs process. The Tokyo Round of the GATT adopted a valuation code to attempt to standardize valuation practices. The U.S. version of that code is §402 of the Trade Agreements Act of 1979.

The usual standard for valuing imports is the "transaction value" of the actual merchandise. In most cases, this is the price the importer pays, less any charges the seller includes in the price for international shipment. The

Customs Service adds to that actual price any packing costs or selling commissions incurred by the buyer, any royalties or license fees the buyer must pay, the value of any "assists," such as tools, dies, or molds provided by the buyer, and any amounts that would accrue to the seller on a subsequent resale.

If it is not possible to use the transaction value for the actual goods, the Customs Service will use the transaction value of identical merchandise (sold to a different buyer) or of similar merchandise. If these methods do not work, the goods may be assigned a "deductive value"; that is, the price of similar goods in the United States, or a computed value, which totals the cost of production and packing as well as an estimated profit level. If these methods fail, the Customs Service may then apply any number of other methods to value the product.

RULES OF ORIGIN

In order to compute the proper tariff, the importer also needs to know where the goods come from. As you learned in Chapter 10, tariffs vary, depending on the source of the imported goods. In the United States, for example, the basic tariff comes from the Smoot-Hawley Tariff Act of 1930, which sets punitive tax rates on imports. Fortunately, most countries have most-favored nation (MFN) status with the United States, and thus have significantly lower tax rates on their products. A country's products may be entitled to even lower tax rates when the country belongs to a tariff preference program like the Generalized System of Preferences (GSP) or the Caribbean Basin Initiative (CBI). Finally, imports from countries in free-trade areas, such as Canada, or under the proposed North American Free Trade Agreement (NAFTA), like Mexico, may have their products qualify for duty-free import. Thus, the place of origin is an important factor in determining the appropriate tariff for imports.

However, in this era of multinational corporations, it is not always easy to determine the source country for imports. The production of goods may take place at any number of places around the globe. Companies have the ability to ship parts and materials to any point for assembly or manufacture in order to take advantage of low taxes, low wages, low energy costs, and tariff preference programs. In some cases, companies subject to antidumping duties have simply shipped the component parts to another country for assembly in what is called a "screwdriver plant," then exported the goods from the second country, which was not subject to a dumping order. In 1990, the United States adopted a procedure designed to prevent the use of screwdriver plants to circumvent antidumping orders.

Problems with determining a place of origin occur when goods from one or more countries are exported to another country during the production process. Goods may have components from several countries. For example, automobiles assembled in Ohio may use sheet metal from the United States, glass from Mexico, engine parts from Japan, and upholstery from Canada. When the automobiles arrive at their final destination, there will be more than one possible place of origin for the goods.

Customs officials have several possible rules they can use to determine a place of origin of the goods. In some circumstances, they will look to the percentage of content from each country to determine the place of origin. The percentage is most often expressed as a percentage of value.

Another rule often used to determine the place of origin is the rule of "substantial transformation." In using this rule, customs officials look at the places where goods are processed to determine whether goods had changed enough in processing to take on a new place of origin. For example, a business might buy vinyl from Mexico and metal hangers from Brazil. If it ships these components to Jamaica, where they are turned into luggage, an importer could probably declare Jamaica as the place of origin, because the goods had undergone a significant change there. In the last few years, variations on this rule, such as "change in character, appearance, identity, and use," "value added," and "change in tariff classification" have been used as alternative tests. The following case illustrates how these rules would apply.

BELCREST LINENS v. UNITED STATES

741 F.2d 1368 (Fed. Cir. 1984)

FACTS:

Belcrest imported pillowcases from Hong Kong that were produced from cotton percale woven in China. In China, the material was woven into a bolt of material, then stenciled with (1) an embroidered design, (2) cutting marks, and (3) a scalloped edge. In Hong Kong, the pieces were cut, sewn, scalloped, whitened, pressed, folded, packed, and shipped.

The Customs Service assessed a 90 percent duty on the goods as products of China. The importer appealed, asserting that the goods should be assessed at a duty rate of 34 percent. The Court of International Trade ruled in favor of the importer, and the government appealed.

ISSUE:

Are the pillowcases a product of Hong Kong?

RESULT:

Yes, the processing in Hong Kong changed the essential character of the goods.

REASONS:

The case most directly on point is Chemo Pure *Mfg. Co. v. United States*, 34 Cust. Ct. 8 (1954), wherein Chinese nutgalls were imported into the United Kingdom and processed into tannic acid. In holding that the United Kingdom was the country of exportation, the court stated:

> The merchandise here in question, in its condition as imported, is tannic acid, not nutgalls. The identity of the nutgalls, produced in China, has been lost, and a new product with a new name, a new use, and a distinct tariff status has been produced in the United Kingdom, the country of exportation. The imported tannic acid is, therefore, an article the growth, produce, or manufacture of the United Kingdom and dutiable as such. . . .

This test, that an article is the "growth, produce, or manufacture" of an intermediary country if as a result of processes performed in that country a new article emerges with a new name, use, or identity, is essentially the test used by the courts in determining whether an article is a manufacture of a given country under other areas of customs law. . . .

The government also argues that the trial court erred when it failed to utilize the "substantially transformed" test as developed under other areas of customs law in determining whether the imported pillowcases were products of China or Hong Kong. Although we decline to advance a definition of this term for all purposes, . . . it is clear that a "substantial transformation" occurs when as a result of a process an article emerges, having a distinctive name, character or use. . . .

In the case at bar . . . the processes performed in Hong Kong were not minor assembly operations which left the identity of the merchandise imported from China intact. The bolts of cloth were cut, the pieces were scalloped, and then sewn with decorative stitching, and the sides were sewn up. As the trial court found, the identity of the merchandise changed as did its character and use: embroidered fabric was transformed into pillowcases which are clearly distinguishable in character and use from the fabric of which they were made. We, therefore, hold that the trial court correctly concluded that the merchandise in this case was a product of Hong Kong.

Various tariff preference programs use alternative tests to discern the place of origin of imported goods. For example, the Canada–U.S. Free Trade Agreement uses several rules of origin. Goods will be deemed to originate in the United States or Canada if they are wholly obtained or produced there. Goods using third-country parts will be eligible for FTA treatment if they undergo processing that changes their tariff classification. For assembled goods, at least 50 percent of the value must derive from materials or processing costs in the United States or Canada. By contrast, under the Caribbean Basin Initiative, 35 percent of the value must originate in an eligible country.

The Uruguay Round of the GATT included a discussion on how to harmonize worldwide the rules of origin for goods. It is likely that over the next several years, an attempt will be made to create a set of generally applicable standards for making decisions about the origins of imported goods.

11.3 NONTARIFF BARRIERS TO TRADE

In addition to worrying about tariffs, importers have a variety of nontariff barriers to trade to worry about. These barriers exist in every country and range from safety standards to absolute quotas.

PRODUCT STANDARDS

Technical standards for goods may exist for a variety of reasons, including safety, environmental protection, and health. For example, the United States requires all imported automobiles to meet federal pollution standards. As a result, some foreign manufacturers either must redesign their production lines to build cars to U.S. standards or must retrofit their cars upon their arrival in the United States. This standard is not imposed to discriminate against imports, but does add costs to those automobiles that do not need to meet such standards in their home markets. Technical standards, because they increase costs, may act as a barrier to entry for smaller foreign automobile manufacturers.

Some standards may be largely targeted at imports, in an attempt to protect domestic industries. For example, in 1989 the EC banned all imports of beef treated with hormones. The EC initially based its decision on health and safety grounds, but later claimed that the ban reflected consumer preferences, much like the U.S. requirement that all imported cheese be pasteurized. The United States, claiming that the ban was an unfair trade practice aimed at U.S. exports, retaliated by imposing 100 percent duties on a variety of EC imports to the United States. The duties were deferred when the whole matter became part of the Uruguay Round of the GATT. This dispute reflected some of the increasing tension over agricultural standards issues, as well as some of the problems that may arise from the unified EC.

QUOTAS, EMBARGOES, AND VOLUNTARY RESTRAINT AGREEMENTS

The United States and other countries have long used quotas and embargoes as part of foreign policy and as protection for domestic industries. As long ago as 1794 the United States imposed a trade embargo against Britain, and in 1990 the United States, as part of an international community, embargoed all trade with Iraq.

As total bans on trade, embargoes tend to be used more often to protect foreign policy interests than to protect domestic industries. A government seeking to protect domestic industries tends to use quotas on specific products to achieve that goal.

In the United States, the Trade Act of 1974 gives businesses, unions, trade associations, Congress, the President, and the U.S. Trade Representative the right to ask the International Trade Commission to investigate cases of increased exports that threaten or cause serious injury to a domestic industry. If the ITC finds the need for protection, it recommends import relief in the form of increased duties, quotas, or adjustment assistance to workers and affected communities to the President.

In most instances, if the ITC finds the need for import relief, the President or the U.S. Trade Representative will negotiate with the exporting countries. During the 1980s, the government negotiated both orderly market agreements and voluntary restraint agreements (VRAs). For example, the Multifiber Agreement is a multilateral agreement to control the import of textiles and textile products. It is legally enforceable and is designed to create an orderly market. In contrast, since 1981 the Japanese government has, through MITI's administrative guidance, asked its automobile manufacturers voluntarily to restrain their exports to the United States. This agreement is not enforceable by the U.S. Customs Service, although the failure of the Japanese automobile industry to honor it would probably result in the imposition of enforceable quotas.

Both advocates of free trade and consumer activists are often dismayed by the application of quotas and VRAs. Free-trade advocates claim that such restraints on trade are inefficient and merely postpone the industrial restructuring that needs to take place in order for the United States to compete effectively in world markets. Consumer advocates point out that the cost of protectionism is increased prices for both domestic and foreign goods. For example, the VRAs on Japanese auto imports mean that the Japanese will not always be able to satisfy the U.S. demand for their vehicles. Thus, their dealers in the United States can add dealer surcharges to the base price of their cars and may order cars loaded with options consumers may not want but must buy in order to get the car. American auto makers also benefit from VRAs because they can keep their prices higher than they could if faced with unlimited competition from Japanese firms.

Those in favor of using quotas and VRAs tend to be organized labor, managers and workers in import-sensitive industries, and politicians from affected areas. They point out that trade restraints help buy enough time for industries to restructure and for workers to retrain. They also have on their side the politically potent argument that protecting U.S. businesses preserves good jobs for Americans. In some cases, advocates of protectionism argue that the nation needs to preserve its basic industries, such as the auto makers and steel mills, in order to preserve the national defense. Finally, they rightfully point out that in many cases the U.S. market is significantly more open to trade than the markets of those nations whose imports are harming U.S. business. They argue that U.S. businesses never get the chance to fight back by exporting to other developing markets.

11.4 EXPORT PROMOTION

Most countries interested in promoting exports provide some form of export assistance to their business community. Such assistance may range from providing technical advice to sponsoring trade fairs in promising markets, or take the form of tax incentives or transportation discounts. The outer limit on export assistance is the GATT's prohibition on unfair subsidies. If a country does too much, it risks having countervailing duties imposed by importing nations.

As the U.S. trade deficit rose in the 1980s, the government intensified its efforts to help businesses export. Government programs now help businesses identify potential markets and customers and obtain financing and insurance for export sales. Exporters may also be eligible for immunity from American antitrust laws for some activities and for tax benefits.

MARKET ASSISTANCE

The International Trade Administration has three departments that offer information to American businesses considering export sales. The International Economic Policy unit has officers on duty around the world, and can offer information on economic and commercial conditions in any country. The Trade Development unit has information on market conditions and trade practices around the world, and the U.S. and Foreign Commercial Service has offices in major markets worldwide. Its officers seek out trade opportunities that could benefit American businesses.

EXPORT FINANCING

Over time, one problem exporters have frequently faced is the inability to obtain financing for specific export deals as well as for their own purchases of the materials and equipment they need to enter into export deals. Private sector banks are one possible source of funding, but if a buyer of U.S. exports comes from a country without a well-developed banking system, it may be difficult to obtain credit. Government agencies are another source of credit, but tend only to fund specific programs rather than general export transactions.

In 1945, the United States established the Export-Import Bank (Eximbank) as a government-owned corporation. Its mandate was to help U.S. exporters compete by making credit easier to obtain. In the main, Eximbank has provided direct loans to customers for U.S. exporters, or has guaranteed commercial bank loans to those customers. Recently Eximbank has also provided more direct help to U.S. exporters by guaranteeing loans for the working capital the exporters need to develop and produce export orders. Eximbank also operates a credit insurance program to insure credit against commercial and political risks. The objective of these programs is to help U.S. exporters compete for business in other countries and to improve the balance of trade by increasing U.S. exports.

ANTITRUST REVIEW

Some other countries, most notably Japan, carefully coordinate export activities. In the United States, the government does not play a role in export strategy, and if competitors in the same industry coordinate their export efforts, they risk criminal or civil lawsuits under the antitrust laws. In response to American exporters' concerns about the possibility of antitrust liability for export trade practices, Congress in 1982 passed the Export Trading Company Act. The Act encourages banks and other business enterprises to form export trading companies to promote American exports. Export trading companies can apply to the Department of Commerce for a Certificate of Review, which, if granted, limits exposure to antitrust liability.

A certificate grants immunity from government antitrust suits to companies whose conduct will not have substantial anticompetitive effects in the United States. A certificate also gives three protections against private actions for violations of the antitrust laws. First, the Act gives a presumption of legality to actions described in the certificate. Second, in a civil antitrust suit, if a court finds that the conduct described in the certificate does not violate the antitrust laws, the losing plaintiff will have to pay the certificate holder's court costs and attorney fees. Third, plaintiffs suing a certificate holder may claim only actual damages, not the treble damages of the usual antitrust suit.

The Certificate of Review allows exporters to create supply and marketing arrangements that might not be legal in the American marketplace. For example, companies can agree to share risks and costs of exporting, act together to reduce shipping rates, create exclusive arrangements with suppliers and distributors, and require resale price maintenance in other countries. Using Certificates of Review, trade associations like the National Machine Tool Builders Association and the American Film Marketing Association have obtained broad antitrust protections for their members.

TAX BENEFITS

The major tax benefit the U.S. government uses to spur exports is the Foreign Sales Corporation (FSC). Businesses that qualify as FSCs can shelter from income tax part of their export income attributable to overseas activities. To obtain FSC status, a business must incorporate and have its main office in an approved foreign country or in Guam, American Samoa, the U.S. Virgin Islands, or the Commonwealth of the Northern Marianas Islands. The FSC cannot have more than twenty-five shareholders, cannot have preferred stock, and must have at least one director who is not a U.S. resident. It must hold all meetings of shareholders and directors abroad, and must make its major disbursements from foreign bank accounts.

CONCLUSION

Many countries now hope to boost their economies by promoting exports. The U.S. has taken several steps to help U.S. exporters. The government provides technical and market information, direct and indirect financing, exemptions from normal competition laws, and some tax advantages to exporters. Businesses considering exporting need to know that there is substantial government assistance available to them and how to take advantage of those resources. Government export promotion programs can help make exports more competitive with the products of other countries.

11.5 EXPORT CONTROLS

Just as governments regulate imports through tariffs, quotas, and other restraints, so governments also regulate exports. When a business signs a contract to sell goods to a buyer in another country, it must know what effect export regulations will have on the contract. Businesses that do not foresee the effect of export regulation in their contracts may face breach of contract cases, loss of export privileges, or even criminal charges.

In the United States, exporting is not a right but a privilege. In fact, every export from the United States requires an export license. While in many cases this requirement is not as onerous as it might seem, unlawful exports may earn the exporter substantial prison time, among other penalties.

Efforts to regulate exports from the United States come from many different government agencies, including Congress, the Commerce Department, the State Department, the Defense Department, and the International Trade Administration. Because so many agencies are involved in export regulation, at times one agency could be promoting an export sale that another agency wants to restrict.

BACKGROUND

Modern American export controls began as emergency measures during World War II, to keep enemy nations from acquiring militarily significant goods, information, and technology. In 1949, Congress passed the first comprehensive legislation regulating exports, largely in response to the threats to national security presented by the Soviet bloc nations.

Exports are now regulated primarily under the Export Administration Act (the EAA) of 1979, as amended in 1985 and 1988, and by the Commerce Department's export administration regulations. The EAA attempts to balance the need to protect national military, economic, and political interests with the need to foster economic growth through export trade.

The EAA gives authority to the President, who in turns delegates it to the Commerce Department, to regulate exports for three purposes:

1. To protect the U.S. economy in times of short supply of products;

2. To protect national security interests; and

3. To further U.S. foreign policy objectives.

Short Supply

Short-supply controls protect the American economy from the inflation and scarcity that might result from foreign demands for American products in short supply. For example, Alaskan crude oil may be exported only

if the export will not reduce the domestic supply and only if the export results in lower prices for U.S. consumers. [See also Western Red Cedar, 50
C.F.R. 377.7 (1985).]

National Security

National security controls restrict the export of goods and technology that
"make a significant contribution to the military potential" of other countries, to the detriment of American security. National security controls extend both to weapons and to "dual use" items, such as computers, chemical equipment, and machinery, that have both civilian and military
applications. These dual-use items have become increasingly important as
the subject of export controls. Many products with peaceful civilian uses
are integral parts of weapons of mass destruction. For example, common
agricultural fertilizers can be used to make chemical weapons.

National security controls would be ineffectual if regulated exports
could be obtained from other countries. The United States, therefore, coordinates many of its national security controls with its allies. COCOM
(Coordinating Committee of the Consultative Group on Export Controls) is
an informal group consisting of the NATO countries (less Iceland) plus
Japan and acts jointly to control the flow of militarily significant goods and
technology to the Eastern bloc nations.

During the late 1980s and early 1990s the application of export controls
for national security purposes changed considerably. With the fall of
Communist governments in Europe and the collapse of the U.S.S.R., businesses found it significantly easier to export to those areas. On the other
hand, the Persian Gulf War in 1991 revealed major gaps in export controls
to countries in the Middle East. Iraq was able to build its military might in
large part as a consequence of purchasing dual-use products. The Persian
Gulf War prompted a tightening of export controls and a reexamination of
COCOM and U.S. practices.

Foreign Policy

The most controversial purpose of export controls is to advance U.S. foreign policy objectives. The United States has maintained long-standing
trade embargoes against Cuba, Vietnam, North Korea, and Kampuchea
under the International Emergency Economic Powers Act, but the foreign
policy provisions included in the 1979 EAA gave the President a means to
impose trade sanctions in response to specific events. For example,
President Carter banned grain exports to the U.S.S.R. and banned U.S.
participation in the 1980 Moscow Olympics in response to the Soviet invasion of Afghanistan. In 1986, President Reagan imposed a total ban on
trade with Libya to protest its support of international terrorism.

Foreign policy controls can be extremely costly to American businesses,
causing loss of markets, breaches of contract, and lost credibility with

foreign customers. For example, prior to trade sanctions against the U.S.S.R. in 1978, Caterpillar Tractor supplied 85 percent of Soviet tractor imports. By 1982, Komatsu of Japan controlled 85 percent of the same market.[1] The 1986 trade sanctions against Libya required U.S. companies to stop work on several hundred million dollars worth of service contracts. Perhaps the most damaging effect of foreign policy–based export controls is their long-term damage to the reputation of American companies as reliable suppliers to world markets. Because political objectives change with the election of new administrations in Washington, foreign customers fear that American companies may have to breach contracts to comply with new export controls. These customers may turn to suppliers from other countries who are perceived as more reliable.

EXPORT LICENSES

If an exporter remembers only one thing about export controls it is that every export from the United States requires an export license. Export licenses are the centerpiece of American export regulation, and are mandatory for all exports of goods, technology, and know-how. While there are many different kinds of specific export licenses, the export regulations categorize licenses as either general or validated.

Most goods and technology exported from the United States require only a *general license*. To obtain a general license, an exporter merely fills out a Shipper's Export Declaration at the time of export. No application or fee is required, and the government does not issue any license document. It is up to the exporter to determine whether the export is eligible for a general license, and what category of general license is applicable. The most widely used designation is the G-DEST, which is a license for a non-controlled destination (for example, New Zealand, for most exports). Other general license types are GIFT, for gift parcels; GLV, for exports of limited value; and G-COM, for general license exports to COCOM countries.

For some exports, an exporter must apply for and obtain a *validated license* from the Commerce Department's Office of Export Administration. The Commerce Department issues many different kinds of validated licenses, including licenses for individual and multiple exports, distribution, comprehensive operations, projects, and the supply of spare or replacement parts. The exporter must obtain the validated license before shipping goods or transferring technology to another country.

The Commerce Department has extensive regulations governing the export licensing process. To determine whether to use a general or a validated license, an exporter must use the Commodity Control List [15 C.F.R. §799.1]. First, the exporter must find the appropriate Export Commodity

---

[1]Lindell, *Foreign Policy Export Controls,* 28/4 California Management Review, p. 32 (Summer 1986).

Control Number (ECON) for the specific product or technology. Controlled items are not always high-technology widgets. For example, scuba diving gear is on the list, as ECON 5938F. The exporter then compares the ECON description with the listing of countries, because the license requirement varies with the destination of the export. The Commodity Control List groups destination countries into seven groups. Table 11.1 indicates the countries in each group and the level of export control.

TABLE 11.1   Country Groups and Controls

Q	Romania
S	Libya
T	Latin America, except Cuba
	Greenland
V	All other free-world countries, except Canada[*]
	China, Yugoslavia, Afghanistan
W	Poland, Hungary
Y	U.S.S.R., Estonia, Latvia, Lithuania, Bulgaria
	Czechoslovakia, Albania, Laos, Mongolian People's Republic
Z	Cuba, North Korea, Vietnam, Cambodia

[*]Except for certain nuclear-related exports, no validated licenses are required for Canada.

DEPARTMENT OF COMMERCE, BUREAU OF EXPORT ADMINISTRATION, COMMODITY CONTROL LIST

15 C.F.R. § 799.1, Supp. 1, Group 3

5398F Self-contained underwater breathing apparatus (scuba gear) and related equipment.
Controls for ECON 5398F
Unit: Report in "$ value."
Validated License Required: Country Groups S and Z and Iran.
GLV $ Value Limit: $0.
Processing Code: TE.
Reason for Control: Foreign policy.
Special Licenses Available: None.
List of Equipment Controlled by ECON 5398F Self-contained underwater breathing apparatus (scuba gear) and related equipment, including, but not limited to, the following:

(a) Self-contained underwater breathing apparatus (scuba gear);

(b) Pressure regulators, air cylinders, hoses, valves and backpacks for the items described in paragraph (a);

(c) Life jackets, inflation cartridges, compasses, wetsuits, masks, fins, weight belts, and dive computers;

(d) Underwater lights and propulsion equipment;

(e) Air compressors and filtration systems specially designed for filling air cylinders.

An exporter who wants to sell any of these listed scuba-related products overseas can use a general license except in the most restricted S and Z categories and Iran. For exports to these listed countries, the exporter must obtain a validated license from the Commerce Department.

In addition to the Commerce Department's review of validated license applications, some exports may need review and approval by the State Department, the Defense Department, or COCOM. In particular, items that have possible military uses may be subject to additional approvals. Exporters have to plan in advance for the delays the review process will cause.

The willingness of the government to grant validated licenses varies, depending on the political events at the time of export. For example, since the fall of the Communist governments in Eastern Europe in 1989, validated licenses for destinations such as Poland have become significantly easier to obtain. By contrast, since the events in Tiananmen Square in China, validated licenses have become more difficult to get for sales to China. This political risk factor is one that U.S. exporters should keep in mind when negotiating contracts in volatile parts of the world.

Penalties

The EAA contains stiff criminal and administrative penalties for violations. Businesses that willfully violate the EAA may be fined the greater of $1 million or five times the value of the illegal exports. Individuals may be fined up to $250,000 or sentenced to jail terms of up to 10 years. The Commerce Department can also levy administrative fines for up to $10,000 per violation, and can suspend, revoke, or deny export privileges to violators. In some ways, the administrative penalties are the most severe, because the loss of export privileges may cripple an export-oriented business, and because these sanctions may be imposed without the delay inherent in criminal indictments and trials. The following case illustrates the kinds of criminal penalties that a court may impose on violators.

UNITED STATES v. ELKINS

885 F.2d 775 (11th Cir. 1989)

FACTS:
As a result of a complex series of negotiations, Elkins arranged to purchase two Lockheed L-100-30 jets from Lockheed and resell them to Contrust, a German business controlled by a Libyan national, Badir. Badir initially wanted to purchase the military version of the jets, but was

unable to do so. Because export licenses to Libya would not have been granted, the planes were routed through France to the allegedly ultimate destination of Benin. Elkins assured the Commerce Department that Badir was a Libyan expatriate, opposed to the government, while at the same time its agent delivered the contract to

Tripoli for signing and discussed the transaction with Badir's Libyan banker.

Once the export licenses were granted, the planes were delivered to Benin, at a profit of $7 million to Elkins. The planes were never seen in Benin again, although one did appear in Cairo, flown by defecting members of the Libyan Air Force, with log books indicating its use by the Libyan Air Force.

Elkins was convicted of one count of conspiracy to defraud the government and one count of violating export laws. He was sentenced to 5 years in prison on the first count and received a consecutive 10-year sentence on the second count. He was also fined $6,600,000. Elkins appealed his sentence as excessive, and as cruel and unusual punishment.

ISSUE:
Was Elkins' punishment unconstitutionally harsh?

RESULT:
No. The court affirmed the sentence and the fine.

REASONS:
Defendant eventually makes one argument that his sentence violated the Eighth Amendment: "Because the harshness of Appellant's sentence far exceeds the sentences imposed in similar export prosecutions in the Northern District of Georgia and elsewhere, Appellant respectfully submits that his sentence is unconstitutionally disproportionate." A sentence is disproportionate for Eighth Amendment purposes if the punishment is grossly disproportionate when compared with the nature of the crime. . . .

. . . These sentences, five years for conspiracy and ten years for violating export control laws, certainly are not grossly excessive compared to the nature of the crime. Additionally, the ten-year sentence imposed for violating export control regulations is not grossly disproportionate to the sentences imposed in other federal jurisdictions for violations of the same federal laws. Defendant unlawfully sold $57 million worth of high technology equipment to an unfriendly nation. . . .

Defendant also challenges the fine imposed on count two. There may be circumstances where an excessive fine constitutes cruel and unusual punishment in violation of the Eighth Amendment. . . . We need not identify those circumstances in this case. Defendant made a gross profit of $13,049,474, a net profit of $7,336,233, and an after-tax profit of $3,368,917 from the sale of these aircraft. Defendant's fine of $6.6 million was less than his gross profit and less than his net profit from the sale of these planes. Although a large amount, we hold that a fine representing an amount less than the net profit of an illegal transaction does not violate the Eighth Amendment absent a showing of severe, particularized hardship suffered by defendant.

. . . Defendant argues that the district court did not consider the impact of this fine on his family. . . . This argument has no merit. That information was before the district court, and the transcript indicates that the court considered these factors.

PROBLEM AREAS

The *Elkins* case highlights two problems that often appear in the context of export controls. The first is the problem of dual-use items; that is, goods, technology, and know-how having both civilian and military applications. The second problem is the issue of controls on reexports.

In *Elkins*, the defendant had a good idea of the ultimate military use of the jets he was exporting. Other cases may not be so clear. A diesel engine can be used to power a tractor or a tank, a heavy truck can help build roads or be modified to serve as a mobile missile launcher, and a personal computer may guide business decisions or missiles. Exporters have sometimes been surprised by their inability to get validated licenses on seemingly innocuous exports.

The problem of controlling reexports has been extremely difficult. Note that Elkins set up his sale not to its ultimate destination, but to a German business taking delivery in France. The Commerce Department is concerned about this intentional diversion of goods and technology to forbidden destinations, but it also wants to control unintended diversions as well.

Ordinarily, both common sense and the legal doctrine of territorial jurisdiction would indicate that once a U.S. exporter completes a sale and delivery in another country, the United States would have no legal ability to control further resale. As an analogy, if you purchase this book from a college bookstore, McGraw-Hill doesn't have the ability to prevent you from selling the book to someone else. Yet the U.S. government regularly asserts the right to control reexport of controlled goods, technology, and know-how, sometimes to the protest of its trading partners.

The main way the United States succeeds in controlling reexports is by conditioning export licenses on assurances that no reexport will occur. For example, suppose an exporter needs a validated license to sell oscilloscopes. The exporter would like to sell its products regularly throughout South America, but does not wish to apply for an individual export license for each sale. The Commerce Department may grant the exporter a distribution license that will cover shipments to approved distributors or manufacturers (using U.S. component part exports). The exporter must agree to have a system of internal controls to prevent diversion of goods; and distributors of U.S. goods, in order to get approval, must agree to let U.S. officials examine records of resales.

Of course, if an exporter knows of an ultimate destination at the time of sale, it must obtain the appropriate license. Failure to do so, as Elkins discovered, defrauds the government and violates export control laws.

COCOM AND EXPORT CONTROLS

One country's export controls will not be effective if the destination country can obtain the products from other sources. COCOM exists to try to coordinate export controls, particularly with respect to Eastern bloc nations. It is a voluntary association, operating by consensus and in secret, and its recommendations are not legally binding on its members. Over time, COCOM members have disagreed about the proper extent of export controls on sensitive goods and technology, with the United States often taking a stricter line than its allies on what products have military significance and on the effectiveness of imposing controls.

COCOM relies on its members to provide enforcement of its decisions, and historically the members have not imposed sanctions on violations occurring in other COCOM countries. However, the Toshiba–Kongsberg incident changed the way the United States viewed the effectiveness of COCOM and led to new sanctions against export violators from other countries.

The Toshiba incident began in 1980 when a Soviet trading company approached Wako Koeki, a small Japanese trading firm, to buy computerized milling machines and the software to run them. The Soviets wanted these machines in order to make super-quiet submarine propellers that would be far more difficult to detect than regular propellers. Wako Koeki approached Toshiba Machine, a subsidiary of Toshiba Corporation, which agreed to sell the machinery to the Soviets, and Toshiba approached a Norwegian firm, Kongsberg Trading, which agreed to provide the needed computer equipment and software.

In order to obtain MITI export permits, Toshiba falsely described the machines and gave a civilian facility in Leningrad as a false destination. The machinery enabled the Soviets to build submarines that are significantly better able to avoid detection by U.S. defense systems. The United States lost a considerable amount of its technological edge in submarine warfare.

The U.S. Congress and the public were outraged by the sale of such sensitive technology to the Soviets. Yet the exports did not originate in the United States or use U.S. technology, so were not subject to U.S. export control laws. In 1988, Congress amended the Export Administration Act to allow the President to impose sanctions against firms violating national export controls imposed pursuant to COCOM rules when those violations compromise U.S. national security interests. The Congress also imposed a 3-year ban on imports and on U.S. government procurement against Toshiba Machine and Kongsberg Trading, and a 3-year ban on U.S. government procurement from Toshiba Corp. and Kongsberg Vaapenfabrikk, the parent companies.

EXPORT CONTROL REFORMS

The growth of the world marketplace and the changing world political situation have led American businesses to press for export control reforms. Congress has responded by increasing the role of COCOM and by easing export requirements for COCOM country-bound exports. In 1988, Congress required the Commerce Department to remove requirements for validated licenses for goods and technology moving to COCOM countries (except supercomputers, spying devices, and exports for use in nuclear applications). It also changed the reexport certification requirements to exempt products made abroad using less than 25 percent U.S. parts. The ultimate goal of the export reforms is to create a "license-free zone" among COCOM countries.

The 1988 export control reforms also deal with another problem that has vexed U.S. businesses. The tension in export regulation lies between promoting U.S. competitiveness and business interests and protecting national security, foreign policy, and supply interests. U.S. businesses complain bitterly when they cannot export products that an end user may readily obtain from foreign sources. The 1988 reforms require the Commerce Department to decontrol most items when it determines that those items are available from foreign sources in sufficient quantities as to make U.S. controls ineffective. When an exporter applies for a determination, the Commerce Department has four months to make its determination of foreign availability, with one additional month for COCOM review. If it does not make a decision in this time, the item is automatically decontrolled.

The entire export control system was established as a weapon in the Cold War, to maintain free-world superiority over Communist-led nations. The appearance of Iraq, among other countries, as a major power in advanced conventional weapons, chemical and biological weapons, and nuclear weapons indicates that the export control policies have large loopholes with respect to nations outside the Eastern bloc. The 1990s will probably see a shift in the view of export controls from the Soviet sphere of influence to the Middle East, parts of Asia, and perhaps Latin America, in an attempt to control the spread particularly of missile systems and nonconventional weapons. Managers in U.S. exporting businesses should be aware of the potential for a change in focus in export control regulations.

11.6 ANTIBOYCOTT REGULATION

Trade boycotts are a traditional tool of foreign policy for many nations. The United States, for example, has boycotted Cuban products for many years. To some extent, they are the most extreme form of export control. One of the broadest trade boycotts of this century is the Arab League's boycott of Israel. Coordinated from a central office in Damascus, Syria, the Arab League boycott is an attempt to cripple Israel's economy.

The boycott takes three forms. The primary boycott forbids Arab League members from trading directly with Israel. The secondary boycott forbids Arab League members from doing business with firms that have significantly contributed to the Israeli economy. In some instances, the boycott has extended to a tertiary level, which forbids firms doing business with boycotting nations from obtaining goods and services from businesses that contribute to the Israeli economy.

The Central Boycott Office in Damascus administers the boycott and recommends a "blacklist" of companies contributing to the economy of Israel. Individual member countries apply the boycott and maintain their own lists of companies with which they will not do business under the boycott. Enforcement varies widely, with the blacklist not being particularly well maintained and Arab countries differing in the zeal with which they apply the boycott.

Congress reacted quite strongly to the boycott, particularly those portions relating to the blacklist. It amended the Internal Revenue Code to require U.S. businesses to report their operations in boycotting countries, to report any requests to comply with the boycott, and to deny a variety of tax benefits to companies complying with the boycott. Congress also amended the Export Administration Act in 1979 to forbid U.S. exporters from complying with the Arab League boycott.

The antiboycott regulations are extremely complex and cover a surprising range of business situations. They apply to all U.S. persons, including citizens or nationals located inside or outside the United States, businesses, including foreign branches of U.S. companies, U.S. branches or subsidiaries of foreign companies, U.S. "controlled in fact" subsidiaries, and affiliates located abroad. The regulations forbid any action taken with the intent to comply with or further the boycott. The regulations apply to activities in foreign or interstate commerce, including the provision of goods, technology, services, know-how, and financing, including letters of credit.

The antiboycott regulations prohibit four main kinds of activities. First, they prohibit refusing to do business with someone in response to a requirement, agreement, or request from a boycotting country. Refusals may be express, including using lists of businesses approved for transactions or prohibited from transactions, or implied from a course of conduct. For example, a contractor building a power plant in Kuwait could not refuse to take a bid from a subcontractor because it is on the Kuwaiti blacklist.

The second prohibition prohibits U.S. persons from discriminating against an individual U.S. person on the basis of race, religion, sex, or national origin in order to comply with the blacklist. Thus, a U.S. company doing business in Syria could not refuse to hire Jewish employees in order to comply with the boycott.

The third prohibition is the most troublesome for U.S. businesses. The antiboycott regulations forbid U.S. persons from providing a variety of information that might further the boycott. This information includes information about the race, religion, sex, or national origin of any U.S. person, including directors, officers, and employees of U.S. persons. The prohibited information also includes information about business relationships with a boycotted country or with businesses in that country, or with businesses subject to the boycott. To comply, a U.S. person may not furnish even publicly available information. The prohibition also extends to providing information about involvement with charitable or fraternal organizations that support a boycotted country.

Finally, the antiboycott regulations prohibit U.S. persons from implementing letters of credit that require compliance with the boycott. These actions would include payment, acceptance of documents calling for compliance, and confirmation of such letters of credit.

The application of these rules in business settings is extremely complex. The Commerce Department regulations contain many exceptions and several pages of examples of the kind of conduct that does or does not violate the law. The key is intent. If one or more reasons for supplying information or for acting is to further the boycott, it is a violation. If a business acts in a manner that incidentally furthers the boycott, without intent, it is not a violation.

Most boycott violation cases are resolved prior to formal litigation, often with the entry of a consent decree not admitting guilt but agreeing to pay a fine. Among the cases reported at the administrative level are settlements involving Safeway Stores, which allegedly maintained a list of approved suppliers for stores in Arab League countries, furnished information about its relationships with Israel, blacklisted businesses and charitable and fraternal organizations, and asked its suppliers to furnish information for a boycott clearance process. It paid $995,000 to settle the charges.[2]

Although the language of the regulations is broadly drawn, it currently applies only to the Arab League boycott. In 1987, the Commerce Department specifically determined that the regulations did not apply to attempts to boycott South Africa, thus leaving U.S. businesses free to comply with attempts to boycott South African products and firms.

11.7 CONCLUSION

Countries use import and export regulation for a variety of purposes, including preserving national security, furthering foreign policy goals, and developing domestic industry. The United States has a particularly complex regulatory structure for both imports and exports.

Managers trading in the world marketplace need to pay particular attention to the legal environment for imports and exports. Contract negotiations should allocate the risk and expense of clearing goods through customs and paying duties and of obtaining appropriate export licenses. Traders doing business in the Middle East need to know that a seemingly innocuous request for information may lead to a violation of the antiboycott regulations. Legal problems in the import–export area may lead to substantial individual and corporate criminal liability, as well as the loss of export privileges. This is a key area for traders to anticipate problems, analyze risks, and act to prevent legal issues from taking control of otherwise sound business arrangements.

[2]Pamela P. Breed and Pleasant S. Brodnax III, "Antiboycott Provisions of Export Administration Act," in W. Willkie II, ed. *The Commerce Department Speaks 1990: The Legal Aspects of International Trade,* Practicing Law Institute, 1990, vol. 2, pp. 797–798.

11.8 QUESTIONS FOR DISCUSSION

1. Loafers, Inc., a shoe company, is thinking about starting to export its high-quality men's shoes to Scandinavia. The president has asked your advice about the markets there for shoes. Where would you look for information about Scandinavian markets? (Don't limit your answer to information in this chapter.)

2. Loafers, Inc., has decided to export its high-quality men's shoes to Sweden, and has found a chain of shoe stores there that has bought 500 pairs of shoes at $60 per pair. Does this export need a license? If so, what kind is Loafers likely to need, and how does Loafers get the license?

3. Suppose you were the manager of a business exporting machinery to a variety of countries in the Middle East and Asia. Are there ways you could guard against changes in export control regulations for foreign policy reasons? What are three advance warning signs of shifting foreign policy?

4. Your company has been accepting orders for machines from customers in many countries, including several countries participating in the Arab League boycott. In the ordinary course of business, one day you receive a substantial order for machines from a buyer in Israel. What are the consequences of accepting this order? What are the consequences of rejecting this order? What are the ethical implications of your decision? What would you recommend?

11.9 FURTHER READINGS

Country of Origin Rules (Seventh Annual Judicial Conference of the U.S. Court of Appeals for the Federal Circuit), 128 *Federal Rules Decisions* 493–516 (1990).

Walter Doherty, "An Introduction to Customs, Law, and Practice," 11 *Suffolk Transnational Law Journal* 301–350 (1988).

Toni Lester, "Does the Government Really Help Small Business Exporters?" *Northwestern Journal of International Law and Business* (1992).

Wende Wrubel, "The Toshiba–Kongsberg Incident: Shortcomings of COCOM, and Recommendations for Increased Effectiveness of Export Controls to the East Bloc," 4 *American University Journal of International Law and Policy* 241–261 (1989).

PART FOUR

INTERNATIONAL BUSINESS RELATIONSHIPS

- **FORMS OF GLOBAL BUSINESS ENTERPRISE**

- **REGULATING GLOBAL COMPETITION**

- **PROTECTING BUSINESS PROPERTY RIGHTS**

- **THE MULTINATIONAL ENTERPRISE AS A WORLD CITIZEN**

FORMS OF GLOBAL BUSINESS ENTERPRISE

12.1 INTRODUCTION

To this point, we have examined international business from a transactional point of view. The focus of study has been on the framework for individual business transactions and on achieving success in planning, negotiating, and executing international business transactions. The remainder of our text will concentrate on the structure of the international business firm, including the ways in which firms organize themselves for international markets, the competitive effects of international business practices, the protection of interests in technology and property, and the social responsibility and accountability of international business enterprises. We will start by examining the different ways in which businesses form and organize to do business globally and the legal implications of their business decisions.

12.2 THE MULTINATIONAL ENTERPRISE

TERMINOLOGY

The first problem in examining the structure of international firms is one of terminology. There is no widespread consensus on the terms and identifying characteristics of international firms. The term academics, politicians, and executives most often use to identify an international business is "multinational enterprise" (MNE). The term was coined in 1960, although MNEs existed long before then. MNE is used interchangeably with the term "multinational corporation" or "multinational company" (MNC), and at the United Nations, "transnational corporation" (TNC).

The traditional definition of an MNE is a firm having ownership in affiliated businesses in two or more countries. Some commentators criticize this definition as too inclusive; for example, covering a Texas company with a single assembly plant in Mexico. They would require a business to have holdings in more than two countries before it qualifies as an MNE.[1] Other commentators see production facilities as the essence of multinationalism, and would require a firm to have production facilities in at least six countries before it qualifies as an MNE.[2] A more important criticism of the traditional definition is that it fails to take into account the explosive growth of international franchising as a method of doing business, and of

---

[1]R. Grosse and D. Kujawa, *International Business Theory and Managerial Applications*, 2d ed., Irwin, Homewood, Ill., 1988; p. 31.
[2]A. Rugman, D. Lecraw, and L. Booth, *International Business: Firm and Environment*, McGraw-Hill, New York, 1985; p. 7.

strategic alliances involving licenses, management contracts, and other nonownership structures.[3] For example, in the fast-food industry, a chain may choose to internationalize by licensing its trademarks in many countries rather than by direct foreign investment. The traditional definition of an MNE would not include the franchisor, no matter how many countries in which it had extensive franchise networks.

Although strictly speaking there is no legal definition of an MNE, two international organizations have developed definitions to apply to guidelines and codes of conduct. Chapter 15 will discuss codes of conduct for MNEs, but the definitions used by the Organization for Economic Cooperation and Development (OECD) and by the U.N. may be helpful here. The OECD, an organization of the leading developed nations, issued voluntary guidelines for the conduct of MNEs in 1976, with amendments in 1984. The guidelines do not attempt a tightly drawn definition of an MNE; instead, they describe MNEs as follows:

> These usually comprise companies or other entities whose ownership is private, state or mixed, established in different countries and so linked that one or more of them may be able to exercise a significant influence over the activities of others and, in particular, to share knowledge and resources with others.

The United Nations Commission on Trade and Development (UNCTAD) is in the process of developing a code of conduct for transnational corporations. The parties to the code negotiations have not yet agreed on all of the wording defining an MNE, but the agreed-upon part of the draft definition defines an MNE as:

> [A]n enterprise . . . comprising entities in two or more countries, regardless of the legal form and fields of activity of these entities, which operates under a system of decision-making, permitting coherent policies and a common strategy through one or more decision-making centres, in which the entities are so linked, by ownership or otherwise, that one or more of them may be able to exercise a significant influence over the activities of others, and, in particular, to share knowledge, resources and responsibilities with the others.

These definitions of an MNE do a better job of including the newer forms of international business, including franchising, licensing, and other forms of strategic alliances.

STRUCTURE

Global businesses form in a variety of different ways. Take as a hypothetical example B-Kleen, Inc., a U.S.-based maker of laundry detergent and other soaps. Starting from a base of domestic sales, B-Kleen may decide to

---

[3]E. Kolde, *Environment of International Business,* 2d ed., Kent, Boston, Mass., 1985.

open an export department to make some direct sales to Canadian customers. B-Kleen may then decide to hire an agent to help it find buyers in South American countries. As its business expands, it may contract with distributors, who purchase soap from B-Kleen for resale. Suppose that high tariffs in South Korea make the price of B-Kleen soaps too high. The company may decide to license its trademarks and its formulas to a Korean manufacturer. The licensing agreement gives the rights to manufacture B-Kleen soaps in Korea and market the soaps there, and perhaps in other countries. At some point, B-Kleen may decide to build factories in Mexico, incorporate a subsidiary in France, or enter into a joint venture with a Polish company. MNEs use a variety of these practices, all with the aim of maximizing competitive advantage on a global basis.

Internally, global businesses organize themselves in a variety of ways, with two predominant patterns. The structure may be product-based, with, for example, a soap division, a cosmetics division, and a detergents division all reporting to B-Kleen headquarters. This structure presumes that managers know their products and that product knowledge is most important for B-Kleen's success. Another method of organization is by geographic area, with, for example, a South American division, a European division, a North American division, and an Asian division all reporting to B-Kleen headquarters. This structure assumes that market knowledge is more important than product knowledge.

In recent years, some MNEs have organized their businesses around functional areas, such as worldwide sales or worldwide manufacturing. Large MNEs will employ many variations on these structures. Some will move from being monocentric—that is, having one headquarters—to being polycentric—that is, having several fairly autonomous centers of authority for the business. Figure 12-1 shows a variety of ways that B-Kleen could organize its business.

12.3 AGENTS AND DISTRIBUTORS

In the example above, one of B-Kleen's first steps into the global marketplace was to find agents and distributors for its products in foreign markets. There are differences between agents and distributors, but in both cases the seller is looking for a third party, located in the overseas market, to act as an intermediary between the manufacturer and the ultimate buyer. The agent or distributor's knowledge of the local market should serve to increase sales beyond what the manufacturer could expect from its own attempts to sell directly in unfamiliar markets.

AGENTS

There are many different kinds of agents, ranging from the sponsors used in many Middle Eastern countries to the *Handelsverträter,* or commercial agent, in Germany. Each nation's legal system has its own rules defining

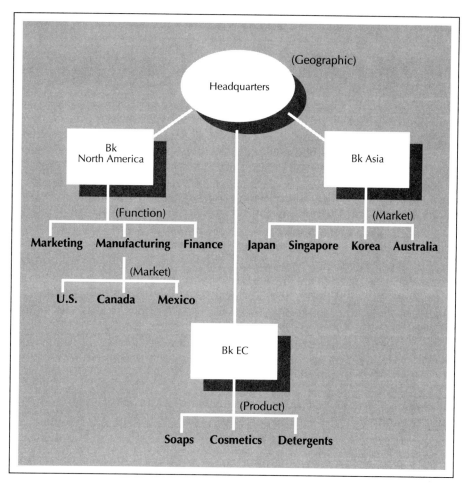

FIGURE 12-1   Sample Organizations for B-Kleen, Inc.

the relationship and obligations between the agent and the principal, usually a manufacturer. Generally, though, agents sell products not for themselves, but for someone else, taking a commission on each sale. The function of the agent is to find buyers for the seller's goods or services.

When giving authority to an agent, a principal should be aware of the same kinds of contract issues that might arise in a domestic agency arrangement. One issue of particular importance is whether the agent will have the authority to enter into contractual obligations on behalf of the principal or whether the agent's authority will be limited to passing on orders to the principal for approval and contract execution. The benefit to allowing the agent to contract on behalf of the principal is efficiency, which may give the principal an edge in the marketplace. The risk, however, is that the agent will bind the principal to unacceptable contract terms, such as warranties, delivery schedules, or even price.

Many different countries regulate the activities of commercial agents. Some countries, such as Algeria, ban the use of agents for foreign sellers, requiring foreign sellers to do business directly with Algerian buyers. Other countries require that agents be citizens. Many civil law countries do not recognize relationships with undisclosed principals, requiring disclosure of the relationship in all of the agent's dealings. Some countries require all commercial agency relationships to be registered with the government, while others limit the commissions an agent may earn on a sale. Obviously, before engaging an agent in a foreign market, the manufacturer needs the advice of local counsel on the laws of that specific market.

Perhaps the most significant problem with commercial agents arises in the context of termination. Many countries, including much of Europe and South America, have protective legislation designed to counteract unfair terminations. These statutes, which vary among countries, generally require terminations to be for good cause (in contrast to the U.S. doctrine that allows agency arrangements to be "at will"), minimum notice of termination, and compensation to agents, often based on length of service or on commission levels.

If the commercial agent is an individual, the principal runs the further risk of the agent being considered an employee. If an agent is found to be an employee, local labor law will apply to the termination. In some instances, local labor laws may make termination prohibitively expensive. In addition, the presence of an employee may establish the employer as present in the country, doing business for jurisdictional and tax purposes. Labor law problems are much less likely if the agent is a separately incorporated business rather than an individual.

DISTRIBUTORS

Contracting with distributors is frequently used as a method of market entry. In contrast to agents, distributors actually purchase goods for resale. They take the risk that the goods won't sell, and they have no ability to bind the manufacturer to contractual obligations to sell. In some instances, the distribution agreement may make the distributor responsible for service and warranty work as well as for the sale.

Distributorship agreements tend to be for fairly lengthy terms. Thus, contract negotiation is critical to developing the boundaries of the business relationship between the manufacturer and the distributor. In particular, the contract may need to provide price adjustment clauses and detailed provisions for default, termination, and dispute resolution. Just as with agents, many countries regulate the termination of distributorships, requiring that termination be for cause. When the distributor has invested substantial amounts of its own money to maintain inventory and promote the product, a court may require high levels of compensation, even for a termination for cause. Chapters 13 and 14 will contain materials concerning antitrust problems and the issue of gray market goods, examining manufacturers' attempts to control the distribution processes using restrictive business practices.

12.4 LICENSING

At some points in its growth, a global business may choose to use licensing agreements to expand its markets. Licensing, which is essentially just a contract between two businesses, takes several forms. One kind of license allows an independent business to manufacture and sell a patented, trademarked, or copyrighted product, generally in a particular geographic area. Another form of licensing agreement is the franchise, a widely used method of internationalizing businesses, particularly in food and service businesses. Franchises are more complex forms of trademark licenses, going beyond mere trademark rights to concerns such as advertising, quality control, and public image.

LICENSING TECHNOLOGY

In the current world economy, many products take their value from their use of legally protected formulas, processes, or other "know-how." The legal protections that confer upon their owners what are known as "intellectual property" or "industrial property" rights take the form of patents, copyrights, and trade secrets. Patent rights give inventors the exclusive right to manufacture and use inventions, including machines, products, processes, and other compositions of matter. Copyright rights give owners of original works of authorship the exclusive right to publish, reproduce, or prepare derivative works, such as translations or films. Trademarks are words, pictures, labels, or designs that indicate the source of goods.

In contrast to the relatively definite protections afforded to intellectual property, "know-how" is protected by contract and by trade secret laws, which vary widely. Know-how is the skill or knowledge about the production, operation, or marketing of a product or service. Know-how may pertain to patentable products that for business reasons (such as a short product life) are not patented or to clearly nonpatentable business areas, such as customer lists.

Intellectual property rights are mostly national in scope. A detergent company that wishes to market its patented detergent formula worldwide would have to obtain patent protection in each of the markets it enters. There are some international agreements, such as the Berne Convention for the Protection of Literary and Artistic Works for copyrights and the Paris Convention for the Protection of Industrial Property for patents and trademarks, that afford some international protection of valid property interests. We will examine those conventions more fully in Chapter 14.

A technology license generally involves a complex contract, granting a foreign business the right to manufacture, use, or sell products or services covered by a patent, copyright, or trademark, in return for a royalty. Often the licensor will provide technical assistance to the licensee, including help in installing machinery, quality control, or marketing assistance. Sometimes the licensor will invest in the business of the licensee or form a joint venture with the licensee to build new production or sales facilities.

Licensing contracts are generally long-term arrangements requiring substantial investments on the part of the licensee. As a result, licensing agreements breed the same kinds of problems seen in distributorship agreements. Provisions for exclusivity may run afoul of antitrust laws. Termination can be a significant problem area, especially after a successful relationship for some time with a licensee. Termination provisions need to provide for the return of any intellectual property rights to the licensor and for nondisclosure of the licensor's commercially valuable information. A court in the licensee's home country may order substantial termination payments to compensate the licensee for its investment. As a result of all these problems, choice of law, choice of forum, or alternative dispute resolution provisions are particularly important in negotiating licensing agreements. The following case illustrates some of the pitfalls a multinational enterprise may face in administering a licensing agreement.

FEN HIN CHON ENTERPRISES, LTD. v. PORELON, INC.

667 F. Supp. 1174 (M.D. Tenn. 1987)

FACTS:

Fen Hin Chon (FHC) had an exclusive license to manufacture and sell pre-inked hand stamps in Hong Kong and Macao, using Porelon's manufacturing know-how, Porelon's premix (ink-impregnated plastic resins), and the Porelon and Perma-Stamp trademarks. Porelon and FHC's business relationship began in 1974, and was operating under a 1983 agreement, providing that FHC would pay a royalty of 5 percent of net sales, with a minimum annual royalty of $20,000. Porelon, headquartered in Tennessee, was a subsidiary of Johnson Worldwide Affiliates and was one of many of the international companies of Johnson Wax.

The parties had a good working relationship until Johnson Wax assigned Wil Ooms from its European subsidiary to be a worldwide marketing agent for Porelon. Ooms did not believe in exclusive licensing agreements, thinking that Porelon would benefit from having competitors market its products. He set about helping one of FHC's distributors, Mark Universal (MU), to become a competitor. Among his actions, Ooms revealed manufacturing know-how to MU, prevented FHC from terminating MU as a distributor, and allowed MU first to become the supplier of premix to FHC, then to cut off FHC's supply.

FHC's problems escalated when MU engaged in talks with the Ministry of Light Industries in China, reporting to Porelon that MU had obtained exclusive rights to import and develop pre-inked hand-stamp technology into China. In order to get the lucrative China business with MU, Porelon agreed to MU's demand to terminate FHC's Hong Kong license. In July 1985,

Ooms wrote to FHC declaring that the licensing agreement would be terminated if FHC did not remedy three alleged breaches: FHC's sales of premix into China; the poor quality of FHC's hand stamps; and the improper use of the name Johnson Wax in FHC's advertising. FHC responded requesting further information and advising Porelon that its operations had halted because of MU's refusal to supply premix. After another year of difficulty in obtaining supplies, FHC received a letter from Porelon terminating the licensing contract. FHC sued Porelon for damages resulting from the interruptions of its business and for lost profits from the wrongful termination of the license.

ISSUE:

Did Porelon's conduct breach the licensing agreement?

RESULT:

Yes. Porelon's reasons for termination were pretextual.[4]

REASONS:

Careful scrutiny of the complaints voiced by Porelon in their July 19, 1986 "breach" letter to FHC reveals their pretextual nature. The objections raised by Porelon were unsubstantiated excuses to avoid FHC's exclusive contract, in a concentrated effort to placate MU and preserve the China opportunity. Porelon's foremost argument in justifying the termination was that FHC was selling premix into China in violation of Porelon's licensing agreement. The proof establishes two sales to China. The first, a sale of three pails of premix, occurred prior to Ooms' April 1985 telex which expressly prohibited sales of Porelon premix directly or indirectly with companies in China. The three pails of premix (one black, one blue and one red) were sold as samples to companies in China in reliance upon Porelon's November 1983 letter which authorized FHC to explore the China market. . . .

---

[4]Porelon appealed this result. The appeals court upheld the findings of the trial judge, but sent the matter back to him for recalculation of the damages for lost profits.

The second sale into China, of manufacturing equipment and raw materials for handstamp production, occurred in two phases, with invoices dated May 22, 1985, and June 4, 1985. The contracts provided for Porelon materials to be sold, but the credible proof establishes that these orders were filled with Wilsolite [a name brand of a different type of premix] due to Porelon's orders to FHC not to sell into China. . . .

In May 1983, Ross Moss, a Porelon chemist and a "troubleshooter" for quality problems, visited FHC's operations in Hong Kong to assist them in remedying a problem with wet violet stamps. Following this inspection, Moss termed the quality of FHC's stamps as "good" and made a number of recommendations regarding manufacturing techniques. David Hedgecoth, Product Development Manager at Porelon, followed up Moss's assessment with a letter to FHC in which he complimented the overall quality of FHC's stamps as very good and made several suggestions based on Moss' memo. The violet premix was subsequently reformulated due to a number of complaints by other licensees. No other negative comments were made to FHC regarding product quality until after Drab [Porelon's president] and Ooms' visit to Hong Kong in January 1985, when they met with MU and the Ministry of Light. They also visited FHC's factory and returned home to write letters criticizing some of FHC's methods. Again, the violet premix was the grievance. Obviously, at this point in time, Porelon, feeling pressure from MU to cancel FHC, had ulterior motives in finding quality problems at FHC's factory. Hedgecoth, who examined a stamp made by FHC during this period, stated that "[i]t looks very good, and I have no concerns about the quality." Moss conceded that the quality of FHC's production did not decline in 1985 and 1986 but was comparable to 1982 and 1983. We find Porelon's claim of quality problems at FHC as justification for termination to be unworthy of credence.

Porelon's insertion of a trademark infringement claim in their breach letter to FHC is manifestly pretextual and requires little discussion. Prior to Porelon's July 19, 1985 letter to FHC, FHC had never been instructed not to use the Johnson Wax name. . . .

The subterfuge and facade of the complaints in Porelon's "breach" letter are further exposed by the following excerpts from the deposition testimony of Drab:

A. . . . We had the China opportunity that I was personally interested in exploring for the good of Porelon; and we had a long-standing relationship with Fen Hin Chon; and I was interested in preserving that. I had no vendetta at all against the Fen Hin Chon organization or the people. They were great people to deal with over the years as businessmen and as individuals. *We had a basic difference in philosophy on how to grow the market at that point in time; and had the China opportunity never come along, I doubt if anything would have ever even come up because at the point in time that we made our decision and extended the Fen Hin Chon contract for five years to the balance of 1989,* we had no contact at all with Mark Universal and just normal relations with Fen Hin Chon; *but then along came the China opportunity; and with the Ministry of Light Industry insisting to deal through Mark Universal, you know, the thing got so dang complicated that it drove everybody nuts.* . . .

Q. Were the items about quality and using the term "Johnson Wax" just put there to beef the letter up?

A. *It could have been.* I didn't participate in that discussion that actually generated the letter that went out. (Emphasis added.)

Additionally, the day before the final termination letter to FHC, Drab's interoffice memo to T. S. Malone contains the following language:

> CONSIDER THE LICENSEE AGREEMENT WITH FEN HIN CHON TERMINATED AND WORK CLOSELY WITH MARK UNIVERSAL
> I have reviewed this action with Russ Barron and he supports official termination of our license agreement with Fen Hin Chon. Therefore, an official letter notifying Fen Hin Chon of the termination of the agreement will be sent via certified return receipt mail (copy attached). This may lead to further legal action by Fen Hin Chon, *but I believe it's a business risk we must take.* (Emphasis added.)

The termination of FHC by Porelon related not to China sales, quality, or the Johnson Wax name; it was a simple matter of dollars and cents to Porelon. The business risk they deliberately chose to take is now one for which they must pay.

The *Fen Hin Chon* case demonstrates some of the strategic consequences of licensing as a method of international expansion. The attractiveness of the Chinese market opportunity blinded Porelon executives to the legal consequences of their actions. Porelon allowed itself, through the actions of one employee, to get whipsawed by two Hong Kong competitors. Licensing decisions are long-term business relationships requiring good faith dealings and mutual respect.

CONCERNS OF DEVELOPING NATIONS

Several additional issues arise in the context of licensing agreements with less-developed countries (LDCs). The area of technology transfer, which largely involves licensing agreements, has been the subject of much commentary and legal regulation in the developing nations. The concerns of developing nations become negotiation points both for the licensor (usually from the more developed nation) and the licensee (usually from the LDC).

The first area of concern is with the validity of the intellectual property rights. Since intellectual property rights are national in scope, their coverage varies among different countries. For example, some developing countries do not recognize patent rights in pharmaceuticals, in order to encourage local industry to manufacture needed medical products at the lowest possible cost. Many countries effectively limit exclusive licenses by having a system of compulsory licensing. In a country with compulsory licensing, any company may produce a patented product, as long as it pays a royalty to the patent holder.

The second area of concern is with the validity of the licensing agreement. LDCs tend to regard the bargaining power of their local businesses as inferior to the bargaining power of businesses from the developed countries. Argentina, Brazil, India, Mexico, and Thailand are among the countries that have required government review and registration and approval of licensing agreements. Without government approval, the licensing contract may not be upheld, which could result in the licensor losing valuable commercial information to the licensee and others in the licensee's country.

One of the areas of review in some LDCs is the match of the technology covered by the licensing agreement with the country's development plans. If the agreement involves a priority economic activity, it is more likely to get approval. For example, a license to manufacture oil-well drilling equipment may be more important to the government of an LDC than a license to make a new kind of detergent for household use. The drilling equipment contract would get priority over the detergent contract in the allocation of the LDC's scarce economic resources.

Another aspect of development plans in LDCs relates to the level of technology and the development of the local workforce. LDC governments are concerned that companies from developed nations may want to exploit outmoded technology in the LDC, saving their best technology for the developed world. Although the licensor may have several business bases for this decision, including concern over the level of intellectual property protection in the LDC, decisions to license outmoded technology are less likely to get government approvals than licenses for current technology. Similarly, LDC governments promote the education, training, and improved quality of life of their local workforces. Licensing agreements that contemplate importing managers and others for the bulk of skilled work are less likely to achieve approval than licenses that provide for skilled positions, training, and education for the local workforce.

The government may also evaluate a licensing agreement for its levels of royalty payments. One of the general features of the economies of LDCs is the scarcity of hard currency. A royalty level the developed nation licensor may see as a reasonable negotiated price may appear to an LDC government to be either the product of an unconscionable agreement or too large a drain on limited hard currency resources.

Finally, the government approval process may involve an evaluation of the agreement for unduly restrictive provisions. Examples would include tying arrangements, which require the purchase of unnecessary or un-wanted products in order to get the desired license; provisions that restrict further innovation for the licensed product in the LDC; provisions that restrict the kinds of uses or products to which the licensee may put the licensed product; and grant-back provisions, which require the licensee to give the licensor intellectual property rights, often on unfavorable terms, to any improvements it makes in the product.

LDC regulation should not prevent licensing agreements in developing countries. Rather, the regulatory environment should put developed country licensors on notice to be aware of economic and social development concerns in their target markets. A business that acts with sensitivity to the needs of a developing nation may well be able to craft a successful relationship with both its licensee and the host government.

FRANCHISING

Much of trademark licensing has evolved into the complex agreements known as franchises. A franchise agreement generally involves the license of both trademark rights and know-how. Additional features of the franchise agreement may provide for employee training, quality control standards, and joint promotional activities.

It may be helpful to think about three different kinds of franchise arrangements. *Production franchises* grant the rights to manufacture and sell trademarked products. Fast food industry franchises are good examples of this kind of franchise. *Service franchises* give franchisees the right to use the franchisor's trademark and know-how to provide services. One example of a service franchise would be Servicemaster, which licenses its trademark and its special expertise at office cleaning. Finally, some franchises are *distribution franchises,* where a franchisee sells products from premises using the franchisor's trade name. In the United States, Ace and TruValue hardware stores are examples of distribution franchises.

Franchising has been a popular method of expanding businesses both domestically and internationally. Franchises are particularly widespread in Europe, North America, and Japan, but are increasingly part of the economies of LDCs as well. Food-related businesses like McDonalds, KFC, International Dairy Queen, and Dunkin' Donuts have led the way for U.S. businesses franchising around the world. Other businesses, such as Holiday Inn and Budget and Dollar Rent A Car, franchise extensively. These companies derive a substantial portion of their overall revenue from their international franchises. More recently, foreign-owned franchisors have entered the U.S. market. One such firm is Imasco, which owns and franchises the Hardees and Roy Rogers food outlets. Another recent entry into the U.S. market is the British-owned business The Body Shop, a chain of natural cosmetics stores.

For the franchisor, a franchise agreement offers the opportunity to enter new markets without making large, long-term capital investments.

Franchising also allows the franchisor to use local managers and workers, familiar with the new market and its customs and preferences. For the franchisee, the franchise offers an opportunity to start a business with the concept, image, and products already developed. The franchisee gets the advantage of the reputation of the entire franchise, and joint advertising and promotion campaigns often make marketing activities more effective than a single small business could manage on its own.

An MNE choosing to use franchising to enter new markets uses as many as three different strategies for its agreements. It may choose to contract with individual franchises for individual locations. Here, the franchisor exerts maximum control over each location and its business practices. Alternatively, the franchisor may use area development agreements. These agreements allow one franchisee to exploit a particular geographic area, operating many franchise outlets. The area development agreement allows the franchisor to deal with larger, usually more sophisticated franchisees, and allows each franchisee to develop a particular market fully. A final kind of franchise agreement often used internationally is the master franchise agreement. Like an area development franchise, the master franchise agreement gives one franchisee the right to develop the market in a particular territory. Unlike the area development agreement, however, the master franchise allows the franchisee to choose either to develop outlets itself or to subfranchise. A franchisor will use a master franchise agreement when it does not wish to exercise tight control over its individual locations.

The worldwide regulatory environment for franchising is quite complex. The European Community, many countries, and even states and provinces within countries may have regulations or legislation affecting contract terms and business practices. As a starting point, franchises involve licensing intellectual property rights and technology, so all of the considerations applying to such licenses also apply to franchise agreements. Additionally, there is an extensive body of antitrust law that applies to franchise agreements. The EC has been quite active recently in creating legal parameters for franchising.

The most significant area of regulation pertaining to franchising contracts relates to rules in various countries mandating financial and operational disclosure prior to beginning the franchise relationship. The United States regulates franchising more extensively than most other countries, at both the state and federal levels. In the United States, for example, the Federal Trade Commission requires extensive disclosure of financial and other information to prospective franchisees, and limits the franchisor's predictions of future earnings. In Canada, the Province of Alberta requires registration of all franchise plans and the filing of a prospectus before a franchisor may solicit franchisees in the province. France recently enacted a law requiring the delivery of extensive disclosure documents, in French, to prospective franchisees at least 20 days before the parties sign a contract or before the franchisee pays any money to obtain trademark rights.

Like any licensing agreement, the franchise is a business relationship, based on contract but relying on flexibility, good faith, and mutual efforts toward success. The holder of trademark rights invests a lot of money and effort in making the product a success, and the franchisor relies on the franchisee's efforts to achieve success in the foreign market. One of the difficult intersections of business and legal interests occurs when a franchisee is not meeting the contractual terms of the franchise contract. If the franchisor allows the deviation, it may lose the legal right to rely on the contract terms in the future. However, if the franchisor insists on observance of the letter of the contract, it may lose a valuable relationship with the franchisee and, perhaps, its best opportunity to enter a particular market. The following case illustrates one licensor's efforts to rehabilitate a failing franchisee rather than terminate the contract.

SEVEN-UP BOTTLING COMPANY (BANGKOK), LIMITED v. PEPSICO, INC.

686 F. Supp. 1015 (S.D.N.Y. 1988)

FACTS:

In 1980, Seven-Up Bottling Company (Bangkok), (the bottler), contracted with Seven-Up International (the company), for a production franchise. The bottler got the right to bottle soft drinks made from the company's extracts and the exclusive right to market those drinks, using the company's trademarks, throughout Thailand. The bottler agreed to certain warehouse and bottling plant improvements, and to further the "good will and reputation" of the company in Thailand.

The contract contained minimum sales obligations of 1.2 million cases in 1981, 2.1 million cases in 1982, 3.3 million cases in 1983, 3.9 million cases in 1984, 4.5 million cases in 1985, and additional amounts in subsequent years. The bottler also agreed to a formula for minimum advertising budgets, and agreed that it would achieve distribution of the soft drinks to 46 percent of all retail sales outlets in Thailand, including bars and restaurants, by 1982.

The parties' business relationship was good in 1981 and 1982. Even though the bottler did not achieve its sales targets, selling 350,000 cases in 1981 and 856,000 cases in 1982, the company selected the bottler for a "World Class Bottling"

award in 1982. However, the bottler got a new managing director in 1983, who stopped improvements, failed to pay bills, and generally allowed the financial and business condition of the bottler to deteriorate. Sales in 1983 were for only 733,500 cases.

In 1984, the company took steps to terminate the franchise. The bottler responded with a reorganization plan, and the company gave the bottler an additional year to improve its performance. The renegotiated sales levels for 1985 were 750,000 cases of 7Up and 200,000 cases of Howdy soft drinks. In 1986, PepsiCo, Inc. purchased Seven-Up International. In November 1986, the company notified the bottler that its franchise would be terminated, and the termination became effective in August of 1987.

The bottler sued the company, alleging wrongful termination under the contract. Because the company had stopped delivering soda extracts, it also sued for tortious interference with business.

ISSUE:

Did the company's conduct waive its right to insist on compliance with the terms of the franchise agreement?

RESULT:

No. The Court entered judgment for the defendant.

REASONS:

It is established that the Bottler never achieved the minimum sales requirements set forth in the 1980 Agreement for any of the years 1981 through 1985. An aggregate of 15 million cases sold was called for throughout this period, but only marginally more than 3 million were actually sold, meaning 80% of the anticipated sales were not achieved. In 1986, the 1980 Agreement required sales of 4.5 million cases, and only 200,000 cases were sold. . . .

Furthermore, Plaintiff has not controverted the evidence submitted by Defendant that the distribution levels of the product reached only 16.5% in greater Bangkok and 5% outside greater Bangkok, far short of the 46% penetration rate required by the 1980 agreement. . . .

. . . [V]alid and enforceable rights under a contract may be waived by a subsequent writing or by a subsequent course of conduct. . . . However, a party's reluctance to terminate a contract upon a breach and its attempts to encourage the breaching party to adhere to its obligations under the contract do not necessarily constitute a waiver of the innocent party's rights in the future. . . . Additionally, waivers of rights in contract will not be inferred unless the intent to waive is clear. . . .

[The court ruled that the company had narrowly modified the minimum sales requirements for 1983, 1984, and 1985 by entering into cooperative marketing agreements using formulas based on lower sales figures than those set in the 1980 agreement.] The Court further concludes that the record demonstrates no subsequent course of conduct . . . by Defendant that modified, contravened or resettled any of the terms of that Agreement as written in 1980. . . . These narrow, subsequent written modifications in no way affected or altered the provisions of the 1980 Agreement relating to distribution levels, submission of business records, or the obligation to effectively promote the brands in Thailand.

Furthermore, upon the basis of the aforesaid findings of fact herein, the Court concludes that Defendant repeatedly, emphatically and unambiguously, orally and in writing, reserved its rights to declare breach under the contract, and terminate Plaintiff's franchise, and that no waiver of rights by Defendant has been established. . . .

Indeed, Plaintiff's claims in this regard give new meaning to the old, cynical aphorism that no good deed (in this case, a series of good deeds) shall go unpunished. The record establishes the almost limitless patience and forbearance on the part of Defendant with respect to Plaintiff's dismal performance under the contract. In this connection, it is useful to bear in mind that Defendant gave more money in marketing funds to Plaintiff than it received in revenues from extract sales to Plaintiff. A Plaintiff's witness testified that the Bottler received approximately $1 million in marketing support from the Company. . . . The Bottler purchased 20,376 units of extract . . . at approximately $36 per unit . . . for a total of $833,526 in revenue to the Company. . . .

The Court concludes that the termination by Defendant of the 1980 Seven-Up Agreement and the 1982 Howdy Agreement, effective August 4, 1987, was in all respects within the legal right and prerogative of Defendant.

12.5 DIRECT INVESTMENT

At some stages of its development, a business working in the global market may decide that its strategic objectives are best served by a long-term presence in a particular foreign market. It may decide to make a direct investment in a country, by acquiring an existing company, establishing a branch, establishing a separately organized subsidiary, or starting a joint venture.

A direct investment actually establishes a legal and physical presence in the foreign market. It is distinct from what is known as portfolio investment, which consists of purchasing and selling the stocks of companies but not managing them. Worldwide portfolio investing has not been seen as one of the functions of an MNE, although that may change through the 1990s as financial services companies become more prominent in the world economy.

The ability to make a direct investment of any kind depends directly on the legal environment of the host country. Historically, some markets, such as the United States, have been relatively open to foreign direct investment. Others, such as many Latin American and African countries, have restricted foreign direct investment, and in some cases, as in some of the Socialist countries of Europe, they have barred foreign direct investment. Still others, like Canada, used foreign investment policy to preserve and protect domestic industry in areas important to the national government, such as culturally related businesses and businesses controlling natural resources.

Today, the legal restrictions on foreign investment are changing rapidly. The worldwide trend is toward opening borders to international business. The trend is particularly strong in Latin America, where countries like Argentina, Chile, Venezuela, and Mexico have made foreign investment much easier than it was just a few years ago. Most of the rest of Latin America is following suit. The trend toward welcoming foreign investment is also particularly strong in the former Socialist countries of Europe, which need foreign investment to make their transition to market economies.

ACQUISITIONS

One method of making a direct foreign investment is to acquire an existing business. The purchase of an ongoing business may have several advantages, including lower start-up costs, an in-place network of distribution or retail outlets, an experienced local workforce, and the goodwill and good reputation of the existing business.

Many countries restrict the ability of foreign businesses to acquire firms. The most common restriction is one requiring some percentage of local ownership. This kind of restriction leads businesses to adopt joint ventures as a preferred method of investment. Some countries restrict foreign ownership of sensitive industries. Canada, to maintain its cultural identity, restricts foreigners from ownership of publishing and media outlets. The United States, too, bans foreign ownership of broadcast media.

Recently, while many of the countries that historically banned or restricted foreign investment have liberalized their regulations, other, historically more open, countries have considered becoming more restrictive. For example, in the United States, the 1988 Omnibus Trade bill gave the President the power to block foreign acquisitions of U.S. businesses on national security grounds. This power, known as the Exon-Florio provisions, after their congressional authors, enables the President to block, suspend, prohibit, or seek divestment of mergers, acquisitions, or other attempts to gain control of U.S. businesses if the President determines that the foreign company's control would affect national security interests.

Since Exon-Florio went into effect in 1989, its provisions have been used several times to challenge acquisitions of U.S. businesses. In one instance, the China National Aero-Technology Import and Export Corporation (CATIC), owned by the Chinese government, acquired MAMCO Manufacturing, Inc., a Seattle-based maker of airplane parts, for $20 million. After an Exon-Florio investigation, the President ordered CATIC to divest its interests in MAMCO within 3 months (later extended for an additional 3 months), based on confidential information made available to him indicating that CATIC's control over MAMCO could, in the future, impair U.S. security interests.

BRANCHES

A second method of making a direct foreign investment is for a business to open a branch office. The laws governing the establishment of branches vary widely among countries. Some countries refuse to allow branch offices, while others merely require registration with a government ministry or commercial registry.

The disadvantages of opening a branch office relate to the fact that a branch has no separate identity from the rest of the corporation. Thus, having a branch office in a country may subject the worldwide operations of the company to the courts of that country. If the host country requires extensive disclosure of financial information, the presence of the branch may reveal information about the worldwide business.

A branch may be advantageous if the main office wants to retain direct control over the operations in the foreign market. Lines of authority and communication are much simpler in a branch than in other forms of direct investment. Opening a branch may also have tax advantages for the company. Many start-up offices operate at a loss for some period of time. If the company is United States–based, for example, those losses are deductible from the company's overall income and may be used to offset profitable operations elsewhere. Finally, some countries require extensive local participation or control of subsidiaries, which may make a branch office a good choice for a direct investment.

SUBSIDIARIES

Another method of making a direct investment in a foreign market is to incorporate a new business entity. In many instances, this new entity will be largely or wholly owned by the foreign business and is thus a subsidiary. The incorporating business is known as the parent company.

Formation

Depending on the specific laws of each country, forming a subsidiary may have many advantages. A separate legal entity with limited liability generally insulates the parent company from liability for acts committed by the subsidiary. Sometimes, as Chapter 15 shows us, the acts of the subsidiary will be imputed to the parent, especially when the parent disregards the separateness of the subsidiary. Disclosure of company activities is also generally limited to the activities of the separately incorporated subsidiaries. Finally, a locally incorporated and managed business may be advantageous from a marketing or government relations point of view.

Once a business decides to form a subsidiary, it must also choose a business form. Unlike the United States, most countries recognize two distinct forms of incorporation. One form is a stock corporation, which may be publicly or privately held and corresponds roughly to larger U.S. corporations. The second form is a type of limited liability company with a relatively large role for the owners, corresponding roughly to U.S. close corporations. The choice the parent company makes will affect the way the subsidiary is governed and managed. Figure 12-2 gives the names of the stock corporations and limited liability companies.

Two of the more important countries for businesses establishing subsidiaries are France and Germany. Both are in the EC, making them popular with businesses worldwide as locations for entering the EC and gaining the advantages of that unified market. French law, due to its importance in promoting the civil law tradition, has served as a model for much of the corporate law in other civil law nations. Germany, apart from being an important member of the EC, also provides a gateway for access to many of the Central and Eastern European countries. Both French and German laws relating to choice of business form for foreign subsidiaries demonstrate some of the choices involved in establishing a subsidiary.

As an example, a Dutch business setting up a subsidiary in France would probably choose between the *société anonyme* (SA) and the *société à responsabilité limitée* (SARL) for its business. Before incorporating by either method, it must get the approval of the Department of the Treasury (Direction du Trésor) for the foreign investment.

The SA is a stock ownership company. It may be publicly or privately held, with a maximum renewable term of 99 years. France has minimum capitalization requirements of F500,000 for a publicly held SA and F100,000 for a privately held SA. Publicly held SAs are also known as quoted SAs, since their shares are quoted on a stock exchange. Most subsidiaries use the privately held, or unquoted form, of the SA. Its charter *(statuts)* contains most of the information that would be found in both the articles of incorporation and the bylaws of a U.S. corporation.

SAs have two possible forms of governance. The *statuts* may provide for a *conseil d'administration*, in which shareholders act as a board of directors, appointing officers. Alternatively, the *statuts* may establish a *conseil*

Country	Stock Corporations	Limited Liability Companies
U.S.	Incorporated (Inc)	(Inc)
Argentina	Sociedad Anonima (SA)	Sociedad de Responsibilidad Limitada (SRL)
Brazil	Sociedade Anonima (SA)	Limitada
Chile	Sociedad Anonima (SA)	Sociedad de Responsibilidad Limitada
France	Société Anonyme (SA)	Société à Responsibilité Limitée (SARL)
Germany	Aktiengesellschaft (AG)	Gesellschaft mit beschränkter Haftung (GmbH)
Italy	Societa Per Azioni (SPA)	Societa a Responsibilita Limitata (SRL)
Japan	Kabushiki Kaisha	Yugen Kaisha
Mexico	Sociedad Anonima (SA)	Sociedad de Responsibilidad Limitada (S. de R.L.)
Republic of Korea	Chusik Hoesa	Yuhan Hoesa
Singapore	Public Company	Private Company
Spain	Sociedad Anonima (SA)	Sociedad de Responsibilidad Limitada (SRL)
Turkey	Anonim Sirkit	Limited Sirkit
U.K.	Public Limited Company (PLC)	Private Limited Company (Limited or Ltd)
Venezuela	Sociedad Anonima (SA)	Sociedad de Responsibilidad

FIGURE 12-2   Examples of Corporate Forms of Doing Business

de surveillance, or supervisory council, which will then select a *directoire,* or directorate, of two to five persons to manage the business.

Whereas the ownership interests in SAs take the form of shares of stock, the ownership interests in SARLs are represented by deeds, known as *parts sociales.* French law requires no fewer than two and no more than fifty participants, called *associés,* in an SARL, who must collectively pay in a minimum capitalization of F20,000. SARLs do not have boards of directors or supervisory councils, but are managed by professional managers, known as *gérants.*

The Germans take a somewhat different approach to organizing limited liability businesses. Government approvals of foreign investment are not required. The two main forms of business used for subsidiaries are the *Aktiengesellschaft* (AG) and the *Gesellschaft mit beschränkter Haftung* (GbmH).

The largest enterprises in Germany tend to use the AG form of doing business. The minimum capitalization of an AG is DM100,000, and ownership of an AG is in the form of shares *(aktien)*. The governing document of the AG is the *Satzung*, which, like its French counterpart, contains the contents of what would be found in the United States in the articles of incorporation and the bylaws.

Governance of an AG resides in three different bodies. The supervisory board (*Aufsichtsrat*) oversees the general direction of the company and appoints the board of management (*Vorstand*). The board of management consists of the operating officers and is responsible for the operations of the company. Finally, like U.S. corporations, the shareholders play a limited role in the major decisions of the AG. The general shareholders' meeting, or *Hauptversammlung*, meets annually to elect members to the supervisory board and to vote on some business actions.

Most subsidiaries of foreign businesses, and most German corporations, take the form of the GmbH. Only one shareholder is required, with a minimum capitalization of DM50,000. Governing powers in a GmbH are split between the shareholders and the managers, with the shareholders having more power to manage than in an AG. GbmHs must have at least one manager (*Gesellschaftsführer*), who bears broad day-to-day managerial responsibility. Smaller GbmHs need not have a supervisory board, although some GbmHs do have supervisory or advisory boards. GbmHs with more than 500 employees must have a supervisory board, one-third of whose members must represent employees.

German law contains one feature that is often unfamiliar to foreign investors. It mandates codetermination—that is, the inclusion of employee representatives in corporate governance—for all corporations of a certain size. As already noted, companies with more than 500 employees must have supervisory boards on which one-third of the members represent employees. The Codetermination Act of 1976 took the concept further, mandating that companies with more than 2,000 employees have a supervisory council with equal numbers of representatives from employees and from shareholders. The employee representatives are proportionately split between the workers, the office staff, and senior executives. In addition, for these qualifying companies, one member of the managing board must be a labor representative, who, as labor director, is responsible for personnel and other labor matters. The codetermination law applies to both AGs and GbmHs. Germany's codetermination law is the basis of current efforts in the EC to introduce codetermination to business across the European Community.

Operating Issues

Once formed, the subsidiary will be subject to all the operating issues encountered in ordinary businesses, such as labor law, accounting standards, marketing practices, and products liability issues. In addition, the subsidiary's role as part of an MNE will raise other problems, such as repatriation of profits and tax problems.

The parent company will have an ongoing interest in getting the subsidiary's profits returned. The ability to repatriate profits is one of the considerations the parent will make in choosing whether to enter a particular market. Profits usually flow back to the parent company in the form of dividends. The issues associated with getting profits out include the convertibility of currency and the existence of exchange controls.

As noted in Chapter 6, some countries still do not have convertible currencies. When investors have a presence in such a market, such as the former Soviet Union, getting profits home may require barter or countertrade. A company may use the profits generated in the inconvertible currency to purchase other local products for export.

Foreign exchange controls respond to uncertain and unstable import–export balances. The controls may take the form of a ban or restriction on the exchange of local currency for foreign currency, taxes on dividends, or restrictions on the level of dividends.

Taxes are perhaps the most important operational issue. Both the parent and the subsidiary will have to assess carefully the impact of all the local, state, provincial, or national taxes on operations. The payment of dividends from a subsidiary to a parent may involve taxable events in both countries. A network of tax treaties exists to prevent the double assessment of taxes. In the United States, foreign taxes paid may be credited against U.S. taxes on the same income, up to the U.S. tax amount. If the subsidiary's country has a lower tax rate than the United States, the U.S. parent will pay only the difference between the two tax rates to the U.S. government. If the subsidiary's country has a higher tax rate, the parent will pay no tax to the United States on that income, but cannot credit taxes paid abroad to other taxes owed. If the subsidiary's country does not have a tax treaty with the United States, the income will be fully taxed in each country, although taxes paid abroad may be deductible as an expense.

From this discussion of operational factors it is easy to see that an MNE might want to structure its business activities so as to produce higher costs for the subsidiary in high-tax or foreign exchange–controlled markets or low costs in nations with lower tax rates or no foreign exchange controls. Using transfer pricing practices, the parent may, for example, charge the subsidiary high prices for parts or services it uses, thus reducing profit and dividend levels shown by the subsidiary. Host countries sometimes react unfavorably and regulate transfer pricing practices as manipulative or unfair, not reflecting the real costs of the business. Aggressive transfer pricing policies may lead to angry public reaction and accusations of tax evasion in the host country. Chapter 15 will discuss transfer pricing in more detail.

JOINT VENTURES

As an MNE grows, it will almost always use joint ventures as a method of expansion into selected markets. The traditional definition of a joint venture has been two or more parties investing together to form a new partnership or corporate entity. This kind of joint venture could be called an equity joint venture. As international business has entered the age of strategic alliances, that definition has become inadequate in reflecting the reality of joint ventures. Today, a joint venture is almost any business combination short of a complete merger. Equity joint ventures fall within this definition, but so do contractual agreements and other forms of alliances for research and development, production, promotion and marketing, and distribution.

Joint ventures have many advantages for their participants. For the MNE, they bring new market opportunities with lower levels of investment than a sole venture would require. The MNE gets the advantage of an experienced local partner with local market presence and goodwill. For the local venturer, the joint venture brings access to the MNE's technology, products, and expertise. Especially in developing countries, the joint venture may be an important vehicle for technological and economic development.

In some nations, the biggest advantage of the joint venture is that it may be the only legal vehicle for foreign investment. Developing nations in particular see the joint venture as a method of developing local capital, creating local managerial and technical expertise, obtaining technology, and preventing foreign domination of key business sectors. Although the current trend is toward opening developing nations to foreign investment, some countries still require substantial levels of local participation.

Joint ventures have expanded dramatically over the past decade. In the United States, they have especially affected such key industry segments as automobiles, where the Chrysler–Mitsubishi joint venture, the Ford–Mazda joint venture, and the GM–Toyota joint venture have led to market success stories like the Dodge Colt, the Mazda Navajo (Ford Explorer), and the Chevrolet Nova. In Europe, joint ventures have been an excellent method of entering the EC and securing the advantages of local presence. In China, the government strongly encourages joint ventures as the preferred means of market entry. Perhaps the most important use of joint ventures has been in the economic restructuring of the formerly Socialist nations of Central and Eastern Europe. A key part of their plans to privatize state-owned business has been the formation of joint ventures with foreign businesses.

The legal and regulatory scheme for international joint ventures varies considerably among countries. In the developed world, joint venture regulation tends to focus on the competitive effects of strategic alliances. Chapter 13 will examine this area in more detail. In the developing world, including the restructuring economies in Central and Eastern Europe, international joint venture regulation is extensive, specifying the allowable percentage of foreign ownership, local and foreign management rights, necessary government approvals, percentage of local content in produced goods, and royalty and dividend levels.

Business issues in the structure and operations of joint ventures tend to be complex, but similar to those found in any partnership or group investment. The first issue is how to value the contributions of the venturers. Problems arise when one party is contributing physical assets, such as factories, while the other contributes skills and technical knowledge, which are more difficult to value. One significant problem for joint ventures in Socialist countries has been the valuation of property when the legal system has not recognized property rights. It is difficult to establish a value for real estate when there is no market for buying and selling property. Similarly, machinery and other tangible assets are difficult to value when replacement prices and sale prices are determined not by the marketplace but by government planners.

A second significant issue in the structure and operation of joint ventures is the sharing of management and control. Some ventures still require 51 percent local ownership to achieve government approval. A foreign investor may be reluctant to cede control over its interest to local partners. In countries requiring majority local ownership, a foreign investor may maintain effective control by spreading out the ownership of the local share among many investors. The foreign investor may also include "supermajority" provisions, requiring, for example, a two-thirds majority vote on key business decisions. These provisions effectively give the minority owner veto power.

The final issue, of course, is the sharing of growth and profits. In some countries, joint venture statutes may help determine this issue for the joint venturers. In other countries, particularly those that do not have a well-developed system of accounting standards, the issue can be quite complex. In the joint venture agreement, the parties will have to negotiate depreciation and amortization, inventory costing methods, and other components of the determination of profit and loss.

12.6 CONCLUSION

Multinational enterprises employ a variety of legal structures to reach their strategic objectives. As a business grows, it will tend to move from direct selling strategies to intermediaries, licensing, and direct foreign investment. The forms it uses to conduct its business are determined by the legal environment of the host country, as well as by the tax environment of both the home and host countries.

MNEs need to be particularly sensitive to the concerns of developing nations when they enter those markets. Restrictions on agents and distributors, technology transfer regulation, and requirements of local participation in capital and management do not exist simply as roadblocks to legitimate foreign investment, but reflect legitimate concerns over the course of economic development, foreign domination of important business activities, and the creation of a local technical and managerial class. MNEs sensitive to these developing-nation concerns can operate successfully in the LDC environment, with the greater support of their customers and the local government.

12.7 QUESTIONS FOR DISCUSSION

1. If you were negotiating a contract to retain a firm to act as your commercial agent in an EC country, what are some of the provisions you might want to consider for the contract? Explain.

2. What reasons might an LDC have for not recognizing patents on pharmaceutical and agricultural products? What reasons might an LDC have for adopting a compulsory licensing scheme? Can you identify advantages to fully recognizing patent rights in pharmaceutical and agricultural products? Explain.

3. After reading the *Fen Hin Chon* case, what advice would you have for Porelon executives to avoid similar situations in the future?

4. Giant Motors Corporation intends to build a new motorcycle manufacturing plant in an African LDC. The plant would make motorcycles for use throughout the African market and for export to the EC. In planning the venture, Giant is considering the choice of a wholly owned subsidiary or a joint venture. What issues should Giant consider in making its choice? Explain.

12.8 FURTHER READINGS

James E. Austin, *Managing in Developing Countries*, Free Press, New York, 1990.

Christopher Bartlett and Sumantra Goshal, *Managing Across Borders: The Transnational Solution*, Harvard Business School Press, Cambridge, Mass., 1989.

J. Bleeke and D. Ernst, "The Way to Win in Cross-Border Alliances," *Harvard Business Review*, November–December 1991, pp. 127–135.

F. Kuebler, R. Mundheim, and I. Shapiro, "Panel Discussion on Corporate Governance: U.S., German and Japanese Perspectives," 8 *Journal of Comparative Business and Capital Markets Law* 401–418 (1986).

Raymond Vernon, *Storm Over the Multinationals*, Harvard University Press, Cambridge, Mass., 1977.

REGULATING GLOBAL COMPETITION

13.1 INTRODUCTION

National governments employ many different methods of regulating competitive business practices within their territories. In centrally planned economies, competition is not an issue, as central planners determine the products businesses will produce and the prices businesses will charge. Other nations allow free establishment of businesses, but regulate prices and wages. In still other nations, the government either controls or maintains a presence in key business sectors by operating businesses. In the market economies of the developed world, however, governments encourage businesses to compete freely for customers, using price and quality as competitive tools.

Regulation of competitive conduct is concentrated in the developed world. Roughly twenty of the developed nations have laws regulating business competitive practices, and about twelve of the developing nations, including Argentina, Brazil, South Korea, and India, have competition laws. The emerging economies of Eastern Europe have just begun developing competition laws, so the number of nations having such laws should increase through the 1990s. In market economies, government regulation of competition serves the function of creating a level playing field for competition.

The focus of regulation is twofold. The first center of regulatory activity attempts to prevent unduly restrictive business practices, such as agreements to fix prices for products and the use of unfair tactics to try to drive competitors out of business. The second focus of competition protects against attempts to monopolize industry and against abuse of dominant market positions.

The multinational enterprise (MNE) will, by the nature of its business activities, encounter government regulation of its competitive activities in its home country and in the markets it enters. The purpose of this chapter is to explore the international dimensions of national regulation of business competition.

13.2 NATIONAL REGULATION OF INTERNATIONAL COMPETITION

THE U.S. APPROACH

The legal structure regulating competitive conduct is known in the United States as antitrust law. Antitrust law originated more than 100 years ago as an attempt to combat the formation of trusts or monopolies in such key industries as oil, sugar, and railroads. The main principles of U.S. antitrust law are expressed in the Sherman Act.

THE SHERMAN ACT OF 1980

15 U.S.C. §§1-7

§1. TRUSTS, ETC., IN RESTRAINT OF TRADE ILLEGAL

Every contract, combination in the form of trust or otherwise, or conspiracy, in restraint of trade or commerce among the several States, or with foreign nations, is declared to be illegal. . . .

§2. MONOPOLIZING TRADE A MISDEMEANOR

Every person who shall monopolize, or attempt to monopolize, or combine or conspire with any other person or persons, to monopolize any part of the trade or commerce among the several States, or with foreign nations, shall be deemed guilty. . . .

The language of the Sherman Act is extremely general. Congress added detail to the Sherman Act prohibitions by enacting the Clayton Act of 1914, which banned certain restrictive business practices. Among the banned practices are exclusive dealing contracts and tying contracts in commodities, and mergers, when these activities may lessen competition or tend to create a monopoly. In 1936, Congress added the Robinson–Patman Act, which bans price discrimination.

The antitrust laws have both criminal and civil applications. Violation of the Sherman Act is a criminal offense, with possible fines and jail terms upon conviction. The government may also bring civil actions for injunctions to stop unlawful conduct and may halt unlawful mergers, even ordering divestment of acquisitions that violate the law. Competitors and others harmed by unlawful conduct also have a powerful remedy. They may sue for treble damages plus their actual attorneys' fees. The treble-damage remedy for competitors is stronger than most remedies available to private parties in other countries. It has been the subject of much unfavorable commentary abroad, and, as this chapter will discuss later, some blocking legislation by other countries.

Interpretation of the antitrust law has been left largely in the hands of the courts, although in recent years the government has issued guidelines indicating the kinds of competitive activities that are likely to face prosecution. The Justice Department's most recent guidelines, reflecting the changes of the Reagan administration, were issued in 1988. Over the years, courts considering Sherman Act cases have developed categories of activities that will always be held unlawful, called "per se activities." Other activities will be judged using a "rule of reason" analysis, which examines the impact of the activity on competition to determine its legality. Among the activities held to be per se illegal are agreements to fix prices on goods, group boycotts or concerted refusals to deal, and tying arrangements, which require a customer to purchase unwanted goods in order to obtain the goods it wants.

Antitrust law in the United States has always reflected current political and economic theories. In the 1980s U.S. antitrust law underwent a major change as a result of the ascendancy of the political policies of the Reagan administration and the economic theories of the "Chicago school" of economists. Current government attitudes toward antitrust enforcement still largely reflect the influence of that decade, which encouraged business activities without government intervention.

Judicial interpretations of antitrust law often reflect the underlying tensions in the purposes of the law. On one side is the desire to prevent monopolization in an industry by preserving as much competition and as many competitors as possible. On the other side is the realization that healthy competition results in realignments and restructuring, with efficient competitors gaining strength and inefficient competitors going out of business. Efficient competition tends toward the ultimate elimination of competitors. The following case illustrates some of the dimensions of this dilemma in a familiar international context.

MATSUSHITA ELECTRICAL INDUSTRIAL CO., LTD. v . ZENITH RADIO CORPORATION

475 U.S. 574 (1986)
United States Supreme Court

FACTS:

Zenith and another television set producer sued twenty-one Japanese makers of consumer electronic products (CEPs), alleging that over a 20-year period the Japanese firms illegally conspired to drive the U.S. manufacturers out of the television manufacturing business. Zenith alleged that the Japanese firms acted together to charge artificially high prices for televisions in Japan, which lowered demand there and increased exports. Zenith further alleged that the Japanese firms priced their TVs below cost in the U.S. market, with the purpose of driving the U.S. makers out of business. Once the Japanese firms attained monopoly power, Zenith alleged they would raise prices on their products. This predatory pricing, if proved, would violate both §1 of the Sherman Act and the Robinson–Patman Act.

The district court granted summary judgment

in favor of the Japanese firms, but the court of appeals reversed, holding that Zenith had raised enough issues of fact concerning the conspiracy to justify a trial. The Japanese firms petitioned the Supreme Court for review.

ISSUE:

Did Zenith allege facts that could show a predatory pricing conspiracy?

RESULT:

No. By a 5–4 vote, the Court held that Zenith failed to show that the actions could not have been the result of independent actions.

REASONS:

. . . Turning to the evidence, the [district] court determined that a fact finder could draw the following conclusions:

1. The Japanese market for CEPs was characterized by oligopolistic behavior, with a small number of producers meeting regularly and exchanging information on price and other matters. . . . This created the opportunity for a stable combination to raise both prices and profits in Japan. American firms could not attack such a combination because the Japanese Government imposed significant barriers to entry. . . .

2. Petitioners had relatively higher fixed costs than their American counterparts, and therefore needed to operate at something approaching full capacity in order to make a profit. . . .

3. Petitioners' plant capacity exceeded the needs of the Japanese market. . . .

4. By formal agreements arranged in cooperation with Japan's Ministry of International Trade and Industry (MITI), petitioners fixed minimum prices for CEPs exported to the American market. . . . The parties refer to these prices as the "check prices," and to the agreements that require them as the "check price agreements."

5. Petitioners agreed to distribute their products in the United States according to a "five company rule": each Japanese producer was permitted to sell only to five American distributors. . . .

6. Petitioners undercut their own check prices by a variety of rebate schemes. . . . Petitioners sought to conceal these rebate schemes both from the United States Customs Service and from MITI, the former to avoid various customs regulations as well as action under the antidumping laws, and the latter to cover up petitioners' violations of the check-price agreements. . . .

We begin by emphasizing what respondents' claim is not. Respondents cannot recover antitrust damages based solely on alleged cartelization of the Japanese market, because American antitrust laws do not regulate the competitive conditions of other nations' economies. . . . Nor can respondents recover damages for any conspiracy by petitioners to charge higher than competitive prices in the American market. Such conduct would indeed violate the Sherman Act . . . , but it could not injure respondents: as petitioners' competitors, respondents stand to gain from any conspiracy to raise the market price of CEPs. . . .

Finally, for the same reason, respondents cannot recover for a conspiracy to impose nonprice restraints that have the effect of either raising market price or limiting output. Such restrictions, though harmful to competition, actually benefit competitors by making supracompetitive pricing more attractive. Thus, neither petitioners' alleged supracompetitive pricing in Japan, nor the five-company rule that limited distribution in this country, nor the check prices insofar as they established minimum prices in this country, can by themselves give respondents a cognizable claim for antitrust damages. . . .

A predatory pricing conspiracy is by nature speculative. Any agreement to price below the competitive level requires the conspirators to forgo profits that free competition would offer them. The foregone profits may be considered an investment in the future. For the investment to be rational, the conspirators must have a reasonable expectation of recovering, in the form of later monopoly profits, more than the losses suffered. . . . Moreover, it is not enough simply to achieve monopoly power, as monopoly pricing may breed quick entry by new competitors eager to share in the excess profits. The success of any predatory scheme depends on maintaining monopoly power for long enough both to recoup the predator's losses and to harvest some additional gain. . . .

Finally, if predatory pricing conspiracies are generally unlikely to occur, they are especially so where, as here, the prospects of attaining monopoly power seem slight. In order to recoup their losses, petitioners must obtain enough market power to set higher than competitive prices, and then must sustain those prices long enough to earn in excess profits what they earlier gave up in below-cost prices. . . . Two decades after their conspiracy is alleged to have commenced, petitioners appear to be far from achieving their goal: the two largest shares of the retail market in television sets are held by RCA and respondent Zenith, not by any of the petitioners. . . . Moreover, those shares, which together approximate 40% of sales, did not decline appreciably during the 1970's. . . . Petitioners' collective share rose rapidly during this period, from one-fifth or less of the relevant markets to close to 50%. . . .

The alleged conspiracy's failure to achieve its ends in the two decades of its asserted operation is strong evidence that the conspiracy does not in fact exist. Since the losses in such a conspiracy accrue before the gains, they must be "repaid" with interest. And because the alleged losses have accrued over the course of two decades, the conspirators could well require a correspondingly long time to recoup. Maintaining supracompetitive prices in turn depends on the continued cooperation of the conspirators, on the inability of other would-be competitors to enter the market, and (not incidentally) on the conspirators' ability to escape antitrust liability for their minimum price-fixing cartel. Each of these factors weighs more heavily as the time needed to recoup losses grows. If the losses have been substantial—as would likely be necessary in order to drive out most of the competition—petitioners would most likely have to sustain their cartel for years to break even. . . .

On remand, the Court of Appeals is free to consider whether there is other evidence that is sufficiently unambiguous to permit a trier of fact to find that petitioners conspired to price predatorily for two decades despite the absence of any apparent motive to do so. The evidence must "tend to exclude the possibility" that petitioners underpriced respondents to compete for business rather than to implement an economically senseless conspiracy. . . . In the absence of such evidence, there is no "genuine issue for trial" . . . and petitioners are entitled to have summary judgment reinstated.

THE EC APPROACH

Given the emphasis in the European Community on opening the market among all the member countries, it is not surprising that the organizing documents of the EC include provisions regulating competitive conduct. EC competition law is playing an important role in the unification of the internal market, and worldwide is the most active area for the development of competition law. The EC Commission and the EC courts are developing many new areas of substantive competition law, affecting business inside and outside the European Community. The Treaty of Rome contains the fundamentals of EC competition law in Articles 85 and 86.

TREATY ESTABLISHING THE EUROPEAN ECONOMIC COMMUNITY (TREATY OF ROME 1957)

ARTICLE 85

1. The following shall be prohibited as incompatible with the Common Market: all agreements between enterprises, all decisions by associations of enterprises and all concerted practices which are apt to affect trade between the Member States and which have as their object or effect the prevention, restriction or distortion of competition within the Common Market, in particular those consisting in:

(a) the direct or indirect fixing of purchase or selling prices or of any other trading conditions;
(b) the limitation or control of production, markets, technological development or investment;
(c) market-sharing or the sharing of sources of supply;
(d) the application of unequal conditions to parties undertaking equivalent engagements in commercial transactions, thereby placing them at a competitive disadvantage;

(e) making the conclusion of a contract subject to the acceptance by the other party to the contract of additional obligations, which by their nature or according to commercial usage have no connection with the subject of such contract.

2. Any agreements or decisions prohibited pursuant to this Article shall be null and void.

3. The provisions of paragraph 1 may, however, be declared inapplicable in the case of:

—any agreements or groups of agreements between enterprises,
—any decisions or groups of decisions by associations of enterprises, and
—any concerted practices or groups of concerted practices,

which contribute to the improvement of the production or distribution of goods or to the promotion of technological or economic progress while reserving to consumers an equitable share in the profit resulting therefrom, and which:

(a) neither impose on the enterprises concerned any restrictions not indispensable to the attainment of the above objectives;
(b) nor enable such enterprises to eliminate competition in respect of a substantial proportion of the goods concerned.

ARTICLE 86

Any abusive exploitation by one or more enterprises of a dominant position within the Common Market or within a substantial part of it shall be deemed to be incompatible with the Common Market and shall be prohibited, in so far as trade between Member States could be affected by it.

Such abusive exploitation may, in particular, consist in:

(a) the direct or indirect imposition of any inequitable purchase or selling prices or of any other inequitable trading conditions;
(b) the limitation of production, markets or technological development to the prejudice of consumers;
(c) the application of unequal conditions to parties undertaking equivalent engagements in commercial transactions, thereby placing them at a competitive disadvantage;
(d) making the conclusion of a contract subject to the acceptance by the other party to the contract of additional obligations which by their nature or according to commercial usage have no connection with the subject of such contract.

EC competition law splits conceptually in ways similar to the U.S. antitrust law. Article 85 deals with agreements among competitors to engage in unfair competitive practices, such as price fixing, refusals to deal, territorial divisions, and tying agreements. Article 86 attempts to prevent abuses of dominant market position by single enterprises or groups of enterprises. It is important to note that businesses doing business in the EC may also be subject to national competition law, which in some instances may be more restrictive than EC law.

EC competition law has different mechanisms for development than U.S. law. Instead of evolving through court decisions, EC law has been strengthened and clarified by regulations, issued by the Commission. The EC courts have become involved in interpreting the treaty and the regulations, but do not generally have the formative legal function that U.S. courts have.

During the past decade, the European Court of Justice has sometimes served as the forum for a test case on certain kinds of business practices. Once the Court ruled in an individual case, the Commission then created regulations for similar activities for other, similarly situated businesses. For example, in 1986 the European Court of Justice ruled that franchise agreements could restrain trade under Article 85, but also could contain clauses necessary to protect the franchisor's know-how, identity, and reputation. The Commission followed this decision with some individual cases involving franchising practices, then with a regulation containing a "white list" of franchise contract clauses that it deemed acceptable under Article 85 and a "black list" of franchise contract clauses that it deemed unacceptable.

One of the distinctive features of EC competition law is found in Article 85(3). Arrangements that would violate Article 85(1) may proceed if they contribute to the production or distribution of goods, or technological or economic progress, if those agreements do not unduly distort trade. Businesses whose agreements would violate Article 85(1) may notify the Commission of their proposed action and apply for an exemption through the application of Article 85(3). The Commission may grant an exemption on an individual basis or on a group basis for similarly situated businesses. An exemption granted under Article 85(3) does not exempt a business from liability under Article 86 if the conduct is an abuse of a dominant market position.

In addition to the exemption procedure under Article 85(3), businesses may take action without fear of challenge by the Commission by obtaining what is called a negative clearance from the Commission. The negative clearance procedure applies to both Articles 85 and 86. If a business (or group of businesses) doubts whether its actions would violate EC competition law, it may request the Commission to agree that it will not challenge the action under Article 85 or 86. The Commission's negative clearance allows the business to go forward without fear of prosecution, as long as its application has disclosed all relevant facts.

The following decision illustrates the Commission's process in granting exemptions under Article 85(3).

RE THE AGREEMENT BETWEEN MOOSEHEAD BREWERIES, LTD. AND WHITBREAD AND COMPANY PLC

[1990] O.J. L100/32, [1991] 4 C.M.L.R. 391
Commission of the European Communities

FACTS:
Moosehead entered into three contracts (the agreement) with Whitbread, which together licensed Moosehead's trademark rights and brewing know-how to Whitbread so that Whitbread could brew and sell Moosehead beer in the U.K. The agreement contained several provisions which could be troublesome under Article 85(1).

Moosehead granted Whitbread an exclusive territory, and Whitbread agreed not to solicit customers outside the territory. Whitbread further agreed for the 10 years of the agreement not to brew or sell any other Canadian beer within the territory. Whitbread also agreed to purchase yeast for the beer only from Moosehead.

The parties sought a negative clearance, or in the alternative, an exemption under Article 85(3).

ISSUE:

Are the parties entitled to an exemption under Article 85(3) for their licensing agreement?

RESULT:

Yes.

REASONS:

(5) The agreements concern the manufacture of a beer in the United Kingdom which is sold by Moosehead in Canada and other countries under the trade mark 'Moosehead' . . . . The product is similar in nature and alcoholic strength to other 'non-premium lagers' presently sold in the United Kingdom, although according to the notifying parties, it has a particular taste typical of Canadian lagers.

(6)1. As was explained in Commission Decision 84/381/EEC (Carlsberg) the following factors distinguish the United Kingdom market from other European markets:

2. Most beer sold in the United Kingdom is sold in draught form in public houses licensed for the consumption of liquor; 81 per cent. of all beer consumed in the United Kingdom is sold in on-licensed premises and 75 per cent. of all beer sold in the United Kingdom is in draught form. In 1987 lager represented 45 per cent. of the beer consumption in the United Kingdom. In order to achieve substantial sales of a new beer in the United Kingdom it is therefore necessary for the seller to have access to a certain number of public houses.

3. Brewers largely distribute their beer in the United Kingdom using their own lorries. No large-scale independent distribution facility therefore exists for beer in the United Kingdom.

4. The majority of public houses in the United Kingdom are operated by tenants who are 'tied' by

contract to purchase beer from one brewer alone. They are, in fact, owned by the brewer with which they sign such agreements. Since . . . 57 per cent. of all on-licensed premises in the United Kingdom are owned by brewers 'tied,' it is very useful, if not indispensable, for a foreign brewer wishing to enter the United Kingdom market to gain the assistance of a large national brewer.

The number of tenants of on-licensed premises that are required to purchase from one brewer alone is likely to decrease by 1 November 1992, when, as a result of implementation of The Supply of Beer Order, all national brewers with more than 2,000 licensed premises must release from all product ties one half of their premises above the 2,000 threshold. Also, all on-licensed tenants tied by national brewers will be free to choose a guest beer as well as to purchase other non-alcoholic drinks from any source by 1 May 1990. Nevertheless, a substantial part of total United Kingdom beer consumption will continue to pass through 'tied' outlets. . . .

The parties have made the following submissions.

(13)1. As Moosehead has no branch in Europe and neither Moosehead nor any of its associate companies has a manufacturing facility in the Community, a distribution network for beer, or any experience of marketing beer in the United Kingdom, it would not, over the short term, be commercially feasible for Moosehead to set up its own manufacturing facility for the product. In view of the nature of the retail market for beer and given the distance and scale on which sales would be established, it would not be economic for Moosehead to establish its own distribution network or to sell through independent wholesalers.

2. Whitbread has limited experience of Canadian lagers and, in particular, has no access to the unique culture yeast that gives Moosehead lager a particular taste that distinguishes it from the other lagers, nor to the technical information held by Moosehead necessary to manufacture the product to which the agreement relates. Whitbread, therefore, lacks the expertise to manufacture the product for the United Kingdom market without assistance from Moosehead. However, its general brewing facilities and experience mean

that it is capable of producing Moosehead beer for sale in the territory if this assistance is given by Moosehead. Furthermore, Whitbread does not possess a well-known Canadian trade mark.

3. The parties argue that as a result of these facts the agreement contributes towards improving production/distribution of the product because (i) in the absence of the agreement, the product could not have been made available as quickly, or over as wide an area . . . and (ii) the agreement enables the product to be produced in the territory, which means it is likely to be fresher and cheaper, since it would be transported over a shorter distance.

The fierce competition in the lager sector of the beer market will ensure that the benefits of the agreement are passed on to consumers and, furthermore, will prevent the agreement from eliminating competition in respect of a substantial part of the products in question.

The clauses to the agreement which are restrictive of competition are indispensable in order to give Whitbread sufficient confidence to invest substantial sums in the launch of a new beer onto an already competitive market, and to enable Moosehead to entrust the brewing and the sale of the product in full knowledge that the licensee will concentrate its efforts, concerning the promotion and sale of Canadian lagers, exclusively on the product. . . .

(15) 1. The exclusive trademark license for the production and marketing of the product, the prohibition of active sales outside the territory and the non-competitive clause. . . fall under the prohibition of Article 85(1) since they have as their object or effect an appreciable restriction of competition within the Common Market.

In this case, the exclusive character of the license has, as a consequence, the exclusion of third parties, namely the five other large brewers in the territory, from the use, as licensees, of the Moosehead trade mark, in spite of their potential interest and their ability to do so.

Likewise, the prohibition of active sales activity outside the territory by the licensee and the ban on marketing competing brands of beer are appreciable restrictions of competition since Whit-

bread, because of its large production capacity, would be able to supply other markets within the Common Market and to distribute other Canadian brands. . . .

2. The other clauses of the agreement do not fall within Article 85(1) because they do not have as their object or effect an appreciable restriction of competition within the Common Market. This applies to Whitbread's obligation to maintain certain qualitative standards, to the know-how clauses, and to the trade mark no-challenge clause. . . .

[16] 2. In light of the particularities of the United Kingdom beer market . . . the Commission considers that the agreement is likely to contribute to the improvement of the production and distribution of the product in the territory and to promote economic progress. In particular, the following considerations are pertinent in this regard:

— The turnover presently achieved by Moosehead would not justify the capital costs involved in building custom production facilities for sales within the territory. . . . Furthermore, production will be at the point-of-sale and the beer need no longer be imported from Canada. The agreement will thereby reduce transport costs and thus contribute to economic progress.

— Through the agreement, the product will automatically benefit from Whitbread's comprehensive distribution network. In the light of a market characterised by a paucity of independent distribution facilities, the Commission considers that the agreement is likely to contribute to the improvement in the distribution of the product in the territory. . . .

After having considered the favourable effect for the production and marketing of beer resulting from the clauses which are restrictive of competition, and in particular the non-competition clause, the Commission considers that they are deemed to be indispensable to the attainment of the objectives of Article 85(3). A decision pursuant to Article 85(3) may, therefore, be adopted.

The EC Commission has strong investigatory and enforcement powers. It has the right of access to business premises, without search warrants, and the right to force disclosure of business documents, including correspondence with in-house counsel and counsel from non–EC countries. In the United States, such correspondence would be exempt from disclosure. Contracts that violate Articles 85 or 86 are void, and the Commission has the power to issue cease-and-desist orders, supported by daily fines, against practices violating the competition law. Finally, the Commission has imposed multimillion ECU fines against violators.

THE JAPANESE APPROACH

Japanese competition law had its start in the attempt by occupying American forces to force the dissolution of the *zaibatsu,* or large trading companies that dominated Japan's economy before World War II. In 1947, the Antimonopoly and Fair Trade Law became the centerpiece of Japanese competition law. Modeled after the Sherman and Clayton acts, the Antimonopoly Law prohibits various anticompetitive activities, including monopolization, unreasonable restraints of trade, unfair methods of competition, and abuse of dominant market power. Enforcement is the responsibility of the Japan Fair Trade Commission, an independent agency, which resolves violations primarily by informal means.

The U.S.-style antitrust law is not a particularly good fit with Japanese culture and business practice. Almost as soon as the U.S. occupying forces left Japan, the Diet began enacting exemptions from the law for various business groups and practices. For example, the Medium and Small Business Organization Law allows business groups to form a cartel and control production, prices, and distribution whenever excess competition threatens the group.

The fundamental conflict in Japanese competition policy is between the Antimonopoly Law and Japanese industrial policy, as articulated by the Ministry of International Trade and Industry (MITI). While the Antimonopoly Law aims to prevent cartels and unfair trade practices, the industrial policy aims to promote research and development, efficient competition, and export growth. Some of the issues that one would expect to find entrusted to the Fair Trade Commission are instead MITI's responsibility. One example is the law governing structurally depressed industries (The Temporary Measure Law for the Structural Adjustment of Specific Industries), which gives MITI the power to order businesses in depressed industries to cut back production, or to establish a cooperative arrangement reorganizing a depressed industry by using cooperation agreements and mergers.

When industrial policy and competition policy clash, industrial policy generally wins. One widely known example comes from the oil cartel cases of the 1970s. In February 1974, the Fair Trade Commission accused oil companies of a conspiracy to fix prices and reduce output. The companies' defense was that they were only following MITI's administrative guidance, which indicated that they should fix prices and reduce output. In 1980, the Tokyo High Court found that the arrangements violated the Antimonopoly Law, but acquitted the defendants because "there was a reasonable possibility they would not have been aware of the illegality of the cartel because of MITI's administrative guidance."[1]

As the *Matsushita* case earlier in the chapter pointed out, the Japanese government encourages domestic business activity that would violate U.S. (and EC) antitrust laws. Many foreign businesses trying to enter the Japanese market have argued that Japanese competitive practices, sanctioned by the government, operate as nontariff trade barriers. Historically, the Japanese government has argued that protective measures are needed to achieve economic recovery and growth. In the face of complaints from foreign trading partners, however, the next decade may see MITI take a more hands-off attitude toward at least some Japanese industries.

13.3 LIMITS ON NATIONAL REGULATION

As markets become more global in scope, the problems of regulating anticompetitive conduct become more complex. For example, if a business is accused of abusing a dominant market position under Article 86 of the Treaty of Rome, how would the Commission measure the relevant market? Is the market restricted to the member states of the EC, or could it be measured worldwide? If two U.S.-based multinational enterprises merge, does the Commission of the EC have the power to block the merger using EC competition laws?

As Chapter 2 discussed, two of the limitations on the ability of national governments to regulate business activity are jurisdiction and enforcement. In both areas, competition law disputes have helped to define the boundaries of national regulation. In neither area are there definitive answers yet to the question of how far a government may go in regulating international competition.

EXTRATERRITORIAL JURISDICTION

Courts and regulators have struggled for a long time with the issue of the reach of their regulatory power. Some cases are relatively simple, involving conduct of foreign-owned businesses within the United States. In those instances, the jurisdictional principle of presence affords a basis for courts or regulatory agencies to act. A more difficult question of authority arises when the alleged illegal conduct took place in a foreign country but inhib-

---

[1]Kenji Sanekata, "Antitrust in Japan: Recent Trends and Their Socio-Political Background," 20 *University of British Columbia Law Review* 379, 382 (1986).

ited competition in a different market. Often, as the *Zenith* case earlier in this chapter illustrates, the conduct an injured competitor complains of is either tolerated or even encouraged by a foreign government.

Because the United States has regulated competition for more than 100 years, it has a long history of disputes over the reach of U.S. legislation. Recall, as a starting point, that the Sherman Act applies specifically to trade between the United States and foreign nations. As early as 1909, the Supreme Court faced the question of whether the Sherman Act extended to actions of U.S. companies in Panama and Costa Rica. In *American Banana Co. v. United Fruit Co.,*[2] Justice Holmes held that the antitrust laws could not apply to acts occurring outside the United States, because the law would make criminal acts that were lawful in other countries.

The Supreme Court revisited the issue of extraterritorial jurisdiction in 1945, when it referred the case of *United States v. Aluminum Company of America (Alcoa)*[3] to Judge Learned Hand. The case concerned the participation of a Canadian company, Aluminum Limited, in a cartel of Swiss, German, French, and British aluminum producers. The cartel agreed to production quotas, with royalties to the cartel for production in excess of quotas. Exports to the United States were included in the production quota amounts. Judge Hand rejected the limits of *American Banana.* He held that extraterritorial acts could be subject to the U.S. antitrust laws if the acts were intended to and did affect American imports.

Judge Hand's decision giving broad extraterritorial scope to the U.S. antitrust laws was widely criticized in other countries. Although the decision limited U.S. power to instances where the foreign conduct was intended to affect imports to the United States, many argued that given the position of the U.S. economy in the post-World War II world, almost any export-related conduct would affect U.S. imports. After *Alcoa*, U.S. courts sometimes found themselves in the position of having the authority to assert jurisdiction over conduct occurring abroad, but facing the possibility that other nations would take offense at a U.S. court passing judgment on conduct in which they had a greater interest. The following case illustrates one widely adopted approach to resolving the problem of whether to hear an extraterritorial case.

MANNINGTON MILLS, INC. v. CONGOLEUM CORP.

595 F.2d 1287 (3rd Cir. 1979)

FACTS:

Mannington, a maker of flooring products, sued Congoleum for violating Section 2 of the Sherman Act. Congoleum had obtained a variety of patents covering vinyl floor coverings in twenty-six countries. Mannington alleged that some of those patents had been procured by fraudulent submissions to foreign patent offices. Mannington al-

[2]213 U.S. 347 (1909).
[3]148 F.2d 416 (2d Cir. 1945).

leged that Congoleum would use these fraudulently obtained patents to bring or threaten patent infringement suits, thus restricting Mannington's ability to export flooring products to other countries. The district court dismissed the complaint, holding that American courts would not question the validity of acts of foreign nations.

ISSUE:

Do U.S. courts have the power to hear cases arising from extraterritorial acts? If so, under what circumstances should they exercise that power?

RESULT:

Yes. The district court's decision was overturned and the case remanded to develop a record from which the court could decide whether to exercise jurisdiction.

REASONS:

The challenge here is to conduct by an American corporation in a foreign country, arguably legal there, and the issue is whether that activity is answerable in the courts of the United States under the Sherman Act's broad and possibly far-reaching language. The extraterritorial application of the Act to "trade or commerce . . . with foreign nations" has been and continues to be the subject of lively controversy. . . . Neither the Act or its legislative history gives any clear indication of the scope of the extraterritorial jurisdiction conferred, leaving such a determination to the courts. . . .

In oft-quoted language, Judge Learned Hand in *United States v. Aluminum Co. of America (Alcoa)* . . . concluded that although Congress did not intend the Sherman Act to prohibit conduct having no effect in the United States, it did intend the Act to reach conduct having consequences within this country—even where the parties concerned had no allegiance to the United States—if the conduct is intended to and actually does have an effect upon United States imports or exports. This wide-reaching "intended effects" test has been cited with approval by the Supreme Court. . . .

It can no longer be doubted that practices of an American citizen abroad having a substantial effect on American foreign commerce are subject to the Sherman Act. . . . This view has been criticized because its failure to abide by the basic tenet that a nation's legislation is valid only in the territory it governs leads to unnecessary international friction. Nevertheless, when two American litigants are contesting alleged antitrust activity abroad that results in harm to the export business of one, a federal court does have subject matter jurisdiction. . . . Therefore, we are satisfied that the district court did have jurisdiction in this case. . . .

Having concluded that . . . there is subject matter jurisdiction, the question remains whether jurisdiction should be exercised. . . .

This may, indeed, be a situation where the consequences to the American economy and policy permit no alternative to firm judicial action enforcing our antitrust laws abroad. But before that step is taken, there should be a weighing of competing interests.

The antitrust statutes enacted by Congress commit this country to the free enterprise system and the exercise of open competition. If an American company is excluded from competition in a foreign country by fraudulent conduct on the part of another American company, then our national interests are adversely affected. In a purely domestic situation, the right to a remedy would be clear. When foreign nationals are involved, however, it is unwise to ignore the fact that foreign policy, reciprocity, comity, and limitations of judicial power are considerations that should have a bearing on the decision to exercise or decline jurisdiction. . . .

In *Timberlane Lumber Co. v. Bank of America* . . . the Court of Appeals for the Ninth Circuit adopted a balancing process in determining whether extraterritorial jurisdiction should be exercised, an approach with which we find ourselves in substantial agreement. The factors we believe should be considered include:

1. Degree of conflict with foreign law or policy;

2. Nationality of the parties;

3. Relative importance of the alleged violation of conduct here compared to that abroad;

4. Availability of a remedy abroad and the pendency of litigation there;

5. Existence of intent to harm or affect American commerce and its foreseeability;

6. Possible effect upon foreign relations if the court exercises jurisdiction and grants relief;

7. If relief is granted, whether a party will be placed in the position of being forced to perform an act illegal in either country or be under conflicting requirements by both countries;

8. Whether the court can make its order effective;

9. Whether an order for relief would be acceptable in this country if made by the foreign nation under similar circumstances;

10. Whether a treaty with the affected nations has addressed the issue.

The record in this case is not adequate to allow a reasoned decision on these highly complex issues even if only one foreign nation were involved rather than 26. Moreover, we do not believe that the extensive inquiry required must yield the same answer in each instance. The legislation and policy of each nation is not likely to be the same, nor is it probable that the effect upon commerce in each instance will be as substantial as others. Although the plaintiff would prefer to have the matter resolved as a unitary one, that cannot be done when the individual interests and policies of the foreign nations differ and must be balanced against our nation's legitimate interest in regulating competitive activity.

We conclude, therefore, that it was an error to dismiss the plaintiff's complaint without preparation of a record which will allow an evaluation of the factors counseling for or against the exercise of jurisdiction.

The approach the *Timberlane* and *Mannington* courts adopted has been cited with both approval and disapproval. Many commentators have noted that it makes an appropriate distinction between the principles of jurisdiction and those of comity, allowing courts to balance interests and recognize the needs of other governments. Other commentators have criticized the balancing approach for leaving the question to the discretion of the trial judge. They would argue for a rule that would be more consistent in application. One could also criticize the approach of the *Mannington* court for not giving managers clear guidance on when their conduct in foreign markets will subject them to antitrust litigation in the United States, with its possible criminal penalties and treble damages.

In an effort to clarify the reach of U.S. regulation, Congress amended the antitrust laws in 1982 to restrict their application to commerce with foreign nations unless the alleged improper conduct "has a direct, substantial and reasonably foreseeable effect" on (1) the U.S. marketplace, (2) exports to the United States from the foreign country, or (3) the business of a U.S. exporter to the foreign country.

The European Community took up the issue of extraterritorial jurisdiction in 1988, using a somewhat different approach from the one U.S. courts had used.

RE WOOD PULP CARTEL ET AL. v. E.C. COMMISSION

[1988] 4 C.M.L.R. 901
European Court of Justice

FACTS:

The EC Commission charged forty-one wood pulp producers and two trade associations, all operating outside the EC, with violating Article 85 of the Treaty of Rome by engaging in concerted activities to set prices for pulp to be sold to customers in the EC. The wood pulp producers, including an American and a Finnish trade association, claimed that the EC did not have jurisdiction over their activities, as the price-setting agreements took place outside the EC. The Commission imposed fines against thirty-six of the pulp producers, holding that it had power to regulate foreign activities that had substantial effects on the EC. The producers appealed to the European Court of Justice.

ISSUE:

Does Article 85 extend to the actions of foreign producers?

RESULT:

Yes.

REASONS:

[11] In so far as the submission concerning the infringement of **Article 85** of the Treaty itself is concerned, it should be recalled that the provision prohibits all agreements between undertakings and concerted practices which may affect trade between member-States and which have as their object or effect the restriction of competition within the Common Market. . . .

[12] It should be noted that the main sources of supply of wood pulp are outside the Community, in Canada, the United States, Sweden and Finland and that the market therefore has global dimensions. Where wood pulp producers established in those countries sell directly to purchasers established in the Community and engage in price competition in order to win orders from those customers, that constitutes competition within the Common Market.

[13] It follows that where those producers concert on the prices to be charged to their customers in the Community and put that concertation into effect by selling at prices which are actually coordinated, they are taking part in concertation which has the object and effect of restricting competition within the Common Market within the meaning of **Article 85** of the Treaty.

[14] Accordingly, it must be concluded that by applying the competition rules in the Treaty in the circumstances of this case to undertakings whose registered offices are situated outside the Community, the Commission has not made an incorrect assessment of the territorial scope of **Article 85.**

[15] The applicants have submitted that the decision is incompatible with public international law on the grounds that the application of the competition rules in this case was founded exclusively on the economic repercussions within the Common Market of conduct restricting competition which was adopted outside the Community.

[16] It should be observed that an infringement of **Article 85,** such as the conclusion of an agreement which has had the effect of restricting competition within the Common Market, consists of conduct made up of two elements, the formation of the agreement, decision or concerted practice and the implementation thereof. If the applicability of prohibitions laid down under competition law were made to depend on the place where the agreement, decision or concerted practice was formed, the result would obviously be to give undertakings an easy means of evading those prohibitions. The decisive factor is therefore the place where it is implemented.

[17] The producers in this case implemented their pricing agreement within the Common Market. It is immaterial in that respect whether or not they had recourse to subsidiaries, agents, sub-agents, or branches within the Community in order to make their contacts with purchasers within the Community.

[18] Accordingly the Community's jurisdiction to apply its competition rules to such conduct is covered by the territoriality principle as universally recognised in public international law.

[The Court then modified some aspects of the Commission's decision on other grounds, and upheld the fines on most of the wood pulp producers.]

The reach of EC jurisdiction using the *Wood Pulp* decision has not yet been fully tested by the Commission. Although the Court did not specifically adopt an "effects" test, some commentators would argue that the Court's decision has the practical effect of extending EC jurisdiction as far as the U.S. courts extended jurisdiction in *Alcoa*.

ENFORCEMENT

One check on a nation extending its jurisdictional reach beyond acceptable limits results from the need for cooperation from foreign governments that is often a part of successfully pursuing an antitrust action. When a government or private party attempts to collect evidence before trial or to enforce a judgment based on the assertion of a court's authority over extraterritorial conduct, it may need the cooperation of courts in other countries. If the foreign country believes that its public policies are being violated by the antitrust action, it may refuse to order parties to give depositions or turn over documents or prevent the enforcement of a foreign judgment. To date, most of the refusals to cooperate relate to actions of U.S. courts. The best-known case of conflict involved Westinghouse and the uranium industry.

IN RE URANIUM ANTITRUST LITIGATION: *WESTINGHOUSE ELECTRIC CORP. v. RIO ALGOM, LTD.*

617 F.2d 1248 (7th Cir. 1980)

FACTS:
In 1975, Westinghouse was sued by twenty-seven electric utilities for breach of contracts to supply uranium. Westinghouse used the defense of commercial impracticability, alleging that a cartel prevented it from meeting its contract obligations. In 1976, Westinghouse sued twenty-nine foreign and domestic uranium producers for antitrust violations. Nine foreign defendants did not appear, and in 1979, Westinghouse obtained default judgments against them.

After obtaining the default judgments, Westinghouse obtained an injunction preventing the defaulting defendants from transferring more than $10,000 from any wholly owned U.S. subsidiaries without court approval. After numerous violations by the nine defendants, Westinghouse obtained an injunction requiring court approval of all transfers from the United States, regardless of amount. The defendants argued that the exercise of jurisdiction and entry of default judgments were an abuse of discretion by the trial judge.

ISSUE:

Did the trial court have jurisdiction to hear the case, enter default judgments, and assess damages?

RESULT:

Yes.

REASONS:

The governments of Australia, Canada, South Africa and the United Kingdom of Great Britain and Northern Ireland have filed briefs as amici curiae [friends of the court]. The principal thrust of the amici's briefs is to call into question the jurisdiction of the United States District Court over this controversy. We view the jurisdictional issue as two-pronged: (1) does subject matter jurisdiction exist; and (2) if so, should it be exercised? . . .

In its complaint Westinghouse alleges that twenty domestic and nine foreign corporations conspired to fix the price of uranium in the world market. The alleged meetings at which Westinghouse claims prices were agreed upon took place in France, Australia, South Africa, Illinois, the Canary Islands and England. At the present state of this litigation, there has been no opportunity for fact-finding. We must therefore accept all properly pleaded allegations as true for purposes of determining jurisdiction. Accordingly, the picture which emerges is one of concerted conduct both abroad and within the United States intended to affect the uranium market in this country. While the governments of the foreign participants in this alleged conspiracy are actively and admittedly sympathetic to the economic determinism of the defaulters, there is no claim that the alleged conduct of the defaulters is mandated by those governments. We therefore conclude that Westinghouse's allegations against the defaulters do fall within the jurisdictional ambit of the Sherman Act, as defined in Alcoa. . . .

In this case, unlike the situation in Timberlane and Mannington Mills, there has been a determination by the District Court as to whether jurisdiction should be exercised. In the order of January 3, 1979, and the order of September 17, 1979, the District Judge considered the unique circumstance presented in this case, and determined, in the exercise of his discretion, to pro-

ceed. Our task is to decide whether he abused his discretion in reaching that conclusion. We find that he did not.

In granting the requested default judgment, the District Court considered three factors: the complexity of the present multi-national and multi-party action; the seriousness of the charges asserted; and the recalcitrant attitude of the defaulters.[4] The District Judge concluded that those factors all weighed heavily in favor of proceeding to judgment and damages.

The amici suggest that the District Court abused its discretion by not considering the factors set out in Mannington Mills in reaching this determination. While the considerations recommended in that case certainly provide an adequate framework for such a determination, we can hardly call the failure to employ those precise factors an abuse of discretion. First, the Mannington Mills factors are not the law of this Circuit. Second, even assuming their adoption by this Court, the circumstances here are distinct from those found in Timberlane and Mannington Mills. In those cases the defendants appeared and contested the jurisdiction of the District Court. In the present case, the defaulters have contumaciously refused to come into court and present evidence as to why the District Court should not exercise its jurisdiction. They have chosen instead to present their case through surrogates. Wholly owned subsidiaries of several defaulters have challenged the appropriateness of the injunctions and shockingly to us, the governments of the defaulters have subserviently presented for them their case against the exercise of jurisdiction. If this Court were to remand the matter for further consideration of the jurisdictional question, the District Court would be placed in the impossible position of having to make specific findings with the defaulters refusing to appear and participate in discovery. We find little value in such an exercise.

[The court then upheld the default judgments, injunction, and damages assessed by the district court.]

---

[4]Indeed, it was asserted by counsel for Westinghouse during oral argument that one defaulter simply tore up the complaint in the presence of the process server.

The response of the governments involved in the Westinghouse litigation was dramatic. Five governments enacted or strengthened "blocking statutes," that is, legislation designed to prevent information collection and judgment enforcement in cases that related to extraterritorial assertions of power over their nationals.

The United Kingdom's Protection of Trading Interests Act, for example, contained several provisions designed to prevent the assertion of extraterritorial power over UK businesses. The Act gives the secretary of state the power to determine that extraterritorial measures would harm UK trading interests, and, upon such a finding, prohibit any person in the UK from complying with those measures, under threat of criminal sanction. If a judgment for multiple damages (such as the U.S. provision for treble damages in antitrust actions) is entered in such a case, the Act forbids a UK court from enforcing it. If overseas assets of a UK business are seized to satisfy a multiple-damage award, the Act allows the UK business to "claw back" by recovering UK assets of the victor in the overseas case.

The strength of the UK's Protection of Trading Interests Act reflects that government's great discomfort with several aspects of U.S. antitrust law, and with the circumstances of *Westinghouse* in particular. First, like many foreign countries, the United Kingdom was (and is) uncomfortable with the wide scope of U.S. discovery before trial. The United States allows parties to seek enormous numbers of documents and interview large numbers of possible witnesses before trial. The discovery process is widely perceived as too intrusive.

Second, the United Kingdom, like many foreign governments, is highly critical of U.S. multiple-damage provisions for competitor lawsuits. The purpose of treble damage awards in the U.S. system is to encourage competitors to police the public policy of fair competition; however, many governments, along with many U.S. executives, feel that treble damages are punitive in nature, rather than compensation for a wrong done.

Finally, note that the *Westinghouse* case involves some special circumstances. The uranium industry, which produces a product used widely in nuclear power generation and in weapons of mass destruction, affects national security interests. It also features much government participation, even if the mining companies are privately owned. Governments are understandably hesitant to allow information about the pricing and production practices of their mining businesses to become part of a public court record, available to all.

13.4 SPECIAL ISSUES

Regulation of competitive practices has seen rapid growth and change in the last few decades. On the government side, the ascendance of the Chicago school of economics in the United States has meant a real change in the enforcement priorities and analytical methods of government regulators. The growing power of the European Community, especially in pursuit of the borderless European market, has led to explosive growth in competition law in the European Community.

On the business side, the growth of international business has been fueled by structural business changes. The use of franchises, licensing, and distribution agreements has risen rapidly. Most importantly, businesses in all parts of the world are invoking "strategic alliances" to achieve globalization. Joint research and development ventures and joint export marketing arrangements are just a few of the ways businesses may act that could raise competition law concerns. The remainder of this chapter examines two areas of recent concern in competition law.

MERGERS AND ACQUISITIONS

The 1980s marked the ascendance of the Chicago school of antitrust analysis in the United States, particularly during the administration of President Reagan. As a result, the government allowed virtually all mergers to proceed without regulatory interference. The lack of government interest in mergers may have been one of the reasons for the boom in hostile takeovers in the United States throughout the 1980s. In contrast, the EC became much more active in merger control during the same period. The passage of the Single European Act in 1986 marked the start of major industrial restructuring across Europe as enterprises in member states sought to increase their community wide presence while firms outside the EC worked to establish a presence in at least one EC nation to avoid anticipated barriers to outsiders and to gain access to the unified market.

In 1990, a new merger control regulation went into effect throughout the EC, regulating large mergers or acquisitions with market impact in more than one member country. The regulation applies to events in which one or more parties acquires control of an enterprise. Thus, passive investments of some amount of stock in a business might not qualify, unless the amount purchased was sufficient to give control. Traditional mergers or acquisitions would qualify, as would joint ventures where the relationship effectively allows a party to gain control over another participant.

The regulation applies only to transactions with a "community dimension." The test is one of size. If worldwide turnover (net sales) of all parties involved exceeds 5 billion ECU (approximately $6.25 billion), at least two of the parties must have European Community turnover of at least 250 million ECU. If more than two-thirds of that turnover is in one country, the transaction will be exempt from the merger regulation.

If a transaction qualifies, the regulation then provides for premerger notification. Within a week of commencing the transaction, the parties must notify the Commission. The Commission then has three weeks to decide whether to clear the merger or open an investigation. If it opens an investigation, the Commission has three months to decide whether the proposed

merger will create or strengthen a dominant position of one or more parties and therefore impede competition within the Community. The Commission can block the merger, order divestiture, or impose fines of up to 10 percent of a party's worldwide turnover.

With the assertion of extraterritorial jurisdiction under the *Wood Pulp* test, the merger regulation applies to a wide variety of mergers. For example, two large U.S. companies merging in the United States might have to notify the Commission if they have combined exports to the EC of more than 250 million ECUs. The Commission has already cleared several large-scale international transactions, including those of Matsushita's acquisition of MCA, the U.S.-based entertainment business, and AT&T's hostile takeover of NCR.

STRATEGIC ALLIANCES

In the 1990s businesses around the world have chosen to internationalize by a variety of methods, including acquisition, joint ventures, distribution agreements, licensing know-how and trademark rights, and joint production and research and development enterprises. Where those activities have not involved traditional methods of business presence, such as acquisitions or establishing branches or subsidiaries, strategic planners often refer to the activities as creating strategic alliances. As a general definition, a strategic alliance is a linkage between two or more companies to develop new products or explore new markets. Because strategic alliances are, by their nature, collaborative activities among potential or actual competitors, they have substantial competition law implications.

Over the past decade, the United States has acted to make strategic alliances easier for U.S. businesses. In 1982, Congress passed the Export Trading Company Act in an attempt to allow U.S. businesses to collaborate in promoting exports. The Act allows U.S. businesses to create export trading companies either to export goods or to assist in exporting services. The Act then allows the export trading company to apply to the secretary of commerce for a Certificate of Review. The Review examines the impact of the export trading company on U.S. commerce. If the secretary of commerce finds that the export trading company's activities would not substantially lessen domestic competition or restrain domestic trade, would not unreasonably affect domestic prices, would not unfairly compete against other exporters, and would not be expected to result in resale of exported goods into the United States, she will issue the Certificate of Review. Once granted, it prevents the government from initiating criminal antitrust proceedings and limits any civil suit remedies to actual, not treble, damages.

Surprisingly few groups of U.S. companies have combined and applied for exemption from the antitrust laws under the Export Trading Company Act. Those that have include machine tool producers, banks facilitating exports, engineering consulting services, and catfish farmers.

Congress passed a second law to help strategic alliances in 1984. The National Cooperative Research Act, designed to aid the semiconductor in

dustry, allows R&D joint ventures to register with the Department of Justice and the Federal Trade Commission. Once they are registered, private suits against such ventures are limited to recovery of actual, rather than treble, damages, and the joint ventures are subject to a rule of reason analysis of their activities rather than a per se analysis. Similar legislation is likely for production joint ventures.

The EC has been extremely active in regulating all kinds of strategic alliances. Many alliances have used the individual exemption or negative clearance features of EC competition law to achieve a regulatory safe harbor for their business activities. In addition, the EC has several regulations establishing lists of acceptable and prohibited activities. Small and midsized firms have enjoyed since 1972 a group exemption from Article 85 under a Specialization Agreement exemption. Under this exemption, groups of businesses can agree to manufacture products jointly and to undertake a reciprocal obligation either to manufacture or not to manufacture certain products.

The EC also has a group exemption from Article 85 for cooperative R&D, containing a list of practices that must exist, such as full access to the work and relatively free exploitation rights; and a list of prohibited practices, such as restrictions on unrelated research, restrictions on output, prices, or customers, or agreements not to challenge future patents.

The EC's group exemptions on patent licensing, trademark and know-how licensing, and distributorships also have an impact on strategic alliances. The merger regulation discussed above also affects strategic alliances, because it covers joint ventures as well as pure acquisitions. The EC has been and continues to be active in regulating strategic alliances, with the aim of creating a single internal market and improving the distribution of goods and services within the Community. As the *Moosehead* decision discussed earlier in this chapter points out, the Commission is favorably inclined toward allowing various kinds of strategic alliances if those alliances promote the economic objectives of the EC.

13.5 CONCLUSION

Competition law is one of the methods governments use to achieve internal market regulation and national industrial policies. Businesses operating in a global marketplace need to be aware that their own domestic competition law will affect their business practices and that the law of other markets may also affect their business practices. The reach of competition law seems to be expanding well beyond the borders of any particular country, to encompass conduct crossing national boundaries.

During the 1990s competition law will probably appear in many of the newly emerging market economies. It is also most likely to be used as a tool to achieve protection from foreign competitors and to promote do-

mestic economic and perhaps political objectives. The manager doing business in this rapidly changing environment must be aware of current trends in competition law and be prepared to use the available regulatory avenues, such as registration under U.S. law or individual exemptions and negative clearances under EC law, to maximize a firm's business position in international markets.

13.6 QUESTIONS FOR DISCUSSION

1. The Organization of Petroleum Exporting Countries (OPEC) is a group of the governments of oil-producing nations that meets regularly to set prices and production quotas. OPEC oil is regularly exported at the set prices to buyers in the EC and the United States. If prosecuting officials in the EC and the United States take action against OPEC, would the EC or the United States be more likely to take jurisdiction? Can OPEC be prosecuted for price fixing and other restrictive business practices?

2. As a part of their restructuring to market economies, many Eastern European nations are considering the adoption of competition laws. If you were advising these governments, would you suggest a Japanese, U.S., or EC style of competition law? What features would you take from each? Explain.

3. Suppose that MacChips, Ltd., is a highly successful chain of fish and chips restaurants in the UK. It is ready to expand its operations in the EC, using franchised stores. It wants its franchisees to sign contracts agreeing to open stores only in specific territories, not to solicit customers by advertising or other means from other franchisees' territories, and to purchase the batter mix, fish, and all paper goods from MacChips. If MacChips is concerned that its actions might create problems under the EC competition laws, what actions can it take? Would your answer be the same under U.S. law? Explain.

13.7 FURTHER READINGS

R. Brumley, "How Antitrust Law Affects International Joint Ventures," *Business America,* November 21, 1988, pp. 3–4.

Comment, "A Critical Review of the Justice Department's Antitrust Guidelines for International Operations," 14 *North Carolina Journal of International Law and Commercial Regulation* 287–313 (1989).

W. Kolasky, Jr., "Recent Developments Affecting Transnational Joint Ventures," 58 *Antitrust Law Journal* 685–701 (1989).

J. Venit, "Technology Licensing in the EC," 59 *Antitrust Law Journal* 485–598 (1991). (The remainder of this issue contains a symposium on EC competition law.)

PROTECTING BUSINESS PROPERTY RIGHTS

RISK MANAGEMENT AND INSURANCE
- planning before expropriations
- insurance

CONCLUSION

14.1 INTRODUCTION

The legal protection of private property rights has been a key factor in the growth of capitalism and of free market economies. Historical records from ancient societies show that people recognized "rights" to possess land and goods, and expected governments to protect their interests in property. One of the early government acts of colonists in North America was to create a system of land records, recording land ownership interests in the New World. Today, a property owner in New England may be able to trace the ownership of her land back to the 1630s by using public land records.

Legal scholars often describe the idea of property as a "bundle of rights." The concept of a bundle of rights may be helpful in thinking about what property really means, and how fluid property rights are over time. A simplistic definition of owning property would be having the right to possess, use, or destroy a thing. But property rights are the creation of governments, through laws, and are subject to changing regulation. For example, the right to use property is subject, in most places, to zoning or other land-use restrictions. Those land-use regulations may interfere substantially with an owner's right to use his property.

Technological change may also affect property rights. Where once the law held that landowners owned the rights into the ground under their land and the sky over their land, the advent of air transportation has changed the rights of landowners to limit activities in what is now known as "public" air space over their land. The kinds of things that can be considered property have also changed over time. Remember that until the mid-19th century the Anglo-American legal tradition widely recognized ownership rights in other human beings. Now, in virtually all societies, slavery is both illegal and morally abhorrent.

Today, legal systems put property into three categories. Most societies recognize private ownership rights in personal property—that is, in tangible things. A second category of property is "real" property—that is, land and buildings permanently attached to land. Until recently, recognition of private property rights in real property was limited in Socialist societies. The third classification of property is known as intellectual or industrial property. The law of most countries recognizes property rights in the products of ideas, in the form of copyrights, patents, trademarks, and trade secrets.

All of these kinds of property are the assets of business enterprises. Their growth and legal protection are essential to the success of businesses in any country. This chapter will examine how businesses can protect valuable property rights, and what rights international law may or may not provide to businesses. Because intellectual property rights are the most difficult area of the law, the chapter begins with a discussion of their legal status, and of the protection business gets from infringers on those rights.

14.2 INTERNATIONAL PROTECTION OF INTELLECTUAL PROPERTY RIGHTS

The products of ideas are an ever-increasing part of the global economy. On one level, they may involve the worldwide market in popular culture, such as international hit movies, the recordings and videos of musical artists like U2, Paul Simon, Madonna, or Hammer, and the prevalence of cultural symbols like McDonald's golden arches. On another level, the products of ideas have brought the world the personal computer revolution, with both hardware and software using forms of intellectual property protection to enhance their value. At still another level, ideas of scientists and other inventors have brought great technological innovation to the global market, including new medical treatments and drugs, products, and production processes.

None of the global growth in these industries would be possible without the legal protection of intellectual property rights. As with much property law, developed nations have been more concerned with increasing the scope and strength of intellectual property law than the less-developed countries (LDCs). LDCs sometimes see intellectual property as unfairly constricting economic and cultural development.

COPYRIGHTS

Copyright law protects the works of authors and artists, by giving the copyright owner the right to control the reproduction and performance of the work. While the scope and length of copyright protection varies among countries, copyright generally protects written works, music, films, and performances. It most often protects works for a substantial period of time, such as the life of the author plus 50 years.

Copyright law has used three different approaches in its development. For civil law countries, copyright has protected both the economic and moral rights of authors. Under civil law systems, owners of copyrights still may have to recognize the rights of the original authors. For example, someone who buys a painting by Peter Max, and thus owns it, may not be able to cut it into 100 pieces, selling each as an "original Peter Max." Such an act would violate the artist's right to maintain the integrity of his work.

Common law legal systems tend to view copyrights as a protection solely of economic interests. Socialist legal systems have historically been less concerned with payment to authors than with the management of culture for the purposes of the revolution.

The orientation of civil law systems toward the moral rights of authors should not be underestimated. Moral rights are rights that stay with the author even though the work may be sold to someone else. They commonly consist of two parts. First is the right of paternity; that is, to be identified as the author of the work. The second is the right of integrity; that is, the author's right to have some control over what subsequent owners do with the original work. The right of integrity affects such practices as "colorizing" old black-and-white movies, as well as other distortions or republication of the work that would impugn the author's creative intent.

Unfortunately, there is no international copyright. Copyright protection is territorially based, so if someone infringes on a copyright, the author will have to go to the place of infringement and bring suit under that nation's laws. There are, however, several multilateral treaties that make international enforcement of copyrights possible.

The most important international agreement on copyrights is the Berne Convention for the Protection of Literary and Artistic Works. The Berne Convention was created in 1886, as an outgrowth of the active efforts of several internationally famous authors of the late 19th century, led by Victor Hugo and Ivan Turgenev. The Convention has since gone through five major revisions, each expanding the rights of copyright owners or authors. The United States became the eightieth member of the Berne Convention in 1988.

The Berne Convention has several important facets. The first is that nations acceding to the Convention agree to provide certain minimum protections for authors. The signatory nations, known as the Berne Union, agree to meet periodically to discuss new developments, such as changing technology, and to improve copyright law protection for authors in all countries.

The Berne Convention's most important provision allows for national treatment for authors publishing in any member country. Thus, an author who publishes a copyrighted book in Canada will have the same copyright protections in Germany as any German author. National treatment eases the burden of suing infringers in other countries, as their courts only have to look to local law to determine the rights of the parties.

The Berne Convention also prescribes some minimum copyright standards. One important minimum standard is the length of copyright protection. Berne Convention members must provide protection for at least the life of the author plus 50 years for most works, with minimum 50-year protections for anonymous or pseudonymous works, works for hire, and cinematographic works, and 25 years of protection for photographic and works of applied art.

Berne Convention members also agree to two other significant provisions. The first is to remove formalities that restrict copyright rights. Thus, for foreign authors asserting copyright rights in the United States, for example, the copyright notice "©" commonly found on most works cannot be required. The second requirement is that Berne Convention members must recognize the moral rights or paternity and integrity for authors. This provision caused the most controversy for the United States, which historically has not recognized the moral rights of authors. The U.S. position is that domestic laws on unfair trade practices offer sufficient protection of the moral rights of Berne Convention authors. In 1990, the United States passed legislation giving minimal protection to the moral rights of authors of limited categories of works.

In addition to the Berne Convention, other multilateral and bilateral agreements grant copyright law protection internationally. The most significant is the Universal Copyright Convention (UCC), which was formed by the United Nations in 1954 as an effort to provide an intermediate level of protection and get nations ultimately to join the Berne Convention. The United States is still a member of the UCC, although joining the Berne Convention made the protections of the UCC largely unnecessary.

PATENTS

A patent is an exclusive right, granted by a government, to manufacture or use an invention for a specific period of time. Like copyright protection, patent protection is primarily territorial. If an inventor has a UK patent on a drug, it does not mean that he can simply assert the validity of the British patent in a court in another country where he does not have a patent. Each country maintains its own patent laws, with differences in the length of patent protection, the procedures for obtaining a patent, and the scope of patent protection. It is important to note that some countries do not yet recognize patents in biotechnology products, such as genetically engineered animals, while other countries, primarily in the developing world, do not recognize patent rights in pharmaceutical products.

There is quite a bit of international activity in the area of patent rights, with the most important development, a harmonized patent system, still in preliminary negotiation stages. The next decade is most likely to see significant changes in international patent protection.

The oldest international treaty affecting patents is the Paris Convention for the Protection of Industrial Property, first signed in 1883. The Paris Convention provides limited but important protection to international businesses using patents. It requires national treatment, so that a patent applicant from France will be treated in the U.S. patent system in the same way the United States treats its nationals. The Paris Convention also establishes a right of priority for international filings. An inventor who files for a patent in her home country will have 12 months to file for patents in other countries, with the filing date in all countries being the original date. The priority right means that inventors looking for international use of their inventions need not file everywhere simultaneously. Finally, the Paris Convention keeps the independence of patents. If a patent is challenged and overturned in one country, it does not automatically follow that the patent is invalid in all Paris Convention countries.

The Paris Convention still left inventors with the problem of having to file patent applications in each individual country, and undergo patent examinations in each country. It specifically allowed for the possibility of inconsistent results, with resulting gaps in patent protection. The first successful attempts to streamline the application and examination processes came in the 1970s, with the European Patent Convention and the Patent Cooperation Treaty.

The European Patent Convention, signed in 1978, had fourteen member nations as of 1991, with more countries expected to join within the next few years. A European inventor uses the Convention by filing once, with the European Patent Office, and designating the member countries in which he seeks patent protection. The European Patent Office examines and issues the patent, which then becomes effective in each of the designated countries. Applicants still have to pay filing fees and sometimes the cost of translating the patent application for additional countries, but the patent is only examined once. The success of the European Patent Convention has resulted in the creation of two other regional patent groups, in eastern and western Africa.

The Patent Cooperation Treaty (PCT), also signed in 1978, works in a similar fashion to the European Patent Convention. As of 1991, the treaty had forty-seven member countries, with several more countries considering joining the treaty group. Under the treaty, an inventor may file in his home country, then, within 12 months, file a PCT application with the World Intellectual Property Organization (WIPO) in Switzerland. Or the original filing may be with WIPO, with the application designating which patent office will conduct the examination of the patent. In either case, the application filed with WIPO must designate the countries in which the applicant wants protection, although WIPO does not charge fees for more than ten countries. If the patent is granted, it becomes effective in all designated countries.

For a business marketing innovative products, the complexity of patent law in international markets is formidable and expensive. The decisions of whether and where to patent turn on the importance of the invention and its potential market. The PCT and European Patent Convention offer some savings of time and money, but some significant countries, in terms of potential markets, do not belong to either group. There are still differences in scope and length of patents, and in the procedures for getting protection. One ready example of such differences is that U.S. law grants patents only to the first person to invent the subject of the patent. In contrast, most of the rest of the world grants patent rights to the first person to file a patent application.

Good patent attorneys are an invaluable asset to businesses needing patent protection on a global basis. The attorneys should be part of the original team devising the strategic plan for new products, so they can help establish the analysis of likely markets and the cost and timing of the product introduction. Until patent law is streamlined for international products, the process of introducing a product on a global basis will include many patent complications. With some luck and a great deal of persistence, negotiators may be able to reach a patent harmonization treaty in the next several years.

TRADEMARKS

A trademark is a symbol, logo, or other indication of the source of goods. Trademark protection gives the owner the exclusive right to use the mark in connection with the marketing of the covered product. There are important national differences in the scope of trademark protection, with some nations still not recognizing marks used in connection with services, and others, such as Japan, having only limited recognition of three-dimensional marks, such as distinctive packaging.

Trademark law is still predominantly national in character, although there are a few treaties to help international marketers. The Paris Convention, which was discussed above in connection with patents, also applies to trademarks, establishing the principles of independence, national treatment, and a 6-month priority from the date of first registration. Since 1973, the Vienna Trademark Registration Treaty has allowed trademark holders to claim rights under the Paris Convention by using a single international filing with WIPO in Switzerland. Trademark owners still must rely on national protection in each country, but the process of filing is simplified.

Several efforts have been made to create a true international trademark system. The oldest is the Madrid Agreement, to which twenty-nine European and North African countries belong. This agreement allows trademarks, once granted in a home country, to have an international filing at WIPO. One application, in one language (French), with all fees and administrative work handled by WIPO, gives trademark protection in whatever member countries the trademark owner designates. The Madrid Agreement underwent substantial revision in 1989 in a document called the Madrid Protocol. Many of the objections the United States and other countries had to the old agreement were removed. The United States is now considering approving the Madrid Protocol. If it does so, U.S. businesses will have an easier process to follow for obtaining international trademark protection for their products.

A business with interests in the EC might think that the single market would provide good opportunities for a single trademark. In 1988, the EC issued a directive for member countries to harmonize their trademark laws in some important respects. As of 1991, the Council of Ministers was quite close to issuing a regulation creating a Community Trade Mark, with registration at a central Community Trade Mark Office, having equal effect throughout the EC.

TRADE SECRETS

The protection of trade secrets is a matter of national law. Some nations, such as China, do not have good records of respecting trade secrets, although China has recently agreed to strengthen its legal protection of trade secrets. At this time, the protection of trade secrets is primarily a matter of contract among the parties who know the secret, and of good practice within corporations to prevent information leaks.

THE SPECIAL PROBLEMS OF COMPUTERS

For the last few decades, the technological innovations brought about by computers have created special problems for intellectual property laws around the world. Neither computer software nor hardware fits neatly within the framework of copyright or patent law.

Computer software is generally protected under copyright laws. The Berne Convention, however, predates the widespread use of computers and makes no mention of computer software being subject to copyright. Thus, a copyright holder will have to look to each country to see whether it covers software with its copyright laws. Many countries do consider software to be copyrightable, but others have not yet considered the issue, or do not consider it protectable.

Computer hardware, particularly chips, has been an even more difficult issue. The United States, in 1984, created a new class of intellectual property for chips. The Semiconductor Chip Protection Act of 1984 created "mask work" protection for chip designs. The protection lasts 10 years from registration. The Act was designed to get other legal systems to create similar mask work protection. For foreign chip designers who seek U.S. protection, the Act requires reciprocity. If the foreign country protects mask works and extends that protection to U.S. chip designers, the foreign designer may get protection for mask works in the United States.

The Act has been quite successful at inducing other legal systems to enact legislation protecting mask works. The EC, Japan, Australia, and other nations have adopted such laws, and there is discussion under way for a multilateral treaty that would protect mask works internationally.

14.3 COUNTERFEITERS AND PIRATES

Once a business has obtained intellectual property protection, it then faces the far more difficult problem of enforcing those property rights in the worldwide marketplace. The most significant problem is one of pirated or counterfeit products, especially for popular products. Both governments and individual businesses have interests in stopping piracy and some gray market practices.

BUSINESS RESPONSES TO COUNTERFEIT GOODS

As anyone who has walked down a city street and been offered counterfeit Gucci bags, pirated cassette tapes, or bogus Levi's 501 jeans knows, it is not easy to protect intellectual property rights. The counterfeit merchandise looks on the surface to be the real article, but is really a knockoff, taking a free ride on the advertising and popular success of the genuine product.

Intellectual property piracy has three consequences for the legitimate trademark, patent, or copyright holder. First, it deprives the owner of revenue from the creation of the product, since the bootlegger pays no royalties. Second, when the quality of the counterfeit goods is poor, buyers who thought they were getting the real product will think poorly of the company that owns the intellectual property rights. Finally, the bootleg sales deprive the legitimate dealers of sales, which affects the success of the distributors' relationships with the rights owner.

Of course, when a property rights owner finds someone selling counterfeit goods in any country where the owner has intellectual property rights, an action for copyright, patent, or trademark infringement is appropriate. Generally, most nations also allow customs officials to seize infringing goods upon import. U.S. law contains some representative provisions allowing customs to stop infringing products at the border. Section 602 of the Copyright Act, for example, prohibits the import of products that infringe on U.S. copyrights, and allows customs to seize any such products (see 17 U.S.C. §602). Similarly, Section 526 of the Tariff Act of 1930 (19 U.S.C. §1526) prohibits imports of goods bearing a U.S. registered trademark without authorization from the trademark owner, and also allows customs to seize those goods. Section 337 of the Tariff Act of 1930 (19 U.S.C. §1337) provides similar protection from imports that infringe U.S. patents.

In 1988, Congress strengthened the methods available for blocking infringing goods from import. Using Section 337 of the Tariff Act of 1930 (19 U.S.C. §1337), any owner of a registered U.S. intellectual property right who believes that an import infringes on that right may apply to the International Trade Commission (ITC) for relief. The ITC has the power to issue orders excluding goods from the United States, ordering unfair trade practices to cease, and in some instances ordering forfeiture of the offending goods. Violations of these orders are subject to penalties of up to $100,000 per day or twice the domestic value of the goods. That the ITC is using its power is apparent from the following case.

HYUNDAI ELECTRONICS INDUSTRIES, LTD. v. UNITED STATES INTERNATIONAL TRADE COMMISSION

899 F.2d 1204 (1990)
Federal Circuit Court of Appeals

FACTS:

Hyundai entered into an agreement in South Korea to produce erasable programmable read only memory chips (EPROMs) for the General Instrument Corporation. The agreement required Hyundai to produce the EPROM chips to General Instrument's specifications, but allowed Hyundai to use excess chips for its own products. General Instrument took possession of the chips in South Korea, flew them to Taiwan for further processing, then imported some of the chips into the United States.

Intel Corporation, a U.S. business, alleged that the EPROMs infringed four of its patents, and filed a complaint under §337 with the ITC. The ITC found that the chips did infringe Intel's patents. It ordered the exclusion of all EPROMs manufactured by Hyundai to General Instrument's specifications, whether imported by themselves or incorporated into circuit boards or other carriers. The order further excluded all Hyundai products that used EPROMs, including computers, computer peripherals, telecommunications equipment, and automotive electronic equipment unless Hyundai certified for each shipment that it had made "appropriate inquiries" and determined that the goods imported in the shipment did not contain EPROMs covered by the exclusion order.

Hyundai appealed the order of the ITC, claiming that, by including secondary products, the relief granted was far too broad.

ISSUE:

Did the ITC exceed the scope of its authority by ordering certification of secondary products?

RESULT:

No. The decision of the ITC is affirmed.

REASONS:

The Commission's remedy determination in this case . . . represents a careful and commonsense balancing of the parties' conflicting interests as well as other relevant factors and is solidly based on the evidence in the record. . . .

The Commission's limited exclusion order requiring Hyundai to certify, as a condition of entry, that certain of its downstream products do not contain infringing EPROMs is a reasonable accommodation. . . . The Commission found that Hyundai had violated section 337; that specific EPROM chips embodied the violation; that Hyundai remained free under its manufacturing agreement with General Instrument to use excess infringing EPROMs for its own requirements; and that Hyundai could easily assemble the infringing EPROMs into and import them as part of other Hyundai product "containers" that require EPROMs to function, including wafers, circuit boards, computers, computer peripherals, telecommunications equipment, and automotive electronic equipment. It concluded that the certification provision "is a reasonable means of ensuring the effectiveness of the remedy to which Intel has proven itself entitled. . . ." We agree.

The Commission fashioned the remedy with sensitivity and objectivity. It declined to include Hyundai automobiles within the scope of the certification provision because to do so "would not significantly increase the relief afforded complainant." . . . It did not extend the exclusion order to Hyundai EPROMs not manufactured under the General Instrument agreement because they either were not subject to the investigation or were covered by an earlier consent order entered by the Commission. . . . And it refused to issue Hyundai a cease and desist order, . . . because there was no evidence that Hyundai maintained significant inventories of infringing articles in the United States.

. . . The Commission's decision in this case to enter a limited exclusion order containing a certification provision is both reasonable and well within its authority. Indeed we have recognized, and Hyundai does not dispute, that in an appropriate case the Commission can impose a general exclusion order that binds parties and non-parties alike and effectively shifts to would-be importers of potentially infringing articles, as a condition of

entry, the burden of establishing noninfringement.

The rationale underlying the issuance of general exclusion orders—placing the risk of unfairness associated with a prophylactic order upon potential importers rather than American manufacturers that, vis-à-vis at least some foreign manufacturers and importers, have demonstrated their entitlement to protection from unfair trade practices—applies here with increased force. Hyundai has not challenged the Commission's determination that it violated section 337 by manufacturing EPROMs that infringe valid and enforceable Intel patents. Given this and the other findings, we cannot say that the Commission abused its discretion by concluding that Hyundai rather than Intel should bear whatever additional burden the certification provision entails.

For managers, the weakness of all of these remedies is that they only stop goods at the border, not at the source. Further, customs cannot inspect all incoming shipments, looking for products that look genuine but are not. Customs relies heavily on property rights holders informing it of incoming shipments or problems with counterfeit products. Thus, the task of policing intellectual property rights falls primarily to businesses, who need to know their markets and the likely trouble spots for their products. Apple Computer, for example, has been very successful at monitoring areas where it believes counterfeiting is taking place, then using local police and other officials to seize products before they leave production sites.

GOVERNMENT RESPONSES TO COUNTERFEIT GOODS

In recent years, the spotlight has shifted from individuals to governments in the struggle to improve intellectual property protection. The U.S. government, in particular, has become an activist toward improving intellectual property protections internationally. It has used two major vehicles to try to get other countries to change their policies: section 301 of the Trade Act of 1974, and the GATT.

In 1988, a Congress frustrated with the lack of protection for U.S. intellectual property rights enacted two new provisions amending section 301 of the Trade Act of 1974. Section 301 is, in general, a trade retaliation statute, requiring the United States to retaliate by imposing higher tariffs or restrictions to the U.S. market in some circumstances, and authorizing retaliation in others. The two 1988 amendments strengthened the authority of the U.S. government to retaliate for unfair trade practices, and to negotiate to improve the protection of intellectual property.

One amendment, known as "Super 301," requires the U.S. Trade Representative to identify unfair foreign trade practices having a major impact on the U.S. economy and identify the countries in which those practices take place. Once the priority practices and countries are identified, the U.S. Trade Representative must undertake negotiations to remove the unfair trade practices. If the negotiations do not result in improvements, the United States must retaliate against the designated country.

The second amendment, known as "Special 301," specifically targets intellectual property practices. It requires the U.S. Trade Representative to identify the countries that deny Americans effective protection of intellectual property rights or deny market access to U.S. businesses that rely on intellectual property law. As with a Super 301 designation, identification triggers a section 301 investigation, which leads to retaliation.

Although many countries believe that the section 301 provisions violate the GATT, the sections have had an impact on world trading practices. Japan, which was targeted under Super 301, has liberalized its markets in several areas. In 1992, China agreed to improve its intellectual property protections and to join the Berne Convention, just before a deadline set for retaliation under Special 301.

The United States has also tried to lead the GATT into a multilateral agreement on intellectual property. Among the items on the agenda for the Uruguay Round were Trade Related Intellectual Property (TRIPS) discussions. As of 1992, new international standards for TRIPS were close to being concluded, although their fate will be determined by the overall outcome of GATT negotiations.

GRAY MARKET GOODS

Intellectual property owners face an additional problem in preserving their property rights. The problem is that under some circumstances legitimate goods will enter a market through unauthorized channels. Such goods are known as gray market goods. Gray market goods appear either because a seller has priced goods differently in different markets or because currency values change, making it profitable to acquire goods in other markets and import them. For example, if the value of the dollar is high against the German mark, it may make sense to buy German cars directly from German sellers, rather than through the authorized American distributors.

Gray market goods pose several problems for intellectual property owners. The primary problem may be the disruption they cause to networks of authorized distributors and dealers, who feel undercut by the lower-priced goods. For consumers, the main problem with gray market goods may be getting warranty service if something goes wrong with the goods. Warranty service is sometimes only available from authorized dealers. In addition, in some cases instructions and safety information may not be in the language of the market in which the sale takes place.

The same laws that bar the import of counterfeit goods may also bar the import of some gray market goods. Many legal systems are beginning to encounter gray market litigation. The United States has struggled with the problem of gray market goods for 70 years. As discussed earlier, by §526 of the Tariff Act of 1930, the owner of a trademark may exclude imports that bear an identical mark. The statute would seem to allow U.S. trademark owners to exclude all gray market goods by simply denying permission for their import. However, the Customs Service over the years interpreted the statute so as to allow many gray market imports.

Gray market practices came before the Supreme Court in 1988, in a case brought by a trade association and by Cartier, Inc., against K Mart and 47th Street Photo, Inc., two of the United States' largest gray market importers. In *K Mart v. Cartier*, 108 U.S. 1811 (1988), the Supreme Court, in an extremely confusing decision with different majorities for different parts of the decision, set out an analytical framework and some guidelines for gray marketers.

The Court set out five structures for gray market imports, and for each, ruled on whether §526 required customs to exclude the goods unless the U.S. trademark owner authorized the import:

CASE 1. A U.S. firm purchases the rights to register and use a foreign firm's trademark in the United States, selling the foreign firm's products in the United States. In this case, the court ruled that imports of the same goods by the foreign manufacturer or by a third party who has purchased the goods from the foreign manufacturer would unfairly jeopardize the value of the U.S. trademark holder's investment. Thus, §526 requires the Customs Service to exclude imports in this case.

CASE 2A. A foreign firm manufactures goods overseas. A U.S. subsidiary of that firm registers the foreign trademark in the United States. The Court held that Customs could allow the gray market goods to enter the United States.

CASE 2B. This case is the reverse of 2A. Here, A U.S. corporation creates a foreign subsidiary to manufacture and sell trademarked goods. Again, the Court held (by a different majority) that customs could allow the goods to enter the United States.

CASE 2C. Here, the U.S. enterprise establishes a branch or a division to manufacture goods offshore. The Court held that these goods were not "of foreign manufacture," as the statute required, so Customs could allow the goods to enter.

CASE 3. In this case, a U.S. holder of a U.S. trademark authorizes a foreign manufacturer to make goods and use a trademark in foreign markets. That manufacturer or a third party then imports the goods. The Court ruled that §526 required the exclusion of those imports, unless the U.S. trademark holder consented to the import.

The net effect of the several different votes on the gray market scenarios is that gray market imports were somewhat restricted. If there is common control between the United States and the foreign firm, either as parent, subsidiary, or branch, the imports may enter. If the U.S. and foreign businesses are independent, the U.S. trademark holder has the right to prevent unauthorized imports.

14.4 GOVERNMENT TAKINGS OF PROPERTY

Just as governments create private property rights, they also can destroy private property rights. In the United States, government takings of private property are known as takings by eminent domain. The Constitution recognizes the government's right to take property, but requires that takings be for public use, and that property owners receive "just" compensation. In business and political usage, government takings of property are known as expropriations. A subset of expropriations are nationalizations, which are takings resulting in government ownership of property. Expropriations and nationalizations may involve real property, personal property, and intellectual property.

The 20th century has seen wide usage of expropriation and nationalization. One large program of expropriation came with the Russian Revolution of 1917. Another came with Mexican land reforms in the 1930s, which affected large-scale foreign holdings of land. The aftermath of World War II involved more large-scale takings of land in eastern Europe, as new Communist governments nationalized industries and real property. The 1940s through the 1960s saw the independence of many countries that had been colonies of the European colonial powers. Many of those countries expropriated the property of foreigners. The developed nations have also taken property of their nationals and of foreigners. One example is France's nationalization of several industrial sectors in the early 1970s, when the Socialist party came to power.

Government takings of property may involve a country's own nationals or foreigners. When the takings involve property rights of nationals, the legal rights of the property owner are governed only by national law. Such is the case when the U.S. government takes land belonging to U.S. nationals in order to build a flood control reservoir. The Constitution mandates compensation, but there is no international law implication to the action. The more difficult question arises when the land taken for the reservoir belonged, for example, to a Japanese citizen. If the Japanese national doesn't believe that U.S. law allows for appropriate compensation, can he ask his government to step in to help? Is there an international standard for when and how governments can take property, and for compensation for its former owners?

THE INTERNATIONAL LEGAL STANDARD

In the early part of the 20th century, the international standards for expropriation were well established. In the *Chorzów Factory Case*, which involved several judgments between 1926 and 1929 by the Permanent Court of International Justice (the predecessor of the International Court of Justice), the Court ruled that governments could expropriate property of aliens for purposes of public utility, without violating international law. However, takings that violated treaties or other agreements would violate international law. Subsequently, the standard has been expanded somewhat, with courts and arbitrators holding that a confiscatory taking, where the government has no intent to pay, and a taking that is discriminatory or retaliatory may also violate international law.

COMPENSATION FOR TAKINGS

The international legal standard for compensation for expropriation is much more ambiguous. The *Chorzów* Court posed two different standards for compensation. For a lawful taking, international law required a government to pay the "just" price for the property, meaning "the value of the undertaking at the moment of its dispossession, plus interest to the day of payment."[1] In contrast, for an illegal taking, international law would require a government to "wipe out the consequences of the illegal act and reestablish the situation which would, in all probability, have existed if that act had not been committed."[2]

The United States further articulated what it believed to be the prevailing international standard for compensation in 1938. In an exchange of diplomatic notes concerning Mexico's nationalization of the oil industry, Secretary of State Hull wrote that international law required an expropriating nation to pay "prompt, adequate and effective" compensation to foreign property owners.[3] The United States still holds that the Hull formula is the appropriate international legal standard for compensation.

In contrast to the views of the United States and of other developed, capital-exporting countries, the nations of the developing world have very different perspectives on the international law governing expropriation. Their concerns are founded in the fact that international law has histori-

---

[1]Factory at Chorzów (Germany v. Poland) (Indemnity) 1928 PCIJ (ser. A), No. 17 (Judgment of September 3), at 47.

[2] *Id.*

[3]The correspondence is contained in G. Hackworth, 3 *Digest of International Law* 655–665 (1942).

cally reflected the interests and traditions of Western, developed nations. These nations were, historically, the colonial powers that ruled and controlled LDCs for centuries. Some LDCs view large multinational enterprises based in the developed world as successors to the former colonial powers. With economies based heavily on natural resources, in many cases LDCs have granted "concession agreements" giving foreign businesses the right to exploit mineral and oil wealth. When the LDCs have attempted to assert sovereignty over natural resources, international law has been an obstacle.

In the decades after World War II, the world underwent large-scale political transformation, as former colonies gained their independence. The newly independent countries found a voice at the United Nations, where they joined with other LDCs to attempt to create new standards of international law, reflecting wider interests than those of the traditional political powers. Throughout the 1960s and 1970s, the U.N. attempted to resolve issues of development, equity, and sovereignty in international law. In 1962, the U.N. reached consensus on the issue of sovereign rights over natural resources. Excerpts from the General Assembly resolution appear below.

UNITED NATIONS GENERAL ASSEMBLY RESOLUTION NO. 1803 (XVII) ON PERMANENT SOVEREIGNTY OVER NATURAL RESOURCES

17 UN GAOR Supp. (No. 17) at 115, UN Doc. A/5217 (1962)

The General Assembly, . . .

Considering that it is desirable to promote international cooperation for the economic development of developing countries, and that economic and financial agreements between the developed and the developing countries must be based on the principles of equality and of the right of peoples and nations to self determination, . . .

Noting that the creation and strengthening of the inalienable sovereignty of States over their natural wealth and resources reinforces their economic independence, . . .

Declares that:

1. The right of peoples and nations to permanent sovereignty over their natural wealth and resources must be exercised in the interest of their national development and of the well-being of the people of the State concerned. . . .

4. Nationalization, expropriation or requisitioning shall be based on grounds or reasons of public utility, security or the national interest which are recognized as overriding purely individual or private interests, both domestic and foreign. In such cases the owner shall be paid appropriate compensation, in accordance with the rules in force in the State taking such measures in the exercise of its sovereignty and in accordance with international law. In any cases where the question of compensation gives rise to a controversy, the national jurisdiction of the State on taking such measures shall be exhausted. However, upon agreement by sovereign States and other parties concerned, settlement of the dispute should be made through arbitration or international adjudication. . . .

Although the debate continued in the U.N., the 1962 resolution marked the last real agreement among both developed and less-developed nations. In 1974, the General Assembly approved the Charter of Economic Rights and Duties of States. The Charter allowed an expropriating government to take into account "its relevant laws and regulations and all circumstances that the State considers pertinent" when setting compensation.[4] The changing U.N. standard, reflecting the needs of LDCs, meant that the international legal standard for compensation for expropriation had become quite fuzzy.

For managers of multinationals, international law gives incomplete guidance, at best. Neither the Hull formula of "prompt, adequate and effective" compensation nor the U.N. formula of "adequate, under the circumstances" contains methods of assessing the amount of compensation. In cases involving long-term concession agreements, arbitrators valuing expropriated property have used discounted cash flow methods, or fixed a rate of return on investment.[5] Other arbitrators have held that a seized business should be evaluated as a going concern, although there is disagreement about including the value of lost future profits.[6] Still other possible methods of valuing seized property include book value, dissolution value, or a lump-sum negotiated price.

The problem of valuation gets more complex using the U.N.'s standard of appropriate compensation, taking into account national laws, regulations, and other circumstances. This standard appears to allow for a number of deductions from compensation for obligations ranging from taxes, unemployment compensation, excess profits removed from the country, or even environmental degradation. "Appropriate" compensation might also involve long-term payments, or payments in a fast-depreciating or nonconvertible currency. The case below illustrates some of the alternative standards for compensation.

---

[4] 29 UN GAOR Supp. (No. 31) at 50, UN Doc. A/9631 (1974).
[5] Kuwait and American Independent Oil Co., 66 ILR 519, 21 ILM 976 (1982).
[6] Amoco International Finance Corporation, AWD 310-56-3, 15 Iran–U.S. Claims Tribunal Reports 189 (1987 II).

BANCO NACIONAL DE CUBA v. CHASE MANHATTAN BANK

658 F.2d 875 (2d Cir. 1981)

FACTS:

In 1959, Fidel Castro came to power in Cuba. His political goals included nationalizing business and agricultural activities and severely restricting foreign involvement in the Cuban economy. By late 1960, relations between the United States and Cuba had soured. At that point, Cuba expropriated all of the assets of three U.S. banks, including Chase, placing them into the hands of Banco Nacional. In response, Chase seized Banco Nacional deposits it held in the United States, and liquidated the collateral on loans it had made to Banco Nacional.

Banco Nacional sued Chase in federal district court in New York, seeking to recover the more than $9 million in Banco Nacional assets in excess of loan amounts held by Chase. Chase admitted the validity of the claim, but counterclaimed for compensation for its expropriated property in Cuba. The district court ruled in favor of Banco Nacional on the original claim, but allowed an offset of about $6.9 million, reflecting the "going concern" value of Chase's four branches in Cuba. Both sides appealed.

ISSUE:

What is the legal standard for compensating the owners of expropriated property?

RESULT:

The international legal standard is appropriate compensation, which does not always require payment of "going concern" value.

REASONS:

We begin with the recognition that our task in determining the standard of compensation with respect to Chase's expropriation claims is to apply principles of international, not merely local law. . . . A review of this area convinces us that there are several strongly espoused views, and that international law is far from clear. [The court

then reviewed the history of expropriation, from the Hull formula through the U.N. resolutions.] . . .

The instant case, however, presents fewer difficulties than some we might envision insofar as the selection of a standard of compensation is concerned. We view the range of choices as including principally (1) no compensation, (2) partial compensation, (3) appropriate compensation, and (4) full compensation. We believe that neither of the first two reflects international law, and that in the circumstances of the present case there is probably no difference between the last two.

First, we reject the position espoused by some states that property may be expropriated without an obligation on the part of the nationalizing state to pay any compensation therefore. Whether or not an expropriation violates international law—and we note that the present expropriations have been held unlawful, and that ruling is not here contested—we believe that the prevalent view is the traditional view, to wit, that the failure to pay any compensation to the victim of an expropriation constitutes a violation of international law. . . .

Nor do we believe that the prevailing view is that international law never requires an expropriating state to pay more than partial compensation. Banco Nacional espouses the partial compensation contention in a way that reveals its unsoundness as a legal standard. It urges that Chase be paid 50% of the value of its branches because most of the past negotiated settlements of expropriation claims have resulted in payments of 40–60% of the value of the claims. The notion that, merely because a negotiated settlement will not result in full payment, a victim of expropriation has no right to more than partial compensation simply confuses adjudication with compromise. . . .

As for the Hull Doctrine and the theory that full compensation is required, we are mindful that it has long been under attack by many commentators as not accurately reflecting international law. . . .

It may well be the consensus of nations that full compensation need not be paid "in all circumstances" . . . and that requiring an expropriating state to pay "appropriate compensation,"—even considering the lack of precise definition of that term,—would come closest to reflecting what international law requires. But the adoption of an "appropriate compensation" requirement would not exclude the possibility that in some cases full compensation would be appropriate. . . .

The principle area of dispute as to the valuation of the Chase branches is whether Chase should receive only their net asset value or whether it is entitled also to a premium for their value as a going concern. Banco Nacional contends that an award for going concern value is inappropriate. We agree. . . .

. . . [T]he circumstances surrounding the taking of the Chase branches were that many of Chase's actual or potential customers had had or were about to have their own businesses nationalized, that many had fled Cuba and been replaced in the ownership of their businesses and properties by the Cuban government, and that Chase's average number of deposits had declined substantially in 1959 and the first eight months of 1960, and that the government would soon decree that

those who remained carry on their banking transactions only with government-owned banks. . . . [W]e regard the prospects of Chase's Cuban branches in September 1960 for future earnings as highly speculative. Future earnings in this case, therefore, are an inappropriate basis for an award of damages. . . .

In short, we see no warrant for believing that, at a time when aliens were fleeing Cuba and many foreign businesses were being abandoned or nationalized, a potential buyer with his eyes open would have paid Chase a premium in anticipation of its future Cuban earnings. This commonsense view is confirmed by the trial testimony of a former executive vice president and comptroller of Chase, who was experienced in bank acquisitions. When asked, if given the political climate in Cuba on August 1, 1960, he would have been willing to purchase a branch of an American bank, he said, "I think it was too far gone by then, you know." We conclude that the appropriate compensation to Chase does not include payment for the going concern value of its branches, and that Chase will be fully compensated by an award that excludes any amount reflecting "lost" future earnings. Accordingly the amount awarded Chase by the district court should be reduced by $1,426,000.

14.5 CHALLENGING EXPROPRIATIONS

Once a business has had its property taken by a foreign government, it has several possible options to try to get compensation for its loss. The business can pursue its claims in the courts of the country expropriating the property. It can also pursue assets that the expropriating country may have in other countries, particularly in the company's home country. One example of that strategy is Chase Manhattan's action in the case discussed above. In yet another strategy, the business may turn to its own government for diplomatic intervention or legal action in the International Court of Justice. Recall from Chapter 2 that the investors in *Barcelona Traction* took this course when their business was seized by the Spanish government. Finally, in many cases, either the terms of the contract between a government and a business or a treaty may allow for arbitration of expropriation claims.

All of these methods of getting compensation have problems. Chief among the problems is delay. In *Banco Nacional*, the expropriation took place in 1960, but was still unresolved in 1981. *Barcelona Traction* involved decades of wrangling over compensation for investors. Even though a court or arbitrator may add an amount for interest in an award, the business is still deprived of its investment for a long time.

A second significant problem in getting compensation for a government taking is the influence of political considerations in the legal process. Many expropriations take place in an atmosphere of political upheaval. In such circumstances, there may or may not be courts or other government agencies available to assess claims by foreign businesses. If such institutions exist, the people in those institutions are most likely to reflect the new political ideology of the successful revolutionaries. They are not likely to be sympathetic to large damage claims by foreign businesses. For example, many U.S. businesses found their property seized by Iran as a result of the revolution there in 1979. The new Iranian politicians and judges were decidedly unsympathetic to the claims of U.S. businesses.

One of the more effective strategies in trying to achieve compensation for expropriations is to look for assets in other countries, particularly in the home country of the business. There, the business can expect to find more sympathetic treatment from its own legal system. There are, however, two major legal problems standing in the way of recovery. One, sovereign immunity, is a time-honored tradition of international law, while the other, the act-of-state doctrine, is a U.S. legal principle stemming from the Constitution's division of foreign affairs powers.

FOREIGN SOVEREIGN IMMUNITY

One of the fundamental principles of public international law is that it regulates the rights among sovereign, independent nations. All nations are legal equals in the tradition of international law. As sovereigns, the nations hold the right to make laws and regulate the conduct of their citizens and other residents. From the notions of independence and sovereignty comes the legal tradition that the sovereign cannot be sued without its consent. This sovereign immunity (which applies domestically as well) extends to international conduct. The actions of one government cannot be challenged in the courts of another country. A foreign government is immune from suits in courts of other countries, unless it consents to be sued. One variation on the doctrine is diplomatic immunity—that the diplomats stationed in a foreign nation cannot be brought before the courts there, even for serious crimes.

The problem with the concept of foreign sovereign immunity has always been one of defining its scope. Governments engage in many different kinds of activities. They may conduct a war or blockade, take property, buy commercial ships, run an airline, or contract for goods and services. Traditionally, Communist countries have conducted all their commercial activity through state-owned trading companies. Historically, some countries, most notably the Communist countries, have maintained that sovereign immunity is absolute, extending both to commercial and to noncommercial activities. Until the mid-20th century, the United States also largely supported the absolute theory of sovereign immunity.

Now, the more widely held view of the scope of foreign sovereign immunity is that it is restrictive; that is, that sovereigns are immune from suits concerning their laws and regulations, including laws expropriating property, acts of their armed forces or diplomatic service, and public loans. When a government engages in a purely commercial activity, however, it should not be treated differently from any other merchant. For example, suppose a state-owned trading company in China were to buy 10,000 tons of wheat from a U.S. seller. Under the restrictive theory, the Chinese trading company would be treated by U.S. courts in the same way as any other commercial buyer if there is a suit for breach of contract.

In the United States, Congress codified the restrictive theory of foreign sovereign immunity in 1976, in the Foreign Sovereign Immunities Act (FSIA). The FSIA states among its provisions that a foreign government is not immune from suit in the United States if (1) it has expressly or implicitly waived its immunity from suit, or (2) the suit is based on commercial acts of the government, carried on in the United States or having a direct effect in the United States, or (3) the suit is based on a taking of rights in property in violation of international law, and that property or property exchanged for it is present in the United States in connection with commercial activity carried on by the government.

The FSIA opens the door to U.S. courts in several different situations. In the *Banco Nacional* case discussed above, the district court held that the Cuban government had waived its right to sovereign immunity by suing Chase in U.S. courts. In a taking of property rights, for example, contained in an oil-drilling agreement between a foreign government and a U.S. company, a court would almost certainly look at the situation as the breach of a commercial contract, subjecting the foreign government to U.S. courts. In takings of tangible property, such as ships or airplanes, for use in commercial activities, a U.S. owner would also be able to use U.S. courts. More difficult, however, are takings of real property, where there is less likely to be a use abroad or an exchange.

It is important to note that getting a judgment against a foreign sovereign does not mean that a business will be able to collect on the judgment. The FSIA allows a successful party to seize assets of the foreign government in the United States that are used for commercial purposes. In some cases, such assets may not exist.

THE ACT-OF-STATE DOCTRINE

If a business can get past the jurisdictional barrier of sovereign immunity, it still faces political impediments to recovery. Governments sometimes have foreign policy objectives that are inconsistent with a private plaintiff using the courts to recover for expropriations. In the United States, as in most other countries, the power to conduct foreign affairs resides with the executive branch of government. Court actions, while giving justice to individual litigants, might interfere with the executive's right to conduct foreign policy.

In the United States, the need to balance due process for litigants with the separation of powers mandated by the Constitution has resulted in the act-of-state doctrine, articulated by the courts in a series of decisions that are not always consistent. The doctrine is one of judicial abstention; that is, even though a court may have the power to act, it will not, out of deference to other branches of government. The act-of-state doctrine is a presumption that acts a government takes on its own territory are legal, and not to be questioned by foreign courts. The best-known articulation of the doctrine came in *Banco Nacional de Cuba v. Sabbatino*,[7] another case involving nationalizations after the Cuban revolution. There, the Supreme Court held:

> . . . [W]e decide only that the Judicial Branch will not examine the validity of a taking of property within its own territory by a foreign sovereign government, extant and recognized by this country at the time of suit, in the absence of a treaty or other unambiguous agreement regarding controlling legal principles, even if the complaint alleges that the taking violates customary international law.

This formulation of the doctrine has not been without its critics. In fact, Congress enacted a law specifically to overrule the *Sabbatino* decision. U.S. courts have not given up the doctrine, however. Its most recent exposition by the Supreme Court came in the case below, which looks at an attempt to use the doctrine in another context.

W. S. KIRKPATRICK & CO. v. ENVIRONMENTAL TECTONICS CORP.

110 S. Ct. 701 (1990)
United States Supreme Court

FACTS:

The plaintiff and defendant were competing for a military procurement contract for the government of Nigeria. After Environmental Tectonics Corp. (ETC) lost the bid, it discovered that Kirkpatrick had paid a bribe to Nigerian officials of 20 percent of the contract price. Nigerian law prohibited such payments, and would make the contract illegal.

The U.S. government charged Kirkpatrick and its executive in charge of the project with violating the Foreign Corrupt Practices Act. Both pleaded guilty. Then ETC sued Kirkpatrick, seeking damages for its lost business opportunity under the Racketeer Influenced Corrupt Organizations Act (RICO), and other statutes. The district court dismissed the case, holding that the act-of-state

[7]376 U.S. 398 (1964).

doctrine prevented the suit. The Court of Appeals reversed, reinstating the suit.

ISSUE:

Does the act-of-state doctrine apply to this case?

RESULT:

No. The case should go to trial.

REASONS:

This Court's description of the jurisprudential foundation for the act of state doctrine has undergone some evolution over the years. We once viewed the doctrine as an expression of international law, resting upon "the highest considerations of international comity and expediency," . . . We have more recently described it, however, as a consequence of domestic separation of powers, reflecting "the strong sense of the Judicial Branch that its engagement in the task of passing on the validity of foreign acts of state may hinder" the conduct of foreign affairs. . . . Some Justices have suggested possible exceptions to application of the doctrine, where one or both of the foregoing policies would seemingly not be served: an exception, for example, for acts of state that consist of commercial transactions, since neither modern international comity nor the current position of our Executive Branch accorded sovereign immunity to such acts . . . or an exception for cases in which the Executive Branch has represented that it has no objection to denying validity to the foreign sovereign act, since then the courts would be impeding no foreign policy goals. . . .

In every case in which we have held the act of state doctrine applicable, the relief sought or the defense interposed would have required a court in the United States to declare invalid the official act of a foreign sovereign performed within its own territory. . . . In the present case, by contrast, neither the claim or any asserted defense requires a determination that Nigeria's contract with Kirkpatrick International was, or was not, effective.

Petitioners point out, however, that the facts necessary to establish respondent's claim will also establish that the contract was unlawful. Specifically, they note that in order to prevail respondent must prove that petitioner Kirkpatrick made, and Nigerian officials received payments that violate Nigerian law, which would, they assert, support a finding that the contract is invalid

under Nigerian law. Assuming that to be true, it still does not suffice. . . . Act of state issues only arise when a court *must decide*—that is, when the outcome of the case turns upon—the effect of official action by a foreign sovereign. When that question is not in the case, neither is the act of state doctrine. That is the situation here. . . .

. . . Petitioners insist, however, that the policies underlying our act of state cases—international comity, respect for the sovereignty of foreign nations on their own territory, and the avoidance of embarrassment to the Executive Branch in its conduct of foreign relations—are implicated in the present case because, as the District Court found, a determination that Nigerian officials demanded and accepted a bribe "would impugn or question the nobility of a foreign nation's motivations," and would "result in embarrassment to the sovereign or constitute interference in the conduct of foreign policy of the United States." . . . The United States, as *amicus curiae*, favors the same approach to the act of state doctrine, though disagreeing with petitioners as to the outcome it produces in the present case. We should not, the United States urges, "attach dispositive significance to the fact that this suit involves only the 'motivation' for, rather than the 'validity' of, a foreign sovereign act," . . . and should eschew "any rigid formula for the resolution of act of state cases generally," . . . In some future case, perhaps, "litigation . . . based on alleged corruption in the award of contracts or other commercially oriented activities of foreign governments could sufficiently touch on 'national nerves' that the act of state doctrine or related principles of abstention would appropriately be found to bar the suit. . . .

These urgings are deceptively similar to what we said in *Sabbatino*, where we observed that sometimes, even though the validity of the act of a foreign sovereign within its own territory is called into question, the policies underlying the act of state doctrine may not justify its application. . . . But what is appropriate in order to avoid unquestioning judicial acceptance of the acts of foreign sovereigns is not similarly appropriate for the quite opposite purpose of expanding judicial incapacities where such acts are not directly (or even indirectly) involved. . . .

The short of the matter is this: Courts in the United States have the power, and ordinarily the obligation, to decide cases and controversies properly presented to them. The act of state doctrine does not establish an exception for cases and controversies that may embarrass foreign governments, but merely requires that, in the process of deciding, the acts of foreign sovereigns taken within their own jurisdictions shall be deemed valid. That doctrine has no application to the present case because the validity of no foreign sovereign act is at issue.

DIPLOMATIC INTERVENTION

In many instances, particularly where large-scale expropriations are involved, a business may find its most effective way to get compensation is through diplomatic channels. The home government of an MNE is often willing to intervene to protect the business. In the case of a large-scale expropriation, the home government may intervene by freezing foreign government assets located within its territory, thus giving the two countries some good reason to negotiate. The governments have the ability to negotiate to submit the dispute to arbitration, or to set up a mutually satisfactory method of resolving the expropriation dispute. Many large-scale expropriation claims in recent years have been resolved by lump-sum payments negotiated by the governments involved, with individual claimants making claims against the fund.

As an example, consider the aftermath of the Iranian revolution. After the seizure of U.S. property in the Iranian revolution of 1979, the United States froze Iranian government assets located in the United States. Then, as part of the settlement ending the hostage crisis in 1981, the United States and Iran agreed to a multinational Claims Commission to hear and determine both sides' claims. Although some claims were not resolved for a decade, the process was faster and probably more satisfactory than it would have been without government intervention.

Governments are also active in trying to establish broader frameworks for resolving disputes over expropriations. In the 1960s the International Bank for Reconstruction and Development (World Bank) established the International Center for the Settlement of Investment Disputes, as an arbitration and mediation service. In a multilateral treaty signed by nearly ninety countries, the ICSID became a method of resolving investment disputes between a government and a foreign investor.

Governments have also attempted to create predispute frameworks for dealing with expropriation problems, using bilateral investment treaties. These are individually negotiated treaties with another country. Usually, the treaty will contain an agreement that expropriations require adequate, full, or "prompt, adequate, and effective" compensation, along with a provision agreeing to submit any claims over expropriated property to international arbitration.

THE CALVO CLAUSE

Not all governments accept the premise that expropriations should be subject to diplomatic resolution. In the late 19th century, the Argentine jurist Carlos Calvo argued that foreign nationals were only entitled to the same treatment as a country's own nationals. By choosing to invest and do business in a country, Calvo argued, businesses willingly agreed to submit their disputes to that country's legal system in the same manner as a national of that country. Thus, a foreigner's remedy for an expropriation was in the local courts only, not with governments and diplomatic exchanges.

Reaction to Calvo's arguments varied widely. His arguments were accepted across most of Latin America. In some cases, foreign nationals would be required to waive any rights to use diplomatic channels when they entered into contracts in a Latin American country. In other instances, such as Mexico and Peru, the Calvo doctrine was written into national constitutions or into foreign investment statutes. For these countries, the Calvo clause was a logical way to assert their authority against the use of "diplomacy" by developed countries with much more diplomatic bargaining power and a history of using military intervention to achieve diplomatic results.

Not surprisingly, the developed nations did not respond as positively to Calvo's assertion. The strongest argument against the Calvo clause is that a nation's decision to use diplomatic channels is a matter of sovereign authority and is not subject to waiver by private individuals or businesses. Another argument against the Calvo clause was that it should not apply to takings that violate international law, since international law is more important than national law. However, many countries did recognize the Calvo clause, at least insofar as they required foreign investors to exhaust local remedies before invoking diplomatic protection. The exhaustion-of-remedies aspect of the Calvo clause is reflected in U.N. Resolution 1903, which does reflect consensus among developed countries and LDCs.

14.6 RISK MANAGEMENT AND INSURANCE

If one concept stands out from this discussion of government takings, it is that a business is not likely to get what it would consider to be complete compensation for the loss of its investment within a reasonable amount of time. With the ambiguity of international law and the confusion of international politics, good planning and risk management are important responsibilities for the manager in an MNE.

PLANNING BEFORE EXPROPRIATIONS

A manager can take many steps to identify and monitor the risk of expropriation and to reduce its impact on a company. First and foremost is to engage in political risk analysis on an ongoing basis. Political risk analysis is an examination of the political stability of a country by looking at events and trends. There are specialized consulting firms that undertake political risk analysis and most large MNEs have employees engaged in risk analysis. For smaller firms, specialized reporting services publish analyses of countries around the world. Of course, managers and employees on location may be an excellent source of information about the political stability of a local government. The analysis can be quite sophisticated; at a minimum, managers should be aware of the political and economic situation in their country, with a special eye out for signs of instability.

If a country shows signs of increased political risk, such as raising restrictions on currency movement, experiencing the rise of radical political parties or movements, or increasing hostility toward foreigners or foreign investment, a manager should take steps to reduce the company's exposure to expropriation. Those steps might include reducing assets in the country by lowering inventory levels, removing sensitive technology, and changing supply arrangements. At this point, a manager might also want to be sure that at least a copy of corporate records exists outside the country, to make it easier to determine asset values in the event of a taking.

If expropriation looks likely, the manager's task becomes one of exploring what local remedies may be available, making sure the home government is fully informed about the prospect of expropriation, and, where necessary, making sure that expatriate employees and their families can leave the country safely.

INSURANCE

One method of helping to manage the risk of expropriation is with insurance. Some private insurance is available, but a U.S. business is most likely to use insurance obtained from the Overseas Private Investment Corporation (OPIC), an agency of the U.S. government. OPIC will insure U.S. businesses against the risks of expropriation, as well as the risk of currency inconvertibility.

In order to obtain OPIC insurance, the company must have its investment in an eligible country. Eligible countries are those that have signed investment agreements with the U.S. government. Generally, these agreements will require host government approval of any U.S. guaranteed investment. They will also recognize the U.S. government's right to make a claim for compensation once it has paid an OPIC policyholder. The agreements also provide for arbitration if the two governments cannot successfully negotiate a claim. OPIC insurance is available in most countries of the world, and has become an important tool for U.S. businesses in managing against the risk of expropriation.

14.7 CONCLUSION

Before placing assets into the stream of international commerce, a business needs to evaluate the protection other governments will give business property rights. Especially in the area of intellectual property rights, the complexity of different legal systems and the absence of effective international protection require businesses to plan carefully for the global introduction of new products. For successful products, businesses need to be vigilant in protecting their rights and to be prepared to use the protections available to them. The next decade should see many improvements in the protection of intellectual property rights.

All kinds of property rights are subject to seizure by governments. International law does require that the takings be for public uses and be compensated. However, complete compensation is difficult to obtain and may take many years. Therefore, managers need to anticipate the possibilities of expropriation and act to minimize the risk of loss and the amount of loss the business may incur. Private or government insurance of foreign investments against the risk of expropriation is one appropriate step to take; an ongoing analysis of the political situation in the host country is another method of managing the risks.

14.8 QUESTIONS FOR DISCUSSION

1. Explain the concept of national treatment for intellectual property rights holders. What do you see as the advantages and disadvantages of using national treatment as the way to achieve international protection for intellectual property rights?

2. Some LDCs do not recognize patent rights in pharmaceutical or agricultural products. If you were a GATT negotiator for a developed nation, how would you persuade the representative of such an LDC that patent protection is in her country's best interest? If you represented the LDC, how would you respond? Is agreement possible?

3. Lever Brothers is a multinational with manufacturing and sales subsidiaries around the world. Lever Brothers Co. (U.S.) makes a scented deodorant soap called Shield. Lever Brothers Ltd. (U.K.) also makes a scented deodorant soap called Shield, although the U.K. version has a different scent and a different color and makes fewer suds. Can the U.S. subsidiary stop the import of the British soap into the United States as a gray market import? Explain your answer.

4. James Douglas, a U.S. citizen, was hired by the minister of health of a small Asian nation to create a computer-based accounting system for that nation's hospitals. While Douglas created the system, he discovered that the minister's son was stealing hundreds of thousands of dollars

worth of equipment, supplies, and money from the hospital system. Douglas reported his findings to the minister and detailed the findings in a letter to the king. Rather than being rewarded, however, Douglas found himself arrested and tortured by the police. The intervention of the U.S. ambassador got Douglas released and deported to the United States. If Douglas sues the government and the minister of health for compensation for his injuries, will he win?

5. As a practical matter, what is the difference between "prompt, adequate and effective" compensation for a taking, and "appropriate compensation"? What do you think the international standard should be? Explain.

14.9 FURTHER READINGS

James Austin, *Managing in Developing Countries*, Free Press, New York, 1990.

F. N. Burton and Hisashi Inoue, "Expropriations of Foreign-Owned Firms in Developing Countries," 18 *Journal of World Trade Law* 396–414 (1984).

Frank Cespedes, E. Raymond Corey, and V. Kastori Rangan, "Gray Markets: Causes and Cures," *Harvard Business Review*, July–August 1988, pp. 75–81.

Note, "Making Intellectual Property Pirates Walk the Plank: Using 'Special 301' to Protect the United States' Rights," 12 *Loyola of Los Angeles International and Comparative Law Journal* 725–752 (1990).

Note, "The Act of State Doctrine: Reconciling Justice and Diplomacy on a Case-by-Case Basis," 43 *University of Miami Law Review* 1169–1202 (1989).

Donald Spero, "Patent Protection or Piracy—A CEO Views Japan," *Harvard Business Review*, September–October 1990, pp. 58–67.

CHAPTER 15

THE MULTINATIONAL ENTERPRISE AS A WORLD CITIZEN

15.1 INTRODUCTION

Multinational enterprises (MNEs) can have significant strategic advantages in the global marketplace. Their presence in many markets enables them to change operating strategies quickly to take advantage of new opportunities. MNEs can use a variety of organizational tools to achieve their goals, and can be flexible, changing the forms of their business activities in response to changing market conditions. The large size of many MNEs means that they have the resources to make capital investments in new markets. MNEs can be a major positive force for economic growth and development in the countries in which they do business.

The same factors leading to the benefits of MNEs also create opportunities for MNEs to damage the countries in which they do business. The organizational and functional flexibility that enhances an MNEs competitive abilities also gives it the ability to shift its operations to avoid national regulation, evade liability for wrongful acts, or even engage in criminal activities. The Bank of Credit and Commerce International (BCCI), which closed, stranding thousands of depositors, is one example of such an MNE.

The large size of MNEs allows them to use capital productively and help countries in their development. On the other hand, it can lead to attempts to corrupt and control political figures, unfairly exploit natural and human resources, and destroy local economies.

MNEs lead change in the societies in which they do business. Whether that change is positive or negative in large measure depends on the choices individual managers make in conducting business. The purpose of this chapter is to investigate some of the areas in which managers of MNEs must make operating decisions and what the legal and ethical consequences of those decisions are for the societies in which the MNE does business.

15.2 INTERNAL OPERATING DECISIONS

The size of MNEs means that their internal operating decisions may have effects going far beyond the balance sheet of the business. A decision to pay bribes in order to obtain a contract, for example, may cause a government to fall when that bribe is discovered. A decision to price goods or technology sold between a parent company and a subsidiary may have tax consequences that substantially affect the budget of the host nation. Seemingly minor day-to-day business practices may have effects going well beyond the company's office, division, or subsidiary.

There is no international law of good corporate behavior. Where there is law governing corporate operations, it is national, and tends to be that of the host country, regulating the conduct of business. As we already saw in

Chapter 13, however, some national law regulating business practices can extend extraterritorially. The United Nations Commission on Trade and Development (UNCTAD) has for many years been drafting a Code of Conduct for Transnational Corporations, which would become an international legal standard. While UNCTAD has made substantial progress, the draft Code is mired in disputes between developing and developed countries. The Organization for Economic Cooperation and Development (OECD), which represents developed countries, has developed a nonbinding set of guidelines for MNEs that has been influential for businesses, although it does not have the force of law. Adopted in 1976, the OECD Guidelines express the consensus of the developed nations on the conduct of MNEs, and provide that the OECD member governments will consult each other when disputes arise over the conduct of MNEs. Their rationale is explained in the following excerpt.

ANNEX TO THE DECLARATION OF 21ST JUNE, 1976 BY GOVERNMENTS OF OECD MEMBER COUNTRIES ON INTERNATIONAL INVESTMENT AND MULTINATIONAL ENTERPRISES

75 Dept. State Bulletin 83 (1976)

1. Multinational enterprises now play an important part in the economies of Member countries and in international economic relations, which is of increasing interest to governments. Through international direct investment, such enterprises can bring substantial benefits to home and host countries by contributing to the efficient utilisation of capital, technology and human resources between countries and can thus fulfill an important role in the promotion of economic and social welfare. But the advances made by multinational enterprises in organising their operations beyond the national framework may lead to abuse of concentrations of economic power and to conflicts with national policy objectives. In addition, the complexity of these multinational enterprises and the difficulty of clearly perceiving their diverse structures, operations and policies sometimes give rise to concern.

2. The common aim of the Member countries is to encourage the positive contributions which multinational enterprises can make to economic and social progress and to minimise and resolve the difficulties to which their various operations may give rise. In view of the transnational structure of such enterprises, this aim will be furthered by co-operation among the OECD countries where the headquarters of most of the multinational enterprises are established and which are the location of a substantial part of their operations. The guidelines set out hereafter are designed to assist in the achievement of this common aim and to contribute to improving the foreign investment climate. . . .

7. Every State has the right to prescribe the conditions under which multinational enterprises operate within its national jurisdiction, subject to international law and to the international agreements to which it has subscribed. The entities of a multinational enterprise located in various countries are subject to the laws of these countries. . . .

General Policies

Enterprises should

(1) take fully into account established general policy objectives of the Member countries in which they operate;

(2) in particular, give due consideration to those countries' aims and priorities with regard to economic and social progress, including industrial and regional development, the protection of the environment, the creation of employment opportunities, the promotion of innovation and the transfer of technology;

(3) while observing their legal obligations concerning information, supply their entities with supplementary information the latter may need in order to meet requests by authorities of the countries in which those entities are located for information relevant to the activities of those entities, taking into account legitimate requirements of business confidentiality; . . .

(6) when filling responsible posts in each country of operation, take due account of individual qualifications without discrimination as to nationality, subject to particular national requirements in this respect;

(7) not render—and they should not be solicited or expected to render—any bribe or other improper benefit, direct or indirect, to any public servant or holder of public office;

(8) unless legally permissible, not make any contributions to candidates for public office or to political parties or other political organizations;

(9) abstain from any improper involvement in local political activities.

While many day-to-day business decisions have implications for the societies in which a large MNE does business, two areas have been the subject of much concern: corrupt practices and transfer pricing.

CORRUPT PRACTICES

In the 1970s, newspapers were full of stories of MNEs bribing prominent politicians around the world in order to obtain lucrative contracts and exercise political influence. The most notorious of the bribery scandals was in the aerospace industry, where Lockheed was charged with paying more than $25 million to foreign officials in order to obtain contracts for airplanes. The prime minister of Japan was forced to resign his post, Crown Prince Bernhard of the Netherlands was forced to abdicate as a result of the scandal, and other governments ranging from Turkey to Colombia felt the repercussions of the illicit payments.

The Lockheed scandal led directly to UNCTAD's efforts to establish a code of conduct for MNEs, as well as to the OECD guidelines for MNEs. However, to date, the only binding legislation on corrupt practices comes from the United States. In 1977, the United States enacted the Foreign Corrupt Practices Act (FCPA), with the hope that it would set a standard for other nations to follow. At present, other countries have not developed similar legislation. In 1988, the United States amended the FCPA, indicating as part of the amendments that if other countries continued not to regulate corrupt practices, the United States would consider repealing the law.

THE FCPA

The FCPA has been extremely controversial from its inception. Many executives have attacked the law as impeding the ability of U.S. firms to compete, claiming that payments, kickbacks, and bribes are simply a part of doing business internationally. When everyone else engages in corrupt practices, why shouldn't U.S. companies do so as well? In support of the law, however, other executives argue that they don't need to pay to compete, and that they want to be judged only on price, service, and quality.

The FCPA actually responded to two perceived problems in international business. The first is making payments to foreign officials in order to get or retain business. In virtually all countries, such payments are unlawful, although many countries allow businesses to take tax deductions for the expense of paying bribes or other corrupt payments. The second problem the FCPA addresses is the practice of concealing such payments by designating them falsely as some other kind of business expense for purposes of financial disclosures to shareholders and others. Here, the FCPA requires all U.S. publicly traded businesses to maintain books and records that accurately reflect the disbursements of the business, including those for bribes.

The corrupt payments portion of the FCPA applies to companies that must register their securities with the U.S. Securities and Exchange Commission, and to "domestic concerns," which the FCPA defines as individuals who are U.S. citizens, nationals, or residents, and businesses having their primary place of business in the United States or organized under U.S.-based law. The law also extends to any officer, director, employee, agent, or stockholder acting on behalf of a business covered by the law. The FCPA prohibits offers, payments, promises, or authorizations to pay or give anything of value to foreign officials, foreign political parties, their officials or candidates, or to anyone else while knowing that the person will offer such a payment to a prohibited party for the purpose of obtaining or retaining business or for directing business to any person.

The FCPA has several provisions designed to address the more legitimate needs of the business community. The first is a provision that payments that are lawful under the written law of the foreign country are not unlawful under the FCPA. The second is a provision that a business may make "reasonable and bona fide" payments to foreign officials, parties, party officials, or candidates when those payments are directly related to promoting, explaining, or demonstrating products or signing or performing contracts. Thus, an airplane manufacturer might pay the travel and lodging expenses of a foreign official for the purpose of having that person see a factory or a demonstration of the planes that might become the subject of a contract.

The FCPA also recognizes that some level of bribery does exist in many countries for purposes unconnected with getting or retaining business. When goods arrive at a crowded port, for example, a small "grease payment" may help get the goods through customs faster. The FCPA allows payments for what it calls "routine governmental action," but carefully defines the kinds of actions it means:

> [T]he term 'routine governmental action' means only an action which is ordinarily and commonly performed by a foreign official in—
> (i) obtaining permits, licenses or other official documents to qualify a person to do business in a foreign country;
> (ii) processing governmental papers, such as visas and work orders;
> (iii) providing police protection, mail pick-up and delivery, or scheduling inspections associated with contract performance or inspections related to the transit of goods across country;
> (iv) providing phone service, power and water supply, loading or unloading cargo, or protecting perishable products or commodities from deterioration; or
> (v) actions of a similar nature. (15 U.S.C. 78dd-2(4) (A)).

The fourth and final provision of the FCPA that should give some comfort to managers deals with the problems of intermediaries. Many companies have argued that they need to employ agents abroad to help them get contracts, and that they do not always know whether commissions paid to such agents end up in the hands of foreign officials. For example, Westinghouse paid a multimillion dollar commission to an agent in the Philippines, who helped it obtain a contract to build a nuclear power plant. When the Marcos government was overthrown, records found in the Presidential Palace indicated that President Marcos had received nearly $25 million from the agent. Although Westinghouse claimed it did not know that a bribe was paid, it still found itself subject to lengthy investigations under the FCPA. It finally resolved its problems concerning this payment in 1992.[1]

The FCPA creates liability for the actions of intermediaries only if the person or business subject to the law knows that the intermediary will act as a conduit to the foreign official. Knowledge is defined as actually knowing or having a firm belief that the result will occur or is substantially likely to occur, or knowing that there is a high probability that an unlawful payment will occur. Thus, a person cannot create structures to keep himself ignorant of the activities of his agent in another country.

The penalties for violating the FCPA are severe. Businesses may be fined up to $2 million, while individuals face fines of up to $100,000 and jail terms of up to 5 years. Fines assessed against individuals may not be paid or reimbursed by their businesses. In addition, as the *Kirkpatrick* case in Chapter 14 shows, competitors who lose business as a result of corrupt payments may bring suit for their damages, in some cases using the FCPA as a basis for a RICO action seeking treble damages and attorneys' fees.

---

[1]For the fascinating story of this deal see "The $2.2 Billion Nuclear Fiasco," *Fortune,* September 1, 1986, pp. 38–46.

ETHICAL IMPLICATIONS OF CORRUPT PRACTICES

As its critics note, the FCPA certainly doesn't solve the problem of corrupt payments in international business. It has a limited reach, not covering lobbying or payments designed to influence political and regulatory environments. It allows "grease payments," even though such payments are explicit bribes. It may affect the competitive positions of U.S. businesses, when businesses from other countries can offer corrupt payments without fear of sanction from their home country. Most significantly, the FCPA fails to take into account cultural difference. In some countries, and particularly in non-Western cultures, business is seen as the process of building relationships, not just transactions between buyers and sellers. In those countries, gift-giving may be a legitimate expression of the creation of relationships, leading to business opportunities. Some gifts, particularly extravagant gifts, could potentially be seen as violations of the FCPA.

One response to the problem of bribery in international business is to look at the issue as one of ethics, rather than strictly as a legal obligation. Looking at ethics allows a business to consider wider implications and longer-term consequences of its decisions. One way of looking at the decision to bribe, for example, would suggest that although a payment may result in getting a particular contract, it may also result in the business getting a reputation among its customers for sharp practices and corner cutting. In the long term, the damage to the firm's reputation may outweigh the benefit of the short-term business gain.

Another way of looking at the decision to bribe stems more from a utilitarian, or even social justice–based approach, rather than the egoistic approach of the first example. Here, a manager might look at the decision as one of balance: the narrow interest of the business in obtaining a contract versus the wider interest of the effect of bribery on the host country. Corruption makes the process of economic and social development extremely difficult. It makes for a politically unstable society that in many cases, as in Iran, Nigeria, and the Philippines, produces social upheaval or even violent revolutions.

A third way of looking at the ethical dilemma posed by bribery is to ask what the duty of the business is. Some may say that the sole duty of a business is to make money for its shareholders. Others see a wider duty, in some cases for the business to act on behalf of a wide range of stakeholders, including employees, the community, and customers. Still others see the role of the business as one of contributing to the well-being of society.

Looking at the problem of bribery as one of ethics gives a business an opportunity to clarify its values. Corporations like Dow Chemical, Borg-Warner, Xerox, and Johnson & Johnson have used the ethical issues of business to establish corporate credos or codes of conduct that strongly express their values. When these statements are properly introduced and reinforced, they give a business the opportunity to create a corporate culture that properly expresses business ethics. In turn, employees then know how to act in a variety of situations so as to further the interests of the company.

TRANSFER PRICING

A second set of operating decisions causing special problems in MNEs is the decision on how to price sales among the different parts of the company. For example, Global Motors, a large, Swiss-based multinational auto maker, may get parts for its cars from subsidiaries in Mexico, Germany, and Venezuela. The cars may then be assembled in its Spanish subsidiary for sale in the EC. The Spanish subsidiary will account for the parts it buys as an expense of doing business, while the other subsidiaries will book the price for which the goods sold as profit.

If the various enterprises were not related, market forces would dictate the price of the goods, and the books of each of the companies would reflect the market price of the goods bought or sold. However, in this example, the companies are related, under the overall control of Global, the parent business. Thus, Global may want to set prices for the sale of component parts that differ from market price. The pricing policy for intracorporate transfers of goods, services, and technology is known as transfer pricing.

An MNE may use transfer pricing for a variety of purposes. The simplest is to take advantage of differences in tax rates among countries. For example, if the tax rate on corporate profits in Mexico is higher than the tax rate in Spain, Global will want to minimize profits in Mexico and maximize profits in Spain. Thus, it may set low prices for the goods its Mexican subsidiary sells to its Spanish subsidiary. If Venezuela restricts foreign companies from taking their profits home, Global may want to set low prices for the purchases its Spanish subsidiary makes, so that the Venezuelan subsidiary shows little profit while the Spanish subsidiary shows higher profit levels. On the other side, particularly if its Mexican subsidiary is relatively new, Global might want to allocate profits in Mexico so as to be able to obtain financing for growth and expansion. Global's own internal compensation policies may also lead to the use of transfer pricing to allocate profits, so that certain managers show profit levels leading to increased compensation.

It is easy to see that every country in which Global does business will have an interest in Global's transfer pricing policies. Given the size of some MNEs, a shift in revenue away from a country may result in significant losses in tax revenues. Even in more developed countries, a large multinational that is perceived to be shifting its income away from the taxing countries may be branded as a tax evader. The Japanese auto manufacturers, for example, regularly face the ire of U.S. politicians, who accuse them of setting artificially high prices for parts sold to their U.S. subsidiaries so as to evade their obligation to pay taxes to the U.S. government.

In response to transfer pricing concerns, countries around the world have regulated the methods that MNEs can use to price their intracorporate transfers of goods, services, and technology. In general, a government will have no problem for tax purposes, in reallocating income between parents and subsidiaries, usually using a standard that tries to find the "arm's length" price; that is, what the free market would charge if the companies were unrelated. In the United States, for example, Section 482 of the Internal Revenue Code allows the taxing authorities to reallocate income, deductions, credits, and allowances between commonly controlled businesses in order to prevent tax evasion or to "clearly reflect" the income of the businesses. The following case shows how the Internal Revenue Service (IRS) may make such a reallocation, and how transfer pricing policies may lead to lengthy litigation.

HOSPITAL CORPORATION OF AMERICA
v. COMMISSIONER

81 T.C. 520 (1983)
U.S. Tax Court

FACTS:

Hospital Corporation of America (HCA) wanted to contract with the government of Saudi Arabia to manage the King Faisal Specialist Hospital (KFSH) in Riyadh. It formed a wholly owned subsidiary in the Cayman Islands, Hospital Corp. International, Ltd. (HCI One), to be its holding company for all international operations. HCI One in turn formed a wholly owned Cayman Islands subsidiary, Hospital Corp. of the Middle East, Ltd. (LTD) to be in charge of obtaining, negotiating, and performing any contract to manage KFSH. The two subsidiaries qualified under Cayman Islands law to pay no income tax.

For the tax year 1973, HCA allocated all of its taxable income ($1,787,030) from the KFSH hospital management contract to the Cayman Islands subsidiary. The IRS used its authority under Section 482 to reallocate 100 percent of the income to HCA. HCA appealed to the Tax Court.

ISSUE:

Did the IRS properly reallocate 100 percent of the income from the KFSH project to HCA?

RESULT:

No. Only 75 percent of the income should have been allocated to HCA.

REASONS:

Respondent [the IRS Commissioner] . . . allocated all of LTD's taxable income to petitioner. By allocating 100 percent of LTD's taxable income to petitioner, respondent has attempted in still another fashion to argue that LTD is a "sham" corporation that should not be recognized for tax purposes. . . . Petitioner organized a separate corporation to contract with the Royal Cabinet of the Kingdom of Saudi Arabia to manage the King Faisal Hospital. We have held that LTD is a valid corporation for tax purposes. In these circumstances, section 482 does not authorize an allocation that would in effect disregard the corporate existence of LTD. . . .

Petitioner [HCA] in Nashville, Tenn., did not exercise day-to-day control over LTD's operations [n.b. no pun intended?] at the King Faisal Hospital in Riyadh, Saudi Arabia. That control was exercised by LTD. We think that this factor is sufficient reason for us to reject respondent's 100-percent allocation under section 482.

Even though we have rejected respondent's 100-percent allocation of taxable income from LTD to petitioner, the evidence indicates overwhelmingly that an allocation is necessary and proper in this case. Unfortunately, there is little quantitative evidence in the record upon which we can determine what a reasonable allocation of profits would be. Neither party has been particularly helpful to the Court in this regard. However, we must do the best we can with what we have.

The regulations provide as a general rule that where one member of a group of controlled entities performs services for the benefit of another member without charge or at a charge which is not an arm's-length charge for the services, appropriate allocations may be made to reflect an arm's-length charge for the services. . . . The regulations also provide that where intangibles are made available in any manner by one member of a group of controlled entities to another member of the group for other than an arm's-length consideration, an allocation can be made to reflect arm's-length consideration for the use of the intangibles. . . .

With undue modesty, petitioner has tried to suggest to this Court that its much-vaunted expertise and experience is a mere nothing: just setting up another corporation and installing an executive director to run the hospital practically on his own. . . . Even discounting some of the sales puffery inherent in annual reports to stockholders or in sales pitches to secure hospital management contracts, we are persuaded that petitioner had a system involving considerable expertise and experience. . . .

Since petitioner performed substantial services for LTD and permitted LTD to use its system without compensation, there was a substantial distortion of income. We have found that LTD had an existence separate and apart from petitioner and that LTD's employees, Todd and Frayer, had day-to-day responsibilities for preparing in 1973 to commence performing the KFSH management contract. Some of the 1973 profits are attributable to their efforts. However, the most important factor in earning those profits was petitioner's managerial expertise and experience which were readily available to and used by LTD. Using our best judgment on the lengthy but inconclusive record before us, we have concluded and found as a fact that 75 percent of the taxable income of LTD in 1973 was attributable to petitioner. We therefore hold that respondent erred in allocating the remaining 25 percent to petitioner.

After reading this decision, one might be tempted to ask whether the Tax Court's allocation of income was any more rational than the IRS allocation. When businesses don't provide good audit trails to establish arm's-length prices, the IRS is left with the difficult task of establishing value. The affected business may not like the result.

In lieu of using an arm's-length transaction pricing standard, it may become tempting to use a formula for what a reasonable profit should be. The IRS has proposed using a formula rather than arm's-length pricing to compute income attributable to U.S. entities. Under this plan, the IRS would set a rate of return for comparable firms, most likely U.S. producers, then impute that income to the MNEs U.S. operations. This proposal has the effect of creating a minimum tax for MNEs that may in fact be wholly unrelated to actual income.

Poorly conceived national regulation of transfer pricing has several adverse effects. It may worsen political relationships with other countries whose MNE operations are affected. It creates the possibility of double taxation, since the overseas country may not recognize the reduction in income there that the home country now claims. Most importantly, it distorts financial reality for MNEs, and will make them less competitive in the world marketplace.

15.3 EXTERNAL OPERATING ENVIRONMENT

One competitive advantage that MNEs have over their single-country competitors is the ability to source their operations in different locations around the world. In response to rapidly changing competitive conditions, the MNE may shift production from place to place, looking for the lowest-cost producer of products or for the most favorable regulatory environment for its activities. For example, suppose that B-Kleen, our hypothetical MNE from Chapter 12, discovered that wages were lower and there were fewer restrictions on its business in Guatemala than in Mexico. Or perhaps an analysis by B-Kleen's corporate planners showed that the regulatory environment for its business was much more favorable in Argentina than in Brazil. The company would have the ability to serve its Central and South American markets by locating its production facilities in the more advantageous markets.

The flexibility MNEs have to locate operations in different countries may benefit consumers by allowing them to buy good-quality products at the lowest possible cost. It also benefits MNEs by allowing them to have the most economically efficient operations possible. However, it also creates possibilities for abuse. A business may decide to create a complex legal structure for the purpose of avoiding legitimate regulation or taxation by the governments where it does business. It may decide to use its separately incorporated subsidiaries as a means of avoiding legal liability for wrongful acts or of evading obligations toward its employees. In these instances, the MNE may do real damage to the economy or the environment of the countries in which it does business. This section will examine the legal and ethical dimensions of evasion of regulation, bankruptcy and shutdown, and environmental liability.

EVADING REGULATION

Ultimately, an MNE has the ability to structure its operations to evade regulation of its activities. On some level, businesses have a legitimate interest in minimizing their taxes and finding the most favorable regulatory environments. However, that interest can be carried to a point where the MNE structures its business for the purpose of helping itself or its customers evade the law. One recent example may be the Bank of Credit and Commerce International (BCCI), which used several evasive techniques to circumvent disclosure requirements for countries in which it did business, and even advertised in some countries its ability to help its customers launder money obtained from illegal activities.

One kind of regulatory evasion with which MNEs have been charged concerns the sale of banned or improperly labeled hazardous products in LDCs. The developed countries that are the home to most MNEs tend to regulate product safety and labeling far more stringently than LDCs do. The lack of regulation by LDCs may be a conscious choice, or may merely reflect higher government priorities in other areas of the legal environment. The nature of the problem appears plainly in the following excerpt.

FRANK CROSS AND BRENDA WINSLETT, "EXPORT DEATH: ETHICAL ISSUES AND THE INTERNATIONAL TRADE IN HAZARDOUS PRODUCTS"

25 *American Business Law Journal* 487 (1987), footnotes omitted

Public outcry has been the strongest with respect to the incidence of "dumping" by American companies of inventories of banned products in Third World countries. Realization of the practice surfaced with the TRIS scandal in 1977. In that year the Consumer Product Safety Commission (CPSC) banned the domestic sale of infants' sleepware treated with TRIS, a flame-retardant compound found to be carcinogenic. CPSC claimed lack of authority to ban exports of the garments and companies responded by exporting large inventories to Third World markets. Under increasing public pressure, CPSC reversed itself seven months later and prohibited any further exports. During those seven months, American manufacturers had managed to "dump" 2.4 million garments. . . .

Criticism of U.S. exports is not limited to products banned in the United States. Critics also charge companies with improper marketing of dangerous products in countries unable to evaluate the risks of the products. Some products may be improperly or inadequately labeled, with no warnings given to the risks associated with their use. The drug industry in particular has been the subject of such criticism. A major problem in the drug industry involved not merely the export of banned drugs, but the improper marketing of drugs which have been domestically approved but which have, nonetheless, potentially dangerous side-effects or risks.

The case of chloramphenicol, a powerful antibiotic, is illustrative. The antibiotic is effective against a wide range of infections but, because of serious and sometimes fatal side-effects, its use has been restricted in the U.S. to the treatment of typhoid fever and a few other relatively rare, life-threatening diseases. Chloramphenicol products sold domestically contain appropriate warnings and prescribing guides. For example, Parke-Davis includes this warning for its chloramphenicol product, Chloromycetin: "It must not be used in the treatment of trivial infections where it is not indicated as in colds, influenza, infections of the throat, or as a prophylactic agent to prevent bacterial infections." The same products sold in Central and Latin America, in Malaysia and in Singapore recommend chloramphenicol for "typhoid and paratyphoid fever, gastrointestinal tract (G.I.T.) and urinary tract infections . . . respiratory infections, pertussis . . . viral, rickettsial and bacterial infections . . . severe infections including typhoid fever, enteric infections, ocular and aural infections." Chloromycetin is reportedly sold in Guatemala, Costa Rica and other Central American countries with *no warnings at all.* McKesson

Laboratories recommends its Cloramfenicol MK for whooping cough, marketing it in Colombia and Ecuador, like Parke-Davis, with no warnings at all.

The danger presented by misprescription of chloramphenicol as well as many other antibiotics is not limited to the risk of side-effects from the drug. Overuse of the drug in the treatment of minor illnesses can lead to the development of bacterial strains which are resistant to the drug. Once this happens, the antibiotic is useless in the treatment of the resistant bacteria. This is precisely what happened with chloramphenicol in Mexico. In 1972, an epidemic of typhoid fever broke out in Mexico. 20,000 victims died before doctors realized that the usual chloramphenicol treatment was not working; the epidemic was caused by bacteria which had developed a resistance to the antibiotic. . . .

Little multinational control exists over international commerce in hazardous materials. At the present time, there are "no binding international controls specifically dealing with trade in hazardous products." Various international organizations exert some influence over the trade in potentially hazardous products, and individual importing nations have some limited laws to protect their citizens from such risks.

United Nations organizations have addressed some aspects of this international trade, and the United Nations Environment Programme adopted a declaration that "there have been unethical practices concerning the distribution of chemicals, drugs, cosmetics and food unfit for human consumption." The [OECD] . . . also has moved to control export of hazardous materials. Unfortunately, these efforts are limited to some notification or other information provisions and have been largely ineffective, due to inconsistencies and jurisdictional disputes among the various international bodies.

Individual nations also exercise controls over the safety of imported products. A substantial percentage of such nations, however, have no legislation specific to hazardous imports. Even among nations that have formal statutory controls, the laws are not comprehensive and the nations "often lack the funds and technical expertise to enforce [them] effectively." In short, both unilateral and multilateral actions have placed some control over potentially hazardous products in the marketplace, but neither can be considered wholly effective.

Since there is little effective international regulation of MNEs' activities, the conduct of the MNE must be guided primarily by the firm's sense of ethics. The OECD Guidelines discussed earlier in this chapter give MNEs some guidance in outlining the kind of regulatory activity a firm should see as legitimate. For example, the section of the Guidelines relating to information disclosure reveals that MNEs should oblige government requests for information about the entire enterprise, not just the portion doing business in a particular country.

ANNEX TO THE DECLARATION OF 21ST JUNE, 1976 BY GOVERNMENTS OF OECD MEMBER COUNTRIES ON INTERNATIONAL INVESTMENT AND MULTINATIONAL ENTERPRISES

75 *Dept. State Bulletin* 83 (1976)

DISCLOSURE OF INFORMATION

Enterprises should, having due regard to their nature and relative size in the economic context of their operations and to requirements of business confidentiality and cost, publish in a form suited to improve public understanding a sufficient body of factual information on the structure, activities and policies of the enterprise as a whole, as a supplement, in so far as is necessary for this purpose, to information to be disclosed under the national law of the individual countries in which they operate. To this end, they should publish within reasonable time limits, on a regular basis, but at least annually, financial statements and other pertinent information relating to the enterprise as a whole, comprising in particular:

(i) the structure of the enterprise, showing the name and location of the parent company, its main affiliates, its percentage ownership, direct and indirect, in these affiliates, including shareholdings between them;

(ii) the geographical areas where operations are carried out and the principal activities carried on therein by the parent company and the main affiliates;

(iii) the operating results and sales by geographical area and the sales in the major lines of business for the enterprise as a whole;

(iv) significant new capital investment by geographical area and, as far as practicable, by major lines of business for the enterprise as a whole;

(v) a statement of the sources and uses of funds by the enterprise as a whole;

(vi) the average number of employees in each geographical area;

(vii) research and development expenditure for the enterprise as a whole;

(viii) the policies followed in respect of intra-group pricing;

(ix) the accounting policies, including those on consolidation, observed in compiling the published information.

DISINVESTMENT AND BANKRUPTCY

An MNE may decide to close its operations in a particular country for many reasons. Often, the decision is based on a cost–benefit analysis, looking at rising prices of labor, materials, or energy. Sometimes, a decision to close may be the product of market analysis, with predictions of growth in other geographic areas or for other products. In some instances, a decision to disinvest involves political judgments, such as predictions of increased political risk. In South Africa in the 1980s, many MNEs decided to disinvest so as not to contribute to apartheid, or because they faced pressure to disinvest from shareholders in their home countries.

In all of these instances, a decision to close an operation has immediate results for employees there, local suppliers, and the community in which the operation is located. When a large MNE has a large operation in a small community or a less-developed country, the closure may have a wider impact. The OECD Guidelines attempt to address at least the employment aspects of disinvestment, stating in part:

Enterprises should . . .
(6) in considering changes in their operations which would have major effects upon the livelihood of their employees, in particular in the case of the closure of an entity involving collective lay-offs or dismissals; provide reasonable notice of such changes to representatives of their employees, and where appropriate to the relevant governmental authorities, and cooperate with the employee representative and appropriate governmental authorities so as to mitigate to the maximum extent practicable adverse effects. . . .

In many countries, an employer closing an operation will have the obligation to pay generous severance payments to the employees put out of work. In such countries, it may be tempting for the MNE to have its subsidiary in that country file for bankruptcy to reduce or eliminate its obligations to pay severance benefits. While such action presents an obvious ethical choice for the parent corporation, the legal system of the host country may not have an adequate way to help the employees reach the assets of the parent company.

In the most famous instance of a business having its subsidiary file for bankruptcy, the Badger Company, a subsidiary of Raytheon, decided to close its Belgian subsidiary and withdraw from doing business in Belgium. Badger's Belgian subsidiary did not have enough assets to pay its creditors, including the severance pay it owed its Belgian employees who were losing their jobs. The government of Belgium, citing the OECD Guidelines, asked for a consultation with the OECD and the U.S. government. In his letters to the U.S. ambassador to Belgium and to the U.S. State Department, the Belgian Secretary of State for Regional Economy wrote:

Apparently the American parent company bears a legal and moral responsibility in this respect. The refusal to take care of the social implications involved in closing down a firm is a deplorable incident and might harm the image of American firms in Belgium. Both the Belgian and American governments signed the OECD declaration establishing rules of behaviour for multinational enterprises. The case Badger could be considered as a test-case in gauging the willingness of the parties involved regarding the application of these rules.[2]

The government of Belgium brought the case on behalf of the Badger employees to the OECD, arguing that this was a case where the Belgian courts hearing the bankruptcy could have the power to claim against the

---

[2]R. Blanpain, *The Badger Case and the OECD Guidelines for Multinational Enterprises*, Kluwer, Deventer, Netherlands, 1977, pp. 105–106.

parent company. The parent, Badger Company, argued that its liability should be limited to its investment in Badger Belgium. After consultations, Badger agreed to make a substantial contribution to Badger Belgium's assets, so as to meet the required severance payments. The Badger case was considered to be the first real test of the strength of the OECD guidelines, and is widely seen as a victory for the guidelines.

ENVIRONMENTAL LIABILITY

One emerging area of regulation that is likely to be significant for MNEs over the next several decades will concern the environment. It is apparent that although industrialization and technological change have brought great improvements in the lives of people, at least in the developed world, it has also led the world toward the brink of ecological catastrophe. Global climate change through the "Greenhouse effect," the erosion of the earth's protective ozone layer, pollution of air and waterways, and the explosive growth in world population that threatens to drain the earth of its resources are all issues increasingly occupying the attention of both political and business leaders.

Current legal and ethical frameworks are grossly inadequate to deal with the problems of the environment. Consider that most regulation of the environment relies on state, provincial, or federal governments pursuing individual violators. Yet most pollution doesn't stop at political boundaries. A power plant in New York may produce fumes that, while within U.S. standards, condense in Quebec in the form of acid rain. A factory in Mexico may discharge waste into the ocean that, while lawful under Mexican law, pollutes beaches in California.

Another significant impediment to environmental regulation is that both legal and ethical thinking tend to be framed in terms of the needs of persons. Look, for example, at the common-law concept of standing; that is, that to sue a polluter, an individual must suffer some specific harm. An organization cannot sue to stop the pollution of a lake or the cutting of a forest, unless the people in that organization have suffered some distinct injury. It is not enough simply to say that the lake will be forever harmed. Similarly, most schools of ethical thought look at decision making in terms of its impact on people. For example, cruelty to animals may be wrong, but it is considered wrong because it debases human goodness, not necessarily because the animal is a sentient being worthy of consideration.[3]

The inadequacy of our frameworks for thinking about the environment shows up in treaties, court decisions, and regulatory actions. For example, in 1991, a dispute resolution panel of the GATT ruled that a U.S. ban on

---

[3]See Christopher Stone, *Earth and Other Ethics*, Harper & Row, New York, 1977.

imported tuna caught by drift net fishing (a fishing method that also ensnares hundreds of dolphins) was an unfair import barrier that violated the GATT. Similarly, the EC has faced the fact that the Treaty of Rome does not mention environmental issues in its statement of purpose. Thus, Denmark was forced to change its recycling laws for disposable beverage cans, because the laws restricted the business practices of beverage companies in the rest of the EC.

To date, most international environmental regulation has taken the form of treaties or conventions, with governments agreeing to pursue policies to reduce various polluting activities. These treaties have only an indirect effect on business, as once signed and ratified, governments enact regulations to carry out the treaty. Perhaps the best-known example is the Vienna Convention for the Protection of the Ozone Layer, a multilateral treaty committing its signers to reducing the levels of ozone-depleting chemicals. While that treaty was signed in 1987, the rapid deterioration of the ozone layer has led to two amendments, known as the Montreal Protocol. The most recent set of amendments requires the signing nations to eliminate the production of ozone-depleting chemicals by the year 2000. The Montreal Protocol will obviously affect businesses that produce and use ozone-depleting chemicals, although enforcement of the rules is left to each nation signing the agreement.

A more recent treaty may indicate a new approach to solving the problems of trans-border pollution. In 1991, the United Nations opened for signature a Convention on Environmental Impact Assessment in a Transboundary Context. The Convention requires signing nations to give notice to other affected nations before granting approvals for activities that will cause trans-border pollution. The Convention would require businesses in designated industries to file an environmental impact statement before building new or expanded facilities. The governments of other affected nations would have an opportunity to respond to the proposed activity before government approvals are granted.

THE ENVIRONMENT AND ECONOMIC DEVELOPMENT

To some degree, the problems of environmental pollution are also problems of economic development. The developed nations have already industrialized, using their own resources and the resources of the developing world. They are the main consumers of products, the main users of energy, and the main generators of waste. Now the industrialized nations are leading the efforts to stop production of ozone-depleting products, save the rain forests (which are mostly located in developing nations), and establish global standards for conservation.

It is not surprising that the reaction to environmental law among the leaders of some developing nations is less than enthusiastic. Some see the attempts to regulate by treaty as just another example of the developed world using its power to prevent development: as a barrier to prevent the less-developed nations from reaching adequate, modern standards of living. Others, like the then minister of the environment of Brazil, use their positions to question the fundamental assumptions of development.

REMARKS OF PROFESSOR JOSÉ ANTONIO LUTZENBERGER, MINISTER OF THE ENVIRONMENT, BRAZIL

Final Proceedings, the Interparliamentary Conference on the Global Environment, Washington, D.C., 1990

. . . [I]f "development" is to be the continuation of the present model and we must help the "developing" countries to reach our levels of affluence, while the "developed" (I'd rather call them overdeveloped or misdeveloped) countries must still continue developing to even higher levels of consumption, then what we are doing is suicidal. Suppose the explicit aim of all development policies had been reached, suppose everywhere in the world consumption patterns, even if we leave out the present orgies of waste, had attained what we today have in the U.S. or Europe or Japan, then we would have, among other things, around three billion private cars. When world population reached ten billion around 2020 or 2030, we would have closer to seven billion cars. This is unthinkable! But if it is impossible to extend the present way of life in the overdeveloped countries to the rest of the planet, then there is something wrong with this way of life. We must reexamine our present model. . . .

We must therefore redefine "progress" and "development." Even the way we measure progress, that is our economic accounting, must be reexamined. When we add up all money flow in an economy to calculate the gross national product (GNP), we do not discount the damage we cause. When we in Brazil export iron ore and aluminum, we add up the foreign exchange that the export brings us, but we do not subtract the loss of ore, the demolition of the mountain, of the forest, the genocide of the Indians and all the other losses. We even add money flow that is the result of the damage caused. Suppose pollution diminishes the

health of a population, the increased costs for hospitals, physicians, nurses, medication, undertakers are added to the GNP. . . . The economists and public administrators even see progress where there is loss and suffering.

With the failure of central planning and in the midst of democratization, the East is now looking to the forces of the market to solve its economic problems. Let us hope they will not repeat the very serious mistakes we committed and continue to commit in the West. By balancing supply and demand, the market is supposed to lead to prices that are fair and to stimulate production of what is needed, while punishing those who produce what is not. But this is only so when the market is complete, when all the supply and all the demand are present. An American economist who thought in more ecological terms, Ezra Mishan, once presented an interesting and relevant metaphor: Suppose the Mona Lisa is being auctioned. But there are only shoe-shine boys in the room. The valuable work of art might be sold for a few dollars. Many of our markets today are like that. Very important bidders are missing. Future generations are absent, so is Nature, and even an important part of present humanity. The market reacts only to demand expressed in money. Millions of poor people are in dire need of food and commodities, but having no money to buy, they don't even appear on the markets. And then, the market is often manipulated by the powerful. We must find ways of making the market reflect a much larger picture. . . .

We must also rethink our technology. Few people realize that much of what is presented as progress in technological development is hard technology, that is, technology conceived, developed and imposed by the powerful, technocracy or bureaucracy, in their interest, not technology conceived to satisfy true human needs, that is, soft technology. Hard or soft, as referring to technology, has nothing to do with sophisticated or simple, it has to do with the aims pursued. Such concepts or policies as planned obsolescence, one-way packaging, misleading publicity to open markets for unneeded things, wasteful use of energy and materials, have nothing to do with true progress or true development. We cannot accept the argument that inevitably is advanced by technocracy that these policies are necessary for full employment. Increased technological productivity could also be used to give us all more free time for activities that are really significant: leisure, friendship, love, art, music, contact with nature, a more beautiful, more harmonious world, healthier agriculture, more healing, less aggressive technologies. The decisions are political, ethical—not technical.

The international community is just beginning to take some steps to address the problems the developing world will have in growing within new environmental boundaries. In 1991, the World Bank established a pilot program, called the Global Environment Facility, to fund projects in LDCs. With the cooperation of the U.N. Development Programme and the U.N. Environment Programme, the Facility identifies and funds projects that protect the ozone layer, limit emissions of greenhouse gases, protect biodiversity, and protect international waters. The object of the program is to coordinate technical and financial assistance to LDCs, to maximize the ability of the LDCs to develop economically as well as environmentally.

In 1992, representatives from more than 170 nations met in Rio de Janeiro, Brazil, for an "earth summit," officially known as the United Nations Conference on Environment and Development. That conference laid a new foundation for international environmental regulation in the coming years. The conference produced four major agreements: a Convention on Global Climate Change, designed to create a framework for reducing the emissions causing the "greenhouse effect"; a Convention on Biological Diversity, which the United States did not sign; a statement of principles on the "Management, Conservation and Sustainable Development of All Types of Forests"; and a general statement of principles known as the Rio Declaration on Environment and Development. These four documents, two of which create new international law, will create the basis for a significant increase in international efforts to preserve and restore the environment in the future.

Currently, however, there is still not much international law to regulate the environmental impact of business activities. In the absence of much effective international regulation of the environment, businesses must again assess their actions as matters of ethics. Some MNEs have looked upon the lack of effective environmental regulation in LDCs as a means of exploiting a competitive advantage. Under this theory, a business should locate where environmental controls are weakest, so as to be the lowest-cost producer of products. It is up to the host country to decide on the appropriate level of regulation: Imposing developed world standards on the host country merely makes production inefficient and expensive, and may even be patronizing toward the host country.

In contrast, other businesses operate in all countries using the highest applicable standards. In their view, one function of their presence in an LDC is to bring new technology and new expertise. Many businesses fall in between these two theories, finding for themselves a standard of conduct that they believe meets their ethical obligations to their host country, even if the law there doesn't establish as high a regulatory standard as the home country. In all approaches, however, the company will face difficulty in the event of a large-scale environmental problem, such as an oil spill or a chemical leak. One example of the difficulty of predicting environmental liability comes from the experience of Union Carbide Corporation in India.

The Bhopal Disaster

Union Carbide Corporation (UCC), a U.S.–based MNE, had a majority interest in a subsidiary in India, Union Carbide of India, Ltd. (UCIL). Among the products made by UCIL were the pesticides Sevin and Temik, both used widely in India. To make the final products, UCIL used a chemical called methylisocyanate (MIC), which reacted with other chemicals to form the final pesticide. The MIC was stored at the UCIL plant at Bhopal.

On December 3, 1984, water somehow entered the tank in which the MIC was stored, setting off a chemical reaction inside the storage tank. The emergency systems designed to prevent an escape of the gas all failed, and early in the morning of December 4, 1984, a cloud of toxic MIC gas escaped the tank and spread in a mist across the city. Between 2,000 and 8,000 people died, and more than 200,000 people suffered injury from the gas.

India's legal system responded to the tragedy in several unexpected ways. When UCC's CEO Warren Anderson arrived soon after the accident, he was arrested and charged with murder, although he was subsequently allowed to leave India. The government of India passed a new law allowing the government to file suit on behalf of all victims of the accident, in *parens patriae* (in the role as sovereign, or parent of the country).

The government sued UCIL and UCC in federal court in New York. It sought to impose a U.S. standard for products liability and negligence on UCC's worldwide operations, and sought to hold UCC liable for the acts of its independent subsidiary. The government, in order to bring suit in New York, found itself in the peculiar position of arguing that the Indian courts were unable to render justice in the case. Union Carbide found itself in what was also the peculiar position of arguing that the case should be returned to India for trial.

The court returned the case to India for trial. Before the trial could actually take place, UCC settled with the government for $470 million, covering

525,000 claims.[4] As of 1992, the criminal complaint against Warren Anderson was not yet finally resolved.

The Bhopal incident provided some difficult lessons for managers. Union Carbide prided itself on its ethical and environmentally sound practices, particularly in the chemical industry. Yet, after the accident, it found itself tried and convicted in the court of public opinion as an irresponsible MNE, locating its plants to avoid regulation.

An outsider looking at Union Carbide before the accident might have thought that the parent had done an excellent job of creating a real, independent subsidiary, run by Indian nationals, with fairly extensive involvement by the Indian government in the planning and construction of the facility. Yet, after the accident, the government immediately looked to hold the parent corporation liable, and Union Carbide ended up paying $237 million in excess of its insurance.[5]

If there is a moral to the story of Union Carbide's experience with the Bhopal disaster, it is that although there is no worldwide standard for corporate environmental liability, in the event of an accident that catches public attention the standards for corporate conduct will be very high. The law of the developing nation is likely to change rapidly, so as to create liability for the parent. Union Carbide was probably wise to settle the case for $470 million rather than be the test case to develop a new standard of liability for MNEs.

15.4 CONCLUSION

MNEs will create change in the host countries in which they do business, particularly when those countries are still developing economically and socially. They have the power to improve living standards, technology, and economic growth, but they also have the power to create political instability and to widen the gap between rich and poor.

In most instances, there is little effective legal regulation controlling the conduct of MNEs. Some countries lack the expertise and the resources to regulate MNEs effectively, while others so need foreign exchange that they will look the other way when MNEs do not act responsibly. Thus, the standard of conduct that MNEs follow is largely a matter of the ethical principles of the company, its top management, and the managers in the field.

---

[4]"Bhopal Payments by Union Carbide Set at $470 Million," *The New York Times*, February 15, 1989, p. Al, col. 6.
[5]Eileen Wagner, *Bhopal's Legacy: Lessons for Third World Host Nations and for Multinational Corporations*, 16 *North Carolina Journal of International Law and Commercial Regulation* 541, 580 (1991).

MNEs face hard decisions in conducting their business. Requests for bribes or other improper payments, decisions about intracompany pricing, decisions to alter or close operations, and choices about product exports and environmental practices are just a few areas in which an MNE has to put its ethical principles into practice. Balancing the need to make profits for shareholders with the interests of other stakeholders in both the home and host countries is not an easy task. To some extent, the OECD Guidelines for the Conduct of MNEs provide a framework to help in decision making, but the Guidelines do not answer many questions.

In the future, MNEs will face increased international regulation, particularly in the area of the environment. MNEs will be less able to evade regulation by moving their operations to ill-regulated LDCs, and even if they can, will find themselves liable in the event of significant accidents and, perhaps, for other conduct. Worldwide regulation is tightening significantly in the area of environmental regulation. Managers in MNEs must therefore take the lead in creating ethical standards for the global operations of their companies.

15.5 QUESTIONS FOR DISCUSSION

1. Suppose you are a Dutch citizen working for a U.S.–based multinational construction firm as the executive in charge of company operations in eastern Africa. You are just establishing operations in one country there, so you hire a national of that country to help facilitate your business. He reports that, due to civil unrest, the country's civil servants have not been paid for a very long time, and most are working other jobs to keep their families fed. Would it be legal for you to authorize your agent to make payments to the civil servants with whom your company is likely to come in contact? Explain.

2. Giant Motors, Inc., a U.S.–based MNE, manufactures its cars at locations around the world. Suppose France proposed taxing intracorporate transfers by setting a profit rate based on the profits of similar businesses in the EC, then imputing that profit to Giant's French operations. As head of government relations in the EC for Giant, would you oppose this proposal? What would your arguments be?

3. Megachemical Corp. has produced Gro-Fast, a chemical fertilizer, for the past 10 years. Unfortunately, recent studies showed that farm workers who inhale fertilizer dust are likely to develop cancer. The U.S. Environmental Protection Agency published a notice of a proposed rule to ban the product, and U.S. sales fell to almost nothing. However, the company still has hundreds of thousands of pounds of the fertilizer in warehouses, ready to sell, and will lose millions of dollars if the product isn't sold. Megachemical's CEO thinks the solution is to export Gro-Fast

to other developing countries. What are the legal and ethical arguments for and against the CEO's plan? If he decides to export the Gro-Fast, what recommendations would you make to be as ethically responsible as possible?

4. As a project, identify manufacturers in your area. Talk to their public relations personnel about the actions the manufacturers are taking to be environmentally responsible. Do any of their actions have international implications? If the manufacturers have foreign facilities, do those facilities follow the same environmental standards? If not, why not?

15.6 FURTHER READINGS

Frances Cairncross, *Costing the Earth,* Harvard, Boston, Mass., 1992.

Jeffrey Fadiman, "A Traveler's Guide to Gifts and Bribes," *Harvard Business Review,* July–August 1986, pp. 124–136.

Charles Irish, "Transfer Pricing Abuses and Less Developed Countries," 18 *Inter-American Law Review* 83–136 (1986).

Jere Morehead and Sandra Gustavson II, "Complying with the Amended Foreign Corrupt Practices Act," *Risk Management,* April 1990, pp. 76–82.

John Ntambirweki, "The Developing Countries in the Evolution of an International Environmental Law," 14 *Hastings International and Comparative Law Review* 905–928 (1991).

Richard Williamson, Jr., "Building the International Environmental Regime: A Status Report," 21 *Inter-American Law Review* 679–760 (1990).

UNITED NATIONS CONVENTION ON CONTRACTS FOR THE INTERNATIONAL SALE OF GOODS[1]

The States Parties to this Convention,

Bearing in mind the broad objectives in the resolutions adopted by the sixth special session of the General Assembly of the United Nations on the establishment of a New International Economic Order,

Considering that the development of international trade on the basis of equality and mutual benefit is an important element in promoting friendly relations among States,

Being of the opinion that the adoption of uniform rules which govern contracts for the international sale of goods and take into account the different social, economic and legal systems would contribute to the removal of legal barriers in international trade and promote the development of international trade,

Have agreed as follows:

PART I
SPHERE OF APPLICATION AND GENERAL PROVISIONS

CHAPTER I. SPHERE OF APPLICATION

Article 1

(1) This Convention applies to contracts of sale of goods between parties whose places of business are in different States:

    (a) when the States are Contracting States; or

(b) when the rules of private international law lead to the application of the law of a Contracting State.

(2) The fact that the parties have their places of business in different States is to be disregarded whenever this fact does not appear either from the contract or from any dealings between, or from information disclosed by, the parties at any time before or at the conclusion of the contract.

(3) Neither the nationality of the parties nor the civil or commercial character of the parties or of the contract is to be taken into consideration in determining the application of this Convention.

Article 2

This Convention does not apply to sales:

(a) of goods bought for personal, family or household use, unless the seller, at any time before or at the conclusion of the contract, neither knew nor ought to have known that the goods were bought for any such use;

(b) by auction;

(c) on execution or otherwise by authority of law;

(d) of stocks, shares, investment securities, negotiable instruments or money;

(e) of ships, vessels, hovercraft or aircraft;

(f) of electricity.

Article 3

(1) Contracts for the supply of goods to be manufactured or produced are to be considered sales unless the party who orders the goods undertakes to supply a substantial part of the materials necessary for such manufacture or production.

(2) This Convention does not apply to contracts in which the preponderant part of the obligations of the party who furnishes the goods consists in the supply of labour or other services.

Article 4

This Convention governs only the formation of the contract of sale and the rights and obligations of the seller and the buyer arising from such a contract. In particular, except as otherwise expressly provided in this Convention, it is not concerned with:

(a) the validity of the contract or of any of its provisions or of any usage;

(b) the effect which the contract may have on the property in the goods sold.

Article 5

This Convention does not apply to the liability of the seller for death or personal injury caused by the goods to any person.

Article 6

The parties may exclude the application of this Convention or, subject to article 12, derogate from or vary the effect of any of its provisions.

CHAPTER II. GENERAL PROVISIONS

Article 7

(1) In the interpretation of this Convention, regard is to be had to its international character and to the need to promote uniformity in its application and the observance of good faith in international trade.

(2) Questions concerning matters governed by this Convention which are not expressly settled in it are to be settled in conformity with the general principles on which it is based or, in the absence of such principles, in conformity with the law applicable by virtue of the rules of private international law.

Article 8

(1) For the purposes of this Convention statements made by and other conduct of a party are to be interpreted according to his intent where the other party knew or could not have been unaware what that intent was.

(2) If the preceding paragraph is not applicable, statements made by and other conduct of a party are to be interpreted according to the understanding that a reasonable person of the same kind as the other party would have had in the same circumstances.

(3) In determining the intent of a party or the understanding a reasonable person would have had, due consideration is to be given to all relevant circumstances of the case including the negotiations, any practices which the parties have established between themselves, usages and any subsequent conduct of the parties.

Article 9

(1) The parties are bound by any usage to which they have agreed and by any practices which they have established between themselves.

(2) The parties are considered, unless otherwise agreed, to have impliedly made applicable to their contract or its formation a usage of which the parties knew or ought to have known and which in international trade is widely known to, and regularly observed by, parties to contracts of the type involved in the particular trade concerned.

Article 10

For the purposes of this Convention:
  (a) if a party has more than one place of business, the place of business is that which has the closest relationship to the contract and its performance, having regard to the circumstances known to or contemplated by the parties at any time before or at the conclusion of the contract;
  (b) if a party does not have a place of business, reference is to be made to his habitual residence.

Article 11

A contract of sale need not be concluded in or evidenced by writing and is not subject to any other requirement as to form. It may be proved by any means, including witnesses.

Article 12

Any provision of article 11, article 29 or Part II of this Convention that allows a contract of sale or its modification or termination by agreement or any offer, acceptance or other indication of intention to be made in any form other than in writing does not apply where any party has his place of business in a Contracting State which has made a declaration under article 96 of this Convention. The parties may not derogate from or vary the effect of this article.

Article 13

For the purposes of this Convention 'writing' includes telegram and telex.

PART II. FORMATION OF THE CONTRACT

Article 14

(1) A proposal for concluding a contract addressed to one or more specific persons constitutes an offer if it is sufficiently definite and indicates the intention of the offeror to be bound in case of acceptance. A proposal is sufficiently definite if it indicates the goods and expressly or implicitly fixes or makes provision for determining the quantity and the price.

(2) A proposal other than one addressed to one or more specific persons is to be considered merely as an invitation to make offers, unless the contrary is clearly indicated by the person making the proposal.

Article 15

(1) An offer becomes effective when it reaches the offeree.

(2) An offer, even if it is irrevocable, may be withdrawn if the withdrawal reaches the offeree before or at the same time as the offer.

Article 16

(1) Until a contract is concluded an offer may be revoked if the revocation reaches the offeree before he has dispatched an acceptance.
  (a) if it indicates, whether by stating a fixed time for acceptance or otherwise, that it is irrevocable; or
  (b) if it was reasonable for the offeree to rely on the offer as being irrevocable and the offeree has acted in reliance on the offer.

Article 17

An offer, even if it is irrevocable, is terminated when a rejection reaches the offeror.

Article 18

(1) A statement made by or other conduct of the offeree indicating assent to an offer is an acceptance. Silence or inactivity does not in itself amount to acceptance.

(2) An acceptance of an offer becomes effective at the moment the indication of assent reaches the offeror. An acceptance is not effective if the indication of assent does not reach the offeror within the time he has fixed or, if no time is fixed, within a reasonable time, due account being taken of the circumstances of the transaction, including the rapidity of the means of communication employed by the offeror. An oral offer must be accepted immediately unless the circumstances indicate otherwise.

(3) However, if, by virtue of the offer or as a result of practices which the parties have established between themselves or of usage, the offeree may indicate assent by performing an act, such as one relating to the dispatch of the goods or payment of the price, without notice to the offeror, the acceptance is effective at the moment the act is performed, provided that the act is performed within the period of time laid down in the preceding paragraph.

Article 19

(1) A reply to an offer which purports to be an acceptance but contains additions, limitations or other modifications is a rejection of the offer and constitutes a counter-offer.

(2) However, a reply to an offer which purports to be an acceptance but contains additional or different terms which do not materially alter the terms of the offer constitutes an acceptance, unless the offeror, without undue delay, objects orally to the discrepancy or dispatches a notice to that effect. If he does not so object, the terms of the contract are the terms of the offer with the modifications contained in the acceptance.

(3) Additional or different terms relating, among other things, to the price, payment, quality and quantity of the goods, place and time of delivery, extent of one party's liability to the other or the settlement of disputes are considered to alter the terms of the offer materially.

Article 20

(1) A period of time for acceptance fixed by the offeror in a telegram or a letter begins to run from the moment the telegram is handed in for dispatch or from the date shown on the letter or, if no such date is shown, from the date shown on the envelope. A period of time for acceptance fixed by the offeror by telephone, telex or other means of instantaneous communication, begins to run from the moment that the offer reaches the offeree.

(2) Official holidays or non-business days occurring during the period for acceptance are included in calculating the period. However, if a notice of acceptance cannot be delivered at the address of the offeror on the last day of the period because that day falls on an official holiday or a non-business day at the place of business of the offeror, the period is extended until the first business day which follows.

Article 21

(1) A late acceptance is nevertheless effective as an acceptance if without delay the offeror orally so informs the offeree or dispatches a notice to that effect.

(2) If a letter or other writing containing a late acceptance shows that it has been sent in such circumstances that if its transmission had been normal it would have reached the offeror in due time, the late acceptance is effective as an acceptance unless, without delay, the offeror orally informs the offeree that he considers his offer as having lapsed or dispatches a notice to that effect.

Article 22

An acceptance may be withdrawn if the withdrawal reaches the offeror before or at the same time as the acceptance would have become effective.

Article 23

A contract is concluded at the moment when an acceptance of an offer becomes effective in accordance with the provisions of this Convention.

Article 24

For the purposes of the Part of the Convention, an offer, declaration of acceptance or any other indication of intention 'reaches' the addressee when it is made orally to him or delivered by any other means to him personally, to his place of business or mailing address or, if he does not have a place of business or mailing address, to his habitual residence.

PART III. SALE OF GOODS

CHAPTER I. GENERAL PROVISIONS

Article 25

A breach of contract committed by one of the parties is fundamental if it results in such detriment to the other party as substantially to deprive him of what he is entitled to expect under the contract, unless the party in breach did not foresee and a reasonable person of the same kind in the same circumstances would not have foreseen such a result.

Article 26

A declaration of avoidance of the contract is effective only if made by notice to the other party.

Article 27

Unless otherwise expressly provided in this Part of the Convention, if any notice, request or other communication is given or made by a party in accordance with this Part and by means appropriate in the circumstances, a delay of error in the transmission of the communication or its failure to arrive does not deprive that party of the right to rely on the communication.

Article 28

If, in accordance with the provisions of this Convention, one party is entitled to require performance of any obligation by the other party, a court is not bound to enter a judgment for specific performance unless the court would do so under its own law in respect of similar contracts of sale not governed by this Convention.

Article 29

(1) A contract may be modified or terminated by the mere agreement of the parties.

(2) A contract in writing which contains a provision requiring any modification or termination by agreement to be in writing may not be otherwise modified or terminated by agreement. However, a party may be precluded by his conduct from asserting such a provision to the extent that the other party has relied on that conduct.

CHAPTER II. OBLIGATIONS OF THE SELLER

Article 30

The seller must deliver the goods, hand over any documents relating to them and transfer the property in the goods, as required by the contract and this Convention.

SECTION I. DELIVERY OF THE GOODS AND HANDING OVER OF DOCUMENTS

Article 31

If the seller is not bound to deliver the goods at any other particular place, his obligation to deliver consists:

(a) if the contract of sale involves carriage of the goods—in handing the goods over to the first carrier for transmission to the buyer;

(b) if, in cases not within the preceding subparagraph, the contract relates to specific goods, or unidentified goods to be drawn from a specific stock or to be manufactured or produced, and at the time of the conclusion of the contract the parties knew that the goods were at, or were to be manufactured or produced at, a particular place—in placing the goods at the buyer's disposal at that place;

(c) in other cases—in placing the goods at the buyer's disposal at the place where the seller had his place of business at the time of the conclusion of the contract.

Article 32

(1) If the seller, in accordance with the contract or this Convention, hands the goods over to a carrier and if the goods are not clearly identified to the contract by markings on the goods, by shipping documents or otherwise, the seller must give the buyer notice of the consignment specifying the goods.

(2) If the seller is bound to arrange for carriage of the goods, he must make such contracts as are necessary for carriage to the place fixed by means of transportation appropriate in the circumstances and according to the usual terms for such transportation.

(3) If the seller is not bound to effect insurance in respect of the carriage of the goods, he must at the buyer's request, provide him with all available information necessary to enable him to effect such insurance.

Article 33

The seller must deliver the goods:
  (a) if a date is fixed by or determinable from the contract, on that date;
  (b) if a period of time is fixed by or determinable from the contract, at any time within that period unless circumstances indicate that the buyer is to choose a date; or
  (c) in any other case, within a reasonable time after the conclusion of the contract.

Article 34

If the seller is bound to hand over documents relating to the goods, he must hand them over at the time and place and in the form required by the contract. If the seller has handed over documents before that time, he may, up to that time, cure any lack of conformity in the documents, if the exercise of this right does not cause the buyer unreasonable inconvenience or unreasonable expense. However, the buyer retains any right to claim damages as provided for in this Convention.

SECTION II. CONFORMITY OF THE GOODS AND THIRD PARTY CLAIMS

Article 35

(1) The seller must deliver goods which are of the quantity, quality and description required by the contract and which are contained or packaged in the manner required by the contract.

(2) Except where the parties have agreed otherwise, the goods do not conform with the contract unless they:

(a) are fit for the purposes for which goods of the same description would ordinarily be used;

(b) are fit for any particular purpose expressly or impliedly made known to the seller at the time of the conclusion of the contract, except where the circumstances show that the buyer did not rely, or that it was unreasonable for him to rely, on the seller's skill and judgement;

(c) possess the qualities of goods which the seller has held out to the buyer as a sample or model;

(d) are contained or packaged in the manner usual for such goods or, where there is no such manner, in a manner adequate to preserve and protect the goods.

(3) The seller is not liable under subparagraphs (a) to (d) of the preceding paragraph for any lack of conformity of the goods if at the time of the conclusion of the contract the buyer knew or could not have been unaware of such lack of conformity.

Article 36

(1) The seller is liable in accordance with the contract and this Convention for any lack of conformity which exists at the time when the risk passes to the buyer, even though the lack of conformity becomes apparent only after that time.

(2) The seller is also liable for any lack of conformity which occurs after the time indicated in the preceding paragraph and which is due to a breach of any of his obligations, including a breach of any guarantee that for a period of time the goods will remain fit for their ordinary purpose or for some particular purpose or will retain specified qualities or characteristics.

Article 37

If the seller has delivered goods before the date for delivery, he may, up to that date, deliver any missing part or make up any deficiency in the quantity of the goods delivered, or deliver goods in replacement of any nonconforming goods delivered or remedy any lack of conformity in the goods delivered, provided that the exercise of this right does not cause the buyer unreasonable inconvenience or unreasonable expense. However, the buyer retains any right to claim damages as provided for in this Convention.

Article 38

(1) The buyer must examine the goods, or cause them to be examined, within as short a period as is practicable in the circumstances.

(2) If the contract involves carriage of the goods, examination may be deferred until after the goods have arrived at their destination.

(3) If the goods are redirected in transit or redispatched by the buyer without a reasonable opportunity for examination by him and at the time of the conclusion of the contract the seller knew or ought to have known of the possibility of such redirection or redispatch, examination may be deferred until after the goods have arrived at the new destination.

Article 39

(1) The buyer loses the right to rely on a lack of conformity of the goods if he does not give notice to the seller specifying the nature of the lack of conformity within a reasonable time after he has discovered it or ought to have discovered it.

(2) In any event, the buyer loses the right to rely on a lack of conformity of the goods

if he does not give the seller notice thereof at the latest within a period of two years from the date on which the goods were actually handed over to the buyer, unless this time-limit is inconsistent with a contractual period of guarantee.

Article 40

The seller is not entitled to rely on the provisions of articles 38 and 39 if the lack of conformity relates to facts of which he knew or could not have been unaware and which he did not disclose to the buyer.

Article 41

The seller must deliver goods which are free from any right or claim of a third party, unless the buyer agreed to take the goods subject to that right or claim. However, if such right or claim is based on industrial property or other intellectual property, the seller's obligation is governed by article 42.

Article 42

(1) The seller must deliver goods which are free from any right or claim of a third party based on industrial property or other intellectual property, of which at the time of the conclusion of the contract the seller knew or could not have been unaware, provided that the right or claim is based on industrial property or other intellectual property:

   (a) under the law of the State where the goods will be resold or otherwise used, if it was contemplated by the parties at the time of the conclusion of the contract that the goods would be resold or otherwise used in that State; or

   (b) in any other case, under the law of the State where the buyer has his place of business.

(2) The obligation of the seller under the

preceding paragraph does not extend to cases where:

   (a) at the time of the conclusion of the contract the buyer knew or could not have been unaware of the right or claim; or

   (b) the right or claim results from the seller's compliance with technical drawings, designs, formulae or other such specifications furnished by the buyer.

Article 43

(1) The buyer loses the right to rely on the provisions of article 41 or article 42 if he does not give notice to the seller specifying the nature of the right or claim of the third party within a reasonable time after he has become aware or ought to have become aware of the right or claim.

(2) The seller is not entitled to rely on the provisions of the preceding paragraph if he knew of the right or claim of the third party and the nature of it.

Article 44

Notwithstanding the provisions of paragraph (1) of article 39 and paragraph (1) of article 43, the buyer may reduce the price in accordance with article 50 or claim damages, except for loss of profit, if he has a reasonable excuse for his failure to give the required notice.

SECTION III. REMEDIES FOR BREACH OF CONTRACT BY THE SELLER

Article 45

(1) If the seller fails to perform any of his obligations under the contract or this Convention, the buyer may:

(a) exercise the rights provided in articles 46 to 52;

(b) claim damages as provided in articles 74 to 77.

(2) The buyer is not deprived of any right he may have to claim damages by exercising his right to other remedies.

Article 46

(1) The buyer may require performance by the seller of his obligations unless the buyer has resorted to a remedy which is inconsistent with this requirement.

(2) If the goods do not conform with the contract, the buyer may require delivery of substitute goods only if the lack of conformity constitutes a fundamental breach of contract and a request for substitute goods is made either in conjunction with notice given under article 39 or within a reasonable time thereafter.

(3) If the goods do not conform with the contract, the buyer may require the seller to remedy the lack of conformity by repair, unless this is unreasonable having regard to all the circumstances. A request for repair must be made either in conjunction with notice given under article 39 or within a reasonable time thereafter.

Article 47

(1) The buyer may fix an additional period of time of reasonable length for performance by the seller of his obligations.

(2) Unless the buyer has received notice from the seller that he will not perform within the period so fixed, the buyer may not, during that period, resort to any remedy for breach of contract. However, the buyer is not deprived thereby of any right he may have to claim damages for delay in performance.

Article 48

(1) Subject to article 49, the seller may, even after the date for delivery, remedy at his own expense any failure to perform his obligations, if he can do so without unreasonable delay and without causing the buyer unreasonable inconvenience or uncertainty of reimbursement by the seller of expenses advanced by the buyer. However, the buyer retains any right to claim damages as provided for in this Convention.

(2) If the seller requests the buyer to make known whether he will accept performance and the buyer does not comply with the request within a reasonable time, the seller may perform within the time indicated in his request. The buyer may not, during that period of time, resort to any remedy which is inconsistent with performance by the seller.

(3) A notice by the seller that he will perform within a specified period of time is assumed to include a request, under the preceding paragraph, that the buyer make known his decision.

(4) A request or notice by the seller under paragraph (2) or (3) of this article is not effective unless received by the buyer.

Article 49

(1) The buyer may declare the contract avoided:
  (a) if the failure by the seller to perform any of his obligations under the contract or this Convention amounts to a fundamental breach of contract; or
  (b) in case of non-delivery, if the seller does not deliver the goods within the additional period of time fixed by the buyer in accordance with paragraph (1) or article 47 or declares that he will not deliver within the period so fixed.

(2) However, in cases where the seller has delivered the goods, the buyer loses the right to declare the contract avoided unless he does so:

(a) in respect of late delivery, within a reasonable time after he has become aware that delivery has been made;

(b) in respect of any breach other than late delivery, within a reasonable time:

(i) after he knew or ought to have known of the breach;

(ii) after the expiration of any additional period of time fixed by the buyer in accordance with paragraph (1) of article 47, or after the seller has declared that he will not perform his obligations within such an additional period; or

(iii) after the expiration of any additional period of time indicated by the seller in accordance with paragraph (2) of article 48, or after the buyer has declared that he will not accept performance.

Article 50

If the goods do not conform with the contract and whether or not the price has already been paid, the buyer may reduce the price in the same proportion as the value that the goods actually delivered had at the time of the delivery bears to the value that conforming goods would have had at that time. However, if the seller remedies any failure to perform his obligations in accordance with article 37 or article 48 or if the buyer refuses to accept performance by the seller in accordance with those articles, the buyer may not reduce the price.

Article 51

(1) If the seller delivers only a part of the goods or if only a part of the goods delivered is in conformity with the contract, articles 46 to 50 apply in respect of the part which is missing or which does not conform.

(2) The buyer may declare the contract avoided in its entirety only if the failure to make delivery completely or in conformity with the contract amounts to a fundamental breach of the contract.

Article 52

(1) If the seller delivers the goods before the date fixed, the buyer may take delivery or refuse to take delivery.

(2) If the seller delivers a quantity of goods greater than that provided for in the contract, the buyer may take delivery or refuse to take delivery of the excess quantity. If the buyer takes delivery of all or part of the excess quantity, he must pay for it at the contract rate.

CHAPTER III. OBLIGATIONS OF THE BUYER

Article 53

The buyer must pay the price for the goods and take delivery of them as required by the contract and this Convention.

SECTION I. PAYMENT OF THE PRICE

Article 54

The buyer's obligation to pay the price includes taking such steps and complying with such formalities as may be required under the contract or any laws and regulations to enable payment to be made.

Article 57

(1) If the buyer is not bound to pay the price at any other particular place, he must pay it to the seller:
 (a) at the seller's place of business; or
 (b) if the payment is to be made against the handing over of the goods or of documents, at the place where the handing over takes place.

(2) The seller must bear any increase in the expenses incidental to payment which is caused by a change in his place of business subsequent to the conclusion of the contract.

Article 58

(1) If the buyer is not bound to pay the price at any other specific time, he must pay it when the seller places either the goods or documents controlling their disposition at the buyer's disposal in accordance with the contract and this Convention. The seller may make such payment a condition for handing over the goods or documents.

(2) If the contract involves carriage of the goods, the seller may dispatch the goods on terms whereby the goods, or documents controlling their disposition, will not be handed over to the buyer except against payment of the price.

(3) The buyer is not bound to pay the price until he has had an opportunity to examine the goods, unless the procedures for delivery or payment agreed upon by the parties are inconsistent with his having such an opportunity.

Article 59

The buyer must pay the price on the date fixed by or determinable from the contract and this Convention without the need for any request or compliance with any formality on the part of the seller.

SECTION II. TAKING DELIVERY

Article 60

The buyer's obligation to take delivery consists:
 (a) in doing all the acts which could reasonably be expected of him in order to enable the seller to make delivery; and
 (b) in taking over the goods.

SECTION III. REMEDIES FOR BREACH OF CONTRACT BY THE BUYER

Article 61

(1) If the buyer fails to perform any of his obligations under the contract or this Convention, the seller may;
 (a) exercise the rights provided in articles 62 to 65;
 (b) claim damages as provided in articles 74 to 77.

(2) The seller is not deprived of any right he may have to claim damages by exercising his right to other remedies.

(3) No period of grace may be granted to the buyer by a court or arbitral tribunal when the seller resorts to a remedy for breach of contract.

Article 62

The seller may require the buyer to pay the price, take delivery or perform his other obligations, unless the seller has resorted to a remedy which is inconsistent with this requirement.

Article 63

(1) The seller may fix an additional period of time of reasonable length for performance by the buyer of his obligations.

(2) Unless the seller has received notice from the buyer that he will not perform within the period so fixed, the seller may not, during that period, resort to any remedy for breach of contract. However, the seller is not deprived thereby of any right he may have to claim damages for delay in performance.

Article 64

(1) The seller may declare the contract avoided:
   (a) if the failure by the buyer to perform any of his obligations under the contract or this Convention amounts to a fundamental breach of contract; or
   (b) if the buyer does not, within the additional period of time fixed by the seller in accordance with paragraph (1) of article 63, perform his obligation to pay the price or take delivery of the goods, or if he declares that he will not do so within the period so fixed.

(2) However, in cases where the buyer has paid the price, the seller loses the right to declare the contract avoided unless he does so:
   (a) in respect of late performance by the buyer, before the seller has become aware that performance has been rendered; or
   (b) in respect of any breach other than later performance by the buyer, within a reasonable time:
      (i) after the seller knew or ought to have known of the breach; or
      (ii) after the expiration of any additional period of time fixed by the seller in accordance with paragraph (1) of article 63, or after the buyer has declared that he will not perform his obligations within such an additional period.

Article 65

(1) If under the contract the buyer is to specify the form, measurement or other features of the goods and he fails to make such specification either on the date agreed upon or within a reasonable time after receipt of a request from the seller, the seller may, without prejudice to any other rights he may have, make the specification himself in accordance with the requirements of the buyer that may be known to him.

(2) If the seller makes the specification himself, he must inform the buyer of the details thereof and must fix a reasonable time within which the buyer may make a different specification. If, after receipt of such a communication, the buyer fails to do so within the time so fixed, the specification made by the seller is binding.

CHAPTER IV. PASSING OF RISK

Article 66

Loss of a damage to the goods after the risk has passed to the buyer does not discharge him from his obligation to pay the price, unless the loss or damage is due to an act or omission of the seller.

Article 67

(1) If the contract of sale involves carriage of the goods and the seller is not bound to hand them over at a particular place, the

risk passes to the buyer when the goods are handed over to the first carrier for transmission to the buyer in accordance with the contract of sale. If the seller is bound to hand the goods over to a carrier at a particular place, the risk does not pass to the buyer until the goods are handed over to the carrier at that place. The fact that the seller is authorized to retain documents controlling the disposition of the goods does not affect the passage of the risk.

(2) Nevertheless, the risk does not pass to the buyer until the goods are clearly identified to the contract, whether by markings on the goods, by shipping documents, by notice given to the buyer or otherwise.

Article 68

The risk in respect of goods sold in transit passes to the buyer from the time of the conclusion of the contract. However, if the circumstances so indicate, the risk is assumed by the buyer from the time the goods were handed over to the carrier who issued the documents embodying the contract of carriage. Nevertheless, if at the time of the conclusion of the contract of sale the seller knew or ought to have known that the goods had been lost or damaged and did not disclose this to the buyer, the loss or damage is at the risk of the seller.

Article 69

(1) In cases not within articles 67 and 68, the risk passes to the buyer when he takes over the goods or, if he does not do so in due time, from the time when the goods are placed at his disposal and he commits a breach of contract by failing to take delivery.

(2) However, if the buyer is bound to take over the goods at a place other than a place of business of the seller, the risk passes when delivery is due and the buyer is aware of the risk that the goods are placed at his disposal at that place.

(3) If the contract relates to goods not then identified, the goods are considered not to be placed at the disposal of the buyer until they are clearly identified to the contract.

Article 70

If the seller has committed a fundamental breach of contract, articles 67, 68 and 69 do not impair the remedies available to the buyer on account of the breach.

CHAPTER V. PROVISIONS COMMON TO THE OBLIGATIONS OF THE SELLER AND OF THE BUYER

SECTION I. ANTICIPATORY BREACH AND INSTALMENT CONTRACTS

Article 71

(1) A party may suspend the performance of his obligations if, after the conclusion of the contract, it becomes apparent that the other party will not perform a substantial part of his obligations as a result of:

(a) a serious deficiency in his ability to perform or in his creditworthiness; or

(b) his conduct in preparing to perform or in performing the contract.

(2) If the seller has already dispatched the goods before the grounds described in the preceding paragraph become evident, he may prevent the handing over of the goods to the buyer even though the buyer holds a document which entitles him to obtain them. The present paragraph relates only to the rights in the goods as between the buyer and the seller.

(3) A party suspending performance, whether before or after dispatch of the goods, must immediately give notice of the suspension to the other party and must continue with performance if the other party provides adequate assurance of his performance.

Article 72

(1) If prior to the date for performance of the contract it is clear that one of the parties will commit a fundamental breach of contract, the other party may declare the contract avoided.

(2) If time allows, the party intending to declare the contract avoided must give reasonable notice to the other party in order to permit him to provide adequate assurance of his performance.

(3) The requirements of the preceding paragraph do not apply if the other party has declared that he will not perform his obligations.

Article 73

(1) In the case of a contract for delivery of goods by instalments, if the failure of one party to perform any of his obligations in respect of any instalment constitutes a fundamental breach of contract with respect to that instalment, the other party may declare the contract avoided with respect to that instalment.

(2) If one party's failure to perform any of his obligations in respect of any instalment gives the other party good grounds to conclude that a fundamental breach of contract will occur with respect to future instalments, he may declare the contract avoided for the future, provided that he does so within a reasonable time.

(3) A buyer who declares the contract avoided in respect of any delivery may, at the same time, declare it avoided in respect of deliveries already made or of future deliveries if, by reason of their interdependence, those deliveries could not be used for the purpose contemplated by the parties at the time of the conclusion of the contract.

SECTION II. DAMAGES

Article 74

Damages for breach of contract by one party consist of a sum equal to the loss, including loss of profit, suffered by the other party as a consequence of the breach. Such damages may not exceed the loss which the party in breach foresaw or ought to have foreseen at the time of the conclusion of the contract, in the light of the facts and matters of which he then knew or ought to have known, as a possible consequence of the breach of contract.

Article 75

If the contract is avoided and if, in a reasonable manner and within a reasonable time after avoidance, the buyer has bought goods in replacement or the seller has resold the goods, the party claiming damages may recover the difference between the contract price and the price in the substitute transaction as well as any further damages recoverable under article 74.

Article 76

(1) If the contract is avoided and there is a current price for the goods, the party claiming damages may, if he has not made a purchase or resale under article 75, recover the difference between the price fixed by the contract and the current price at the time of avoidance as well as any further damages recoverable under article 74. If, however, the party claiming damages has avoided the contract after taking over the goods, the current price at the time of such taking over shall be applied instead of the current price at the time of avoidance.

(2) For the purpose of the preceding paragraph, the current price is the price prevailing at the place where delivery of the goods should have been made or, if there is no current price at that place, the price at such other place as serves as a reasonable substitute, making due allowance for differences in the cost of transporting the goods.

Article 77

A party who relies on a breach of contract must take such measures as are reasonable in the circumstances to mitigate the loss, including loss of profit, resulting from the breach. If he fails to take such measures, the party in breach may claim a reduction in the damages in the amount by which the loss should have been mitigated.

SECTION III. INTEREST

Article 78

If a party fails to pay the price or any other sum that is in arrears, the other party is entitled to interest on it, without prejudice to any claim for damages recoverable under article 74.

SECTION IV. EXEMPTIONS
Article 79

(1) A party is not liable for a failure to perform any of his obligations if he proves that the failure was due to an impediment beyond his control and that he could not reasonably be expected to have taken the impediment into account at the time of the conclusion of the contract or to have avoided or overcome it or its consequences.

(2) If the party's failure is due to the failure by a third person whom he has engaged to perform the whole or a part of the contract, that party is exempt from liability only if:
   (a) he is exempt under the preceding paragraph; and
   (b) the person whom he has so engaged would be so exempt if the provisions of that paragraph were applied to him.

(3) The exemption provided by this article has effect for the period during which the impediment exists.

(4) The party who fails to perform must give notice to the other party of the impediment and its effects on his ability to perform. If the notice is not received by the other party within a reasonable time after the party who fails to perform knew or ought to have known of the impediment, he is liable for damages resulting from such non-receipt.

(5) Nothing in this article prevents either party from exercising any right other than to claim damages under this Convention.

Article 80

A party may not rely on a failure of the other party to perform, to the extent that such failure was caused by the first party's act or omission.

SECTION V. EFFECTS OF AVOIDANCE

Article 81

(1) Avoidance of the contract releases both parties from their obligations under it, subject to any damages which may be due. Avoidance does not affect any provision of the contract for the settlement of disputes or any other provision of the parties consequent upon the avoidance of the contract.

(2) A party who has performed the contract either wholly or in part may claim restitution from the other party of whatever the first party has supplied or paid under the contract. If both parties are bound to make restitution, they must do so concurrently.

Article 82

(1) The buyer loses the right to declare the contract avoided or to require the seller to deliver substitute goods if it is impossible for him to make restitution of the goods substantially in the condition in which he received them.

(2) The preceding paragraph does not apply:
(a) if the impossibility of making restitution of the goods or of making restitution of the goods substantially in the condition in which the buyer received them is not due to his act or omission;
(b) if the goods or part of the goods have perished or deteriorated as a result of the examination provided for in article 38; or
(c) if the goods or part of the goods have been sold in the normal course of business or have been consumed or transformed by the buyer in the course of normal use before he dis-

covered or ought to have discovered the lack of conformity.

Article 83

A buyer who has lost the right to declare the contract avoided or to require the seller to deliver substitute goods in accordance with article 82 retains all other remedies under the contract and this Convention.

Article 84

(1) If the seller is bound to refund the price, he must also pay interest on it, from the date on which the price was paid.

(2) The buyer must account to the seller for all benefits which he has derived from the goods or part of them:
(a) if he must make restitution of the goods or part of them; or
(b) if it is impossible for him to make restitution of all or part of the goods or to make restitution of all or part of the goods substantially in the condition in which he received them, but he has nevertheless declared the contract avoided or required the seller to deliver substitute goods.

SECTION VI. PRESERVATION OF THE GOODS

Article 85

If the buyer is in delay in taking delivery of the goods or, where payment of the price and delivery of the goods are to be made concurrently, if he fails to pay the price, and the seller is either in possession of the goods or otherwise able to control their disposition, the seller must take such steps as are reasonable in the circumstances to preserve them. He is entitled to retain them until he has been reimbursed his reasonable expenses by the buyer.

Article 86

(1) If the buyer has received the goods and intends to exercise any rights under the contract or this Convention to reject them, he must take such steps to preserve them as are reasonable in the circumstances. He is entitled to retain them until he has been reimbursed his reasonable expenses by the seller.

(2) If goods dispatched to the buyer have been placed at his disposal at their destination and he exercises the right to reject them, he must take possession of them on behalf of the seller, provided that this can be done without payment of the price and without reasonable inconvenience or unreasonable expense. This provision does not apply if the seller or a person authorized to take charge of the goods on his behalf is present at the destination. If the buyer takes possession of the goods under this paragraph, his rights and obligations are governed by the preceding paragraph.

Article 87

A party who is bound to take steps to preserve the goods may deposit them in a warehouse of a third person at the expense of the other party provided that the expense incurred is not unreasonable.

Article 88

(1) A party who is bound to preserve the goods in accordance with article 85 or 86 may sell them by any appropriate means if there has been an unreasonable delay by the other party in taking possession of the goods or in taking them back or in paying the price or the cost of preserva-

tion, provided that reasonable notice of the intention to sell has been given to the other party.

(2) If the goods are subject to rapid deterioration or their preservation would involve unreasonable expense, a party who is bound to preserve the goods in accordance with article 85 or 86 must take reasonable measure to sell them. To the extent possible he must give notice to the other party of his intention to sell.

(3) A party selling the goods has the right to retain out of the proceeds of sale an amount equal to the reasonable expenses of preserving the goods and of selling them. He must account to the other party for the balance.

PART IV. FINAL PROVISIONS

Article 89

The Secretary-General of the United Nations is hereby designated as the depositary for this Convention.

Article 90

This Convention does not prevail over any international agreement which has already been or may be entered into and which contains provisions concerning the matters governed by this Convention, provided that the parties have their places of business in States parties to such agreement.

Article 91

(1) This Convention is open for signature at the concluding meeting of the United Nations Conference on Contracts for the International Sale of Goods and will re-

main open for signature by all States at the Headquarters of the United Nations, New York until 30 September 1981.

(2) This Convention is subject to ratification, acceptance or approval by the signatory States as from the date it is open for signature.

(3) This Convention is open for accession by all States which are not signatory States as from the date it is open for signature.

(4) Instruments of ratification, acceptance, approval and accession are to be deposited with the Secretary-General of the United Nations.

Article 92

(1) A Contracting State may declare at the time of signature, ratification, acceptance, approval or accession that it will not be bound by Part II of this Convention or that it will not be bound by Part III of this Convention.

(2) A Contracting State which makes a declaration in accordance with the preceding paragraph in respect of Part II or Part III of this Convention is not to be considered a Contracting State within paragraph (1) of article 1 of this Convention in respect of matters governed by the Part to which the declaration applies.

Article 93

(1) If a Contracting State has two or more territorial units in which, according to its constitution, different systems of law are applicable in relation to the matters dealt with in this Convention, it may, at the time of signature, ratification, acceptance, approval or accession, declare that this Convention is to extend to all its territorial units or only to one or more of them, and may amend its declaration by submitting another declaration at any time.

(2) These declarations are to be notified to the depositary and are to state expressly the territorial units to which the Convention extends.

(3) If, by virtue of a declaration under this article, this Convention extends to one or more but not all of the territorial units of a Contracting State, and if the place of business of a party is located in that State, this place of business, for the purposes of this Convention, is considered not to be in a Contracting State, unless it is in a territorial unit to which the Convention extends.

(4) If a Contracting State makes no declaration under paragraph (1) of this article, the Convention is to extend to all territorial units of that State.

Article 94

(1) Two or more Contracting States which have the same or closely related legal rules on matters governed by this Convention may at any time declare that the Convention is not to apply to contracts of sale or to their formation where the parties have their places of business in those States. Such declarations may be made jointly or by reciprocal unilateral declarations.

(2) A Contracting State which has the same or closely related legal rules on matters governed by this Convention as one or more non-Contracting States may at any time declare that the Convention is not to apply to contracts of sale or to their formation where the parties have their places of business in those States.

(3) If a State which is the object of a declaration under the preceding paragraph subsequently becomes a Contracting State, the declaration made will, as from the date on which the Convention enters into force in respect of the new Contracting

State, have the effect of a declaration made under paragraph (1), provided that the new Contracting State joins in such declaration or makes a reciprocal unilateral declaration.

Article 95

Any State may declare at the time of the deposit of its instrument of ratification, acceptance, approval or accession that it will not be bound by subparagraph (1)(b) of article 1 of this Convention.

Article 96

A Contracting State whose legislation requires contracts of sale to be concluded in or evidenced by writing may at any time make a declaration in accordance with article 12 that any provision of article 11, article 29, or Part II of this Convention, that allows a contract of sale or its modification or termination by agreement or any offer, acceptance, or other indication of intention to be made in any form other than in writing, does not apply where any party has his place of business in that State.

Article 97

(1) Declarations made under this Convention at the time of signature are subject to confirmation upon ratification, acceptance or approval.

(2) Declarations and confirmations of declarations are to be in writing and be formally notified to the depositary.

(3) A declaration takes effect simultaneously with the entry into force of this Convention in respect of the State concerned. However, a declaration of which the depositary receives formal notification after such entry into force takes effect on the first day of the month follow-

ing the expiration of six months after the date of its receipt by the depositary. Reciprocal unilateral declarations under article 94 take effect on the first day of the month following the expiration of six months after the receipt of the latest declaration by the depositary.

(4) Any State which makes a declaration under this Convention may withdraw it at any time by a formal notification in writing addressed to the depositary. Such withdrawal is to take effect on the first day of the month following the expiration of six months after the date of the receipt of the notification by the depositary.

(5) A withdrawal of a declaration made under article 94 renders inoperative, as from the date on which the withdrawal takes effect, any reciprocal declaration made by another State under that article.

Article 98

No reservations are permitted except those expressly authorized in this Convention.

Article 99

(1) This Convention enters into force, subject to the provisions of paragraph (6) of this article, on the first day of the month following the expiration of twelve months after the date of deposit of the tenth instrument of ratification, acceptance, approval or accession, including an instrument which contains a declaration made under article 92.

(2) When a State ratifies, accepts, approves or accedes to this Convention after the deposit of the tenth instrument of ratification, acceptance, approval or accession, this Convention, with the exception of the Part excluded, enters into force in

respect of the State, subject to the provisions of paragraph (6) of this article, on the first day of the month following the expiration of twelve months after the date of the deposit of its instrument of ratification, acceptance, approval or accession.

(3) A State which ratifies, accepts, approves or accedes to this Convention and is a party to either or both the Convention relating to a Uniform Law or the Formation of Contracts for the International Sale of Goods done at The Hague on 1 July 1964 (1964 Hague Formation Convention) and the Convention relating to a Uniform Law on the International Sale of Goods done at The Hague on 1 July 1964 (1964 Hague Sales Convention) shall at the same time denounce, as the case may be, either or both the 1964 Hague Sales Convention and the 1964 Hague Formation Convention by notifying the Government of the Netherlands to the effect.

(4) A State party to the 1964 Hague Sales Convention which ratifies, accepts, approves or accedes to the present Convention and declares or has declared under article 92 that it will not be bound by Part II of this Convention shall at the time of ratification, acceptance, approval or accession denounce the 1964 Hague Sales Convention by notifying the Government of the Netherlands to that effect.

(5) A State party to the 1964 Hague Formation Convention which ratifies, accepts, approves or accedes to the present Convention and declares or has declared under article 92 that it will not be bound by Part III of this Convention shall at the time of ratification, acceptance, approval or accession denounce the 1964 Hague Formation Convention by notifying the

Government of the Netherlands to that effect.

(6) For the purpose of this article, ratifications, acceptances, approvals and accessions in respect of this Convention by States parties to the 1964 Hague Formation Convention or to the 1964 Hague Sales Convention shall not be effective until such denunciations as may be required on the part of those States in respect of the latter two Conventions have themselves become effective. The depositary of this Convention shall consult with the Government of the Netherlands, as the depositary of the 1964 Conventions, so as to ensure necessary coordination in this respect.

Article 100

(1) This Convention applies to the formation of a contract only when the proposal for concluding the contract is made on or after the date when the Convention enters into force in respect of the Contracting States referred to in subparagraph (1)(a) or the Contracting State referred to in subparagraph (1)(b) of article 1.

(2) This Convention applies only to contracts concluded on or after the date when the Convention enters into force in respect of the Contracting States referred to in subparagraph (1)(a) or the Contracting State referred to in subparagraph (1)(b) of article 1.

Article 101

(1) A Contracting State may denounce this Convention, or Part II or Part III of the Convention, by a formal notification in writing addressed to the depositary.

(2) The denunciation takes effect on the first day of the month following the expira-

tion of twelve months after the notification is received by the depositary. Where a longer period for the denunciation to take effect is specified in the notification, the denunciation takes effect upon the expiration of such longer period after the notification is received by the depositary.

DONE at Vienna, this day of eleventh day of April, one thousand nine hundred and eighty, in a single original, of which the Arabic, Chinese, English, French, Russian and Spanish texts are equally authentic.

IN WITNESS WHEREOF the undersigned plenipotentiaries, being duly authorized by their respective Governments, have signed this Convention.

NOTE

[1]Source of text: U.N. Document A/CONF.97/18, Annex I, English version reprinted in 52 Fed. Reg. 6264 (1987) and in 19 I.L.M. 668 (1980)

UNIFORM COMMERCIAL CODE: SELECTED PROVISIONS ON RISK AND LOSS

§2-319. F.O.B. and F.A.S. Terms

(1) Unless otherwise agreed, the term F.O.B. (which means "free on board") at a named place, even though used only in connection with the stated price, is a delivery term under which

(a) when the term F.O.B. the place of shipment, the seller must at that place ship the goods in the manner provided in this Article (Section 2-504) and bear the expense and risk of putting them into the possession of the carrier; or

(b) when the term is F.O.B. the place of destination, the seller must at his own expense and risk transport the goods to that place and there tender delivery of them in the manner provided in this Article (Section 2-503);

(c) when under either (a) or (b) the term is also F.O.B. vessel, car or other vehicle, the seller must in addition at his own expense and risk load the goods on board. If the term is F.O.B. vessel, the buyer must name the vessel and, in an appropriate case, the seller must comply with the provisions of this Article on the form of bill of lading (Section 2-323).

(2) Unless otherwise agreed, the term F.A.S. vessel (which means "free alongside") at the named port, even though used only in connection with the stated price, is a delivery term under which the seller must

(a) at his own expense and risk deliver the goods alongside the vessel in the manner usual in that port or on a dock designated and provided by the buyer; and

(b) obtain and tender a receipt for the goods in exchange for which the carrier is under a duty to issue a bill of lading.

(3) Unless otherwise agreed in any case falling within subsection (1) (a) or (c) or subsection (2) the buyer must seasonably give any needed instructions for making

delivery, including, when the term is F.A.S. or F.O.B., the loading berth of the vessel and, in an appropriate case, its name and sailing date. The seller may treat the failure of needed instructions as a failure of cooperation under this Article (section 2-311). He may also at his option move the goods in any reasonable manner preparatory to delivery or shipment.

(4) Under the term F.O.B. vessel or F.A.S., unless otherwise agreed, the buyer must make payment against tender of the required documents and the seller may not tender nor the buyer demand delivery of the goods in substitution for the documents.

§2-320. C.I.F. and C. & F. Terms

(1) The term C.I.F. means that the price includes in a lump sum the cost of the goods and the insurance and freight to the named destination. The term C. & F. or C.F. means that the price so includes cost and freight to the named destination.

(2) Unless otherwise agreed and even though used only in connection with the stated price and destination, the term C.I.F. destination or its equivalent requires the seller at his own expense and risk to
(a) put the goods into the possession of a carrier at the port for shipment and obtain a negotiable bill or bills of lading covering the entire transportation to the named destination; and
(b) load the goods and obtain a receipt from the carrier (which may be contained in the bill of lading) showing that the freight has been paid or provided for; and
(c) obtain a policy or certificate of insurance, including any war risk insurance, of a kind and on terms then

current at the port of shipment in the usual amount, in the currency of the contract, shown to cover the same goods covered by the bill of lading and providing for payment of loss to the order of the buyer or for the account of whom it may concern; but the seller may add to the price the amount of the premium for any such war risk insurance; and
(d) prepare an invoice of the goods and procure any other documents required to effect shipment or to comply with the contract; and
(e) forward and tender with commercial promptness all the documents in due form and with any indorsement necessary to perfect the buyer's rights.

(3) Unless otherwise agreed, the term C. & F. or its equivalent has the same effect and imposes upon the seller the same obligations and risks as a C.I.F. term except the obligation as to insurance.

(4) Under the term C.I.F. or C. & F., unless otherwise agreed the buyer must make payment against tender of the required documents and the seller may not tender nor the buyer demand delivery of the goods in substitution for the documents.

§2-321. C.I.F. or C. & F.: "Net Landed Weights"; "Payment on Arrival"; Warranty of Condition on Arrival

Under a contract containing a term C.I.F. or C. & F.

(1) Where the price is based on or is to be adjusted according to "net landed weights," "delivered weights," "out turn" quantity or quality or the like, unless otherwise agreed the seller must reasonably estimate the price. The payment due on

tender of the documents called for by the contract is the amount so estimated, but after final adjustment of the price a settlement must be made with commercial promptness.

(2) An agreement described in subsection (1) or any warranty of quality or condition of the goods on arrival places upon the seller the risk of ordinary deterioration, shrinkage and the like in transportation but has no effect on the place or time of identification to the contract for sale or delivery or on the passing of the risk of loss.

(3) Unless otherwise agreed, where the contract provides for payment on or after arrival of the goods the seller must before payment allow such preliminary inspection as is feasible; but if the goods are lost, delivery of the documents and payment are due when the goods should have arrived.

§2-322. Delivery "Ex-Ship"

(1) Unless otherwise agreed, a term for delivery of goods "ex-ship" (which means from the carrying vessel) or in equivalent language is not restricted to a particular ship and requires delivery from a ship which has reached a place at the named port destination where goods of the kind are usually discharged.

(2) Under such a term, unless otherwise agreed
  (a) the seller must discharge all liens arising out of the carriage and furnish the buyer with a direction which puts the carrier under a duty to deliver the goods; and
  (b) the risk of loss does not pass to the buyer until the goods leave the ship's tackle or are otherwise properly unloaded.

§2-323. Form of Bill of Lading Required in Overseas Shipment; "Overseas"

(1) Where the contract contemplates overseas shipment and contains a term C.I.F. or C. & F. or F.O.B. vessel, the seller unless otherwise agreed must obtain a negotiable bill of lading stating that the goods have been loaded on board or, in the case of a term C.I.F. or C.& F., received for shipment.

(2) Where in a case within subsection (1) a bill of lading has been issued in a set of parts, unless otherwise agreed, if the documents are not to be sent from abroad the buyer may demand tender of the full set; otherwise only one part of the bill of lading need be tendered. Even if the agreement expressly requires a full set
  (a) due tender of a single part is acceptable within the provisions of this Article on cure of improper delivery (subsection (1) of Section 2-508); and
  (b) even though the full set is demanded, if the documents are sent from abroad the person tendering an incomplete set may nevertheless require payment upon furnishing an indemnity which the buyer in good faith deems adequate.

(3) A shipment by water or by air or a contract contemplating such shipment is "overseas" insofar as by usage of trade or agreement it is subject to the commercial, financing or shipping practices characteristic of international deep water commerce.

§2-504. Shipment by Seller

Where the seller is required or authorized to send the goods to the buyer and the contract does not require him to deliver them at a particular destination, then, unless otherwise agreed, he must

    (a) put the goods in the possession of such a carrier and make such a contract for their transportation as may be reasonable having regard to the nature of the goods and other circumstances of the case; and

    (b) obtain and promptly deliver or tender in due form any document necessary to enable the buyer to obtain possession of the goods or otherwise required by the agreement or by usage of trade; and . . .

§2-505. Seller's Shipment Under Reservation

(1) Where the seller has identified goods to the contract by or before shipment

    (a) his procurement of a negotiable bill of lading to his own order or otherwise reserves in him a security interest in the goods. His procurement of the bill to the order of a financing agency or of the buyer indicates in addition only the seller's expectation of transferring that interest to the person named.

    (b) a nonnegotiable bill of lading to himself or his nominee reserves possession of the goods as security but except in a case of conditional delivery (subsection (2) of Section 2-507) a nonnegotiable bill of lading naming the buyer as consignee reserves no security interest even though the seller retains possession of the bill of lading.

(2) When shipment by the seller with reservation of a security interest is in violation of the contract for sale it constitutes an improper contract for transportation within the preceding section but impairs neither the rights given to the buyer by

shipment and identification of the goods to the contract nor the seller's powers as a holder of a negotiable document.

§2-509. Risk of Loss in the Absence of Breach

(1) Where the contract requires or authorizes the seller to ship the goods by carrier.

    (a) if it does not require him to deliver them at a particular destination, the risk of loss passes to the buyer when the goods are duly delivered to the carrier even though the shipment is under reservation (Section 2-505); but

    (b) if it does require him to deliver them at a particular destination and the goods are there duly tendered while in the possession of the carrier, the risk of loss passes to the buyer when the goods are there duly so tendered as to enable the buyer to take delivery.

(2) Where the goods are held by a bailee to be delivered without being moved, the risk of loss passes to the buyer

    (a) on his receipt of a negotiable document of title covering the goods; or

    (b) on acknowledgement by the bailee of the buyer's right to possession of the goods; or

    (c) after his receipt of a nonnegotiable document of title or other written direction to deliver, as provided in subsection (4)(b) of Section 2-503.

(3) In any case not within subsection (1) or (2), the risk of loss passes to the buyer on his receipt of the goods if the seller is a merchant; otherwise the risk passes to the buyer on tender of delivery.

(4) The provisions of this section are subject to contrary agreement of the parties and

to the provision of this Article on sale on approval (Section 2-327) and on effect of breach on risk of loss (Section 2-510).

§2-510. Effect of Breach on Risk of Loss

(1) Where a tender or delivery of goods so fails to conform to the contract as to give a right of rejection, the risk of their loss remains on the seller until cure or acceptance.

(2) Where the buyer rightfully revokes acceptance, he may to the extent of any deficiency in his effective insurance coverage treat the risk of loss as having rested on the seller from the beginning.

(3) Where the buyer, as to conforming goods already identified to the contract for sale, repudiates or is otherwise in breach before risk of their loss has passed to him, the seller may to the extent of any deficiency in his effective insurance coverage treat the risk of loss as resting on the buyer for a commercially reasonable time.

§2-513. Buyer's Right to Inspection of Goods

(1) Unless otherwise agreed and subject to subsection (3), where goods are tendered or delivered or identified to the contract for sale, the buyer has a right before payment or acceptance to inspect them at any reasonable place and time and in any reasonable manner. When the seller is required or authorized to send the goods to the buyer, the inspection may be after their arrival.

(2) Expenses of inspection must be borne by the buyer but may be recovered from the seller if the goods do not conform and are rejected.

(3) Unless otherwise agreed and subject to the provisions of this Article on C.I.F. contracts (subsection (3) of Section 2-321), the buyer is not entitled to inspect the goods before payment of the price when the contract provides
  (a) for delivery "C.O.D." or on other like terms; or
  (b) for payment against documents of title, except where such payment is due only after the goods are to become available for inspection.

(4) A place or method of inspection fixed by the parties is presumed to be exclusive but, unless otherwise expressly agreed, it does not postpone identification or shift the place for delivery or for passing the risk of loss. If compliance becomes impossible, inspection shall be as provided in this section unless the place or method fixed was clearly intended as an indispensable condition, failure of which avoids the contract.

§2-514. When Documents Deliverable on Acceptance; When on Payment

Unless otherwise agreed, documents against which a draft is drawn are to be delivered to the drawee on acceptance of the draft if it is payable more than three days after presentment; otherwise, only on payment.

INDEX